Essentials of International Human Resource Management

Essentials of International Human Resource Management

Managing People Globally

David C. Thomas

University of New South Wales, Australia

Mila B. Lazarova

Simon Fraser University, Canada

Los Angeles | London | New Delhi
Singapore | Washington DC

Los Angeles | London | New Delhi
Singapore | Washington DC

FOR INFORMATION:

SAGE Publications, Inc.
2455 Teller Road
Thousand Oaks, California 91320
E-mail: order@sagepub.com

SAGE Publications Ltd.
1 Oliver's Yard
55 City Road
London EC1Y 1SP
United Kingdom

SAGE Publications India Pvt. Ltd.
B 1/I 1 Mohan Cooperative Industrial Area
Mathura Road, New Delhi 110 044
India

SAGE Publications Asia-Pacific Pte. Ltd.
3 Church Street
#10-04 Samsung Hub
Singapore 049483

Acquisitions Editor: Patricia Quinlin
Associate Editor: Megan Koraly
Editorial Assistant: Katie Guarino
Production Editor: Melanie Birdsall
Copy Editor: Karin Rathert
Typesetter: C&M Digitals (P) Ltd.
Proofreader: Laura Webb
Indexer: Sheila Bodell
Cover Designer: Candice Harman
Marketing Manager: Liz Thornton
Permissions Editor: Jennifer Barron

Printed in the United States of America

Library of Congress Cataloging-in-Publication Data

Thomas, David C. (David Clinton), 1947–
Essentials of international human resource management: managing people globally / David C. Thomas, Mila B. Lazarova.

pages cm

ISBN 978-1-4129-9591-7 (pbk.)

1. International business enterprises—Personnel management. 2. International business enterprises—Management—Cross-cultural studies. 3. Management—Cross-cultural studies. I. Lazarova, Mila B. II. Title.

HF5549.5.E45T456 2014
658.3—dc23   2013008304

This book is printed on acid-free paper.

SFI label applies to text stock

13 14 15 16 17 10 9 8 7 6 5 4 3 2 1

Brief Contents

Detailed Contents

List of Tables and Figures

List of Tables

List of Figures

Preface

This book is about managing people in the context of a global business environment. The field of international human resource management has its roots in the study of managing expatriates in the multinational firm and in comparisons of management practice in different countries. In recent years, the strategic management of human resources in the multinational firm has been the dominant consideration. However, globalization has created the need to understand human resource management more broadly across countries, cultures, and organizational types. In this book we consider the broad global spectrum for the context for HRM, including cultural, institutional, and organizational contexts. Our coverage is not limited to the multinational firm but considers all types of organizations that are embedded in the global context. And we integrate comparative approaches to HRM with an understanding of the strategic management of people in organizations that operate in a global context.

A unique feature of this book is that it balances U.S. and non-U.S. schools of thought with regard to HRM. That is, as opposed to treating HRM strictly as a set of functions in the service of strategic management of the multinational firm that can be reduced to best practice, we take a more pluralistic view of the relationship of people within organizations in a global context. While recognizing this complexity, we present concepts in an easy to read user-friendly way, but provide extensive references that allow the reader to follow up on concepts in more depth.

Because the book is an essentials volume that extracts key concepts in the management of people in a global context and presents them in a concise form it allows a number of options for use in the classroom. It can be used as a standalone text for advanced undergraduate and postgraduate courses in International Human Resource Management. In that regard we have provided some of our favorite case studies to supplement the text. While recognizing that cases often present multiple issues, we have presented them in an order that parallels the development of topics in the text. However, they are at the end of the book to facilitate their use at any stage in the course. In addition, the text can be combined with selected readings to create a more rigorous in-depth treatment of global HRM or used as a supplement to introduce the international dimension to more general HRM courses. Finally, we hope that scholars, particulary those without a deep background in IHRM, will find it a concise reference to key issues in the field.

In Chapter 1, we introduce HRM in a global context and define the scope of the book. This chapter moves beyond the traditional focus of management of human resources in the multinational enterprise (MNE) to discuss the continually changing context in which IHRM exists and the changing nature of MNEs themselves. It addresses trends, such as the aging of the workforce in the developing world and international migration that result in workforce demographic changes, outsourcing and its influence on workforce characteristics, rapid technological changes, and cultural differences in attitudes toward work influence the way work itself is organized. And uneven distribution of talent around the world creates a playing field in which talent shortages in one area contrast with labor surpluses in another resulting in a worldwide competition for talent.

The goal of Chapter 2 is to overlay the country context on the global context to define the external challenges facing global HRM. In it we focus on the cultural and institutional factors that influence HRM within a national context. We also discuss differences in national business systems including political, legal, social, and economic institutions and their effect on HRM, including coverage of the unique context of less developed countries. Further, we include a discussion that contrasts models of HRM and outline the differences in institutional constraints and choices available to HR managers.

Chapter 3, completes the contextual picture by introducing the organizational context of IHRM. It focuses on how organizational differences influence global HRM, including a discussion of types of MNEs (international, multidomestic, global, transnational, metanational), but also describes a shift from MNEs alone to the broad domain of firms for whom global HRM is relevant. This involves an examination of emerging players on the global stage, including small- and medium- sized enterprises and MNEs in the developing world. It includes a discussion of the strategy and structure of the MNE, including emerging organizational forms on HRM.

In Chapter 4, we move the discussion from a description of HRM in global context to the influence of crossing contextual boundaries on HRM policies and practices. In this chapter, we discuss the issues involved in transferring HRM policies and procedures across boundaries, including the direction of transfer and the effects of outsourcing of HRM on transfer. We include a discussion of the global diffusion of employment practices, global best practices, the influence of home and host country on inhibiting or facilitating transfer, and country of origin effects. Finally, we review the often unanticipated effect of cultural recontextualization of practices as they are transferred.

In Chapter 5, we present a systematic understanding of HRM issues that are present in joint ventures, mergers, and acquisitions. In this chapter, we highlight issues in a variety of functional areas of HRM because of disparities in practices among firms, the need to eliminate duplication in the new entity, the need for consistent HRM practices, the integration or merging of practices, and the dominance of one firm's practices over the other. The need for HR due diligence as part of the process of joining firms is an additional important area of discussion.

In Chapter 6, we focus on how the changing nature of the global workforce influences attracting, engaging, and retaining employees for competitive advantage. We include discussions of issues such as talent availability, workforce mobility, and outsourcing and also provide a comparison of recruitment and selection methods across countries. Also covered in this chapter are issues involved in staffing managerial positions in MNEs and a discussion of the reasons for using expatriates and expatriate selection issues.

Chapter 7 examines and categorizes training and development activities, including global leadership development, in such a way that their utility in different and dynamic contexts can be clearly understood. The global context forces an examination of cultural differences in learning styles and training methods and the need to design and deliver training and development programs across borders. We also give attention to the special needs of training expatriates, repatriates and their families, including discussions of program types, predeparture versus in-country training, and so on.

This goal of Chapter 8 is to examine how to achieve the best return on the investment made in employees by matching performance management systems with the firm. The global environment requires a consideration of both cultural differences in motivation and performance management and institutional differences in compensation practices. A key area of consideration is the need for internally consistent versus locally adapted performance management and compensation systems. Compensation and tax issues related to international assignments are also discussed.

In Chapter 9, we expand the traditional discussion of expatriates to cover all types of mobility and its relationship to both firm and individual outcomes. We examine international career issues both from the perspective of the employee and the employer and also discuss the adjustment, performance, and repatriation of expatriates and the relationship of overseas assignments to career. An associated topic area involves family issues, women on overseas assignments, and dual-career couples. From the perspective of the organization, a key issue is the relationship of the organization (support) to the expatriate assignment and the ROI of expatriate assignments.

In Chapter 10, we include both a comparative perspective in which such issues as cultural differences in ethical HR practices are examined and an organizational perspective covering such elements as the formulation and implementation of corporate codes of social responsibility. A second but related focus is on differences in the development of and current state of industrial relations and differences in employment law. We integrate stakeholder perspectives to understand the important role that the HRM practices have in CSR.

Chapter 11 is dedicated to sensitizing the reader to areas that are likely to have the biggest impact on future global HRM. We outline a number of important, if less-studied, issues that are on the horizon with regard to managing a global workforce. These involve demonstrating the link between global HRM and firm performance, the role of global HR in championing sustainable business, the numerous challenges under the heading of global talent management, and the way in which global mobility is being shaped by the changing needs, locations, and types of international assignments combined with an increasing focus on cost reduction. Finally, the changing nature of careers and the need to create policies and procedures that are fair across employee categories, countries and regions will also be central issues for global HR in the future.

With this book we have tried to capture the broad spectrum of global HRM to include comparative aspects as well as the importance of HRM in the multinational enterprise. Global HRM has come a long way from the study of how to manage expatriates. In this volume we have tried to reflect the fact that globalization requires an understanding of human resource management across countries, cultures, and organizational types.

Acknowledgments

We are grateful for the support and assistance of a great number of people and institutions that contributed to the completion of this project. The Beedie School of Business, Simon Fraser University, Koç University, Istanbul (thank you Zeynep), the Australian School of Business, University of New South Wales, and Wirtschaftsuniversität Wien all provided support in various ways. Mila's association with the Cranfield Network on International Human Resource Management (CRANET) has been invaluable. And our colleagues in the International Organizations Network (ION) are a continuous source of information and inspiration. We thank Patricia Quinn and all the professionals at Sage for allowing us the latitude to do the book the way we wanted and in the time available to us. Thanks to Vicki L. Baker, Albion College, Albion; Diya Das, Bryant University, Smithfield; Linda Kuechler, Daemen College, Amherst; Denise Lanfear, Oakland University, Rochester; Fidelis Ossom, Northeastern State University, Tahlequah; and Kern Peng, Santa Clara University, for providing reviews of the book. We are especially grateful to Karin Rathert for her superb job of copyediting the manuscript and to Echo Yuan Liao for research assistance. Finally, we are both grateful for the tolerance and support of our partners in life and families. Lisa works hard to keep Dave centered and mostly succeeds, and Mila is fortunate to have the love and support of Gancho and Boyan.

Globalization and Human Resource Management

LEARNING OBJECTIVES

After reading this chapter you should be able to

- describe what is meant by the term *globalization*,
- define global *human resource management* (HRM),
- discuss the factors in the external environment that influence global HRM,
- outline the important differences in global and domestic HRM,
- outline the historical development of global HRM, and
- describe the role of the global human resource (HR) professional.

Goldstar Mining[1]

Trevor Hackett scooped his 2-year-old daughter Sally into his arms as he walked into the arrivals area of Toronto's Pearson International Airport. "I don't think I'll be going back to Colombia anytime soon," he said cheerily to reporters as he made his way through the crowd. Even the blowing snow outside could not dampen his spirits today. He was home! Home, after being held captive for 94 days by *Fuerzas Armadas Revolucionarias de Colombia* (*FARC*) high in the mountains of remote Santander province.

the dynamic interconnectedness that results from shifts that are taking place across a range of contexts, including technological, political, economic, and cultural spheres. Figure 1.1 is a graphic representation of the fact that organizations operate in an increasingly interconnected world.

As shown in Figure 1.1, these interconnections operate within and across levels. For example, Thomas Friedman talks about how ten events and forces, including political (fall of the Berlin Wall and later the opening of China, Russia, and Eastern Europe), technological (the advent of Netscape and later other online search and collaborative tools such as Google), cultural (the popularization of the Internet), and economic (the use of thousands of Indian software engineers to work on the Y2K problem from all over the world and waves of outsourcing, offshoring, and global supply chaining) that converged to flatten the world.[7] These forces have created a world that allows for multiple forms of collaboration without regard to geography, time zones, or in many cases even language. While presented as independent elements in Figure 1.1, these environments interact with and influence each other. As an event occurs in any one of the external environments (the introduction of Netscape in the technological sphere) it influences other spheres (the popularization of the Internet in the cultural sphere). These interrelated shifts in the four external environments affect organizations whose leaders respond by integrating *people, processes,* and *structures* to shape organizational

Figure 1.1 Global Interconnections

Source: Adapted from Parker (2005, p. 37).

outcomes. In addition, other elements such as intergovernmental and nongovernment organizations (IGOs and NGOs), buyers, sellers, competitors, unions, and other mediating organizations influence elements of the external environment on the firm. For example, while the fall of the Berlin Wall touched off a worldwide rush to capitalism, NGOs, in representing the interest of society, advocate (either through opposition to or through dialog with organizations) for workers' rights in the absence of unions or legal protection.[8] Thus, these four spheres are not independent. Together they create a complex interconnected external environment in which the organization operates and across which the global organization must function. Despite their interconnectedness, it is useful to consider each individually with respect to global HRM.

Global Technology

The aspect of globalization with perhaps the most potential to shape the organizational environment is the dramatic advances being made in information and communication technology.[9] Technological breakthroughs seem to be occurring on an almost daily basis with the latest communication or computing device even more powerful, smaller, less expensive, and more user-friendly than its predecessor. The pace of technological change is breathtaking. For example, the computer in your cell phone today is a million times cheaper, a thousand times more powerful, and about a hundred times smaller than the one computer owned by the Massachusetts Institute of Technology (MIT) in 1965.[10] The effects of technology largely result from two interlinked activities. First, advances in information technology reduce the cost of communication, leading to more global goods and capital markets. This globalization in turn increases competition and contributes to the spread of technology and to its further development. The decreasing price and increased sophistication of computing systems has placed in the hands of a wide range of organizations capabilities that were available only to large multinational firms only a few years ago. And access to information, resources, products, and markets are all affected by this improved technology. This means that small firms can now compete globally. This is of considerable significance given that across countries of all levels of development, the majority of firms are small and medium sized (SMEs). Now even they have to think globally about HRM. It also means that all organizations are less limited by physical place; for example, making it possible for teams of individuals to be rapidly assembled and just as rapidly disassembled throughout the world, even creating virtual organizations in which employees do not meet face to face but are linked by computer technology.[11] Organizational boundaries are less rigid, and the value chain functions of production, sales and marketing, and distribution might all be located in different countries. As for their influence on HR, technological advances allow for various administrative functions to become easily automated or outsourced.[12] As recently as 30 years ago, there was a widespread belief that technology is largely irrelevant in HR as computers do not have people skills and can not handle HR work. While the "transition from paper to pixels" has taken a couple of decades, today there are very few HR tasks that do not require technology. Organizations in many countries depend on it to manage recruitment, hiring, employee evaluation, compensation, and outsourcing.[13] Therefore, rapid technological change is challenging traditional thinking about organizing and the HR function. And of course, the work roles of employees in all organizations will change to reflect an increasingly information-driven environment.

Global Economics

It is possible to argue that globalization is nothing new—just business as usual. For example, international trade as a percentage of gross world product was only slightly higher at the end of the 20th century than it was before 1914.[14] However, the number of new economic entrants to the international business arena is difficult to ignore. And global economic interconnections are increasingly evident in shifting patterns of trade, foreign direct investment, capital, and labor. In particular, globalization has resulted in worldwide capital markets that were previously closely aligned with nations, allowing both large and small firms around the world to participate in the global economy. A "flat world" is one in which the economic playing field has been leveled for all participants, small and large from developed countries and emerging economies, and one in which value chains in both manufacturing and service industries are becoming (or can become) truly global.[15] While U.S. multinational firms dominated the international business landscape just after World War II, in 2011 as shown in Table 1.1, Tokyo, Beijing, and Paris were home to most of *Fortune* magazine's Global 500. In addition, the service sector of the global economy is increasing rapidly with as much as 70% of advanced economies contained in this sector and with trade in services now about 20% of world exports.[16] Research on patterns of foreign direct investment (FDI) predicts that the relative share of investment in manufacturing will decline, as services and primary sectors offer more attractive FDI opportunities. Further, developing and transition economies are expected to absorb and generate increasing shares of global FDI, with Asia being a primary destination for FDI. While established economies are expected to remain the main sources of FDI, investments from China, India, and Russia will increase substantially.[17]

In summary, the players on the global economic stage are now more likely to include firms headquartered in Asia or Europe as opposed to the United States. They are also more likely to be small-to medium-sized businesses and to be involved in the service sector. It has been suggested that globalization is not a trend or a phenomenon, it is rather an "overarching international system" that shapes not only economic activity but also domestic politics and foreign relations of every country on the planet.[18]

Related to the increased interconnectedness of economies and permeability of political boundaries, the number of permanent migrants is changing the composition of the workforce in many countries. The magnitude of migration is large and increasing. Between 1990 and 2005, the world gained 36 million international migrants. In 2005, the number of international migrants in the world was over 190 million, which was 3% of the world population, or roughly equivalent to the population of the world's fifth largest country, Brazil.[19] Developed countries, as shown in Table 1.2, are the largest recipients of migrants, with China, India, and the Philippines leading the list of sources. A relatively small number of countries are the recipients of the majority of migrants, with 75% of all migrants going to the top 28 countries in 2005.

Table 1.1   Host Cities: Global Fortune 500 in 2011

Rank	City	Country	Number of Global 500 Companies (City)	Global 500 Revenues $ Millions (City)
1	Tokyo	Japan	47	$2,268,640
2	Beijing	China	41	$2,222,366
3	Paris	France	23	$1,285,432
4	London	United Kingdom	18	$1,170,270
5	New York	United States	18	$955,291
6	Seoul	South Korea	12	$640,586
7	Osaka	Japan	8	$376,607
8	Toronto	Canada	7	$197,294
9	Houston	United States	6	$377,702
9	Moscow	Russia	6	$348,084
9	Madrid	Spain	6	$323,345
9	Zurich	Switzerland	6	$221,818
9	Mumbai	India	6	$207,156
14	Amsterdam	Netherlands	5	$261,933
14	Shanghai	China	5	$165,751
16	Munich	Germany	4	$386,355
16	Rome	Italy	4	$283,454
16	Atlanta	United States	4	$184,416
16	Essen (Rhine-Ruhr)	Germany	4	$173,644
16	Brussels	Belgium	4	$144,833
16	Hong Kong	China	4	$141,495
16	Frankfurt	Germany	4	$140,929
16	Sao Paulo	Brazil	4	$135,406

Rank	City	Country	Number of Global 500 Companies (City)	Global 500 Revenues $ Millions (City)
24	Stuttgart	Germany	3	$213,108
24	Mexico City	Mexico	3	$169,776
24	Milan	Italy	3	$109,943
24	Philadelphia	United States	3	$94,643
24	Taipei	Taiwan	3	$90,537
-	Washington D.C.	United States	2	$220,877
-	San Francisco	United States	2	$205,333
-	Minneapolis	United States	2	$87,908
-	Chicago	United States	2	$87,535
-	Melbourne	Australia	2	$74,849
-	Sydney	Australia	2	$70,992
-	Hannover	Germany	2	$56,589
-	Los Angeles	United States	2	$54,614
-	Nagoya	Japan	2	$47,669
-	Detroit	United States	1	$135,592
-	Dallas	United States	1	$124,629
-	Seattle	United States	1	$34,204
-	Boston	United States	1	$33,193

Source: Host Cities, *Fortune* Global 500 (2011).

Two trends in migration have important implications for global HRM. First, the number of women migrants is increasing. In 1976 fewer than 15% of migrants were women, but in 2005 the proportion of women among all international migrants was 50%.[20] Second, the traditional pattern after World War II was that low-skilled workers moved from less developed to more developed countries. While economic factors continue to be a major pull, today's migrant is much more likely to be highly skilled.[21]

Table 1.2   Migrants as a Percentage of Total Population (Countries With at Least 20 Million Inhabitants)

Country	Percentage of Population
Saudi Arabia	26%
Australia	20%
Canada	19%
Ukraine	15%
United States	13%
Germany	12%
France	11%
Spain	11%

Source: Population Division of the United Nations Secretariat (2005).

Note: Migrants as a percentage of total population.

The ease of movement of workers of all skill levels across borders combined with low birthrates in the developed world have changed the characteristics of the workforce in many countries, with increased levels of cultural diversity and more women in the workforce becoming key features. Therefore global HRM policies and procedures must reflect the differing needs of this new workforce demographic. On a larger scale, nation-states that receive migrants become more multiethnic and multicultural and face the increased challenge of integrating migrants and maintaining their own national and cultural identity.[22]

Global Political and Legal Environments

Many of the economic interconnections described previously are forged or brokered by intergovernmental financial institutions, which underscores the link between economics, politics, and organizations.[23] Political systems are the structures and processes by which a nation integrates the parts of society into a functioning unit. At the core of every political system is the need to balance between individual and national interests. The global shift from command to market-based economic structures suggests that many countries believe that free markets can help to achieve that balance. However, the world continues to be organized around nation-states that operate with different political structures and the different laws, rules, and regulations that apply to organizational practices.

There is a wide range of political systems around the world. However, they can be roughly classified along a continuum that represents the degree to which citizens participate in decision making. The two extremes are the pure democracy advocated in ancient Greece at one end and totalitarianism at the other. Totalitarianism typically takes one of two forms, theocratic or secular. In theocratic totalitarianism, religious leaders are also the political leaders, as in Islamic countries in the Middle East such as Iran and Saudi Arabia. Secular totalitarianism includes socialism and communism, where ideological as opposed to religious concepts form the basis of the political system and leaders rely on bureaucratic power, military power, or both. Key elements of political systems affecting organizations are political rights and civil liberties. The extent to which these freedoms exist in a country is often used to anticipate the degree of government interventions with business. For example, in their 2011 report, Freedom House ranked 194 countries on a scale of 1 to 7.[24] Twenty five percent of the world received a rating of 1 as the most free including Australia, New Zealand, Canada, the United States, and most of Europe, while 5% were classified as the least free with a rating of 7 on the index including, Libya, North Korea, and Burma.

The last two decades have produced enormous political change and have transformed the world's political landscape. After four decades of the Cold War, the fall of the Berlin Wall in 1989 marked the beginning of a democratization process in many former secular totalitarian countries, notably those in Central and Eastern Europe. Many of these countries have seen great improvements in political rights and civil liberties. These political changes were closely intertwined with economic liberalization and privatization, leading to the increased participation of these countries in the global marketplace. But economic liberalization is not always matched by political change within countries.[25] For example, China is currently implementing some characteristics of a market economy while still maintaining a political hard line. While pressures to democratize are visible, the government has shown readiness to use various unpopular measures to suppress dissent and maintain order. Other countries have started on the path to democracy only to find themselves regressing back to totalitarianism. Thus, according to the 2011 "Nations in Transit Report," nine of twelve non-Baltic former Soviet states, including Russia, were classified as either semiconsolidated or consolidated authoritarian regimes. Only three (Georgia, Moldova, and Ukraine) fell into more democratic categories. Even in those three states, the state of democracy is very frail, with new governments implementing changes in direct reversal of democratic changes, as in the case of the Ukraine.[26]

Until recently, the Middle Eastern countries were excluded from this democratization process. But the arrival of the Arab Spring in late 2010 signaled that these countries too are ready for a change. Throughout 2011, prodemocracy rebellions erupted throughout the Middle East.[27] The wave of protests was sparked by popular discontent with unlimited political power concentrated in the hands of a small minorities, corruption, lack of political freedom and civil liberties, and extremely high unemployment, especially among youth, which represents the majority of the population in the region. As of early 2012, three governments have been overthrown, others have announced their intent to step down or have made significant concessions, and protests in some countries continue. But whether the events of the Arab Spring will lead to a true democratic revolution is still uncertain. Resistance from authoritarian leaders is still strong, and protest is often met with repression. Even in countries that have implemented changes, the challenge of solidifying the transformations on the path to democracy remains.[28] The interconnectedness of the spheres of globalization is again illustrated as technology is credited with having played a significant role in the events in the Middle East, as protesters used social media to plan their protest and mobilize support.

These shifts in the political landscape underscore the need to estimate the likelihood that a government will undergo political changes and how these changes may affect the organization. It is also important to consider the extent to which governments are involved in the activities of organizations and the overall legal environment associated with doing business in a particular country. With respect to global HRM, companies in some countries have relative freedom when it comes to handling HR issues, whereas in other countries many HR activities are strictly regulated by legislation (e.g., employment discrimination, minimal wage, maximum work hours, unionization rights, pension benefits). Further, some countries, notably members of the European Union, are partially harmonizing their legislation. There is also rising pressure to comply with voluntary guidelines introduced by international organizations such as the United Nations (UN), the Organization of Economic Cooperation and Development (OECD), or the International Labour Organization (ILO), especially in the area of corporate social responsibility, which is often tightly linked to HR issues.

In this context, political and legal pressure for organizations to be consistent with the local environment can sometimes conflict with a more global orientation toward economic activities. For example, organizations may wish to strategically deploy personnel wherever in the world they are most needed, but laws regarding immigration or the national composition of a workforce within a country can limit this ability.

Globalization of Culture

Culture stems from the fundamental way in which a society learns to interact with its environment. The economic, legal, and political systems that have developed over time are the visible elements of a more fundamental set of shared meanings in the society. As described in more detail in the next chapter, culture also affects the goals of the institutions of society, the way the institutions operate, and the reasons that their members have for their policies and behavior. The cultural context deserves special attention because unlike the economic, legal, and political aspects of a country, which are observable, culture is largely invisible. That is, the influence of culture is difficult to detect and is often overlooked.

Some people suggest that the rapid technological and economic development associated with globalization will have a homogenizing effect on culture.[29] For example, products ranging from cola beverages to denim jeans are consumed throughout the world, English is increasingly the global language for business, global travel is inexpensive and fast, and popular culture from films and television is transmitted worldwide. However, others argue that cultural diversity will persist or even expand, as people with different cultural orientations respond differently to this development.[30] For example, while values associated with economic development are converging, this is not true for other elements of culture,[31] and these aspects of culture can be seen to affect behavior in societies.[32] The seemingly identical McDonald's restaurants that exist almost everywhere actually have different meanings and fulfill different social functions in different parts of the world.[33] Although the physical facilities are similar, eating in a McDonald's is a very different social experience in Japan, or China, or the United States, or France.

Both convergence and divergence of culture are probably oversimplifications. The reality is that, although different environments produce different social systems, different environments can also produce similar social systems, and similar environments can produce vastly different cultures.[34] Thus, a reliance on the idea that the influence of the cultural context on global HRM will diminish as a result of globalization is probably not well founded. Global HRM must consider the systematic differences in values, attitudes, beliefs, and assumptions about appropriate behavior that exists across societies and among members of today's increasingly culturally diverse workforce.

Organizational Integration

Organizations function within the envelope established by the interconnected environmental elements of technology, economics, culture, political, and legal systems as shown in Figure 1.1. Organizations respond to this environmental context through different configurations of people, *processes,* and *structures.*[35]

All organizations create structure to coordinate and control the actions of their members. However, the forms that organizations take both domestically and around the world vary considerably. The influence of these different organizational forms on global HRM and the relationship of HRM to the overall organization structure is the subject of Chapter 3. However, it is important to note here that because structures are related to both processes and people, change in one results in changes in the others. For example, when Ford changed from a geographic to a product line structure it saved billions of dollars, but sales processes and the roles of some managers were affected, and new managers were needed in its European operations. To remedy the problems, Ford relocated some employees but also restored some of the authority that regional managers had lost.[36]

Organizational *processes* are flows of activity that link together to accomplish the goals of the organization. Organizational processes are of course linked to both structures and people. For example, process innovations such as just-in-time manufacturing or concurrent engineering can transform the way organizations are structured and the way in which people do their jobs.[37] Of particular importance to HRM is the strategic management of the organization, which is a continuous process involving specifying the organization's mission, vision, and objectives and developing policies and plans to achieve these objectives. Sometimes an organization's business strategy can be its human resource strategy. That is, developing human capital can be a competitive advantage, and it is therefore a strategically important consideration for global HRM.[38]

Organizations are created by and consist of *people.* As organizations globalize, differences in how people think about their jobs, the time they are willing to devote to work, the skills and abilities they have, and the compensation they expect become apparent.[39] Designing and implementing structures and processes require engaging a diverse workforce. Additionally, despite the economic slowdown following the 2008 worldwide financial crisis, many firms continue to report how difficult it is to find the people they need. For example, in 2010 in a survey of 35,000 employers in 36 countries, 31% of firms (up from 30% in 2009) reported that they had difficulty filling positions because of a lack of suitable talent. In Japan the percentage was 76% and in Brazil, 64%.[40]

In summary, organizations must engage with a dynamic and complex set of factors in the global environment. They do this through different configurations of *people*, *processes*, and *structures*. The remainder of this book focuses on how an organization can attract, engage, develop, and retain the employees that it needs to thrive in today's global environment. To set the stage for this discussion, it is useful to examine the historical development of HRM.

Evolution of Global HRM

The roots of modern human resource management in an international context can be traced to the Industrial Revolution of the late 18th century.[41] The forces of industrialization drove employment policies and practices until the rapid internationalization of organizations that followed World War II. The idea of internationalization was a dominant factor until the 1990s when the distinction between domestic and international business began to blur with the vast majority of firms becoming exposed to international competition. While the seeds of globalization had been sown much earlier, it was from the early 1990s on that forces of globalization began to have a significant influence on HRM policies and practices. Therefore, the three broad phase of development of global HRM can be categorized as the eras of *industrialization*, *internationalization*, and *globalization*.

Era of Industrialization

The spread of industrialization in Europe and the United Sates prompted a global search for the raw materials to fuel this development. Trading firms, shipping companies, banks, and utilities were all involved in international expansion. By the mid-19th century cross-border manufacturing began to emerge. The level of development of transportation and communications made it difficult to exercise control over geographically distant operations. Family members were often sent abroad to ensure that distant subsidiaries acted in the best interest of the parent firm. For example, when Siemens set up a factory in Saint Petersburg in 1855, a brother of the founder was put in charge, and in 1863 another brother established a manufacturing subsidiary in Britain.[42]

During this era, the way in which firms were organized was influenced by new manufacturing techniques such as interchangeable parts and the resultant division of labor. To alleviate punctuality, attendance, and supervision problems created by the mechanical pacing of work, some individuals, such as Scottish textile mill operator Robert Owen in 1810, began attending to the welfare of employees. Under his direction, workers were provided with housing, dining facilities, recreation centers, and so on, and the minimum wage and schooling for children were introduced. By the late 1880s, these ideas had spread to the United States in the form of a philosophy called *industrial betterment*.[43] The industrial betterment movement resulted in the creation of the first managers whose main responsibilities revolved around the workers rather than the work process, called *welfare secretaries*, who were initially engaged in education, health and safety, and social issues.[44]

By the early 1900s, multinational activity had become an important element of the world economy, with numerous, large, multinational manufacturing firms supported by a global infrastructure of service firms. This period saw the emergence of the *scientific management* movement in the United States with its emphasis on making the most efficient use of a poorly educated immigrant labor pool. The focus of what were now increasingly called *personnel* directors shifted to conducting time and motion studies, preparing job specifications and financial incentive programs, as well as a continuing focus on employee morale. Thus, modern HRM has a dual legacy in both the industrial betterment and scientific management initiatives.

Two world wars and the Great Depression saw a retrenchment of international business activity while *personnel management* emerged as a function quite separate from line management with an emphasis on systematic recruitment, testing, and assessment of employees, some of which had spilled over from the psychological testing used by the military.[45] The personnel department was further strengthened during this time because of its role in managing the relationship with labor unions.

Era of Internationalization

While international commerce had long existed in Europe and Asia, it was the rapid post World War II international expansion of U.S. firms that gave rise to institutions that truly transcended national borders—the modern multinational corporation. The drivers of this internationalization were the fact that the United States had emerged as the unprecedented leader of the world economy following the war, coupled with advances in transportation and technology such as the introduction of commercial jet travel, transatlantic telephone links, and the use of computer technology. The rush to internationalize created an increase in the international job market that could not be filled by the sons of internationally experienced military or diplomatic fathers. The focus of the expanding *personnel* departments was on expatriation.[46] Initially this activity focused on persuading managers to accept overseas assignments, usually through financial incentives. In the 1970s, the costs of expatriation, reports of expatriate failure, and increased employee resistance to moving overseas refocused activities to support for expatriates to assure success. The use of the term *human resource management* became popular[47] at this time, and coupled with the study of expatriation, gave rise to the academic study of international HRM.[48]

The rapid growth of multinational organizations created issues with regard to the coordination and control of far flung operations. The problem of how to best organize to meet this challenge resulted in two approaches to organizational structure, both of which contributed to the internationalization of HRM. One approach was implementing matrix organizational structures involving both product and geographic reporting lines, while the other was to have more headquarters staff in coordinating roles. In the first case, the difficulties associated with matrix structures, in particular dual authority relationships and horizontal communication linkages, created people management challenges that involved HRM as opposed to strategy and structure. In the second case, the increase in headquarters staff required for coordination led to top-heavy bureaucracies that eroded competitiveness. Downsizing staff bureaucracies began with the U.S.-based firms but was followed by European, and then following the financial crisis of the 1990s, by Asian firms. Therefore, HRM turned its attention to outplacement and redesigning jobs to manage this change. Coupled with expatriation, the need to coordinate and control the activities of the multinational organization recognized during this era continues to be a major element of global HRM.

During the 1980s, the idea that the management of human resources could be a strategic advantage began to take hold, which in turn questioned the notion that there was a single best approach to HRM. Growing research on cultural differences in management practice[49] along with the ability of Japanese firms to make such an amazing recovery after World War II, with people as their only natural resource, awakened Western managers to the fact that very different approaches to the management of people could be successful. The recognition that organizations who were expanding overseas did not necessarily have superior management practices coupled with pressure from local governments to hire and develop local employees shifted HRM focus to also include recruiting and developing local executives to run foreign subsidiaries. As organizations began to adopt the approach that talent mattered more than nationality, the challenge for global HRM became how to identify, develop, and transfer and repatriate talent that was spread out across the world.

Era of Globalization and Beyond

The accelerating global completion of the 1990s caused organizations of all sizes and types to consider the global context in which they were operating. Previously HRM had a heavily functional focus primarily on managing international assignments. However, the erosion of traditional sources of competitive advantage by the forces of globalization emphasized the need for organizations to create sustainable competitive advantage through HRM. This has brought HRM to center stage with regard to management practice and stimulated many innovations that have improved operational effectiveness. More important perhaps is the recognition that in order to be competitive in today's global environment HRM must be aligned with organizational strategy. An important development in thinking about the alignment of HRM and strategy is what is called the *resource-based view* of the organization.[50] The idea that the organization can be viewed as a bundle of resources gave rise to notion that HRM-related capabilities (such as staffing practices, performance appraisals, training and development, compensation, or union-management relationships) could be sources of competitive advantage.[51] For example, Hewlett-Packard's (HP) organizational strategy requires continuous innovation of products and services. HP's competitive advantage stems in part from the entrepreneurial behavior that is stimulated by their reward system.[52] Globalization has also caused multinational organizations to recognize that a critical aspect of maintaining their competitive advantage is the ability to learn across its geographic boundaries.[53] Valuable knowledge can originate anywhere in the network of subsidiaries, and concerted efforts are needed to ensure that knowledge and innovative practices are transferred not only from headquarters to subsidiaries but within and across all organizational units, regardless of their geographic location. The importance of transferring and recombining knowledge effectively reinforces the role of HRM as central to organizational effectiveness. While explicit knowledge can be easily passed on to others through texts or manuals, complex tacit knowledge (knowledge you don't know you have), which is based on experience and is difficult to put into words, can be a source of competitive advantage.[54] This knowledge is embodied in individuals. In order for organizations to leverage it these individuals must be retained and assigned to roles in which the knowledge can be used.

HRM in the age of globalization continues to be concerned with the challenges of foreign assignments and the coordination and control of geographically distributed organizations. However, there is a growing recognition that organizational effectiveness involves tracking and developing a global talent pool and that talent not nationality is key. Furthermore, while HRM was initially seen as a means to implementing organizational strategy, it is increasingly viewed as a source of competitive advantage, in particular as the transfer and recombination of knowledge increases in its strategic importance.

Global Versus Domestic HRM

The globalization of business requires HRM in all types of organizations to consider the broader context of its activities and the interests of different stakeholders.[55] However, global organizations need to manage the additional challenge of successfully navigating diverse institutional, social, cultural, political, and economic environments. It is the need to leverage all these differences that makes the HRM activities in global organizations much more complex than the HRM activities of purely domestic organizations.[56] This complexity affects the people, processes, and structures required to deliver the functions of HRM. Global HRM must (a) consider more and different contextual influences, (b) operate under higher levels of risk, (c) engage in a broader set of activities, (d) fulfill many strategic roles, and (e) balance the forces toward differentiation versus internal consistency of HR operations.[57]

More and Different Contextual Influences

In a purely domestic context, HRM is concerned with a single national context, including its legal, economic, political, and cultural elements. In global HRM, policies and procedures must be constructed and implemented with the variety of national contexts in mind. This requires more in-depth knowledge of countries and cultures as well as a broader understanding of issues. For example, as discussed in Chapter 8, compensation programs that provide incentives for employees to accept an overseas assignment can create serious inequities with local managers at the same level.

Operating across national boundaries increases the number, type, and variety of external factors with which HRM must contend, and the relative importance of factors external to the organization is hugely variable. For example, in Islamic countries religion dictates numerous work practices, including time and space for daily prayers, a work week that includes a Saturday through Wednesday (e.g., Saudi Arabia) or a Sunday through Thursday (e.g., Egypt, Jordan, United Arab Emirates) schedule. In addition, international nongovernmental organizations (NGOs) and human rights groups are more active and influential in some parts of the world compared to others. For example, variations in labor standards around the world attract the attention of such groups as the International Labour Rights Forum and Amnesty International's Human Rights Division requiring global HR managers to understand and interact effectively with these groups.

Higher Risk Exposure

Global HRM often involves higher levels of risk than domestic HR activities. This additional risk takes a number of different forms. For example, the additional expense associated with sending expatriates on overseas assignments creates a financial risk associated with the potential for these employees to return without completing the assignment or to underperform. In addition, globalization has reduced boundaries not only for business organizations but for international gangs, terrorist groups, and political activists as well.[58] While the case that opened this chapter may be somewhat unusual, multinational organizations now routinely consider political risk and terrorism in planning international assignments, meetings, and so on. Finally, the simple fact that international organizations operate in multiple geographies exposes them to greater risk from both natural and manmade sources. As described earlier, in the first quarter of 2011, prodemocracy demonstrators in Egypt staged a massive protest that led to the downfall of the Mubarak government and spread across North Africa to Tunisia, Syria, Jordan, Yemen, and Libya, while across the world a massive 8.9 magnitude earthquake and subsequent tsunami in Japan left tens of thousands dead, hundreds of thousands displaced, and created a massive economic shock.

Broader Set of HR Activities

Operating in multiple national environments makes a number of activities necessary that are not required in a purely domestic context. In addition to the multiple activities associated with managing international mobility of employees (e.g., family relocation, international tax services), global HR departments are engaged in complex processes such as global redistribution and relocation of work, the integration of organizational units following international mergers, acquisitions or joint ventures, and providing input in the designing of HR practices in greenfield investments overseas. Global HR is also involved in creating conditions for successful transfer of HR practices across contexts, disseminating corporate culture, facilitating knowledge transfer across borders, and creating and maintaining formal and informal HR networks that span the globe.[59]

Balancing Differentiation and Internal Consistency[60]

In contrast to HRM in domestic organizations, which operate in fairly homogenous national contexts, global HRM needs to continuously balance two conflicting principles that stem from the dual pressures in international operations. This is the need to be both responsive to local environments *and* internally consistent (discussed in more detail in Chapter 3). On the one hand, multinational enterprises (MNEs) need to ensure that the HR policies and practices they introduce will be accepted in the various national environments. They must fit with local employment regulations, broader institutional conditions, and local cultural values. For example, introducing a compensation practice that foregoes union consultation in a country with a strong union presence may not only alienate workers but may be in violation of local laws. This means that to fit well with local environments, organizations may need to introduce different HR practices in the different countries where they operate.

On the other hand, global HRM also needs to create coherence and internal consistency between HRM strategy and the HRM policies and practices in different locations of the organization. To achieve this, HRM practices should display a consistent theme or message that reflects a clear and coherent management philosophy that the organization embodies. Local adaption of HR practices in each national subsidiary may diminish the competitive advantage of the organization. That is, by choosing to adopt local practices the MNE runs the risk of becoming like every other local organization and of losing the rare and unique capabilities that made it successful in the first place.

This dilemma between local adaptation and internal consistency brings about the need to carefully balance the two principles and to decide which structures, processes, and core HR practices will achieve the optimum balance between responding to local workforce requirements and maintaining consistency and integration. As the dynamic global work environment changes, organizations respond with different configurations of people, processes, and structures. This means that HRM must constantly be prepared to shift emphasis among different sets of employees and activities. For example, as an organization involved in a particular country matures it may seek to fill managerial position with local nationals as opposed to parent country nationals. This changes the emphasis of HRM from recruiting, selecting, training, and supporting expatriates to the training and development of locals. The need to shift emphasis as the environment and organizational needs dictate adds considerable complexity to the global HRM function.

Mapping Global HRM

Models of HRM vary depending on the extent to which they emphasize the fit between HRM and business strategy with a goal to improving organizational effectiveness[61] or a more pluralistic perspective that considers multiple stakeholders and situational factors as antecedents to HRM policy choices.[62] Here we map the domain of HRM onto the multiple contexts that influence HRM in a global environment. This framework is presented in Figure 1.2.

These include factors in the external environment, including culture and the institutions that reflect different legal, political, and economic systems and also differences in the organizational context. In this book, Chapter 2 focuses on the external (cultural and institutional) factors, while Chapter 3 deals with the internal (organizational) context for global HRM. These factors interact with the core functions of HRM to result in different configurations of people, processes, and structures involved in decision making about the human resources of the organization. The result is not only the definition of particular policies or practices but also the priority ranking or relative importance of a particular domain, the feasibility and mechanisms for implementing a particular policy or procedure, and how that policy or procedure might be organized.[63] For example, by drawing on the various elements outlined in Figure 1.2 we could define the domain of a particular HR activity as attracting computer technicians in a joint venture in the petroleum industry to work on drilling rigs off the coast of Norway. The feasibility of engaging particular people (HRM professionals and/or line managers), a particular process (university on-campus recruiting or professional associations), or particular structures (local Norwegian HR, headquarters HR, or both) might vary depending on other factors, such as the human resource strategy of the firm or its organizational culture. This framework does not prescribe the configuration

Figure 1.2 Map of Global HRM

of global HRM activities nor does it suggest a strictly contingent relationship. For example, the configurations of HRM activities might be as influential in shaping organizational strategy as the reverse, and as we discussed at the outset, the interconnectedness of the environmental and organizational factors means that a change in one affects the others. However, this static diagram is useful in mapping the various elements that must be considered by HRM in a global context.

An outgrowth on mapping global HRM in this way is that it highlights the additional complexity of the role of the global HR professional. While the responsibility for managing human resources does not reside exclusively with HR professionals, it seems clear that the perspectives and competencies of the global HR manager must be greatly expanded to deal with the multiple countries and cultures with which they must engage. The need for global HR professionals to have specific competencies is reflected in the criteria that the Society for HRM in the United States sets for certification as a *global professional in HR*[64]. According to the society, a global professional in HR

- has HR responsibilities that cross national borders;
- understands the strategies of globalization versus localization of HR policies and programs;
- establishes HR policies and initiatives that support the organization's global growth and employer reputation;
- designs organizational programs, processes, and tools to achieve worldwide business goals;
- develops, implements, and evaluates programs, processes and tools;
- ensures that programs, processes, and tools align with competitive practice, the organization's objectives, and legal requirements;
- oversees practices that balance employer needs with employee rights and needs; and
- has core knowledge of the organization's international HR activities.

The broad competency domains assessed in the certification process are

- strategic management (26%);
- global talent acquisition and mobility (22%);
- global compensation and benefits (18%);
- organizational effectiveness and talent development (22%), and
- workforce relations and risk management (12%).

While this description may reflect a particular functional perspective of the role of HR, the fact that such a certification exits indicates the recognition of the substantial additional challenges faced by HR professionals in a global context.

Chapter Summary

This chapter examines human resource management in global context. The global context includes the cultural, political, legal, economic, and technological aspects of the various national environments in which firms might operate. However, it also includes the dynamic interconnectedness called *globalization* that has resulted from recent shifts that have occurred across contexts. Organizations engage with this dynamic and complex set of factors through different configurations of people, processes, and structures. The people, processes, and structures involved in making decisions concerning the human resources of organizations in today's global environment is the core focus of this book. Global HRM has its origins in responses to the forces of industrialization, later of internationalization, and now globalization. HRM in the era of globalization is still concerned with the challenges of foreign assignments and the coordination and control of geographically distributed organizations. However, it is increasingly engaged in the development and utilization of a global talent pool and viewed as a source of competitive advantage. While all organizations need to consider how the global context influences HRM, organizations that operate in multiple countries face a number of additional challenges that are not present in a purely domestic context. This increased complexity has implications for the activities, policies, and procedures of HRM and also for the role of HR professionals.

Questions for Discussion

1. Discuss the key elements of the external environment that shape global HRM.

2. Describe how international HRM differs from purely domestic HRM.

3. Describe how the eras of industrialization and internationalization influenced HRM.

4. Give an example of how an organization might engage with its environment by configuring its people, processes, and structures.

5. In what ways is the role of the global HR professional different from his or her domestic counterpart?

Notes

1. This case is fictional but based on the true story of Norbert Reinhardt reported in *Mclean's* magazine, January 25, 1999.
2. See Beer, Spector, Lawrence, Mills, & Walton (1984) for a discussion of this definition of HRM.
3. For more on globalization and business, see Parker (2005).
4. See Ohmae (1995); Renesch (1992).
5. See Friedman (2005); Robertson (1995).
6. Parker (2005).
7. Friedman (2005).
8. Chen, E. (2009, May 26). "NGOs in China: The rise of civil-awareness," *People's Daily.*
9. See Naisbitt (1994).
10. Mcleod, S., Fisch, K., & Bestler, L. (2009). XPLANE. *Economist,* http://mediconvergence .economist.com.
11. See Erez & Earley (1993).
12. See Marler (2009).

13 Caudron, Gale, Greengard, & Hall (2002).

14. Farnham (1994).

15. Friedman (2005).

16. Parker (2005).

17. Word Investment Report, 2010. UNCTAD.org.

18. Friedman (1999).

19. Population Division of the United Nations Secretariat, *Trends in total migrant stock: The 2005 revision.* Retrieved from http://www.un.org/esa/population/publications/migration/UN_Migrant_Stock_Documentation_2005.pdf.

20. Ibid.

21. Carr, Inkson, & Thorn (2005).

22. Menipaz & Menipaz (2011).

23. See Parker (2005) for a discussion.

24. http://www.freedomhouse.org/report/freedom-world/freedom-world-2011.

25. See Napier & Thomas (2004).

26. Walker (2011).

27. *The Guardian.* http://www.guardian.co.uk/world/interactive/2011/mar/22/middle-east-protest-interactive-timeline.

28. Puddington (2012).

29. For example, see Dunphy (1987).

30. For example, see Lincoln, Olsen, & Hanada (1978).

31. Inglehart & Baker (2000).

32. See Smith & Bond (1999).

33. Watson (1997).

34. See Cohen (2001).

35. See Parker (2005).

36. Lublin (2000).

37. See Carter & Baker (1991).

38. See Evans, Pucik, & Barsoux (2002).

39. See Thomas, Au, & Ravlin (2003).

40. 2010 Talent Shortage Survey Results, Manpower Inc.

41. Our discussion of the historical development of HRM draws on Evans, Pucik, & Barsoux (2002).

42. Evans, Pucik, & Barsoux (2002).

43. George (1968).

44. Crichton (1968).

45. Jacoby (1985).

46. See Thomas (1994) for a discussion.

47. The term possibly originated from the Japanese word *jinzai* (human material), which gained use in post war Japan, or from early economics research on "human capital."

48. For a discussion see Thomas (2008).

49. See Hofstede (1980).

50. See Barney (1991) for a discussion from a management strategy perspective.

51. Schuler & Macmillan (1984).

52. *Business Week.* (2009, September 23). How Hewlett-Packard turns strategy into action.

53. See Kogut & Zander (1992).

54. See Nonaka & Takeuchi (1995) for a discussion.

55. See Beer, Spector, Lawrence, Mills, & Walton (1984) for a discussion of the stakeholder interests served by HRM.

56. Dowling et al.; Sparrow, Brewster, & Harris (2004).
57. This classification is based on Dowling (1988), Evans, Pucik, & Bjorkman (2011), and Farndale, Scullion, & Sparrow (2010).
58. See Parker (2005) for a discussion.
59. Sparrow, Brewster, & Harris (2004).
60. Discussion based on Evans, Pucik, & Bjorkman (2011).
61. Fombrun, Tichy, & Devanna (1984).
62. Beer, Spector, Lawrence, Mills, & Walton (1984).
63. Murray, Jain, & Adams (1976).
64. http://www.hrci.org/HRCertification.aspx?id=67.

2

Cultural and Institutional Context of Global Human Resource Management

LEARNING OBJECTIVES

After reading this chapter you should be able to

- describe the basic characteristics of culture and explain how cultural dimensions can be used in global HRM,
- describe how the institutions of society can shape HRM policies and procedures,
- discuss the possibility of the convergence of HRM across countries,
- explain how the heritage of state socialism continues to influence the context of HRM in transition economies, and
- discuss the effects of cultural and institutional context on the HRM role and on employee expectations.

Springtime in Paris

As she savored the last bite of her croissant, Martha Pereaux, HR director for C3 Technologies, thought about how she would approach her latest "cross-cultural collision," as she had come to think of them. In the year since she had moved to Paris from Houston, there had been many, but none quite as bizarre as this one.

Martha had taken the big promotion to head up the HR division of the joint venture between Houston-based SuperChem and the French company. C3 developed technology for the oil industry, primarily new types of concrete that formed the barrier wall for offshore oil and gas wells. The joint venture was meant to take on the likes of the giant Schlumberger on its own turf and compete with them for valuable technical staff.

Everyone said she was the perfect choice, having grown up in a bilingual family in Canada, with a chemical engineering degree and an MBA with an emphasis in international management. But nothing had really prepared her for the day-to-day challenges she faced in Paris. Every time she thought she had the French figured out something new would arise that mystified her. They could be so "French" she thought.

She had called the meeting this morning with the lead chemist Dr. Bertrand to discuss his rejection of her recruit Frank Reynolds, a recently graduated PhD from MIT and an expert in synthetic polymer chemistry, which C3 desperately needed. Despite what to Martha seemed impeccable credentials Bertrand had refused even to interview him. "The graphology report shows him to be unreliable," said Bertrand. Graphology—handwriting analysis—thought Martha, what will it be next?

It's still early, she thought as she paid for her breakfast. I might as well walk the few blocks over to the office in the seventh arrondissement and try to figure out where Bertrand's thinking is coming from. It's a lovely spring morning and I could use the exercise. The bread in France is wonderful, but it's not doing much for my figure.

Introduction

While the use of handwriting analysis as a selection technique, as mentioned in the opening vignette, may be peculiar to a few countries such as France, HRM policies and practices do vary significantly in different countries in which global firms operate. Thus, global HRM is not only about understanding the HRM practices of international organizations but also about the ways in which the context that different countries provide influence human resource management.[1] In this chapter we discuss both cultural and institutional factors of societies that shape HRM.[2]

Cultural Context

Culture is a widely recognized word, but its exact meaning can be elusive. A useful way of thinking about culture is that it is the mental programs that are shared by groups of people and that condition their responses to their environment.³ Therefore, in terms of establishing the context for HRM, culture consists of values, attitudes, beliefs, and assumptions about appropriate behavior that are shared in a society. In order to understand how this cultural context influences HRM, it is important to know some basic characteristics of culture, the way in which cultures vary in a systematic way, and how culture has its influence.

Characteristics of Culture

Several general characteristics of culture are important to keep in mind in order to understand the effect that the cultural context has on HRM. These are that culture is *shared,* it is *learned,* and it is *systematic and organized.* Also, cultures can be *tight* or *loose.* By definition, culture is something that is shared by a specific group of people and is not readily available to individuals outside this group. This may be one of the reasons that Martha in the opening vignette is having a difficult time understanding the French culture even though she speaks the language fluently. If we think of culture as mental programming, culture exists at the middle of three levels as shown in Figure 2.1.

Figure 2.1   Three Levels of Mental Programming

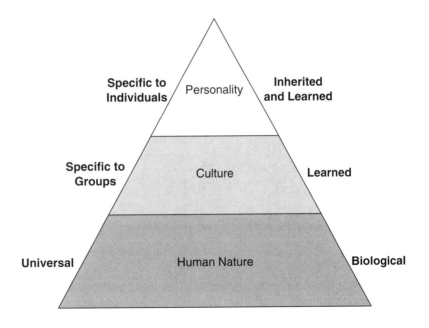

Source: Adapted from Hofstede (1980).

At the base level, all human beings share certain biological characteristics. At the highest level are the personality characteristics that are unique to each of us. Culture occurs at an intermediate level and consists of the elements of mental programming that we share with others in our specific group. Also, as indicated in Figure 2.1, culture is transmitted through the process of learning and interacting with the environment. Over time, societies develop patterned ways of dealing with their environment, and this is passed on from generation to generation. For example, guidance about appropriate behavior in a particular culture is often contained in the stories parents tell their children.[4]

A third important characteristic of culture is that culture is not a random assortment of customs and beliefs but is an organized system of values, attitudes, and meanings that are related to each other. The visible artifacts of culture (language, customs, dress, etc.) are related to a deeper set of meanings that are not accessible to outsiders but are taken for granted by members of a cultural group. Thus, because of the mental programming imposed by our own culture, the cultures of others often seem strange and illogical, as indicated in Martha's feelings about graphology in the opening vignette. Because much of culture is hidden, the superficial and visible elements of culture have been likened to the tip of an iceberg, with more fundamental aspects well below the surface.[5] Icebergs have as much as 90% of their mass below the surface of the water, leaving only a small percentage visible. Like the iceberg, it is the deep underlying assumptions of culture that are the ultimate source of values and action. It is at this level that the logic and coherence of a culture can be understood. Thus, a deeper understanding can often reveal the logic in beliefs and behaviors that seem strange and illogical on the surface.

Cultures differ not only in their details but also in the extent to which they are shared among members of society. Some cultures have widespread agreement about correct behavior, while others have greater diversity and tolerance of difference.[6] So-called *tight* cultures, such as Japan's, have broad agreement on cultural norms and are often based on homogeneous populations or the dominance of particular religious beliefs. Countries with diverse populations, such as Canada, have relatively *loose* cultures with a greater degree of variability of thought and action accepted and even encouraged. Thus, it is important to remember that there can be very different degrees of consensus among members of society on culturally-based values, attitudes, beliefs, and assumptions about appropriate behavior.[7]

Comparing Cultures

Societal culture is best expressed in the complex interactions of values, attitudes, and behavioral assumptions among its members. However, in order for the concept of culture to be useful in management studies, much of our understanding has been achieved by reducing the analysis to the study of values. Value differences arise from the solutions that different societies have devised over time for dealing with fundamental problems. Because there are a limited number of ways in which a society can manage these problems, it is possible to develop a system that categorizes and compares societies on this basis.[8] By examining the choices that societies have made we can infer their values, that is their preferences for the way things ought to be or the way one should behave.

Despite being devised at widely different times and with different methods, some very similar sets of cultural dimensions have been identified. Because none of these dimensional approaches is entirely satisfactory as a basis for cultural comparison, we briefly review the major frameworks that have been devised for categorizing and comparing cultures. This review leads to a more in-depth look at the concept of individualism and collectivism and its relationship to other elements of the socio-cultural system.

Kluckhohn and Strodtbeck's Framework

Early studies in comparative anthropology produced a framework that has influenced the way the management literature has conceptualized cultural variation.[9] This categorization identified six dimensions along which a society can be categorized. These variations in value orientations concern the following issues:

- *Relationship to nature*—People have a need or duty to control or master nature (domination), to submit to nature (subjugation), or to work together with nature to maintain harmony and balance (harmony).
- *Beliefs about human nature*—People are inherently good, evil, or a mixture of good and evil.
- *Relationships among people*—The greatest concern and responsibility is for one's self and immediate family (individualist), for one's own group that is defined in different ways (collateral), or for one's groups that are arranged in a rigid hierarchy (hierarchical).
- *Nature of human activity*—People should concentrate on living for the moment (being), striving for goals (achieving), or reflecting (thinking).
- *Conception of space*—The physical space we use is private, public, or a mixture of public and private.
- *Orientation to time*—People should make decisions with respect to traditions or events in the past, events in the present, or events in the future.

Hofstede's Study

A framework that has received a great deal of attention is Hofstede's now classic study of work values.[10] Based on attitude surveys of 117,000 employees of a large U.S. multinational corporation (later identified as IBM), Hofstede extracted four dimensions with which he could classify the 40 different countries represented. These dimensions were named *individualism-collectivism, power distance, uncertainty avoidance,* and *masculinity-femininity.*

Individualism-collectivism is the extent to which one's self-identity is defined according to individual characteristics or by the characteristics of the groups to which the individual belongs on a permanent basis and the extent to which individual or group interests dominate. Power distance refers to the extent that power differences are accepted and sanctioned in a society. Uncertainty avoidance is the extent to which societies focus on ways to reduce uncertainty and create stability. Masculinity-femininity refers to the extent to which *traditional* male orientations of ambition and achievement are emphasized over *traditional* female orientations of nurturance and interpersonal harmony. By giving each of the 40 countries (later 50) a score, ranging from 0 to 100 on each of the four dimensions,[11] Hofstede derived a classification of national cultures. In an effort to investigate the possibility of a Western bias in this classification, a subsequent study in 23 countries[12] revealed a new cultural value orientation important in Chinese culture, *Confucian work dynamism* (later called *long-term/short-term orientation*),[13] interpreted as dealing with society's search for virtue. Societies with long-term orientation tend to show preference for order, thrift, and persistence. Recently, a sixth value orientation called *indulgence versus restraint* was identified. Indulgence stands for pursuit of gratification of basic needs and desires and hedonistic behaviors, while restraint describes societies with strict social norms where gratification of needs is suppressed.[14]

It is particularly important to point out that Hofstede's value scores were the average score for all participants in each country. Therefore, it is not appropriate to infer that because two nations differ on a particular value dimension that any two individuals from those countries will differ in the same way. Within each nation there might be variation on a particular dimension, such that a particular individual will not be at all representative of the mean score. For example, Figure 2.2 shows the hypothetical distribution of individual scores on individualism-collectivism between a collectivist country (Malaysia) and an individualist country (New Zealand).

As shown in Figure 2.2, it is entirely possible to find an individual in New Zealand who scores lower on individualism than someone in Malaysia.

Figure 2.2   Hypothetical Distribution of Individualism–Collectivism Scores

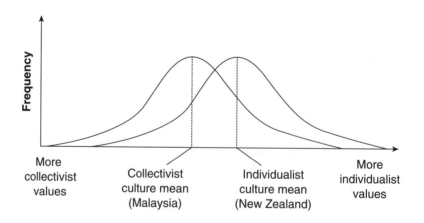

Source: Thomas (2008, Figure 3.2).

Schwartz Value Survey

In what can be seen as a refinement of Hofstede's earlier work, several additional large-scale surveys of values have been conducted.[15] Each of these studies adds something new to our understanding of cultural differences. The first of these is the Schwartz Value Survey.[16] Based on a review of previous theory and research, Shalom Schwartz and his colleagues conducted a series of studies on the content and structure of human values based on three universal human requirements. The first is the nature of the relationship between the individual and the group, the second is the preservation of the society itself, and the final problem relates to the relationship of people to the natural world. From these requirements that all societies share, Schwartz and his team derived values that reflected various ways of satisfying these needs.

To define cultural dimensions at the level of national culture, Schwartz and colleagues performed an analysis that yielded seven value types that were labeled as the following:

1. *Egalitarianism,* recognition of people as moral equals

2. *Harmony,* fitting in harmoniously with the environment

3. *Embeddedness,* people as embedded in the collective

4. *Hierarchy,* unequal distribution of power is legitimate

5. *Mastery,* exploitation of the natural or social environment

6. *Affective autonomy,* pursuit of positive experiences

7. *Intellectual autonomy,* independent pursuit of own ideas

A procedure that generates a two-dimensional graphic representation of the relationship of countries to each other on all seven dimensions simultaneously produces the diagram shown in Figure 2.3.[17]

As shown in Figure 2.3, the location of countries along the seven value vectors indicates their relationship to each other. The direction of the vector indicates the increasing importance of the value type in relationship to the center of the diagram marked by the X. For example, the line drawn on Figure 2.3 indicates the importance that each country attributes to *intellectual autonomy.* To locate a country on this dimension, a perpendicular line is drawn from the position of the country to the vector. The lines drawn on the figure indicate that this dimension is very important in France, less so in Norway, India, and Singapore, and very unimportant in Ghana.

The GLOBE Study

The most recent study of cultural differences in value orientations was undertaken as a part of the Global Leadership and Organizational Behavior Effectiveness (GLOBE) program.[18] One of the outcomes of the GLOBE research was the construction of nine dimensions of cultural variation. The first four of these dimensions are

Figure 2.3 Co-Plot of Value Dimensions Across 57 National Cultures

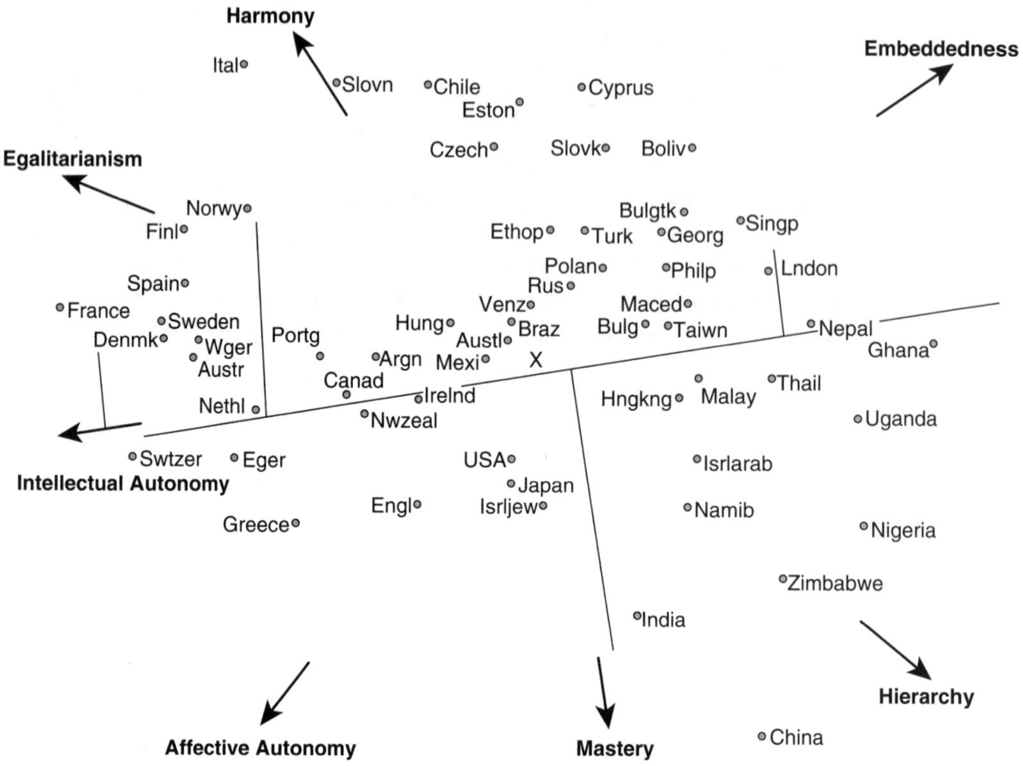

Source: Sagiv & Schwartz (2000).

described as direct extensions of Hofstede's work, with the exception that two dimensions of collectivism are presented. These four dimensions are the following:

- *Institutional Collectivism*—The degree to which organizational and societal institutional practices encourage and reward collective distribution of resources and collective action
- *In-Group Collectivism*—The degree to which individuals express pride, loyalty, and cohesiveness in their organizations or families
- *Power Distance*—The degree to which members of a collective expect power to be distributed equally
- *Uncertainty Avoidance*—The extent to which a society, organization, or group relies on social norms, rules, and procedures to alleviate unpredictability of future events

The next two dimensions can be seen as reconceptualization of Hofstede's masculinity-femininity dimension. They are the following:

- *Gender Egalitarianism*—The degree to which a collective minimizes gender inequality
- *Assertiveness*—The degree to which individuals are assertive, confrontational, and aggressive in their relationships with others

The next two dimensions have their origins in the work of Kluckhohn and Strodtbeck on the nature of people and time orientation presented previously and are the following:

- *Humane Orientation*—The degree to which a collective encourages and rewards individuals for being fair, altruistic, generous, caring, and kind to others
- *Future Orientation*—The extent to which individuals engage in future-oriented behaviors, such as delayed gratification, planning, and investing in the future

The final dimension is derived from work on achievement motivation,[19] but is also related to Hofstede's masculinity concept.[20] This dimension is the following:

- *Performance Orientation*—The degree to which a collective encourages and rewards group members for performance improvement and excellence

The country scores for GLOBE data are presented in the Appendix. However, an additional way of understanding similarities and differences across cultures is to examine which countries cluster together in their positions on measures of cultural values. Based on the GLOBE data these clusters are shown in Figure 2.4.

As shown in Figure 2.4 the clusters of countries reflect such factors as common language, common religion, common climate, common economic systems, and shared political boundaries, some aspects of which are discussed ahead in this chapter as culture and the institutions of society share a common history.

As the previous discussion indicates, the results of the major studies of national variation in value orientations have some remarkable similarities, despite being conducted at widely different times, with different samples, and using different methods. This consistency of findings shows the utility of this approach to describing cultural variation. In addition, however, because they appear in some form in all of the frameworks, individualism-collectivism and power distance (verticality) are perhaps more important to understanding cultural variation. These dimensions relate to two of the three fundamental issues that have been identified as being common among societies.[21] The first has to do with boundaries between individuals and groups and the second with the preservation of order in society.

Horizontal and Vertical Individualism and Collectivism

Because they relate to fundamental differences among societies, individualism and collectivism are perhaps the most useful and powerful dimensions of cultural variation in explaining a wide range of behavior.[22] Individualism refers to viewing one's self as independent of others and to be more concerned about the consequences of a particular behavior for one's self. Alternatively, collectivism refers to viewing one's self as interdependent with selected others, to being concerned about the consequences of

Figure 2.4   Country Clusters According to GLOBE

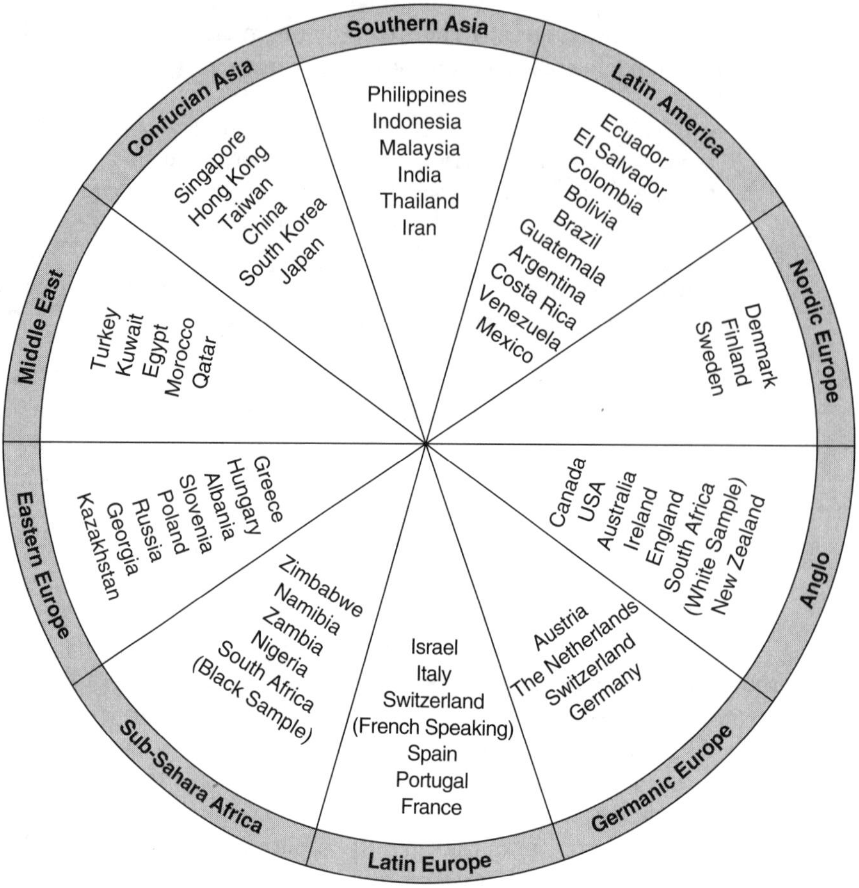

Source: Reprinted from House et al. (2004).

behavior for one's reference group, and to being willing to sacrifice personal interests for the good of this group. However, individualism-collectivism is not a dichotomy of self-interest and group interest. Both individualists and collectivists derive their sense of self, in part, from the groups with which they identify—their in-groups. Although both generally behave similarly toward members of their in-group, they differ in the way in which they decide who is a member of this group. Collectivists have very few of these groups, but the groups are broad in scope, encompassing many interrelated relationships. By contrast, individualists have many groups with which they identify, but their relationships within these groups are more superficial.

In addition to the differences in motives and in the specification of reference group members noted earlier, it is possible to differentiate between different kinds of individualism and collectivism. Most significant are the concepts of vertical and horizontal dimensions that relate to the way in which people view their status relationship with others.[23] In combination with individualism and collectivism, these two additional dimensions identify four types of self—independent or interdependent[24] and same or different.

Table 2.1 indicates how these different combinations of vertical and horizontal individualism and collectivism correspond to how people define themselves, their value orientations, their dominant political systems, and their typical patterns of social behavior. As shown in Table 2.1, this distinction between vertical and horizontal individualism and collectivism results in four different cultural profiles. However, vertical collectivism and horizontal individualism might be the dominant cultural profiles around the world.[25]

Vertical collectivists see themselves as an aspect of an in-group, but members of the in-group are different in terms of status. These cultures are characterized by patterns of social relationships that emphasize communal sharing according to need and authority ranking, or the distribution of resources according to rank. They typically have social systems that do not reflect the values of individual freedom or equity. Inequality is the accepted norm, and serving and sacrificing for the in-group feature prominently.

Table 2.1 Culture, Self-Orientation, and Politics

	Vertical		Horizontal	
	Collectivism	**Individualism**	**Collectivism**	**Individualism**
Kind of self	Interdependent	Independent	Interdependent	Independent
	Different from others	Different from others	Same as others	Same as others
Fiske orientation	Communal sharing	Communal sharing	Communal sharing	Communal sharing
	Authority ranking	Authority ranking	Equality matching	Equality matching
Rokeach values	Low equality	Low equality	High equality	High equality
	Low freedom	High freedom	Low freedom	High freedom
Political system	Communalism (e.g., Indian village)	Market democracy (e.g., United States, France)	Communal living (e.g., Israeli kibbutz)	Democratic socialism (e.g., Sweden, British Labour Party)

Source: Triandis (1995).

In horizontal individualism, the self is autonomous and people are generally equal. These cultures are characterized by patterns of social behavior that emphasize equity in resource sharing according to contribution and distribution of resources equally among members. They have social systems that emphasize both the values of equality and individual freedom. What these two dominant syndromes suggest is that verticality serves to reinforce collectivism, and horizontalness reinforces individualism.

The previous discussion has examined the main attempts that have been made to identify dimensions along which cultures could be systematically described and compared. Of the dimensions identified, the constellation of concepts encompassed by individualism and collectivism appear to be especially important in describing and comparing social behavior.

Use of Cultural Dimensions

Being able to systematically define cultural variations provides a foundation for explaining and predicting HRM on a comparative basis. However, the ability to profile national cultures along a limited number of dimensions also opens up the possibility for a dramatic oversimplification of the effect of culture. This oversimplification results in stating that people from this particular type of culture behave this way, whereas those from that other type of culture behave like that. Often, this is done by referring to an existing typology of attributes of national culture (very typically Hofstede's now almost 30-year-old numeric ratings). In effect, by suggesting that culture works in this way, we have substituted *sophisticated stereotypes* of a culture for the complex reality that exists.[26] Therefore, instead of explaining cultural effects, this dimensional approach can have the opposite effect of constraining the way in which people regard members of another culture. For example, we run the risk of thinking of all Japanese people as high on *masculinity* and *uncertainty avoidance,* low on *individualism,* and moderate on *power distance.* The fallacy of this approach is apparent to anyone who has encountered behavior in members of another culture inconsistent with the picture painted by the profile. However, these problems do not render the systematic description of cultural variation useless. On the contrary, they can be valuable in selecting national cultures to compare when trying to assess the degree of similarity or difference on responses to particular HRM questions. In addition, they are useful tools, as long as their limitations are understood. It is also important to understand how culture exerts its influence. It is this topic that we discuss next.

Influence of Cultural Context on HRM

To avoid the oversimplification of the influence of cultural context that suggests that all people in a country behave in a particular way, we discuss the individual-level mechanisms through which variation in national culture influences global HRM. It is important to understand that individuals are embedded in specific national-level cultures and are affected by and express their cultural orientation through both *cognitive* (what is perceived and interpreted) and *motivational* (what is desired) individual-level mechanisms.[27] Each individual will be different in the degree to which aspects of their culture are influential, but in general there is more similarity within cultural groups than between cultures.[28] First, from a *cognitive* perspective, culturally different individuals learn different sets of values (as discussed previously), which develop into cognitive frameworks (mental programs) that are used to help organize and process information about situations and events such as human resource management practices. Different priorities for what activities deserve attention, and the meaning we attach to these activities, are formed by gradually internalizing prevailing cultural patterns.[29] Individuals only attend and respond to those things that they have learned in their culture are important. From a motivational perspective, the appropriateness of human resource practices is fundamentally tied to how people view themselves and their relationship to others. Everyone evaluates activities according to the extent to which the activities contribute to personal self-worth and well-being[30]. Motives to maintain a positive self-image are probably universal. However, what constitutes a positive self-view depends on the extent to which individuals see themselves as connected to or separate from others as learned in their culture. The extent to which a policy or practice has benefit to the individual or to others with whom they feel connected can be seen as more of less appropriate in different cultures.

In sum, the mechanisms of cultural influence at the individual level fall into these cognitive and motivational domains. Together, these mechanisms produce a reasonably complete picture of the mechanics of cultural influence. They are the mechanisms through which cultural factors influence individuals to see a particular policy or practice as important and also evaluate the extent to which it is beneficial. For example, the reasons that employee ownership plans are more likely to be found in some countries than others is influenced by individual preferences based on the cultural values of low power distance, high individualism, and low uncertainty avoidance.[31]

Cultural differences have been found to exist in a wide variety of HRM practices, including recruitment and selection (Chapter 6), reward allocation policies and compensation programs (Chapter 8), and social benefits programs. For example, organizations in countries which culture is characterized by high uncertainty avoidance are more likely to offer seniority-based compensation than organizations from low uncertainty avoidance cultures. However, the fact that societies might, in general, exhibit a culturally-based preference for a particular set of policies or practices should not be interpreted as requiring that firms adopt these practices in order to be effective.

While the idea that culture influences HRM across countries has long been embraced, culture can become "the catchall for complexity"[32] if any differences between countries are quickly attributed to culture. Cultural differences are only one of many country differences, and variations in HR practices can be caused by a multitude of factors. Also, the assumption that culture drives HRM practices implies that organizations have only very limited managerial discretion in adopting HR practices.[33] While HRM practices may be culture-bound on average, diversity within countries does exist, and some evidence suggests adopting counter-cultural practices may pay off for the organization.[34] For example, pay for performance systems would seem to be

It had all started when Trevor, president of Goldstar Mining, had sent Ken Powers to Colombia to head up drilling operations. The contract with Vancouver-based Megametals for core samples was just what his small firm had needed. And while everyone knew that Colombian revolutionary forces were financing their operations by kidnapping, people in the mining business didn't give the risks much thought. In fact, they often paid so called "vaccination money" to groups like *FARC*. Ken had jumped at the opportunity to go, and diamond drillers of his caliber were in short supply.

When Ken was kidnapped by *FARC*, Trevor felt responsible. The rebels wanted a share of the gold that would be extracted from the mine, and Trevor couldn't deliver because the site was owned by Megametals. However, he had scraped together $100,000, and through intermediaries, he had finally negotiated contact with the rebels, who had agreed to release Ken for that amount. Despite the protests of his wife and the Canadian government, he had made his way up that winding mountain trail to find Trevor and tell him that after four months "his shift was over and he could come home." The *FARC* rebels released Ken but saw that Trevor was a much bigger prize, and thus his own captivity began.

The details of his own release were shrouded in mystery, but he knew it resulted from some very complex negotiations involving the guerillas and both the Columbian and Canadian governments as well as a local Catholic priest.

Introduction

HRM activities may not often involve rescuing an employee from revolutionaries in a foreign country. However, human resource management in a global context must respond to a dynamic and complex set of factors. HRM consists of the activities, policies, and practices of *attracting*, *engaging*, *developing*, and *retaining* the employees that an organization needs to accomplish its goals. It involves all of the management decisions that affect the relationship between employees and the organization.[2] Global HRM means conducting these activities across countries, cultures, and institutional contexts. And not only must global HRM bridge across environments, it must also operate in a worldwide context characterized by the rapid and discontinuous change that is called *globalization*.[3]

Globalization

Definitions of the term globalization vary widely. Some see it in economic terms as the absence of borders and barriers to trade and economic activity or more broadly as the overlapping of the interests of business and society.[4] Others focus on the rapid advances in information and communications technology, suggesting that the world is flat or has crystalized as a single place.[5] Here, we focus on the central idea that globalization is the process whereby worldwide interconnections in every sphere of activity are growing.[6] Globalization is not an end result or caused by a single force but incompatible with collectivist cultures but in fact have been implemented with some success in China.[35] In fact, it is doing things that are unique (i.e., not average) that can result in a competitive advantage and make an organization more successful. Adopting atypical practices may also attract employees that are more open to change, easily adaptable, and less constrained by prevalent norms, which can result in additional benefits for the organization.[36]

In the absence of clear evidence that shows that adapting HRM practices to local cultural values results in better organizational performance, organizations are best advised to use cultural values as only very general guidance as to what practices may or may not be culturally appropriate. Specific decisions on HRM practices should be driven not by the desire to achieve cultural fit but rather to build strong organizational identity and achieve superior performance.[37] This reminds us that culture is only one aspect of the context in which global HRM must operate and that other factors such as the institutions of society, discussed next, and the organizational context (Chapter 3) are important.

Institutional Context

Institutions are the structures and activities that provide stability to a society; they consist of the family, education, economic, religious, social, and political systems. These institutions shape organizations in that they are built into the fabric of society and constrain and set conditions on the actions of organizations and organization members. Failure to conform to these demands of society can be costly, increase risk, and reduce the organization's legitimacy.[38] One way of thinking about the influence of institutions on global HRM policies and practices is in terms of three mechanisms through which institutions have influence. These are *coercive* mechanisms that stem from institutions that are more powerful than the organization, *mimetic* mechanisms that result from response of the organization to uncertainty, and *normative* mechanisms that result from adopting standards associated with a particular context, such as an industry. With regard to global HRM, coercive mechanisms involve not only legislation and government policies regarding HRM but also the influence of trade unions and works councils. Mimetic mechanisms involve benchmarking against and imitating other similar and successful organizations. And, normative mechanisms result from engagement with professional bodies, employers' associations and the like.[39] Thus, as HRM policies and procedures are developed, implemented, and coordinated, they are influenced by the institutional context in which this occurs.[40]

Another important consideration in understanding the effect of the institutional context is the extent to which particular institutional features in combination have an effect on how organizations interact with the institutions of society.[41] In order to accomplish their goals, organizations need to interact with societal institutions in five spheres. First, they must interact with the industrial relations system to regulate wages and working conditions. Second, they need to ensure that employees have the requisite skills through their interaction with the vocational training and education system. Third, they must secure the cooperation of the workforce by interacting with employees. And finally, they must interact with institutions to raise capital and also secure access to inputs and technology. These spheres combine in a variety of ways in capitalist econo-mies. However, it is possible to simplify this effect by looking at two ends of the coordi-nation spectrum. At one end are *liberal market economies* in which competitive markets coordinate the interaction of the organization with other aspects of the environment. At the other, are *coordinated market economies,* in which organizations typically engage more directly and strategically with trade unions, financial institutions, and other aspects of the institutional context. Whether a firm coordinates its endeavors through market relations or strategic interaction depends on the overall institutional setting. The characteristics of these two opposing settings are presented in Table 2.2.

Table 2.2 Comparison of Institutional Settings Based on Varieties of Capitalism

Institutional Sphere	Coordinated Market Economies	Liberal Market Economies
Education and training	Industry associations have a major influence on the establishment of industry and legal standards and provide collaborative training schemes on industry specific skills.	Industry associations are weak, collaborative training programs for industry-specific skills are not well established, and workers invest in skill development that can be transported to other jobs.
Industrial relations	Strong trade unions, powerful works councils, and high levels of employment protection make labor markets less fluid and allow for longer job tenure.	Trade unions are relatively weak, employment protection low, and labor markets are fluid.
Firm-employee relations	Trade unions coordinate wage setting and employers and managers must rely on a more consensual style of decision making because of constraints imposed by workforce representatives and business networks.	Relationships are primarily contractual between the employer and individual employees, and managers have a great deal of authority over organizational activities, including layoffs.
Interfirm relations	Organizations are connected by important networks of cross shareholding and membership in strong employer associations, which allow the exchange of private information.	Technology transfer is accomplished primarily by licensing or taking on expert personnel, and standards are usually set by market races.
Financial markets	Access to capital is based on reputation as opposed to share value.	Large transparent equity markets—access to external finance depends on market valuation.
Examples	Austria, Germany, Japan, South Korea, Sweden, Norway, Finland, Denmark, Belgium, the Netherlands, and Switzerland	United States, Canada, United Kingdom, Australia, and New Zealand

By examining the characteristics of each setting, the way in which the five institutional spheres complement each other becomes clear. For example, long-term employment is more feasible where the financial system makes capital available based on terms that are not sensitive to current profitability. This approach helps us understand that the formal institutions of society allow for the coordination among organizations through the exchange of information, by monitoring firm behavior and also by sanctioning deviant behavior.

The institutional context has been found to influence HRM policies and practices even among countries that are relatively similar in terms of national culture.[42] For example, the extent to which organizations employ a *calculative model* of HRM (aimed at ensuring that production activities are at all times efficiently supplied with the necessary input of human resources) versus a *collaborative model* of HRM (a humanistic focus, based on the value of employees to the firm and ethical matters related to the employment relationship) has been found to vary across the European countries of England, France, Spain, Germany, Norway, and Denmark.[43] Similar results have been found when comparing the institutional contexts of the subsidiaries of U.S. firms in Germany, the United Kingdom, Australia, Ireland, Denmark and Norway.[44] Therefore, we should expect variations in human resource management practices insofar as dissimilar institutions exist in the context in which the firm operates, regardless of similarities in culture. However, multinational organizations can influence the local context by creating organizational units that cross national and institutional contexts, lobbying for change in national regulations and exerting influence on the way in which national as well as international institutions function.[45]

Convergence, Divergence, or Equilibrium

Because of the effects of globalization (discussed in Chapter 1) and the tendency of multinational organization to be consistent wherever they operate (discussed ahead in Chapter 3), it can be argued that HRM policies and procedures are in the process of becoming more similar around the world. The key argument to support this idea is that as the world adopts a single economic system[46] and technology produces an increasingly information-driven business environment, business executives receive the same type of training, and as a result organizations and their HRM systems become more similar. This suggests the possibility of a universal set of best HRM practices that all organizations should adopt in order to be successful.[47] However, as discussed in this chapter, HRM systems are embedded in the cultural and institutional context of their home country. HRM may be somewhat resistant to the forces of globalization because its ability to change is limited by regulatory structures, interest groups, public opinion and cultural norms, which are relatively slow to change.[48] In fact, national differences in HRM practice in Europe persist in the face of globalization.[49] The reality is probably somewhat more complex than simply converging or diverging practices.

Two examples are provided by the concepts of *directional similarity* and *club convergence*. Directional similarity implies that over time organizations from different countries move in the same direction, but because of different starting points they remain relatively parallel, maintaining the same relationship with each other. Directional similarity is indicated by the presence of similar trends across countries but without final convergence. For example, between 1992 and 2004 organizations in both Norway and Greece decreased their investment in employee training and development. However, despite moving in the same direction, they ended up in different places at the conclusion of this 12-year period because of different initial levels.[50] Research across Europe suggests limited directional similarity in some but not all core HRM elements. For example, there is clear evidence for an increased use of performance-related and flexible pay elements, but no significant directional trends have been observed in the investment of time and money spent on employee training and development.

Club convergence[51] is the idea that countries with similar degrees of labor legislation tend to cluster together and that they look more like other countries belonging to the same cluster over time.[52] This means that HR practices are more similar within than across clusters of countries. Groupings include a Latin cluster (including Spain, Italy, and France), a Nordic cluster (Sweden, Norway, Denmark), an Anglo-Saxon cluster (United Kingdom, United States, Canada, Australia, New Zealand), and a Germanic cluster (Germany, Austria, Switzerland) among others. While any classification of countries into clusters has its inherent problems, countries do exhibit certain similarities to other countries, and framing the study of HRM in terms of clusters may be a useful point of departure when examining HRM across the globe.

Global changes in HRM are a result of the complex, dynamic interaction of forces of convergence and the embeddedness of national business systems.[53] It may be that some practices are converging, others exhibiting directional similarity, and some may actually be diverging. Organizations may develop hybrid approaches in which they maintain local management values and practices but are very adaptable and flexible with regard to using best practices developed in other countries.[54] Also, different environments produce different institutional systems, but different environments can produce similar systems, and similar environments can produce vastly different cultures and institutions.[55] This creates multiple different equilibrium conditions in the institutional environments with which organizations must attend.[56] Institutions result from social interaction and form the structure of society based on patterns of thinking that persist over time.[57] Any change must consider the historical as well as current conditions that create the present institutional environment. The remnants of state socialism in transition economies provide a case in point, which is discussed in Box 2.1.

Box 2.1   Legacy of State Socialism

The essence of economic transition is the replacement of one set of institutions that govern economic activity with another. In former socialist countries, the institutions that support a Western-style, market-based economy have had to be adopted very

(Continued)

(Continued)

rapidly, but they must also be acceptable within their society.[58] Therefore, it is not surprising that the institutions in transition economies retain some vestiges of their socialist past. Understanding the institutional context of former socialist countries requires some understanding of the previous environment.

The key to understanding state socialism is recognizing the importance of three factors; undivided political power, state ownership of key elements of the economy, and bureaucratic coordination. These three factors motivated all the actors in the social system. In pretransition socialist economies, the single party system set rules for organizations as a form of legal power. There was no need for laws regarding business since formal constraints on organizations were part of the central planning regime. The various institutions of society were designed to have a monopoly in their own field: one labor union movement, one association of engineers, one academy of sciences, and so on. Power and prestige were determined by one's level in the hierarchy, with appropriate privileges (e.g., housing, medical care, access to goods and services, holidays) proportionate to rank. Individuals in power maintained their position through paternalism. Also, a kind of labor aristocracy in which reliable and skilled workers were recruited into the party existed.[59] With the transition to a market orientation, a shift in the balance of power came about, with the previous hierarchical distinctions becoming blurred.

A fundamental tenet of socialism is that labor is not a commodity but a resource to be employed. A central belief of the labor collective is that a worker has a right to a job and its associated benefits.[60] For example, in China factories approximated institutions, providing for all of the worker's needs: They fed, housed, hospitalized, and generally protected the working class as part of the wider social contract. The bureaucratic control of employment began with education, where choices open to individuals were severely limited or individuals were channeled to a particular type of work, and extends through all aspects of organizational life, including central determinations of wage rates. Pre-transition managerial behavior was also influenced by this bureaucratic control. As the state gradually relinquished its role in controlling organizations, institutions were required to fill the void. However, developing an institutional framework takes time, and the capacity of society to accept institutions and enforce their norms is questionable.[61]

Former socialist countries have faced a number of difficulties, including a slower than expected pace of change, growing differences between rural and urban areas, large income disparities, and in some cases declines in health care and life expectancies as well as social unrest.[62] In some countries, the reality of economic transition is causing a resurgence of communist parties and move toward more conservative policies. Thus, the institutional context in these societies is far from stable.

The HR Function Across National Contexts

The institutional context has been found to influence not only HRM policies and practices but also the role, status, and position of the HRM function. The role and status of HRM varies considerably across countries. A key indicator of the status of HRM in the organization is the extent to which HRM is represented at the board level in organizations. Consistent with their cultural and institutional contexts, France, Spain, Sweden, and Japan report that 70% to 80% of organizations have an HR director on the main decision-making body of organizations (board of directors in publicly held companies).[63] In general, the figures in Central and Eastern Europe and Israel are much lower. The United Kingdom and Australia indicate that less than half of the organizations have HR representatives at the board level. In Germany and the Netherlands, employees have a legal right to be represented on the board, and in Germany the level of board representation has been increasing.[64] Another indicator of the role of HRM is the size of the HRM department relative to the size of the organization. Despite organizational downsizing and the introduction of new technology to automate or outsource some HR functions, the relative size of HRM departments has remained relatively stable.[65] Finally, the extent to which line managers versus HRM professionals are directly involved with personnel issues is indicative of the role and status of the HRM function. The trend toward giving line managers more responsibility and reducing HRM involvement in this regard, which was prevalent in the 1990s, seems to have reversed itself in some countries.[66] However, the relative positions with regard to the propensity to center this responsibility in an HR department has been relatively stable with, for example, Italians most likely to house these functions in HR, followed by the British, while in Denmark much more responsibility is given to line managers. Table 2.3, based on data drawn from the Cranfield Network on International Human Resource Management (CRANET) project, provides key data points about these developments over time.

Table 2.3 Data on HR Representation Around the World[1]

Representation of HR on Board of Directors	1995	1999	2004	2008
Liberal market economies	52.1%	45.7%	44.1%	64.0%
Coordinated market economies	56.0%	58.1%	65.0%	65.6%
Mediterranean economies	63.8%	48.7%	48.1%	59.3%
Nordic economies	63.3%	65.4%	69.0%	75.8%
Central and Eastern European economies		48.6%	37.4%	61.9%

(Continued)

Table 2.3 (Continued)

Ratio of HR Employees Per 100 Organizational Employees	1999	2004	2008
Liberal market economies	1.57	1.26	1.48
Coordinated market economies	1.56	1.47	1.37
Mediterranean economies	1.30	1.36	1.43
Nordic economies	1.33	1.24	.97
Central and Eastern European economies	1.33	1.20	1.30

Assignment of HR Responsibilities to Line Managers[2]	1995	1999	2004	2008
Liberal market economies	2.60	2.67	2.69	2.71
Coordinated market economies	2.48	2.55	2.50	2.58
Mediterranean economies	2.34	2.55	2.57	2.49
Nordic economies	2.20	2.19	2.24	2.41
Central and Eastern European economies		2.13	2.21	2.08

[1] For all tables, *Liberal Market Economies* include Australia, Canada, Ireland, New Zealand, the United Kingdom and the United States; *Coordinated Market Economies* include Austria, Belgium, France, Germany, Netherlands, and Switzerland; *Mediterranean* countries include Cyprus, Greece, Italy, Spain, Portugal, Turkey, and the Turkish Cypriot Community; *Nordic* countries include Denmark, Finland, Iceland, Norway and Sweden; and *Central and Eastern European Countries* include Bulgaria, Czech Republic, Estonia, Hungary, Lithuania, Russia, Serbia, Slovakia, and Slovenia. Due to data restrictions, country configuration for each cluster varies in each year analyzed.

[2] The higher the number, the more responsibilities are assigned to line managers.

Psychological Contract Across National Contexts

In addition to the influence of the cultural and institutional context on the role and status of HRM is the effect that this context has on the expectation that employees have for their relationship with their organization. This expectation of a particular type of relationship with an organization is called the *psychological contract*. The term psychological contract refers to a set of individual beliefs or perceptions concerning the terms of the exchange relationship between the individual and the organization.[67] These beliefs are conditioned by the cultural and institutional environment in which individuals grow up.[68] Individuals learn what they should expect from their job both from the values that have been instilled by their family and by the work relationships that are considered normal in society. Specific differences in the psychological contract have been documented in 13 countries; and another project has conducted an analysis of the psychological contracts in six European countries and Israel.[69] The nature of these beliefs about what organizations promise employees and what they are obligated to do in return can take a wide variety of forms. And the institutional context influences the kinds of employment relationships that are negotiable in that many conditions of employment can be prescribed by legal or other societal institutions. However, within this *zone of negotiability,*[70] it is possible to classify these forms according to the extent that employees expect long-term, broad, socio-emotional relationships characterized by commitment and loyalty (*relational*) or short-term, specific, pay-for-services rendered (*transactional*) relationships and the differences in power between employees and the organization. *Instrumental* contracts are transactional, and the parties have symmetric power. *Exploitive* contracts are also transactional, but the power between the parties is asymmetric. *Communitarian* contracts are relational with symmetric power, and *custodial* contracts are relational with asymmetric power. National-level cultural values predict the dominant form of the psychological contract with vertical individualist cultures (France is an example) describing their psychological contracts as primarily exploitive, horizontal individualist cultures (such as Canada) as primarily instrumental, vertical collectivist (such as China) as primarily custodial, and horizontal collectivist (such as Norway) as primarily communitarian. Understanding the expectation of employees is important for global HRM because meeting these culturally and institutionally based expectations about the employment relationship results in higher employee satisfaction, employee loyalty, and less turnover.[71]

Chapter Summary

This chapter examines the cultural and institutional context that shapes HRM in different countries. Culture exerts its influence and constraints informally, through internalized socially acceptable norms for behavior, while the influence of institutions is formal and backed by enforceable sanctions.[72] Numerous attempts have been made to categorize national cultures on a set of value dimensions. While these dimensional approaches are an oversimplification, they provide a systematic basis for explaining and predicting HRM on a comparative basis. They are useful as long as their limitations are understood. Institutions are the structures and activities that provide stability to a society and set the conditions under which organizations and organizations' members must act. Institutions do not operate in isolation but combine to form a contextual system in which organizations are embedded. This context influences global HRM through coercive, mimetic, and normative mechanisms. The external environment of transition economies is a composite of the new global context in which all firms must operate combined with institutions that to some degree contain the vestiges of state socialism. This highlights the fact that changes in the cultural and institutional context must consider the historical as well as the current conditions that support a particular set of institutions. The cultural and institution context influences not only HRM policies, including the role and status and position of the HRM function but also the expectations that employees have about their relationship with organizations.

Questions for Discussion

1. What are the three key characteristics of culture?

2. Discuss how the major studies of cultural values are similar.

3. What are the differences in collaborative and calculative models of HRM?

4. What is implied by convergence and divergence of HR practices? Do studies provide support for either idea?

5. Describe some of the ways in which state socialism affects the institutional environment in transition economies.

6. How might employee expectations about their relationship with their employer be different in different countries?

Notes

1. While we recognize that the academic literature is typically divided into international HRM (the study of HRM in international organizations) and comparative HRM (the study of differences in HRM policies and practices across countries, see Boxall, 1995), this distinction is largely irrelevant to practice. We consider global HRM to incorporate both of these perspectives.

2. In distinguishing between these two factors, we do not take a position as to whether culture is an institution of society or if institutions of society reflect the more fundamental societal characteristic of culture. Again, this academic debate is largely irrelevant to practice.

3. Hofstede (1980).

4. Howard (1991).

5. Schein (1985).

6. The idea of tight and loose cultures comes from Pelto (1968) as cited in Triandis (1995). See also Chan, Gelfand, Triandis, & Tzeng (1996).

7. Au (1999); Gelfand et al. (2011).

8. Kluckhohn & Strodtbeck (1961).

9. Kluckhohn & Strodtbeck (1961); Maznevski, DiStefano, & Nason (1993).

10. Hofstede (1980, 2001).

11. This was later extended to five dimensions with the addition of Confucian-Dynamism (Chinese Culture Connection, 1987) and most recently to a sixth with the addition of Indulgence versus Restraint (Hofstede, Hofstede, & Minkow, 2010).

12. Chinese Culture Connection (1987).

13. Hofstede (1991).

14. Hofstede & Minkow (2010).

15. Smith & Bond (1999).

16. Sagiv & Schwartz (1995); Schwartz (1992, 1994); Schwartz & Bilsky (1990).

17. Sagiv & Schwartz (2000).

18. House, Hanges, Javidan, Dorfman, & Gupta (2004).
19. McClelland (1962).
20. Peterson (2004).
21. See work by Schwartz and colleagues.
22. Triandis (1995).
23. This concept is conceptually similar to Hofstede's (1980) power-distance dimension and relates to the SVS (Schwartz, 1992) value orientations of hierarchy and harmony.
24. Markus & Kitayama (1991).
25. Triandis (1995).
26. Osland & Bird (2000).
27. See Thomas (2008) for an expanded discussion of these mechanisms.
28. Schwartz & Sagie (2000).
29. Markus & Kitayama (1991).
30. Erez & Earley (1993).
31. Schuler & Rogovsky (1998).
32. See Evans, Pucik, & Barsoux (2002).
33. Milkovich & Bloom (1998).
34. Caprar (2011).
35. Du & Choi (2009).
36. Gerhart (2008); Gerhart & Fang (2005).
37. Milkovich & Bloom (1998).
38. Lawrence & Shadnam (2008).
39. Paauwe & Boselie (2003).
40. We do not suggest that these forces are deterministic. However, a discussion of the influence of organizational agents in this regard is beyond the scope of this chapter. See Kostova, Roth, & Dacin (2008).
41. This section draws heavily on the work of Hall & Soskice (2001) and Hall & Gingerich (2009).
42. Dobbin, Sutton, Meyer, & Scott (1993).
43. Gooderham, Nordhaug, & Ringdal (1999).
44. Gooderham, Nordhaug, & Ringdal (2006).
45. Edwards & Rees (2006).
46. Eisentadt (1973).
47. See Mayrhofer, Brewster, Morley, & Ledolter (2011) for a discussion.
48. Brewster (2006).
49. Gooderham & Nordhaug (2011).
50. Mayrhofer, Brewster, Morley, & Ledolter (2011).
51. Fischer & Stirböck (2006 cited in Mayrhofer et al., 2011).
52. Mayrhofer, Brewster, Morley, & Ledolter (2011); Mayrhofer & Brewster (2005); Brewster (2004); Brewster (2007); Sparrow, Schuler, & Jackson (1994).
53. See also McGaughey & De Cieri (1999); Tregaskis & Brewster (2006).
54. See Rowley, Poon, Zhu, & Warner (2011) for a discussion.
55. Cohen (2001).
56. Dewettinck & Remue (2011).
57. See Rozin (1998) for a discussion from an evolutionary theory perspective.
58. Napier & Thomas (2004); Rock & Solodkov (2001).
59. Clark (1996).
60. Lee (1987).

61. Peng (2000).
62. Napier & Thomas (2004).
63. Mayrhofer & Brewster (2005).
64. Brewster & Mayrhofer (2011).
65. Brewster (2006).
66. Mayrhofer & Brewster (2005).
67. Rousseau (1995).
68. Thomas (2008).
69. Rousseau & Schalk,(2000); Psycones (2006).
70. Rousseau & Schalk (2000).
71. See Robinson & Morrison (2000); Robinson & Rousseau (1994); Turnley & Feldman (1999).
72. Tayeb (2005).

3

Organizational Context of Global HRM

LEARNING OBJECTIVES

After reading this chapter you should be able to

- describe the fundamental elements of organizational structure,
- discuss the ways in which national culture influences the structure of organizations,
- describe what is meant by the term organizational culture,
- contrast the HRM structures of small and medium enterprises (SMEs) with large organizations,
- describe the implications of different multinational structures for global HRM, and
- discuss the multiple roles of global HRM and global HRM professionals.

Global HR at Technica[1]

Emma Taylor knew that the new executive management team was depending on her to engineer a human resources function that reflected the new reality at Technica. As a result of changes in the external environment, Technica had been pared down to about half its mid-1990s size, but its organization was scattered across six continents. She had recently read *Flight of the Buffalo*,[2] and the idea of an organization that was "similar to a flock of geese flying in a 'V' formation" stuck with her. Each goose was responsible for getting itself to wherever the gaggle was going, changing roles whenever necessary, and whenever the task changed the geese would be responsible for changing the structure of the group to accommodate, similar to geese flying in a "V" but landing in waves. That's the HR organization I want, she thought, but how to get it in the context of Technica's strategy, international structure, and cultural differences?

Technica, founded in the early 1980s in Utah, is now a world leader in the development and marketing of Internet networking software. Technica markets its products and support around the world through a partner and leverage model that begins with one-person outposts in widely dispersed targeted geographic areas. Technica began using local people when country offices were first set up, with anyone who could speak the local language and was willing to sell Technica products recruited to head an international operation. As the market grew, additional people were required, and initial distributors were replaced with more sophisticated personnel and a more formal structure. Technica delivers uniform products worldwide—only the language differs. The user interface on the screen is in different languages, but behind the scenes the products all operate the same. One of Technica's secret weapons is that it has at headquarters (because of its location) an arsenal of people who speak languages other than English and have high levels of technical skill. This had proven a real benefit in initial communication with foreign markets and in product translation. However, aligning the perspective of Technica's associates around the globe with the organization's vision has been a continuing challenge. Technica's global strategy requires that employees and customers encounter a uniform look and feel when they interact with Technica offices worldwide. However, the balance between headquarters' control and local autonomy had been uneven. Local laws, customs, and political events have often required Technica to adapt its business model—for example, allowing an exclusive distributorship in Brazil and a joint venture in Japan.

Emma wondered if creating a global HR function was as feasible as building a global IT product in which everything was identical except the language. What will this HR organization look like? One thing she knew for sure was that she would be expected to work fast. This was an IT company where a one-year plan is long term.

Introduction

The HR function does not operate in a vacuum but is influenced by and influences the larger organization in which it is embedded. As discussed in previous chapters, organizations are not independent of their surrounding context but are open systems that continuously take inputs from the environment (including human resources), transform them, and then return output to the environment in the form of products or services.[3] All organizations create formal structure to control and coordinate the activities of their members. In addition, the shared perceptions of organizational work practices, the informal organization, is an important influence on the behavior of organization members. Both the formal and informal structures of organizations vary considerably around the world. And the multinational enterprise (MNE) is a special organizational form that faces the unique challenge of determining the extent to which it should be internally consistent or adapt to the local environments in which it operates. As Emma discovers, in the case that opened this chapter, the answer to this question is as important for HRM as it is for the organization as a whole.

Organizational Structure

Organizations are systems of people that are intentionally structured to achieve goals. This structure consists of a differentiation of roles (what jobs need to be done and who does them) and a hierarchy of authority (who makes what decisions) to achieve the organizational mission. The structure of any organization can be described in terms of its degree of complexity, formalization, and centralization.[4]

The *complexity* of an organization is the extent to which it is differentiated along three dimensions: horizontal, vertical, and spatial. *Horizontal differentiation* refers to the number of different types of jobs that exist in an organization. The greater the number of different occupations in an organization, the greater its horizontal differentiation. *Vertical differentiation* is the number of levels in the hierarchy of the organization. For example, large banks might have as many as eight or nine layers between the teller at the bottom of the hierarchy and the CEO at the top while a small software developer might have as few as two, consisting of the entrepreneurial founder and employees. *Spatial differentiation* is the extent to which an organization's physical facilities and personnel are geographically dispersed. Large multinational organizations are often very complex with high levels of all three types of differentiation.

Formalization is indicated by the extent to which rules and procedures govern the activities of organization members. Formal organizations allow little discretion in the way people do their jobs and often have numerous explicit policies and procedures. The degree of *centralization* is indicated by the extent to which decisions are made at a single point in the organization. In centralized organizations, most decisions are made at one location, typically at headquarters by top management, while in decentralized organizations, decision making is dispersed throughout the organization.

There are any numbers of ways that the three elements of organizational structure can be combined, with two fundamental types *organic* and *mechanistic* at the extremes.[5] Mechanistic or bureaucratic organizations are centralized and have high formality and high complexity. In contrast, organic organizations have low formalization and complexity, with decisions being made throughout the organization. Figure 3.1 presents a graphic representation of these two fundamental types of organizational structure.

These two general organizational forms are helpful in demonstrating how the various elements of structure might combine. However, the reality for most organizations is that they fall somewhere on the continuum between these two extremes. For example, the elements of structure may vary depending on the size of the organization, its strategy or technology, and the extent of its internationalization and its needs for

Figure 3.1 Fundamental Organizational Designs

Mechanistic

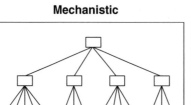

Organic

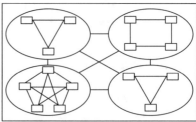

- High horizontal differentiation
- High formalization
- Centralized decision authority

- Low horizontal differentiation
- Low formalization
- Decentralized decision authority

Source: Thomas (2008, p. 193).

knowledge exchange.[6] To some extent, the contingencies that organizations face operate in a similar way to affect organizational structure regardless of the country in which they exist. For example, large organizations in one country look very much like large organizations in another.[7] However, a number of cross-national differences have been found in structural variables.[8] It is the way in which national culture might influence the organizational context for global HRM that we discuss next.

Culture and Organizational Structure

As discussed in the previous chapter, the institutions of society—that is, the political, social, and legal ground rules of a society, form a significant element of the context in which global HRM must function. These institutions present a broader context for the influence of culture, but one that includes its influence. However, it is important to recognize that culture may have a more direct effect on the structure of organizations, which in turn influences global HRM.

Two mechanisms through which culture can influence organizational structure have been identified.[9] First, organizational structure can be seen as a manifestation or symptom of management's cultural values. Organizational structures are logical extensions of the specific value orientations of the managers who create them. Managers may not be aware of these subconscious influences and simply make choices about structure that feel right. For example, in high power distance cultures, such as Germany, organizations tend to be more hierarchical and centralized, and the flat organizational structures in Swedish automotive firms can be seen as consistent with Sweden's egalitarian cultural values.[10] Second, national culture influences the extent to which different ways of organizing are accepted by members (and the institutions) of society. Pressures from the cultural environment dictate the type of structure that is seen as correct or legitimate. For example, normative pressures influence the tendency of Chinese firms to stay small and family owned. The Chinese family firm centers on paternalism, which results in simple structures that restrict the focus to a single aspect of business, and the societal characteristics of mutual obligation, familism, and personal contacts (*guanxi*) support the effectiveness of this organizational form.[11]

Examples of other organizational forms that reflect culturally-based societal pressures are the *keiretsu* in Japan, the *chaebol* in Korea, and the system of *putting out* in the knitwear industry in the Modena region of Italy. The Japanese *keiretsu* has its basis in the family-based *zaibatsu* that existed in Japan prior to World War II. While the family name often survived, as in Mitsui, Mitsubishi, and Sumitomo, the modern *keiretsu* is no longer family owned but consists of a complex interfirm network including a trading company (*sogo shosha*) and is usually anchored by a bank. However, it functions like an extended family with coordination and control facilitated by reciprocal ownership and a focus on long-term success.[12] The Korean *chaebol* are family dominated multi-industry conglomerates such as Hyundai, Samsung, LG, and Daewoo. They differ from the *keiretsu* in that they are heavily populated by family members, particularly in key positions, and are financed by the government. Like other types of family businesses *chaebol* are paternalistic and highly centralized, but because of a societal preference (supported by government policy) they are very large. In the Modena region of Italy, a system of production called *putting out* has resulted in a unique organizational form that economists consider archaic and inefficient. In this system the manufacturer *puts out* raw material to a network of independent artisanal firms (averaging less than nine workers) who cut, assemble, dye, press, and package knitwear, often in their homes. The success of the system rests on the presence of cohesive family units and cooperative relationships based on centuries of societal engagement in cooperative endeavors, dating back to the straw hat weaving in the 1600s.[13]

These examples suggest that there may be systematic variations in the structure of organizations based on cultural factors. Not only do these organizational forms dictate the relationship among (hierarchy of authority) and roles of organization members (i.e., we would expect that most HR decisions would be made by the senior family member in a family oriented business), but they also affect the way in which the organization conveys expectations about appropriate behavior. Consider the situation in Box 3.1 in which a selection policy is interpreted in two different organizational contexts.

Box 3.1   Selection in Two Contexts[14]

HR Policy. Attributes of individuals must not be used for differential treatment of individuals, unless they are clearly connected to the goals and tasks required. *American MNE Manager.* I must hire the best person for the job regardless of class, race, religion, gender, or national origin.

(Continued)

(Continued)

Chinese Family Business Manager. I must hire people whom I know or who belong to my network of friends and relatives, because I can trust them to be dependable employees.

The interpretation of the formal policy in this case is influenced by factors not represented on the organization chart or in the job descriptions but by norms for behavior that are informally shared among the organization's members. It is this informal aspect of organization that is discussed next.

Informal Organization

The informal organization refers to a set of assumptions shared by organization members that guide behavior. This set of normative behaviors and relationships is called *organizational culture*. Organizational culture can produce both functional behavior that contributes to the goals of the organization but also dysfunctional behavior that has negative effects. The primary positive effects of organizational culture are to provide a sense of identity for the organization that differentiates it from other organizations and a mechanism for socializing organization members into ways of doing things that are consistent with the organization's goals. This may be particularly important in complex multinationals that have a high degree of geographic differentiation. For example, Johnson & Johnson manufactures and markets consumer and health care products through 250 subsidiary companies in more than 175 different countries. Its strong organizational culture (codified in "The J & J Credo," which is translated into 36 languages) tells managers who and what to care about and in what particular order, regardless of where in the world they are located.[15] Negative effects of culture result from the fact that organizational culture gives organization members a set of behaviors that have served them well in the past and can therefore be a barrier to change in the organization or create conflict between merged firms with different cultures (See Chapter 5 for an example).

While there has been little systematic study of differences in organizational cultures in different countries, some attempts have been made to identify the types of organizational cultures that are predominant in different cultural contexts. The categorization of organizational cultures into four types—*family culture, Eiffel Tower culture, guided missile culture,* and *incubator culture* (shown in Table 3.1)—is a useful tool to relate prototypes of organization cultures to their societal context.[16] In reality of course, organization cultures are influenced by a host of factors in addition to the cultural context in which they are embedded.

Another view of organizational culture in a global context is that the forces of globalization are shaping the cultures of global organizations to be similar. New, shared meanings of individuals result from the fact that they work in a global context, and this

Table 3.1 Characteristics of Four Organizational Culture Types

Factor	Family	Eiffel Tower	Guided Missile	Incubator
Relationships	Diffuse, bonded to whole	Specific role in mechanistic system	Specific tasks with shared objectives	Diffuse, spontaneous roles
Authority and Status	Parent figures	Superior roles	Contributing members	Achievers
Thinking Patterns	Intuitive	Logical, analytical	Problem centered	Creative, ad hoc
Employees	Family members	Human resources	Specialists, experts	Cocreators
Change	By leader	By rules or procedures	As target moves	By improvisation
Reward Basis	Intrinsic	Promotion	Performance	Participation
Management	By subjectives	By job description	By objectives	By enthusiasm
Conflict Resolution	Turn other cheek, save face	Procedures arbitrate	Constructive, task related	Creative
Preferred in	Singapore, Korea, Japan, France, Belgium, India, Greece, Italy, Spain	Denmark, Germany, Netherlands	United States, Canada, United Kingdom	Silicon Valley, CA; Route 128, Boston; Sweden

Source: Adapted from Trompenaars & Hampden-Turner (1998).

influences organizational policies and procedures with regard to the nature of competition, response to uncertainty and change, acceptance of diversity, social responsibility, and the focus on people.[17] The emergence of a *global work culture* is consistent with the demands on organizations to function in a global context. The structure of these organizations is discussed next.

Multinational Enterprise Structure

An organization's choice of structure involves addressing questions of the relationships among individuals and the specification of organizational roles. For geographically differentiated organizations, the additional question of where these jobs are located is important. MNEs need to coordinate and control operations across multiple environments, and various approaches to placing foreign activity in the organizational structure have been used. The particular approach taken depends on the location and type of foreign subsidiary, the influence of international operations on corporate performance, the way in which international operations have developed over time, and the country of origin of the firm.[18] Five ways of integrating international operations are common. These are the *international division structure,* the *product division structure,* the *functional division structure,* the *geographic division structure* and the *matrix.*[19]

- *International division.* This structure groups all international activities together in a single organizational unit and is more popular with U.S. than European MNEs. This structure has also been the initial choice of a significant number of firms as they expand internationally.
- *Product division.* This structure groups all units involved with like products together around the world. In this case, it is possible for foreign subsidiaries in the same country to have a different relationship to the firm depending on the product line. This is the most popular structure among organizations who market a diverse portfolio of products. For example, LVMH, the world's largest luxury goods company markets, in addition to Louis Vuitton luggage, products as diverse as Tag Huer watches, Christian Dior perfume, and Moët & Chandon champagne through its five product-based divisions.
- *Functional division.* This structure expands its domestic functional units into its foreign counterparts (e.g., Marketing Europe, Marketing North America, etc.) based on geography. It is popular among companies offering a limited range of related products, such as oil and mining companies. One company that uses a functional design is British Airways. The company is focused on providing air transportation services and has company-wide functional operations dedicated to engineering, marketing, HR, and so forth. Lenovo also used this design in the early years of its existence.[20] A weakness of this structure is its inability to respond rapidly to environmental change.
- *Geographic division.* This structure groups all functional areas into geographic units (e.g., North American Division, European Division, etc.). It is typical in organizations that have large foreign operations and are not dominated by one country or region. Historically this structure was more popular in Europe than in North America. One example here is the Swiss temporary employment company Adecco. A global leader in HR services, Adecco is the world's largest temporary employment agency and is organized in ten areas. The areas are based mostly on geography (e.g., North America, Northern Europe), with some countries of strategic importance to the organization constituting separate divisions (e.g., France, Switzerland) and two divisions based on mixed criteria: not only geography but also similarity of the markets (Iberia and South America, and Italy, Eastern Europe and India).[21] A limitation of this approach is that it requires an organization to conduct similar activities in several locations rather than combining them into a more cost-efficient central location. And for better or worse, it allows for a wide variation in the manner in which subsidiaries in different locations are managed.
- *Matrix structure.* In this structure each subsidiary reports to more than one group (product, geographic, or functional) for the purpose of integrating international operations with functional areas, product areas, or both. The popularity of this type of structure has waxed and waned as the advantages of integration versus the disadvantages of dual reporting were weighed against each other. The Swedish-Swiss company ABB (ASEA Brown Boveri), operating in the power and automation technology sectors, is often given as an example of a matrix organization. The company adopted a matrix structure in the 1980s but has since been reorganized. Some organizations may use a

global matrix organization for specific projects. For example, Texas Instruments uses a matrix design for new product development with the respective matrix group dissolving after new product launch.[22]

Few multinational organizations have structures that exactly match the five ideal types presented here. In reality, while a particular organizational form may be preferred, changes in industry conditions, firm capabilities, market trends, and so forth, mean that organizations seldom have all activities corresponding to a single type of organizational structure. In addition, the dynamic and complex nature of the global environment may require a perspective on global organizations that does not focus on trying to find a fit between structure and the environment. One approach involves taking into account the need of these organizations to use human resources more efficiently in order to be more responsive to their environment. A popular and influential categorization considers the configuration of the organization's capabilities, the role of overseas operations, and the development and diffusion of knowledge.[23] This categorization is presented in Table 3.2.

In *international* organizations, subunits are loosely aligned, and the focus is on transferring technology developed at headquarters throughout the organization. The *multinational* is decentralized and adapts to the local environment. *Global* organizations

Table 3.2 Categorization of MNEs

Organizational Characteristics	Multinational	Global	International	Transnational
Configuration of assets and capabilities	Decentralized and nationally self-sufficient	Centralized and globally scaled	Sources of core competencies centralized, others decentralized	Dispersed, interdependent and specialized
Role of overseas operations	Sensing and exploiting local opportunities	Implementing parent company strategies	Adapting and leveraging parent company competencies	Differentiated contributions by national units to integrated worldwide operations
Development and diffusion of knowledge	Knowledge developed and retained within each unit	Knowledge developed and retained at the center	Knowledge developed at the center and transferred to overseas units	Knowledge developed jointly and shared worldwide

Source: Bartlett & Ghoshal (1989).

are centralized with subunits resembling headquarters, while in the *transnational*, global standards are shared throughout the organizational network.

Subsidiary Structure and Global HR

Regardless of the overall form of the organization, the subunits of the MNE operate in distinct local environments. These environments create a unique context for global HR as discussed in Chapter 2. In addition however, the local environment influences HRM through its effect on the organization of the foreign subsidiary. An idea helpful in understanding this effect is that the organizational structure and management practices of subsidiaries of MNEs are influenced by the opposing forces toward adaptation to the local environment (local responsiveness) and consistency within the organization (global integration).[24] The pressures for consistency among subsidiaries in the international firm (global integration) stem from two factors: *organizational replication* and the *imperative for control*.[25] Organizational replication is the tendency of organizations to duplicate, in new environments, existing structures and procedures that are effective. For example, Procter & Gamble initially designed each new foreign subsidiary to be an exact replica of the U.S. organization because of a belief that the same policies and procedures that were successful in the United States would work equally well overseas.[26] The imperative for control means that organizations standardize policies and procedures to try to reduce the complexity and uncertainty involved in controlling international operations. However, in new environments subunits also face pressures for local adaptation because of the social nature of organizations. Organizations have a tendency to reflect the values, norms, and accepted practices of the societies in which they operate.[27]

The pressures for conformity to local norms and for internal consistency with the rest of the organization can vary from subsidiary to subsidiary, resulting in a variety of structures across the organization. Overall HRM policies and practices of foreign subsidiaries often more closely resemble their local competitors than they do their parent company. Also, some HR policies and practices are more susceptible to environmental influence than others. Thus, a complex pattern emerges with elements of foreign subsidiaries having various degrees of conformity to local demands for some practices and not others, and the subsidiaries in different countries resembling each other to varying degrees. The extent to which subsidiaries' practices reflect the local context as opposed to being consistent with the overall organization is taken up in more detail ahead in Chapter 4.

The four organizational types discussed previously (Table 3.2) are a reflection of the different emphases organizations place on local responsiveness and global integration. Organizations following a *multinational* strategy give primary importance to local responsiveness; *global* organizations strive for global efficiency, which requires a focus on consistency and global integration; and *transnational* organizations attempt to achieve both local responsiveness and integration, a goal they accomplish through being highly flexible and continuously adapting to changing circumstances. Finally, *international* organizations do not strive for efficiency, as do global companies, nor do they pursue local responsiveness to the extent of multinational companies—but they pay some attention to both of these goals.[28]

One implication of the typology is that any combination of structural forms might be effective in differing contexts. As important, however, is that each of these structural configurations may have different implications for the HRM function. The relationship between organization structures and the global HR function is not well studied. However, the limited research that is available[29] allows a conceptual map of global HR against structural configurations. As shown in Table 3.3, the global HR function can be categorized along two dimensions of centralization and interdependence (the extent to which functional activities are coordinated or integrated among units in different countries)[30] that map against the organization configurations of *international, global, multinational* and *transnational*.

Multinational organizations give rise to a decentralized and independent global HR function because of the focus on exploiting local opportunities. Local units are largely independent from other subsidiaries. Knowledge is developed within each unit and is generally not well integrated throughout the organization. This type of HR organization is typically housed in firms with product-based or geographic-based structures. The headquarters HR role is typically limited to dealing with the elite corporate structure, with most functions devolved to the subsidiaries. Corporate HR can sometimes be effective in using informal processes to introduce a degree of corporate integration—for example, in influencing operating companies and divisions to support international transfers for development purposes.

Global organizations are characterized by centralized and dependent HR functions with strategies formulated at headquarters and implemented throughout the organization—local units having a one-way relationship to headquarters. This type of HR organization is often housed in firms with product-based or matrix organizational structures. The primary role for HR is to establish and maintain control over all high-grade management positions worldwide. Centralized control is established over the careers and mobility of top management positions and over expatriate transfers. The HR function in these companies is large, well resourced, and responsible for a wide range of functions. The majority of this type has group-wide appraisal and performance management systems for top management.

International organizations like global organizations give rise to centralized and dependent HR functions. However, headquarters processes are adapted as they are transferred throughout the organization, with subunits somewhat loosely connected.

Table 3.3 Map of Global HR on Organizational Characteristics

Organizational Characteristics	Multinational	Global	International	Transnational
Global HR function	Decentralized Independent	Centralized Dependent	Centralized Dependent	Decentralized Interdependent
Corporate HR role	Influencing	Implementing	Process champion	Coordination and integration

Management development and the management of careers and mobility of expatriates are under centralized control. Formal structures reflect a centralization philosophy. However in practice, there may be a significant amount of informal influence from the center with regard to local activities. The HR managers' role is largely that of champion of the process.[31]

Transnational organizations foster decentralized but interdependent global HR functions. The headquarters' HR function is typically staffed by a relatively small group of corporate HR executives who are primarily engaged in coordination and integration activities but are also the guardians of the organizational culture. HR practices from throughout the organization are replicated across the organization both by aligning formal systems and also through the informal mechanisms of instilling shared objectives.[32]

In summary, in centralized/global firms the corporate HR function undertakes a wider range of activities, and key roles are management development, succession planning, career planning, strategic staffing, top management rewards, and managing the mobility of expatriate managers. In the highly decentralized firms and those pursuing a more multidomestic strategy, corporate HR executives are often confined to a more limited range of activities, and the roles of coordination and integration become more important.

Global HR and Control Mechanisms in MNEs

Along with organizational strategy, reporting systems, and budgets, organizational structure is a central mechanism for formal control and coordination in MNEs. However, as the level of interdependencies among different units of the MNE increases, the effectiveness of the formal control mechanisms decreases. This creates a vacuum that must be filled by more complex and flexible integrating mechanisms, such as organizational culture (discussed previously), informal communication, and networks of personal relationships.[33] Building and maintaining a perfect organizational structure is probably not possible for MNEs. Therefore, these organizations must devote resources to building the capability in individuals to resolve complex and contradictory issues or what has been called a "matrix in the mind of managers."[34]

This capability is derived from social ties, networks of personal relationships, and communication, all of which are core components of *social capital*.[35] Three types of social capital have been identified: structural, relational and cognitive. *Structural* social capital consists of the network of relationships that an individual has within the organization. *Relational* social capital involves trust and reciprocity as well as the willingness of a member of the organization to be flexible and forego individual goals for organizational goals when necessary. Finally, *cognitive* social capital is the shared norms and behaviors of organization members as well as adherence to common goals and a common approach to accomplishing tasks.[36] Social capital facilitates information exchanges and knowledge transfers between individuals and organizational units and thus acts as an informal mechanism of control.

Global HR is central to the development of organizational social capital and other informal control mechanisms in MNEs, because of its role in managing the relationships among organization members. For example, the global HR department manages all forms of international mobility of employees, including short-term project work or long-term expatriate assignments. It can manage job assignments of boundary spanners in strategic ways, so that networks among key individuals are created and maintained. Boundary spanners are key in carrying important information from one organizational unit to another and also in creating perceptions regarding what other organizational members or units are doing. For example, if the boundary spanner had a positive experience with an organizational unit in a different country, he or she can convey this to his or her immediate colleagues and build good will between the two units; if the experience was negative, it can taint the broader interunit relationship.[37] Global HR can also provide resources to virtual team leaders to ensure that (in addition to accomplishing work-related tasks) personal networks are actively built that can be utilized even after virtual teams disband. Global HR can also facilitate information sharing and knowledge transfer within the MNEs. For example, it can organize corporate events that enable and encourage socializing among employees across organizational units in a way that ensures interactions among employees from different units are productive, meaningful, and directed towards mutually beneficial work-related goals.[38] It is important to remember that as the level of interdependencies within MNEs increases (from relatively low in the case of multidomestic organizations to very high in transnational organizations), informal control mechanisms become essential. The contribution of global HR is critical to building these mechanisms in global and transnational MNEs.

Global HR in SMEs

Small and medium enterprises (SMEs), the majority of which are family owned, are an increasingly important economic player on the international stage. In the mid-1990s, more than 25% of all exporting firms had fewer than 100 employees,[39] and SMEs may now account for as much as 80% of global economic growth.[40] (By some estimates, 95% of all firms worldwide could be classified as SMEs.)[41] Technology facilitates the entry of small firms into the international business environment.[42] However, as they grow, these firms are increasingly faced with human resource issues. The specific HRM issues vary over the life cycle of the firm, with training issues dominating in high growth firms, compensation issues dominant in moderate growth firms, and recruiting dominant in no-growth firms.[43] Family owned SMEs in particular face the problem of attracting and retaining strong nonfamily executives as well as generally having insufficient and poorly trained personnel at all levels.[44] A skills shortage (along with a decrease in productivity or a specific performance issue) is one of the most important issues triggering an SME to consider HR practices.[45]

SME performance seems to be positively related to the adoption of effective HRM strategies.[46] This is especially true for practices that promote discretionary behavior knowledge sharing and organizational learning, which positively influences entrepreneurial performance.[47] However, SMEs often lack the capacity to develop formal HRM practices. It is important to recognize that SMEs face unique HRM challenges. Small firms, regardless of age, face the liabilities of smallness and must often form alliances, purchase opportunities, or mimic larger, more successful firms in order to gain access to resources. Where resources are limited there may be a small number of HR professionals, increased difficulty in recruiting and retaining employees, and a reluctance to engage in costly or restrictive practices. In addition, small firms may face additional challenges, such as an ambiguous identity, lack of legitimacy as an employer, and difficulty in maintaining sustainable HR policies.[48] Therefore, it is important to remember that HRM in small business does not rely on the same principles as large organizations only on a smaller scale.

The adoption of formal HRM by SMEs is more likely if the organization employs highly skilled workers, is networked with other organizations,[49] or is unionized.[50] However, the specific HR practices adopted are highly variable among SMEs. Table 3.4 presents the results of a survey of 100 SMEs in the United Kingdom.

As shown in Table 3.4, only three practices—equal opportunities, appraisal, and employee development—were highly used by more than 30% of SMEs surveyed, and a majority of firms had no formal HR strategy. Thus, the HRM practices of SMEs are often characterized as ad hoc and informal. While the level of formality of HR management increases with firm size, many HR practices are similar in both large and small firms. Table 3.5 presents a comparison of the rank order of HR practices in a sample of small and large firms in the United States.

Table 3.4   Use of Human Resource Practices in 100 British Firms

HR Practice	Low Use/Not Used	Medium Use	High Use
Formal HR strategy	64	13	20
Recruitment/selection procedures	38	30	31
Equal opportunity policies	21	21	57
Appraisal systems	39	16	42
Invests in people (IIP)	62	6	27
Incentive schemes	58	17	23
Nonmonetary benefits	67	16	15
Wide-ranging employee development	44	23	31
Empowerment	44	26	29

Source: Cassell et al. (2002, p. 680).

Note: Figures represent the percentage of companies using the practice ($n = 100$).

Table 3.5   HRM Practices in Small and Large Manufacturing Firms

Practice	Large			Small		
	Sample Size	Mean	Rank	Sample Size	Mean	Rank
Open communication	21	3.90	1	77	4.19	1
Pay based on performance	21	3.76	2	78	3.53	4
Competitive wages	21	3.71	3	78	3.47	5
Training for new employees	21	3.67	4	79	3.72	2
Job security for employees	21	3.62	5	78	3.62	3
Employee participation initiatives	21	3.43	6	78	3.41	6
Training to enhance group orientation	20	3.25	7	77	3.00	9
Collective responsibility	21	2.81	8	75	3.24	8
Training to enhance quantitative skills	20	2.80	9	78	2.85	10
Pay based on acquired skills	21	2.76	10	79	3.31	7
Job rotation	21	2.57	11	79	2.65	12
Group incentive programs	21	2.38	12	77	2.42	13
Specialized career paths	20	2.20	13	78	1.91	16
Pay based on seniority	21	2.10	14	79	2.30	14
Profit sharing schemes	21	2.10	14	77	2.68	11
Rapid promotions	20	1.80	16	78	1.83	17
Individual incentive programs	21	1.62	17	78	2.08	15

Source: Deshpande & Golkar (1994, p. 54).

The comparison shown in Table 3.5 suggests that the categorization of HRM in SMEs as unsophisticated may be overstated. In fact, some characteristics of SMEs may actually be an advantage in managing HRM. For example, the informality of the SME results in lower levels of internal uncertainty. In small firms the owner/manager is closer to the work force and thus better able to

- deliver information and decisions personally and consistently,
- receive immediate feedback from employees, and
- monitor progress with regard to how decisions are being carried out.[51]

However, this reliance on the discretion of the manager and the ad hoc nature of HRM in SMEs can result in a wide variation across countries and firms with regard to HRM practices. The two extremes of HR in SMEs has been described as the *bleak house* model versus the *happy family* model. The bleak house model describes a situation characterized by low wages, numerical flexibility, and an exploited workforce, while the happy family model is characterized by a workforce with reasonable pay, a flexible and informal approach to management, and close interpersonal relationships between employees and owners. Of course, the majority of firms probably fall somewhere between these two extremes.[52] The extent to which SMEs adopt a particular model of HRM is highly influenced by the industry in which they operate (with the imitation of the practices of competitors a key factor influencing the HRM approach) along with the values of managers and owners and characteristics of the workforce.[53] However, the willingness of managers to employ innovative and formal HRM systems is constrained by indigenous beliefs about the management of people. For example, in many societies the management of people is not seen as a technical matter necessitating any special expertise,[54] which argues against the adoption of formal HRM systems. In Chinese SMEs for example, the adoption of HRM is strongly influenced by cultural factors (for example, *guanxi*), such that the practice that emerges is endowed with Chinese characteristics.[55] This is particularly true with regard to the way in which the HR function is organized in China, where HR takes on a very operational role. Ahead, we discuss the more general issue of how global HRM is organized.

Organizing Global HRM

As described in Chapter 1, the role of HRM has evolved from the welfare secretaries of the 1800s to that of strategic partner in the 21st century—a role in which HRM must contribute value to the firm. However, HRM must also make sure that the basics of human resource management are in place and that they function consistently. And just getting the basics right can contribute to creating competitive advantage for the organization as shown in Box 3.2

Box 3.2   HRM at SAS Institute, Inc.

The SAS Institute based in Cary, North Carolina, is the largest privately owned software company in the world. It is a global leader in business analytic software, with revenues in the billions of dollars. However, its approach to HRM in the more than 50 countries in which it operates might be viewed as extremely traditional and reminiscent of the best practices of 30 years ago. For example, in the United States, employees enjoy a beautifully landscaped campus-like environment with private offices, workout rooms, medical services, and so on. Employee salaries are average for the industry, with little in the way of bonuses or stock options, but benefits are very generous. The organizational structure is flat with a great deal of cross-functional mobility. The benefit of this approach is that the turnover rate is around 4% in an industry that averages 20%. Thus, while at competitor companies a project team might consist of one third of the team learning the job and one third looking for their next job, thereby leaving only one third working on the project, at SAS everyone is focused on the customer project, and many have long-term relationships with customers.[56]

However, globalization is changing the HRM function and its professionals. Global HRM has multiple roles in that it must deliver basic HR functions, such as building HR infrastructure and championing employee concerns, while also making the changes required to integrate HRM and business strategy in a dynamic global environment.[57] In seeking to add value to the firm, global HRM faces the challenge of organizing in such a way as to deliver effectively on all its roles. The first step in this organizing is the recognition that there are numerous delivery options for human resource *activities* ranging from those that can be outsourced to those that must be tightly integrated and coordinated. By categorizing HR domains along the two dimensions of *integration* and *differentiation*, the general categories of HR delivery mechanism can be identified.[58] This categorization is shown in Figure 3.2.

Figure 3.2 Delivery Mechanisms for Different Global HR Functions

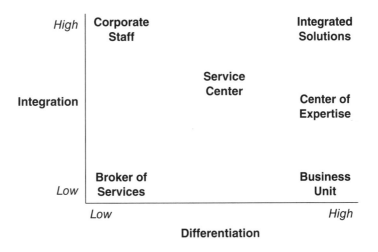

Source: Evans, Pucik, & Barsoux (2002, p. 466).

Low Integration-Low Differentiation

The first category of HR activities are those activities that are low on integration (not closely tied to the strategy of the firm) and low on differentiation (relatively standardized across the organization). Examples of these activities are payroll processing, handling inquiries regarding benefits, pensions, employment rules, generic types of training, and occupational health and safety. While there can be variability among these examples along the two dimensions, all are typically standardized to a large extent. These types of activities are candidates for outsourcing to a third party who can often deliver high quality at a lower cost than if they were performed internally. Also, advances in information technology have made the cost effective delivery of these types of activities broadly available.

High Differentiation-Low Integration

A number of HR activities need to be adapted to the local environment, but their relationship to overall organizational strategy is low. For example, the recruitment, selection, and training of the nonmanagerial workforce is typically the domain of the local business unit. Also, labor relations activities have strong pressures toward being handled locally because of large variability around the world. However, local responsibility does not necessarily mean lack of coordination across the firm. For example, best practices in all of these domains might be shared across organizational units.

Low Differentiation-High Integration

In the opposite quadrant are those activities that are important strategically (highly integrated) but need not be differentiated across the organization. These activities, which require tightly integrated solutions, vary according to the strategy of the organization. For example, if a firm's strategy involves growth through repeated mergers and acquisitions then training in the methodology required to accomplish this complex task is an HR function that needs tight central coordination. In addition however, there may be some functions that require integrated solutions regardless of strategy. For example, some have argued that the most strategic of the HRM functions in all organizations is the management development of individuals with the potential to occupy key positions in the organization.[59] This argument is consistent with the often reported global shortage of talent and the need for highly integrated structures for talent development.

High Integration-High Differentiation

The most complex set of global HR activities are those that are strategically important but have high demands for differentiation. Internally consistent processes for recruitment or performance management (see Chapter 8) can fall into this domain with both local units and headquarters having a vested interest in this function. A common structural mechanism for providing solutions to these types of issues, at least on a short term basis, is the cross-functional team. Other intermediate structural mechanisms for handling complex organizational challenges are *service centers* (or *centers of expertise*) in which the expertise necessary to manage a particular function is brought together (physically or virtually and from within or outside the organization) to deal with an issue. A number of different functions might be handled in this way, including such activities as diversity management, organizational change consulting, and global knowledge management. For example, Sun Microsystems organizes many of its HR functions through the use of such centers.

In summary, the structure of HRM at the subsidiary (local subunit) level is influenced by the overall pressures on the organization for internal consistency and local adaptation. However, the organization of HRM in the local subsidiary is also influenced by the extent to which different HRM activities are central to firm strategy (integrated) and the degree to which they face local pressures for differentiation. This creates a complex matrix in the organization of global HRM resulting in multiple and varied roles for HR professionals.

Role of the Global HR Manager

The organization of global HR to accomplish its mission in a global environment requires that HR professionals perform a number of different and sometimes conflicting roles. These roles include partnering with management to align HR with business strategy (strategic partner), managing transformation and change in the organization (change agent), increasing employee commitment and capability (employee champion), as well as building an efficient infrastructure to deliver HR services (administrative expert).[60] Thus, being an effective HR manager in a global context means more than just moving from an operational to a more strategic focus. It means, for example, being able to balance the tension inherent in being a strategic partner with management while also acting as the champion for employees. As strategic partners with management, HR professionals can alienate employees if they are seen only as agents of management. Alternatively, a management view of HR as only championing the needs and concerns of employees can jeopardize HRs strategic partnership. Likewise the roles of administrative expert and change agent are potentially in conflict. Global HR professionals must balance the need for innovation with the need for efficiency. They must get the basics of the HR infrastructure right, while also creating structures that respond effectively to a dynamic and complex global environment.[61]

Chapter Summary

This chapter examines how differences in the structure of organizations influence global HRM. Basic organizational structures can be described in terms of their complexity, formalization, and centralization, which when combined form structures ranging from mechanistic to organic. These structures are influenced by the societal context in which they exist, based on what is perceived as legitimate in society and what is consistent with management values. In addition to formal structure, all organizations have an informal structure comprised of a set of normative behaviors and relationships. Global HR is central to the development of social capital and other informal control mechanisms in the MNE. Multinational organizations have found a variety of ways to integrate their international operations. These different configurations of the multinational organization have implications for the extent to which global HR functions are centralized and independent. Regardless of the overall structure of the organization, the local subsidiaries face conflicting pressures for consistency with the overall organization and adaptation to the local environment. Some HRM functions are more susceptible to the forces for local adaptation than are others. In addition, the extent to which an HRM activity is central to the strategy of the firm and varies across subunits affects how the function is organized and delivered. Finally, the organization of HRM to accomplish its mission creates a number of different and conflicting roles for HR professionals, which they must keep in balance to be effective.

Questions for Discussion

1. Describe the three basic dimensions along which an organizations structure can be determined.

2. What are the reasons that an international organization faces the conflicting pressures of internal consistency and local adaptation?

3. What type of HR organization best fits with global, multinational, international and transnational organizations?

4. Discuss how organizational strategy influences the delivery of different HR activities.

5. Describe the conflicting roles of the Global HR Professional.

Notes

1. This case is fictional but is based loosely on the development of Novell as described in the case "Novell: Transforming Culture," by Marjorie McEntire in Mendenhall, M. E., & Oddou, G. (2000) *Readings and Cases in International Human Resource Management,* South Western College Publishing.
2. Belasco & Stayer (1994).
3. Katz & Khan (1978).
4. Pugh, Hickson, Hinings, MacDonald, & Turner (1963).
5. Burns & Stalker (1961).
6. Lawrence & Lorsch (1967); Birkinshaw, Nobel, & Ridderstråle (2002).
7. See Hickson & Pugh (1995); Hickson & McMillan (1981).
8. See for example Azumi & McMillan (1975).
9. See Gibson (1994) and Thomas (2008).
10. Child & Kieser (1979); Ellegard et al. (1992).
11. Chen (1995); Wu (1999).
12. Ghauri & Prasad (1995).
13. Lazerson (1995); Putnam (1993).
14. Based on Phatak & Habib (1998).
15. From "Organizing 'People, values, and environment' at Johnson & Johnson" in Daniels, Radebaugh, & Sullivan (2011).

16. Trompenaars & Hampden-Turner (1998).
17. Erez & Shokef (2008).
18. Stopford & Wells (1972); Leksell (1981); Marschan (1996).
19. Daniels, Radebaugh, & Sullivan (2011).
20. Griffin & Pustay (2013).
21. Griffin & Pustay ((2013); Adecco corporate web-site: http://www.adecco.com/en-US/About/Organisation/Pages/default.aspx (accessed Feb 17th, 2012).
22. Griffin & Pustay (2013).
23. Bartlett & Ghoshal (1989).
24. Bartlett (1986); Porter (1986).
25. Rosenzweig & Singh (1991).
26. Bartlett & Ghoshal (1989).
27. See Westney (1993).
28. Harzing (1995).
29. Adler & Ghadar (1990); Farndale et al. (2010); Scullion & Starkey (2000).
30. Roth (1995).
31. See Evans, Pucik, & Barsoux (2002).
32. See Morris, Snell, & Wright (2006).
33. Dowling, Festing, Engle, Gröschl (2009); Kostova & Roth (2003).
34. Bartlett & Ghoshal (1989).
35. Kostova & Roth (2003).
36. Burt (1992); Nahapiet & Ghoshal (1998); Leana & Van Buren (1999); Inkpen & Tsang (2005).
37. Kostova & Roth (2003).
38. Kostova & Roth (2003).
39. Aharoni (1994).
40. Osman, Ho, & Galang (2011).
41. Wong (2011).
42. Thomas (2008).
43. Rutherford, Buller, & McMullen (2003).
44. Carlson, Upton, & Seaman (2006).
45. Cassell, Nadin, Gray, & Clegg (2002).
46. Diamantidis & Chatzoglou (2011).
47. Hayton (2003).
48. For a review of HRM in small firms see Cardon & Stevens (2004).
49. Bacon & Hoque (2005).
50. Wagar (1998).
51. Hill & Stewart (2000).
52. Richbell, Szerb, & Vitai (2010).
53. Tsai (2010).
54. See for example Saini & Budhwar (2008).
55. Cunningham (2011).
56. Adapted from O'Reilly & Pfeffer (2000).
57. Ulrich (1997)
58. This discussion draws heavily on Evans, Pucik, & Barsoux (2002).
59. Evans, Doz, & Laurent (1989).
60. Ulrich (1997).
61. See also Welch & Welch (2012).

4

Transfer of HRM Across Boundaries

LEARNING OBJECTIVES

After reading this chapter you should be able to

- explain why firms might want to transfer HRM practices throughout the organization,
- identify the key factors that account for the level and types of HRM practices transferred,
- describe the effect of the local cultural, institutional, and subsidiary context on the transfer of HRM practices, and
- discuss the probable causes of the various patterns of diffusion of HRM practices throughout multinational enterprises (MNEs).

Working for the Mouse[1]

As Jean François prepared to go "on stage" to his "role" (job) at the Euro-Disney Fantasyland shop where he had been a "cast member" (employee) for a week, he wondered how long he would stick it out. Almost all of the staff at the shop in which he was working had left, and he had heard that about 50% of the entire theme park had quit since it opened just two months ago. That's almost as bad as the retention rate for students at the French medical school he attended, he thought. The hour-long commute from his flat in Paris to Marne le Valée was bad enough, but when he got to work he had to put up with all the cast member rules.

At first he had felt lucky to be selected. The interview process had involved talking with other cast members and then a 45-minute ordeal with a Disney HR manager. And at the weekend "brain washing" session, as he now thought of it, he had been told that Disney cast members must follow the same rules at all the theme parks, Anaheim, Orlando and Tokyo. It had sort of made sense at the time—maintaining services standards, delivering a consistent experience, exceeding customers' expectations every day, and so on—but the reality was that he couldn't dress the way he wanted, couldn't take his lunch at the normal time, had to bathe and shave every day, had to be constantly "on stage," and when he asked questions the answer more often than not was, "That's not the way we do it at Disney." Do Disney managers really think all Europeans are alike and that we all think the same way? he wondered.

Some days he just didn't feel like smiling all the time!

Introduction

A distinctive feature of global HRM is that it must operate across a number of different contexts. In the previous three chapters, differences in the cultural, institutional, and organizational contexts affecting global human resource management were discussed. In this chapter, we take a more in-depth look at the transfer of HRM practices across contexts. As Disney discovered upon opening its theme park near Paris, just because practices work well in one context is no guarantee that they will transfer effectively to a new one. However, the ability to develop an expertise in one country and then implement it in another is one of the key advantages of the MNE.[2] Since, as discussed in previous chapters, the contexts across which global organization must operate differ significantly, the transfer of practices involves more than the simplistic "Think global, act local" mantra that dominates much of the thinking in this regard.

Why Firms Transfer Practices

The wide variety of contexts across which multinational organizations must operate along with the inherent pressure for adapting to local practices raises the question of why firms would engage in transfer of practices at all. Three basic motives for the transfer of practices have been identified. These are *market, cultural* and *political* motives.[3]

Market Motives

Market motives refer to the idea that the transfer of practices is seen as a means to enhance the efficiency of the organization by sharing *best practices* throughout the organization. This is based on the idea that organizations need to develop an integrated network of subunits that share expertise and knowledge with each other in order to survive in an internationally competitive environment.[4] HRM practices are central to developing and sharing the organizational competencies required to enhance the organizations' relative competitive position. For example, a Japanese firm's Singapore affiliate may develop efficient HRM selection policies to cope with high turnover in the labor market. If the MNE can successfully transfer these policies to other environments that also experience high labor mobility, this can increase the efficiency of the overall organization.[5]

Cultural Motives

Cultural motives involve the influence that national culture has on the MNE by encouraging it to take aspects of the national culture with it as it expands internationally. The premise is that the organizational culture (discussed in the previous chapter) is influenced by the national culture of the country of origin and that this explains the desire to implement home country practices in terms of organizational replication. The transfer of Japanese employment practices to Europe and the United States during the 1980s and 90s is often cited as an example in which Japanese firms attempted, as they expanded abroad, to employ those practices that had been so successful for them at home.[6]

Political Motives

Political motives involve any number of organizational actors who, in order to advance their own interest or to gain legitimacy, initiate the transfer of practices. And managers throughout the organization may wish to engage in sharing practices to enhance their legitimacy as good corporate citizens and/or as key players in the organizational network.[7] Headquarters personnel, for example, may wish to portray themselves as key agents in controlling the transfer of practices in order to advance their status. And as shown in Box 4.1, political motives may even obscure the source of an innovative practice.

Box 4.1   Whose Idea?

Borislav Draganov, HR manager of the Bulgarian subsidiary of an Austrian industrial goods company, was proud of the standardized practice for socializing new employees he had implemented in the Bulgarian subsidiary. When the regional headquarters HR manager Rudolf (Rudy) Spreckels had visited a few months earlier, he had been skeptical and discouraged Boris from using the practice. Boris, however, had not been discouraged and had decided to present his idea to the vice president (VP) of HR at the company's Vienna headquarters. Imagine his surprise when at the completion of his presentation, the VP of HR said, "That's a great idea Boris, but Herr Spreckels is already implementing it here."[8]

While these three broad factors may represent the primary motivation for the transfer of HR practices, they do not explain the nature and form of this transfer. In order to do this, we must consider differences in national business systems and the growing internationalization of economic activity in combination with such other factors as the competitive pressures of international markets, the cultural and institutional context that shapes MNE behavior, and the role of the various actors in initiating, engaging in, or obstructing the transfer of practices.[9] However, in order to provide a solid basis for understanding the complexity of the various patterns of diffusion of practices, we begin by considering transfer as a single event.

Factors Influencing Transfer of HR Practices

The ability of organizations to successfully transfer HR practices involves both characteristics of the organization and the environments in which it is operating. Employment practices are particularly susceptible to the influence of context because these practices are deeply embedded in the culture and institutions of society. Factors affecting their successful transfer across contexts include, country-of-origin effects, dominance effects, strategic international human resource management (SIHRM) orientation, host-country effects, and the type of practice transferred. We discuss each of these elements ahead.

Country of Origin

Even the largest MNEs seem be influenced by the way business is done in the country in which the organization originates. However, this truism applies to MNEs from some countries more than it does to MNEs from other countries. For example, the subsidiaries of U.S. multinationals have HR practices that are more similar to U.S. practices when compared to subsidiaries of European MNEs—where the practices are less likely to resemble practices in the respective parent country.[10] One reason for this is that U.S. MNEs are often not as *multi*-national as their name implies. General Electric, the second largest multinational in terms of assets, has a ratio of foreign assets to total assets that is only about 40% and Wal-Mart, one of the world's largest employers, has a ratio of only about 32%.[11] These large multinational organizations are still dominated by operations and practices that are common in their country of origin—in this case, the United States. Further, their domestic growth is often supported by replicating a standard set of practices in multiple locations. In contrast, large multinationals headquartered in locations with small domestic markets, such as Swiss-based ABB with almost 95% of its assets outside Switzerland[12], are less likely to have a tradition of replicating home country practices in foreign locations. Another factor that contributes to the country-of-origin effect is that in organizations in which there is a concentration of activities in the country of origin, parent-country nationals tend to dominate senior management positions. The CEOs of the vast majority of MNEs are citizens of the respective country of origin of the MNE. In addition, parent-country nationals are disproportionately represented on management boards.[13] Country-of-origin effects continue to be a factor throughout the life of the firm. However, as might be expected, these effects tends to diminish as firms internationalize.

MNEs from different countries of origin are also systematically different in their overseas operations because of the influence of expatriates. Expatriate managers tend to have taken for granted ideas about what practices are most effective and are likely to introduce these practices in the overseas subsidiary. These views will of course have been shaped by the home country culture and national business systems. For example, Japanese expatriate managers made attempts to transfer practices associated with lean production, team work, and functional flexibility in the 1980s and 1990s, while U.S. managers transferred performance-related pay and direct forms of communication to their subsidiaries.[14] Also, expatriate managers interact both socially and professionally with other expatriates from their home country. This interaction can result in the diffusions of similar practices among firms from the same country of origin because of the tendency to mimic what is perceived to be best practice.[15]

Dominance Effects

Examinations of the HRM practices of the subsidiaries of multinationals from a variety of countries of origin have found that there is high degree of convergence toward a dominant best practices model.[16] An explanation for this can be found in the concept of *social dominance*.[17] Social dominance is the idea that within every complex society certain groups are dominant over others and thus enjoy a disproportionate amount of privilege. At the global level, there may be a generally accepted hierarchy of nations based on status. For example, such a hierarchy has been suggested to exist because of different levels of economic development.[18] The logic is that because a country has a high level of economic development it is assumed that this results from good management practices. Therefore, these practices are more likely to be emulated than practices from those countries lower on the economic hierarchy. This would explain the strong influence of U.S.-based practices following World War II in which the United States was the world's dominant economy and also the high interest in Japanese management practice during the late 1970s and 1980s when Japan was a world leader.[19]

Both country-of-origin effect and dominance effects result in the standardization of HRM practices in the MNE as opposed to adaptation of HR practices to the local environment (localization). However, worldwide consensus on best management practice can challenge the country-of-origin effect. These ideas are shown graphically in Figure 4.1.

Some research indicates that of the three effects—localization, country of origin, or dominance—the dominance effect is more important in determining local subsidiary HRM practices. Despite the fact that HRM is often considered to be the most localized of functions, there are also examples of convergence toward worldwide best practices. It may be that MNEs limit the export of practices to their core competencies and converge to best practices in other areas.[20]

Figure 4.1 Effect of Country of Origin, Dominance, and Localization on HRM Practice

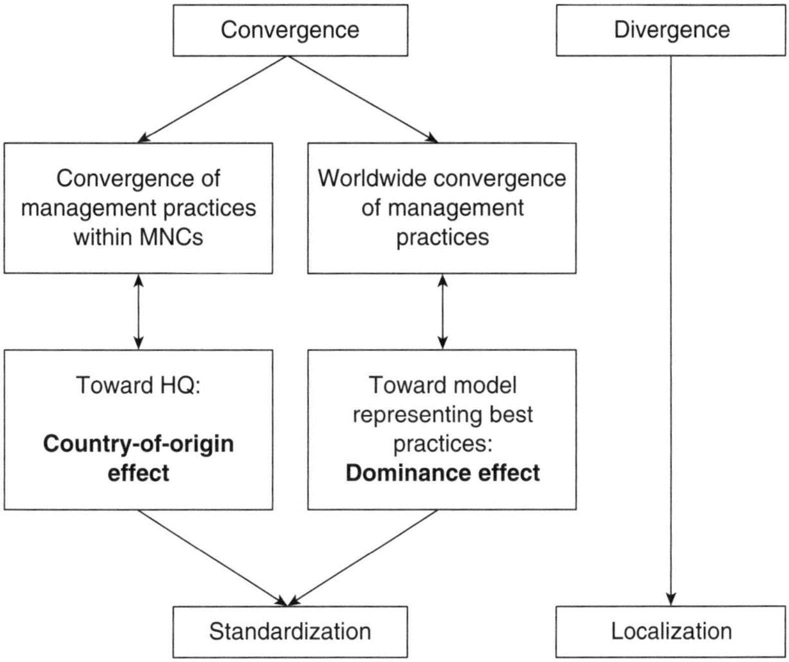

Source: Pudelko & Harzing (2007).

Additional opportunities for the influence of dominance include the fact that managers familiar with the dominant best practice can use this knowledge to their advantage. Therefore, as discussed ahead, the notion of dominance may also affect the politics of transfer of practices and support "reverse" transfer from subsidiaries to the parent, as MNEs headquartered in developing countries adopt practices originating in subsidiaries located in developed economies.

Strategic IHRM Orientation and Organizational Context

An important determinant of the level of HRM practice transfer is the extent to which the organization sees its HRM policies and practice as a source of competitive advantage. Human resource management can be viewed as a strategic resource that can be leveraged to the benefit of the organization.[21] The particular strategic international human resource management (SIHRM) approach stems from the international strategy of the firm and management beliefs about their HRM competence. In order to be a candidate for transfer, HRM practices must be considered a strategic resource and also be able to be used outside the specific context in which they were developed. Based on these dimensions, SIHRM can take one of three general forms: *adaptive, exportive,* or *integrative.*[22] These are the general approach or philosophy of the organization in the design of its HRM systems used in its overseas affiliates.

Adaptive SIHRM

Adaptive SIHRM approaches create HRM systems for foreign affiliates that reflect the local environment. This results in low internal consistency among MNE subsidiaries. This approach is consistent with a *multinational* strategy and a belief that the firm's HRM competence is context (location) specific. In MNEs with an adaptive approach, we would expect to see little if any transfer of HRM policies or practices from the parent to overseas affiliates or among the affiliates.

Exportive SIHRM

In exportive SIHRM approaches, the parent firm's HRM practices are transferred wholesale to foreign affiliate replicating home country HRM practices in its overseas affiliates (thus achieving high internal consistency). We would expect to find this approach in firms with a *global* strategy and a belief that their HRM competence is generalizable across context (locations). MNEs with exportive approaches are likely to engage in significant transfer of HR practices from headquarters to subsidiaries.

Integrative SIHRM

MNEs with integrative SIHRM approaches combine characteristics of their overseas affiliates with the parent company's HRM system. Transfer of HRM policies and practices occur but are just as likely to be between affiliates or from affiliates to parent as they are between the parent and affiliates. This SIHRM approach attempts to take the best HRM approaches and use them throughout the organization. It is consistent with a *transnational* strategy and a belief that practices can be adapted to fit in more than one context.

Other aspects of the organizational context can affect the level of transfer of practices. As discussed in the preceding chapter, the extent to which the structure of the organization is globally integrated affects the organization of HR in subsidiaries. Global integration (internal consistency) encourages the tendency of organizations to duplicate practices that are effective in one environment in new contexts. It also leads to standardization of practices to try to reduce the complexity and uncertainty of operating in multiple environments. The informal organization, or organizational culture (Chapter 3), is another important factor in the transfer of practices. For example, transfer is facilitated if the culture of the receiving unit supports learning, change, and innovation.[23]

The *degree* of transfer of practices is influenced by the subsidiaries method of founding, local dependence, the presence of expatriates, and the amount of communication with the parent. Resistance to transfer is greater for organizations that are embedded in the local environment, such as acquired organizations (which presumably have local practices in place) and those that are dependent on raw materials and intermediate parts from the local environment. Thus, the transfer of standard practices is also more likely in subsidiaries that are *greenfield* investments (newly formed) than in acquisitions, which are more embedded in the local context,[24] as shown in the example in Box 4.2.

Box 4.2   Morning Calisthenics at Fuji Photo Film Corporation

Fuji Film's operation in Greenwood, South Carolina, was a greenfield plant built to produce photographic plates for the printing industry. Professor Clarence Ritchie from the University of South Carolina had arranged a visit for his class to see one of the best examples of a continuous process machine, which started with a huge role of aluminum on one end and ended up as plates with many layers of photosensitive emulsion on the other. The class arrived very early, before the first shift had started. The receptionist ushered them past the stunning Japanese garden off the reception area into a large conference room saying, "Mr. Tokuzawa will be with you shortly."

"Well this place is certainly different from our previous Japanese plant tour at Showa Denko Carbon," said one of the students. "Yes," replied Clarence, "That company was acquired by the Japanese firm from its British parent." Just then, he thought he heard singing from the door that lead from the conference room to the factory floor. By pushing the door open a crack, Clarence was presented with a view of the entire local workforce clad in identical company uniforms being lead in calisthenics and the company song by the Japanese plant manager. Clarence wondered how those rural South Carolinians had been convinced to do that.[25]

Finally, the extent to which communication flows is largely from the parent to the subsidiary through the use of expatriates and/or frequent communication with the parent has a negative influence on the degree to which the HRM policies and practices resemble local competitors.[26] In this case, the tendency to replicate practices that have been proven or are in favor at headquarters is reinforced through frequent contact.

Host Country Effects

Both the *level* and *type* of practices transferred are influenced by the institutional and cultural factors in the local context. A number of elements of a national business system can influence the ability of an MNE to transfer practices. Employment law and labor market institutions, such as unions and works councils, influence labor relations in foreign subsidiaries as discussed in more detail in Chapter 10. Research has found that MNEs are more likely to transfer practices to affiliates located in *liberal market economies*, which tend to have fewer employment regulations than in *coordinated market economies*, where labor markets are more tightly regulated[27] (see Chapter 2). MNEs have little choice but to abide by the labor laws in a particular country, and practices that contravene such legislation are unlikely to be transferred. For example, China restricts the ability of managers in such core HR functions as recruitment, selection, and dismissal.[28] Labor unions may have to rely on more indirect means of influence but can still limit the ability of MNEs to unilaterally decide on the transfer of policies and practices. The success of transfer of HRM practices from the parent is also likely to be negatively associated with how different the institutional context of the subsidiary is from that of the parent.[29]

Host country culture exerts its influence on transfer through differences in the perception that culturally different individuals have about whether or not a particular policy or practice is important and/or beneficial. Practices that are viewed as inconsistent with good management by local managers are unlikely to be implemented. For example, the transfer of high involvement Japanese management practices was resisted by British managers who were not comfortable with giving responsibility of operating decisions to shop floor workers.[30] What is considered good management can be influenced not only by the broad sociocultural norms but also by local professional norms.[31] The host country context does not necessarily block the transfer of practices but can alter both the scope of the transfer (discussed ahead under affiliate responses) and the character of the practice being transferred (discussed ahead under recontextualization).

Types of Practices Transferred

Not all policies and practices are equally transferable across organizational types and institutional and cultural contexts. HRM policies and practices for which there are well-defined local norms or legal mandates and which affect the rank and file (time off, benefits, gender composition of workforce, etc.) are most likely to reflect the local context. However, practices for which there are not well-defined local norms or which are central to internal consistency in the organization or have to do with executives (executive bonuses, participation in decisions) are likely to be internally consistent throughout the organization.[32]

Local Affiliate Response to Transfer

As indicated in the previous discussion, the response of affiliates to the mandate that parent company practices should be adopted is not uniform across subsidiaries. And variation in the level of adoption can occur, even on policies and practices that are objectively superior or more efficient. Adoption of a particular practice or process involves not only *implementation* but also *internalization*. Implementation requires that the behaviors and actions required by the practice are exhibited, and internalization means that the practice is viewed as valuable for the unit and members become committed to the practice.[33]

The extent to which practices are adopted (implemented *and* internalized) depends both on institutional factors and the relationship of the affiliate to the parent. Institutional factors are those regulatory (laws and rules), cognitive (widely shared beliefs), and normative (norms and values) factors that differ from country to country. The relationship of headquarters to the affiliate can vary according to the extent to which the affiliate is dependent on the parent, the extent to which there is trust between these entities, and the extent to which the foreign affiliate identifies with (feels they are a part of) the parent organization. It is important to point out that implementation does not automatically result in internalization. Rather, four patterns of adoption are possible, as presented in Table 4.1.

In *minimal* adoption, the affiliate has low levels of implementation and internalization, essentially disavowing the practice. In this case, the institutional environment is unfavorable, and the relationship with the parent is characterized by low levels of trust and identity—very low dependence. In *assent* adoption there is a perceived value in the practice, but there is a low level implementation of the behaviors indicated by the practice. As with the minimal adoption situation the institutional context is not favorable, but the level of dependence is high. Given that the value of the practice is recognized, the lack of implementation may reflect insufficient capability in the subsidiary. In *ceremonial* adoption there is a high level of implementation but a low level of internalization. The distinguishing feature of this group is that they face a very high level of regulatory pressure. The regulatory context exerts pressure to adopt the practice but has little effect on commitment to the practice. Finally, in *active* adoption, affiliates are high on both implementing the practice and on believing in and recognizing the value of the practice. This represents the ideal level of adoption but requires a favorable institutional context as well as high levels of identification with and trust in the parent. Thus, regardless of the objective effectiveness of a practice, its adoption by a foreign affiliate depends a great deal on the perceptions of the practice by the affiliate.

Recent studies of transfer of practices have also pointed out that the process of transfer can be political (and sometimes contentious). There may be agents in the headquarters or the subsidiaries that can be motivated to either facilitate or sabotage the successful transfer of practices.[34] For example, employees at headquarters may not want to engage in transfer if they believe that doing so will cause them to lose an internal competitive advantage (i.e., they did something special that is now being adopted throughout the organization and is thus no longer unique). On the other hand, they can also be motivated to advocate strongly for transferring a practice as they may raise

Table 4.1 Patterns of Practice Adoption

	Low Internalization	High Internalization
High Implementation	Ceremonial adoption	Active adoption
Low Implementation	Minimal adoption	Assent adoption

their status as key agents in the organization. As suggested in our discussion on the difference between adoption and internalization of practices, actors in subsidiaries may refuse to engage in the transfer of a practice if they do not believe the practice is necessary, fitting, or valuable for the local context. Or they may want to go along with a practice transfer only because doing so will allow them to receive benefits from headquarters which they might not get in the absence of cooperation.[35] Studies have also suggested that the success of transfer is dependent on the relationship of employees from the headquarters and employees at the subsidiaries to which the practice is being transferred (i.e., the extent to which there is regular and meaningful interaction between the units or the level of mutual trust that exists between the units) and the extent to which employees at the headquarters are committed to identify with and trust the parent company.[36]

Recontextualization

Another perspective on the transfer of HRM policies and practices across the global organization highlights the fact that transfer does not always result in a practice being rejected or accepted "as is." Instead, practices are often modified in some way or given different meaning as they are transferred to a new institutional and cultural context. In some cases, this modification or *hybridization* of the practice is planned and anticipated.[37] For example, Japanese MNEs reduced the requirements for Brazilian workers to rotate across a range of tasks when implementing lean production techniques in Brazil. This was in recognition of the fact that Brazilian workers lacked the breadth of skills required for this rotation among tasks.[38] However, in other cases the policy or practice is reinterpreted in unpredictable ways. In these cases the policy or practice can be said to be *recontextulized.*

Recontexualization is the idea that when procedures and processes are transferred from one country to another they take on new meanings in the new sociocultural context.[39] The concept of recontextualization allows the tracking of meanings attached to procedures and processes as they move from one sociocultural context to another. Figure 4.2 is a graphic representation of the key elements of transnational transfer.

In this diagram the term *semiosis* is used to indicate the production of meaning.[40] In the first instance (initial semiosis, S1), when procedures or polices are transferred across a sociocultural boundary, new meanings are attached as people make sense of them using their preexisting frame of reference. An example is the U.S. understanding of sushi as raw fish. In Japan, sushi refers to the pickling agents used in the rice as opposed to the topping.[41] However, in the United States, the strangeness of eating the raw fish that is commonly used as a topping was what received attention. Therefore sushi was recontextualized as raw fish. A second type of meaning transformation occurs as policies and procedures evolve in the new environment (ongoing semiosis, S2). Continuing with the sushi example, the *California roll*—sushi made with cooked crab and avocado—is a further recontextualization that is more palatable for Americans. Finally, a third kind of recontextualization (reflexive semiosis, S3) or diffusion, can

Figure 4.2 Process of Recontextualization

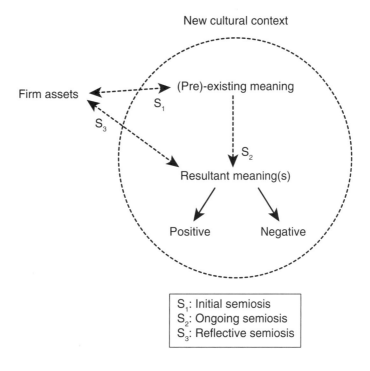

New cultural context

Firm assets

(Pre)-existing meaning
S_1

S_3

S_2

Resultant meaning(s)

Positive   Negative

S_1: Initial semiosis
S_2: Ongoing semiosis
S_3: Reflective semiosis

Source: Brannen (2004).

occur if the policy or procedure is repatriated to its country of origin. The example would be finding the California roll offered in sushi bars in Japan.

It is important to note that recontextualization can be either positive or negative, as shown in Figure 4.1. In the vignette that opened this chapter, the attempted transfer of Disney HRM practices that were seen as part of their distinctive competitive advantage had very negative results in France, ultimately resulting in Disney being charged with violating French labor laws.[42] Disney's strategy depends on creating the "Happiest Place on Earth" through well-developed HRM practices that create a clean, safe, and friendly environment.[43] For example, in order to achieve what Disney calls *a wholesome American look*, it has strict grooming and dress requirements for its employees (cast members) who must deliver "service with a smile." For women this includes the wearing of appropriate undergarments, specifically transparent as opposed to colored or designed pantyhose, skirts no shorter than 4 centimeters above the knee, fingernails no longer than the fingertips, and naturally colored hair. Men must be clean shaven with short haircuts and are not allowed to wear earrings. In France where freedom of personal expression and dress are highly valued, these *foreign* practices were seen as invasive. No such problems were encountered with the same practices in Tokyo Disney however, where these same HR practices fit in very well with the existing societal context. Thus, whether or not the foreignness of a practice is seen as a liability or an asset depends on the extent to which it is legitimate or marginalized in the new context. Figure 4.3 provides a humorous look at a practice that worked really well in one context but was ineffective in a different context.

The lesson is that recontextualization does not always conform to strategic intent. Positive recontextualizations may be a source of sustainable competitive advantage, but negative ones can come as an unwelcome shock.[44]

Figure 4.3   HRM Practice in a New Context

Source: BIZARRO © 2008 Dan Piraro, distributed by King Features.

Diffusion of Practices and Knowledge Transfer

Thus far in this chapter the discussion of the transfers of policies and practices has for the most part assumed that the transfer was from the parent to the local subsidiary. However, the transfer of practices need not originate with the parent and can also involve transfer back to the parent or among foreign operations (called reverse transfer or *diffusion*).[45] In fact, as many as eight different patterns of diffusion of practices have been identified based on the order and direction of transfer and the number of adopters (presented in the order of how commonly they occur in MNEs).[46]

- *Flow*—Practices from one subsidiary are implemented in both the MNE home country operations and other foreign subsidiaries.
- *All-together*—All subsidiaries from a region develop practices addressing a problem specific to their common business environment. Such jointly developed practices are then implemented region wide but not in the MNE home country operations.
- *Horizontal*—Practices from one subsidiary are implemented at another subsidiary.
- *Smorgasbord*—A subsidiary signals the existence of a novel practice to headquarters and other units, but adoption is voluntary and decided by individual country units. This type of reverse diffusion takes its name from the Swedish "*smorgasbord*," a buffet-style serving of food where guests select individually what to have and when to have it.
- *Strict reverse*—Practices from a subsidiary are implemented at the MNE home country operations.
- *Re-import*—Following a forward transfer (from headquarters to subsidiary), one subsidiary introduces innovations to the diffused practices, which make the new practice superior to the originally transferred practice. The amended version then becomes reintroduced by the headquarters and the other units.
- *Chain*—This is a process whereby a practice from one subsidiary is diffused to other subsidiaries and eventually reaches the headquarters, which in turn transfers the practice to additional subsidiaries.
- *Multisource*—Two or more country units (possibly including the headquarters) introduce a similar practice simultaneously. The practice is then picked up by other organizational subsidiaries.

It is important to note that this typology of diffusion patterns includes the possibility that practice innovations can progress through multiple repeated attempts, in which a practice might be reintroduced after modification to address initial transfer difficulties.[47] Not all of these patterns will exist in every organization, and the *flow* pattern appears to be the most prevalent type of reverse transfer. As discussed ahead, this may be partly the result of the fact that despite the popularity of network types of organizational structures, the majority of MNEs are very hierarchical.[48]

The particular pattern for *diffusion* of HR practices is dependent on four main factors. These are the nationality of the parent firm, the configuration of the MNE, the organizational conduits through which the practices may be diffused, and the relative influence of each of the national operations.[49] The effect of the nationality of the parent firm on diffusion is consistent with the country of origin and dominance effects discussed previously. It seems that the openness to new policies and procedures modeled on foreign operations is somewhat less hindered by these effects. For example, some German MNEs have accorded *vanguard* status to their operations in some foreign countries, enabling them to lead initiatives on which global HRM policies are based.[50] However, there is a good deal of variation of this influence with, for example, U.S. and French MNEs being much more resistant to reverse diffusion.[51]

The second main factor that influences the pattern of diffusion is the organization characteristics of the MNE. This includes the organizational structure, the similarities among subsidiaries and degree of integration, and how the firm has grown. The network form of organization, with its flexible links among organizational units, is obviously the one in which the subsidiaries have the greatest opportunity to exert influence on the organization.[52] And the more similar organization units are to each other the more scope there is for them to share practices. This includes similarity that extends across the organization, referred to previously as integration. Finally, consistent with the previous discussion of transfer of practices, the fact that a subsidiary is a greenfield start-up or an acquisition could influence reverse transfer. Growth though greenfield investment tends to rely on policies and practices that exist in the parent, while in acquisitions there may be more potential for the acquired subsidiary to influence the parent with its preexisting polices and practices. As discussed ahead in Chapter 5, the distinctive practices of the subsidiary are sometimes part of the motive for the acquisition.[53] Firms may see the opportunity to access, absorb, and transfer HR practices as an attractive aspect of an acquisition.

The third factor affecting diffusion is the richness of the transmission channels available among subsidiaries to support diffusion. Explicit, easily codified knowledge concerning HR practices can effectively be transferred through such mechanisms as international committees, information systems, databases, and management audits. However, these procedural channels are less likely to be effective for tacit knowledge (knowledge that cannot be codified, sometimes called *in the bones expertise*), which requires people-based channels, such as cross-national work groups and international assignments for diffusion.[54] For example, practices in the area of pay and performance management tend to be transferred through procedural channels, while training practices are more likely to be diffused through people-based mechanisms.[55]

A final source of influence on the diffusion of practices has to do with the relative influence that each subsidiary has on the MNE. At the outset of this chapter, the importance of the political aspect of the transfer of practices was identified. We should not assume, therefore, that HR managers in foreign operating units will always be willing to share practices that they have developed. However, the more resources and greater the influence of the subsidiary the more likely they will be a net supplier of practices to the rest of the organization.[56]

The preceding discussion highlights the fact that standardization or the export of practices from the parent to the subsidiaries is not the only way to achieve competitive advantage through integrating best HR practices throughout the organization. Increasingly, MNEs are recognizing that good practices can originate in foreign subsidiaries. Furthermore, these practices can permeate the organization through a variety of diffusion patterns.

Chapter Summary

This chapter focuses on a distinctive aspect of global HRM—the ability of the MNE to develop expertise in HRM in one context and then transfer it to other units or diffuse it throughout the organization. The motives for the transfer of practices may be cultural, political, or market driven. There are numerous factors that influence the nature and form of this transfer including, country-of-origin effects, dominance effects, strategic IHRM orientation, host country effects, and the type of practice that is being transferred. A key factor in the transfer of practices is the extent to which the organization sees HRM policies and practices as a source of competitive advantage. This fact coupled with the extent to which a practice can be used outside of the context in which it was developed accounts for a significant amount of the diffusion of practices. Local affiliates of the MNE do not respond uniformly to the mandate that parent company practices should be adopted. Adoption of a particular practice involves both implementation and internalization and is influenced by both the institutional context of the affiliate and the relationship that the affiliate has with the parent. HRM policies and practices do not always transfer across sociocultural contexts in a way that achieves their original strategic intent. Sometimes the practice is given a new meaning through the process of recontextualization, which can have either positive or negative results for the organization. The transfer of HR policies and practices occurs not only from the parent to local affiliates, but practices can be diffused throughout the organization through a variety of different patterns based on the order, direction of transfer, and the number of adopters. The particular pattern of diffusion is dependent on the nationality of the parent, the configuration of the MNE, the channels available to transfer the practice, and the relative influence of the various national operations.

Questions for Discussion

1. Describe how an HRM policy or practice can be a source of competitive advantage.

2. Discuss the difference between implementation and internalization of an HRM practice.

3. Explain how the process of recontextualization changes the meaning associated with an HRM policy or practice.

4. Outline the possible patterns of diffusion of an HRM practice. What factors would be likely to generate each pattern?

5. Explain how SIHRM orientation of the firm determines the level of HRM practice transferred.

Notes

1. This vignette is based on various accounts of the Disneyland Paris case.
2. Bartlett & Ghoshal (1998b).
3. See Edwards (2011b).

4. Bartlett & Ghoshal (1998b).
5. Taylor, Beechler, & Napier (1996).
6. Abo (1994).
7. Edwards (2011b).
8. Adapted from a case in Lemanski, Björkman, & Stahl (2011).
9. Edwards (2011b).
10. Gunnigle, Murphy, Cleveland, Heraty, & Morley (2002).
11. http://www.unctad.org/en/docs/gdscsir20041c3_en.pdf.
12. http://www.unctad.org/en/docs/gdscsir20041c3_en.pdf.
13. Edwards (2011a).
14. See Oliver & Wilkinson (1992); Muller (1998).
15. Björkman (2006).
16. Pudelko & Harzing (2007).
17. Sidanius (1993).
18. Smith & Meiskins (1995).
19. See Ouchi (1981).
20. Pudelko & Harzing (2007).
21. See Kostova (1999).
22. Taylor, Beechler, & Napier (1996).
23. Kostova (1999).
24. Kostova (1999).
25. This case is fictional but based on the experience of the first author.
26. Rosenzweig & Nohria (1994).
27. Parry, Dickmann, & Morley (2008); Farndale, Brewster, & Poutsma (2008).
28. Von Glinow & Teagarden (1988).
29. Kostova (1999).
30. Broad (1994).
31. Björkman (2006).
32. Rosenzweig & Nohria (1994).
33. This section is based on Kostova (1999) and Kostova & Roth (2002).
34. Edwards (2011a).
35. Edwards (2011a).
36. Kostova (1999); Kostova & Roth (2002); Björkman & Lervik (2007).
37. Zhu & Dowling (2002).
38. Humphrey (1995).
39. See Brannen (2004) for a detailed discussion of this process.
40. This is a simplified interpretation of the term. See the work of C. S. Pierce in Houser & Kloesel (1992) for a more complete description.
41. What all sushi has in common is *shari* (cooked vinegared rice), which can be combined with a variety of other ingredients.
42. Brannen (2004).
43. See Peters & Waterman (1982).
44. Brannen (2004).
45. Edwards (1998); Edwards, Edwards, Ferner, Marginson, & Tregaskis (2010); Edwards & Tempel (2010).
46. Lemanski, Björkman, & Stahl (2011).
47. Thory (2008).
48. Bartlett & Ghoshal (1998b).

49. Edwards, Edwards, Ferner, Marginson, & Tregaskis (2010).
50. Ferner & Varul (2000a).
51. Edwards, Almond, Clark, Colling, & Ferner (2005); Thory (2008).
52. Harzing & Noorderhaven (2006).
53. See Schuler, Jackson, & Luo (2004).
54. See Tregakis (2003).
55. Edwards, Edwards, Ferner, Marginson, & Tregaskis (2010).
56. See Harzing (2001a); Kirstensen & Zeitlin (2005); Minbaeva (2007).

5

HRM in International Joint Ventures, Mergers and Acquisitions, and Collaborative Alliances

LEARNING OBJECTIVES

After reading this chapter you should be able to

- describe the influence of HR at the various stages of the mergers and acquisitions (M&A) process,
- discuss the people and cultural factors important to the success of international M&As,
- describe the HR aspects of the "due diligence" process,

- outline the HR issues associated with the various stages of international joint ventures (IJV) formation, and
- describe and discuss the importance of strategic alliance learning.

Flight BA 92

Charles W. "Chuck" Wilson accepted the complimentary glass of champagne offered to him as he adjusted his fully reclining business class seat on British Airways flight 92. At least I can get some sleep on the overnight flight to London, he thought. It's going to be a stressful day tomorrow!

Chuck was executive vice president and director of human resources for U.S.-based New Dominion Bank, and he knew what he had to do. The bank could not afford the kind of wholesale departure of personnel that had occurred during its last merger. The takeover of Bancoverde had been a disaster. Called a "merger of equals" by the CEOs of both organizations, Chuck knew at the outset it was going to be anything but. New Dominion, originally headquartered in Charlotte, North Carolina, but now based in New York had grown rapidly by acquiring smaller banks in attractive markets. This expansion had taken it international, and the target organizations were much larger. Still, its success depended on introducing competitive lending practices and extremely efficient backroom operations. This inevitably meant headcount reductions and staff relocations; it would be New Dominion policies, procedures, and personnel that would prevail.

Bancoverde's international lending division had been headquartered in Miami to take advantage of strong ties to its Latin American base. However, it had always been assumed at New Dominion that this activity would be moved to New York post merger. Chuck remembered vividly that sinking feeling in the pit of his stomach when he had first walked into the Bancoverde International Division offices in Miami. The entire 23rd floor that had been occupied by more than 20 loan officers and their support staff was vacant. Unbelievably, they had left over the long holiday weekend, taking most of their customer base with them, and were now working at a competitor institution almost across the street.

This time it had to be different. Tomorrow, when he met with the senior executives of Celtic Shield bank in London, he would outline his plan to give all employees a very clear and realistic picture of what would happen to their job after the merger. He hoped they would agree to let him proceed.

Chuck settled back into his seat and turned on the aircraft entertainment system, hoping that there was at least one movie he hadn't seen.

Introduction

M&As have become an increasingly popular alternative to greenfield investment for achieving international diversification and growth. In 2010, cross-border M&As

increased by 37% to $341 billion[1] while international greenfield projects fell both in number and in value.[2] The driver of this activity is of course the reduction of boundaries resulting from globalization discussed in Chapter 1 coupled with an increase in global competition. In today's competitive environment, target firms can no longer be acquired and left as independent operations but must be integrated in order capture their added value. However, it is the inability to effectively integrate that is the major cause of the unspectacular performance of the majority of M&As.[3] And the failure of M&As can often be attributed to problems of integrating the different cultures and workforces of the combined firms.[4] In this chapter, we discuss the HRM challenges associated with international M&As and then go on to discuss the related issues in international joint ventures and other types of international collaborative alliances.

Reasons for M&As

From a legal perspective, a *merger* occurs when two companies join together to create a new entity, while in an *acquisition* one company acquires sufficient shares to gain control of the other. These ventures may be structured one way or the other for accounting, tax, or public relations purposes. However, there are actually very few mergers among equals. As indicated in the case that opened this chapter, once the agreement is signed, most mergers look very much like acquisitions with one organization the dominant partner.

There are a number of reasons that firms engage in international M&As, including response to political or economic conditions, diversifying risk, vertical integration, and reducing costs. Two of the main reasons for M&As are to achieve competitive size or to increase market share by adding brands or distribution channels.[5] While larger firms aim to gain market power by acquiring companies in areas where they are not represented (as in the case of Bancoverde), smaller firms may try to leverage their niche competencies through cross-border deals. In this way, M&As allow a much more rapid response to the pressure of global competition than does a greenfield investment. In some industries, the key motive for an acquisition is access to talented people with the value of the deal calculated accordingly. For example, when the semiconductor firm Broadcom bought chipmaker SiByte it was reported to have paid $18 million per engineer.[6] Alternatively, the key factor in many M&As is cost cutting and workforce reduction, which may be as difficult in some countries as is retaining engineers in Silicon Valley.[7] International mergers and acquisitions occur for both strategic and tactical reasons, while some are the result of corporate egos. Box 5.1 provides some recent examples.

Box 5.1   M&A Strategies

Market Dominance
Banks and insurance companies in Scandinavia are merging across the region to create Nordic financial institutions, such as Nordea and SEB, in order to achieve economies of scale and control distribution channels.

Geographic Expansion

Brewing companies, such as Kirin, Heineken, and Interbrew, are using acquisitions to extend their geographic reach and global market share.

Leveraging Competence

Foreign companies, such as GE and Axa, have made large-scale acquisitions in the financial industry in Japan to leverage their competence in new product development, credit risk evaluation, and debt management.

Resource Acquisition

In the petroleum industry firms such as BP and Exxon acquire existing companies with proven oil reserves as a more cost-effective way to grow than through oil exploration.

Capability Acquisition

As the market shifted from voice to data transmission, European wireless makers, such as Nokia and Ericsson, acquired small start-up companies with competence in emerging data communication technologies.

Adjusting to Competition

Companies are sometimes forced into acquisitions in order to counter the acquisitions strategies of their competitors. For example Matsushita launched a series of ultimately disastrous acquisitions in Hollywood after Sony acquired Columbia Pictures.

Executive Arrogance

While most companies launch acquisitions for sound strategic reasons, there are also cases, regardless of what the press release says, in which the logic of an M&A seems to make no sense beyond the CEO's desire to run a bigger company.

Source: Adapted from Evans, Pucik, & Barsoux (2002).

M&A Success and Failure

Some M&As are successful, some have little effect on the performance of the acquiring firm, and some are spectacular failures, such as the much publicized Daimler-Chrysler merger.[8] While estimates of M&A success vary, it has generally been the case that the majority of them do not create value for the acquiring firm, and a significant number actually reduce value.[9] A 1999 survey by KPMG found that 17% of deals had added value to the combined company, 30% produced no discernible difference, and 53% actually destroyed value.[10] More recent research has suggested more positive results, indicating that companies may be getting better at M&A, but by all accounts failures outnumber successes.[11]

There are many potential causes for the failure of the combined company to achieve its goals, but they fall into four categories. These are *lack of a shared vision, loss of key assets, high transition costs*, and *lack of cultural fit*. First, an M&A can fail because there is a difference in the vision of what the two parties want to achieve in the combined firm. Sometimes for the sake of making the deal, these differences are glossed over and only become a problem in the post-merger integration phase (discussed ahead). Second, the M&A can fail because assets that were key to achieving the potential value of the combined firm are lost. These assets can be tangible—as in the case of the international division employees who left Bancoverde, described in the vignette that opened this chapter. Or they can be intangible, such as relationships with suppliers, government, or the local community; if the new organization is perceived as insensitive these relationships may be damaged. These concerns can be even greater in cross-border M&As because of different legal and regulatory environments, accounting standards, and employment systems.[12] International differences also contribute to the next general reason for M&A failure—high transition costs. Linking the new entities can be difficult across national contexts and can also incur higher coordination costs because of geographic distance. And managers can be so consumed with overcoming these coordination problems that they become distracted from the original goals of the M&A. Finally, the integration of organizational cultures, human resource systems, managerial views, and other aspects of organizational life can lead to severe organizational conflict.[13] The significant cultural mismatch between Daimler and Chrysler and the inattention to people-related dimensions is often cited as the key reason for the failure of that merger as shown in the news report presented in Box 5.2.

Box 5.2   DaimlerChrysler Merger a Fiasco

It was supposed to be a perfect union of carmakers.

When the two companies merged in 1998, Daimler Chairman Jürgen Schrempp promised a "merger of equals." But it wasn't long before Chrysler executives complained the bullheaded Germans wouldn't listen to the Americans.

"We don't demand things of people; we seek people's cooperation," said Gerald Meyers, former chairman of American Motors and now a professor at the University of Michigan business school. "These two cultures were therefore bound to collide."

And collide they did.

Americans Feel Deceived

From the beginning, the high command in Stuttgart issued orders to Detroit about everything from where the headquarters would be located (Germany) to what kind of business cards would be used.

The relationship began to fall apart quickly. Since the merger, the company has lost nearly half its value. Somebody had to go, and it was the Americans. Daimler eventually sent in a German management team.

Schrempp's promise of a "merger of equals" had been fiction, and he even admits as much. He told the *Financial Times* that if he had been honest with the Americans about German dominance before the merger, they never would have made a deal.

So what was the reaction at Chrysler?

"[I was] one of [the] people who'd been deceived," says Meyers. "People who'd been hoodwinked. This wasn't just a small, a small decision. This was just plain dishonest."

The two cultures had never been compatible. Take the Daimler annual meeting, where stockholders are fed sausages and dumplings. In Germany, there's more attention paid to wining and dining the shareholders than to giving them precise information.

That's the reason Kirk Kerkorian, Chrysler's largest shareholder, sued Daimler for $9 billion, charging fraud. "Apparently in Germany, one can say pretty much whatever one wants to the shareholders of a company," says Terry Christensen, Kerkorian's lawyer. "Here in the United States, what you say to the shareholders has to be true."

Dejected Employees

All of this has demoralized Chrysler's workers. "Most of them are disgusted and frustrated because they seem like they have been shafted," says one.

The rank and file now expects big layoffs, and they worry the company will be sold. Schrempp insists that isn't true, but few of the Americans he has dealt with are willing to take him at his word a second time.

Source: Bob Jamieson, ABC News, http://abcnews.go.com/WNT/story?id=131280&page=1# .TtVGnLJCqU8

Are international M&As more or less successful than domestic M&As? This is especially salient question given that M&A failure often stems from problems related to integrating cultures. The answer to the question is far from straightforward. Cross-border M&As demand a "double-layered acculturation,"[14] as organizations must align both organizational and national cultures; one may conclude that they will be significantly more challenging than domestic M&As. Differences in national culture imply differences in commonly accepted norms, management styles, and prevalent practices, all of which can impede building a sense of shared identity or development of trust between the M&As partners. While a number of studies provide some support for such negative impact of culture distance between parties in an M&A deal, there are also studies that reach an opposite conclusion and suggest that cultural distance is an asset rather than a liability. A key argument to support this line of reasoning is that, in addition to being a potential source of conflict, cultural distance can also be a source of value creation, as it provides access to potentially valuable capabilities, resources, and learning opportunities. Further, cultural issues (at the level of the organization) are often ignored in domestic M&As and may remain under the radar for far too long. When involved in international M&As, organizations have increased awareness of the importance of cultural issues for the integration process. They tend to pay much more attention to them, and subsequently, engage in culture integration more purposefully. While we take note of all these possible ways in which culture can impact M&As, as of now there is no compelling evidence for a relationship (be it positive or negative) between cultural distance between M&A parties and post-M&A performance. Looking for such a direct relationship may be too simplistic. A balanced perspective suggests that the outcomes of cross-border M&A depends on not whether the cultures are different but on the nature and extent of culture differences, and more importantly, on strategic intent, integration approach and specific interventions chosen to manage the integration of the two entities across borders.[15]

To that end, it seems clear that even in the most well thought out M&As their ultimate success may depend on the ability to integrate across boundaries effectively.[16] However, what *integration* means may differ depending on the strategic intent underlying the M&A.

Types of M&A Integration

One way to understand the implications of the process of combining the two firms is to consider the strategic intent behind the acquisition. Most M&A transactions are one of two types, either *traditional* or *transformational.* Traditional M&As leverage existing capabilities through rationalization or transfer, while transformational M&As involve more complex exploration skills so as to create new capabilities or to do things differently.[17] The difference is important because it influences the focus of HR issues and ultimately the kind of organization that will emerge from the deal.

A useful framework for predicting the character of the organization that results from an M&A is to examine the situation in terms of the amount of cultural change required in both the acquiring and acquired companies in order to achieve the desired goal.[18] Figure 5.1 shows how these factors result in five types of strategies for post-merger outcomes.

When no cultural change is required the resulting company is called a *preservation* acquisition, while when large amounts of change are required in both the acquired and acquiring company the result is a *transformation.* When large change is required in the acquired company but little change is expected in the acquirer, the result is *absorption.* The rare case of the opposite cultural change requirements in which the acquiring company is blended into the acquired is called a *reverse merger.* The case in which the best practices of both sides are integrated is labeled *best of both.*

Figure 5.1   Strategies for Post-Merger Outcomes

	Low		High
High	**Absorption** Acquired company conforms to acquirer–cultural assimilation		**Transformation** Both companies find new ways of operating–cultural transformation
Degree of Change in Acquired Company		**Best of Both** Additive from both sides–cultural integration	
Low	**Preservation** Acquired company retains its independence–cultural autonomy		**Reverse Merger** Unusual case of acquired company dictating terms–cultural assimilation

Degree of Change in Acquiring Company

Source: Mirvis & Marks (1994).

Preservation M&As

In this case the end goal is that the acquired company will preserve its independence and cultural autonomy. This is often the case when the motive for the merger involves securing talent or other soft skills or when imposing the acquiring companies policies and procedures could harm the company's competitive advantage. However, this independence rarely survives because operational pressures often require some functions to be merged with the rest of the organization.[19]

Transformation M&As

In transformation M&As, the goal is that the newly formed entity will break sharply with the past, do things differently—in effect, reinvent the firm. This type of M&A is difficult to implement and requires a commitment to the vision for the new entity by both parties. A recent example is Lenovo's acquisition of IBM's PC business.[20]

Absorption M&As

Absorption M&As are common when there are differences in the size or sophistication of the two parties involved in the deal, when the acquired company is performing poorly, or when market conditions force consolidation. Often, much of the benefit is derived from cost cutting and headcount reduction in the acquired company. However, employees of the acquired firm can benefit if they see the new owner as helping them to remain competitive, when the previous management style was unpopular, or when higher pay, benefits, or prestige accompany the merger. Cisco Systems is well known for acquiring firms to gain access to technology, but while they are assimilating their acquisitions into Cisco culture, Cisco Systems tries to retain most of the employees, including top management.[21]

Reverse Merger

The exact opposite of the absorption M&A is the situation in which the acquiring company wants to gain capabilities from the acquired organization. Typically this takes the form of the acquired company absorbing a parallel unit from the acquiring firms. For example, when Nokia bought a high tech firm in Silicon Valley, it gave the acquired unit global responsibilities. This meant that part of the business in Finland reported to California.[22]

Best of Both

Adopting the best practices from both parties in the merger might seem a painless way of achieving cultural integration. However, in practice this approach almost never occurs. The internal consistency of the organization's culture is lost when practices are adopted piecemeal, and the process of deciding which practices are "best" can often become very political. Where this approach has had success, the merging organizations were very similar, as in the case of Exxon/Mobile.

Few M&As fit cleanly into any of these categories, and cross-border mergers add another complicating factor. In international M&As there may be parts of the organization or units in some countries or regions where a particular approach works well and other parts where it does not.[23]

Critical HRM Issues at Different Stages of M&As

People and cultural issues are key determining factors in the success of M&As. Surveys consistently rank such factors as *retention of key talent*, *selecting the management team*, *resolving cultural issues*, and *communications* as the key people factors in M&A success.[24] Thus, HRM has an important role to play in all stages of the M&A process. The process is typically divided into three stages: the *initial planning stage*, including due diligence; the *closing the deal stage*; and the *post-merger integration* stage. Box 5.3 provides an overview of the HRM activities at each stage.

The stages are for illustration only, and some HRM activities will occur across stages. For example, communication is a key element of any change process and will cut across all stages.

Box 5.3   HRM Activities in the Cross-Border M&As

Initial Planning Stage

- Participating in selection of M&A targets
- Forming the M&A leadership team
- Determining how success will be measured
- Assuring that the due diligence process deals with HRM considerations

Closing the Deal and Company Integration

- Advising on implementation (staffing plan)
- Integration planning (integration manager and team)
- Deciding on HR policies and procedures
- Planning "how to learn"

Post-Merger Integration

- Communication to alleviate anxiety and stress
- Retaining key talent
- Building the new culture
- Assessing and revising as required

Initial Planning Stage

In international M&As, human resource strategy cannot be separated from its cultural and social context. Cultural compatibility or incomparability is one of the most discussed issues in cross-border M&As and needs to be assessed at the initial selection of targets.[25] Here HR can offer an initial assessment of the quality of human assets before committing to a full due diligence assessment (discussed ahead). A second important consideration at this stage is making sure the company has the appropriate leadership team in place to head the M&A process.[26] For example, the success of the Renault acquisition of Nissan is largely attributed to the leadership ability of Carlos Ghosn, while the failed DaimlerChrysler merger had three different top management teams in its first two years.[27] And at the planning stage, it is important to clearly understand the goals of the M&A and how success will be measured. If, for example, the motive for the acquisition involves talent acquisition, the retention of employees is a key metric, perhaps at the cost of efficiency. Finally, the most important contribution that HR can make during this stage is to ensure that the due diligence process covers the critical people issues, which involve a *cultural assessment* and a *human capital audit*.

Due Diligence Process

Due diligence in an M&A of course involves gaining a complete and accurate understanding of the legal, financial, and operational issues associated with the deal. However, as important is learning about the culture and HR policies and practices of the target organization. As indicated previously, these people issues are often at the core of M&A success or failure, and it is therefore important to try to gain an understanding of these issues before signing the deal. Box 5.4 outlines the broad list of topics that might be covered in a due diligence audit of a target company.

Box 5.4   A Human Resource Due Diligence Checklist

Organization and Management

Organization charts
  Job title hierarchy
Management committees
Succession plans
Employment contracts
Employment agreements

HR Policies

Hiring procedures
Employment documents
Job descriptions
Work rules
  Vacation policy
  Discipline
Performance management
Early retirement

Termination/severance

Compensation/Benefits

Executive compensation
General compensation
Incentive compensation
  Bonus eligibility
  Stock plans
Pension plan
  Coverage
  Assets and liabilities
Nonmonetary rewards

Labor Relations

Litigations and Claims

HRIS (Human Resource Information Systems)

Employee records

Source: Evans et al. (2002, p. 268); Schuler et al. (2004, pp. 102–103).

Some of this information is needed in order to protect the company from potential financial exposure, while other information involves the strategy of the M&A. However, HR due diligence is more than just collecting data to avoid financial liability or to assess strategic fit. It means a complete assessment of the HR environment of the firm, including its culture. Before an integration strategy can be developed, the cultures of the two companies must be understood. The *organizational culture assessment* evaluates factors that may influence organizational fit, such as core philosophy and values, leadership styles, time orientation, risk tolerance, team versus individual performance, and so on, and allows the firm to prepare a plan of how cultural issues should be addressed before the deal is signed. Some information will address the leadership of the target company and their philosophy such as the following:

- What are their core beliefs about what it takes to succeed?
- Is the company business strategy driven by tradition or innovation?
- Is the company long- or short-term oriented?
- How much risk is the company willing to accept?
- Who are the important stakeholders in the organization?

Other information will examine how the company manages key activities such as the following:

- Is the company results or process oriented?
- Is the power concentrated at the top, in certain functions, or diffused?
- Are decisions made by consensus, by consultation, or by authority?
- Is the information flow in the company wide or narrow?
- Are employees valuable because of their values, skills, and competencies or because of getting results?
- Is the culture oriented toward teamwork, individual performance, or both?
- Who are the "heroes" in the organization, and what are its key "rituals"?[28]

Some companies use the organizational cultural audit to assess fit, with the view that it would be difficult to integrate the target if there are large differences in organizational culture. Cisco, for example, avoids acquisitions of companies that are substantially different in the belief that it would be difficult to retain key staff.[29] However, it may be that the best partner is not always the one with the best cultural fit. For example, while large cultural difference may create difficulties, too small a difference may provide little opportunity to leverage unique competencies. Similarity can in fact lead to redundancies and conflict between the acquirer and the target.[30] A moderate degree of organizational culture difference might be most beneficial in that it prompts discussion about the most appropriate policies and practices for the new organization.[31] What seems to be very important is the complementarity of cultures and managing the integration process (discussed ahead) to build on the unique contributions that each partner brings to the new organization.[32] As noted above, it is also important to remember that the culture of the organization is embedded in the nationality of the country.[33] Therefore, cultural due diligence means evaluating the sociocultural context in which the company exists as well.

A second aspect of due diligence in HRM is the *human capital audit*. The human capital audit has both a *preventative* dimension (focused on liabilities, such as outstanding employee litigation and grievances, labor contracts, and differences in compensation and benefits—any employment related constraint on the M&A), and a *talent identification* dimension. The talent identification dimension involves understanding if the target company has the talent necessary to execute the acquisition strategy, identifying key individuals, and assessing any weaknesses in the management team. Examples of information required include the following:

- What unique skills do employees have?
- How does the target company's talent compare to our own?
- What is the background of the management team?
- What are the reporting relationships?
- What effect will losing some of the management team have?
- What is the compensation philosophy?
- How much pay is at risk at various levels of the firm?[34]

The difficulty in gaining access to information about the target's employees causes some firms to ignore this issue in the early stages of the M&A process. However, early talent assessment can identify potential risks and allow time to develop strategies to deal with them. And this assessment will help with decisions about who to retain in the target organization.[35] Without such an assessment, firms run the risk of not having talent with the skills important to the success of the new organization.

Closing the Deal

Prior to signing the deal, the HR involvement in the M&A process will likely have been conducted behind the scenes. And the amount of time from signing the agreement to implementation can be quite long (and in some cases the deal may not go through because of shareholder approval or changes in the market and so on). However, this is an important period of time because as soon as there is public awareness of the M&A, the communication process must kick into gear.[36] This is where first impressions of new *foreign* partners (owners) are formed, and communication with all parties, including employees and unions, begins at this time. Managers from the acquiring company need to become familiar with the organizational culture of the acquired company and also the national culture context in which the firm operates. Because both organizations are unfamiliar with each other, there is a tendency for both to display defensive behavior.[37] Additionally, at this preclosing stage, the firm will now typically have complete access to data to confirm the due diligence assessment. At this stage, the HR roadmap (organizational structure, reporting relationships, and so on) for the post-merger integration phase is finalized. Finally, at this time the integration manager and transition team are identified.[38] Because the new management team is not yet in place, M&As typically turn to a dedicated integration manager and transition team to guide the integration process. Box 5.5 describes the process at Cisco.

Box 5.5   The BD Group at Cisco

"My experience with most companies is that they do acquisitions infrequently and integration is somebody's nighttime job," says Brett Galloway, the former CEO of Airespace, a wireless networking company Cisco acquired. "Cisco has people who do this full time--it's a core function of the company."

The nucleus of the company's acquisitions machine is its business development group, a 40-person team tucked into a nondescript cubicle farm in Cisco's sprawling San Jose office complex. The BD group, as it's called, has a diverse staff, ranging from PhDs in engineering to experts in silicon chips to MBAs with investment banking experience. Together, they identify potential buys, conduct due diligence on target companies, negotiate with senior execs, and integrate new companies into the greater Cisco whole. (The company now has more than 48,000 employees.) For over a decade, the group has operated under the same set of basic principles: Buy small, buy early in the product's life cycle (that is, preferably before it becomes the next big hit), and most importantly, put the people you're acquiring above everything else. "At the end of the day, it's always an art, not a science," says Dan Scheinman, the senior vice president for corporate development, who has overseen the group since 2001—and who reports directly to Chairman and CEO John Chambers.[39]

Post-Merger Integration

The value creation that produces a successful M&A occurs after the acquisition.[40] The integration process required to create new value for the firm involves the separate elements of human and task integration. Both are required to achieve success. However, as suggested in the Cisco example, it is the human integration consisting of activities that foster the participation of the employees of the acquired company that leads to the more comprehensive integration in terms of organizational culture convergence and mutual respect. And then, additional task integration takes place after the human integration process is complete.[41] Figure 5.2 shows graphically these two integration processes.

All M&As require integration to some extent, and it is important that the integration be tailored to the goal of the M&A. There are three activities that seem to be critical to the human aspect of effective post-merger integration. These are *communication, retaining key talent* and *building the new culture*.

Communication

Post-merger integration can be a delicate and complicated process as dysfunctional employee mindsets can lead to numerous HR problems. M&As alter the established order and pattern of activities in the target firm and employee attitudes have been found to decline immediately after the announcement and deteriorate over time.

Figure 5.2 Impact of Human and Task Integration on Acquisition Outcome

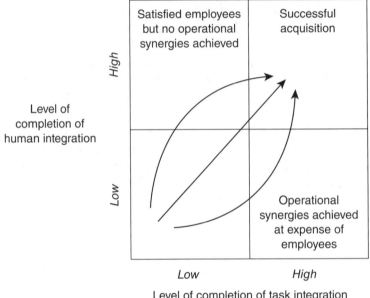

Source: Birkinshaw, Bresman, & Håkanson (2000).

Regardless of the reality of the situation employees fear job loss, question the validity of their skills and knowledge, and generally are uncertain about the future.[42]

Communication is the most basic action that organizations can take to reduce employee anxiety, lack of trust and other negative feelings following the announcement of an M&A. Communicating the organization's intent increases employee perceptions that the company is trustworthy, honest, and caring and it also helps them understand how they fit in the new company.[43] Communication is also critical to help employees understand the new identity of the merged organization. Additional care must be taken in cross-border M&As where there are language differences. Written documents describing the M&A that are drafted in a foreign language tend to be abstract and limited in scope, which reduces their usefulness.[44] And cross-cultural communication competence does not receive the attention it should in cross-border M&As.[45]

Communication is necessary but insufficient to reduce employee uncertainty surrounding M&A integration. A related aspect of the process is employee involvement. Employee involvement reduces psychological stress, leads to more successful functional integration, facilitates partnerships and collaborative work environments, and is a key predictor of achieving synergistic outcomes in cross-border M&As.[46] Employee involvement can be achieved through open information exchange, face-to-face personal relationships, by using in-house integration teams consisting of managers from both firms, and by identifying integration entrepreneurs (employees who naturally take on the integration role) and supporting them.[47] In effect, employee involvement distributes responsibility for the success of the integration to a wider group of employees across both firms.

Talent Retention

Retaining key talent is widely recognized as one of the most (if not *the* most) important element in the success of international M&As.[48] However, as shown in the case that opened this chapter, many acquired firms lose key employees soon after the acquisition. And there is some evidence (in U.S. acquisitions) that the chance of executives leaving is higher if they are acquired by a foreign firm.[49] Retention of talent is especially important where the value of the M&A lies in the intangible assets, such as the knowledge and skills of people in the acquired firm.

The key elements of retaining key talent in an M&A involve, first of all, knowing who the talented people are, effectively and openly communicating with them, providing financial motivation to stay, and finally integrating these key employees into the leadership development of the organization. Despite the well-known competition for talent, there is little evidence that MNEs do talent management in any sort of effective way.[50] One report suggested that only about 16% of executives surveyed believed that they could identify their high performers.[51] In an M&A situation, obtaining performance information may be even more difficult and complicated by the fact that performance criteria are likely to vary (see Chapter 8). Also, local managers may protect their top people by withholding information about them.[52]

As indicated previously, communication is the most basic intervention, and this applies to retaining talent as well. Once top talent is identified, it is important that immediate clear and open communication from the acquiring firm gives individuals a realistic expectation of their role in the new organization. This communication also involves providing financial motivation to remain. Some employees will be offered financial incentives (stock options, bonuses, etc.) to stay until a specific point in time or until merger-related projects are completed. Others will need to be integrated into the longer-term leadership development plans of the company in order to retain them after the initial impact of the financial incentives wears off.

Building the New Culture

A final element of the post-merger integration phase that lasts long after the combination of the two firms is building the new culture of the new entity. Conflict in M&As is often attributed to lack of understanding of the partner's organizational culture. Minimizing cultural conflict involves understanding the behavioral norms and routines of both the acquirer and target. Compatibility between M&A partners is achieved through learning within the organization that results in the construction of a shared culture. Identifying cultural differences and learning from them are the only way in which key elements of both organizations will be valued and preserved in the new organization.[53] A number of interventions have been proposed to accomplish this, including collaborative problem solving and intergroup workshops between the merging management teams, and merger workshops that engage employees in determining best practices for the new organization.[54] However, the success of these interventions requires those involved to first have a good understanding of the culture of their own organization.[55] Strong leadership seems to be a key factor in this regard. For example, cross-border teams sharing knowledge, implementing direct contact among managers to break down stereotypes, and extensive training workshops were just some of the measures introduced by Carlos Ghosn to break down the "us versus them" mindset in the Renault/Nissan merger.[56]

Cultural Differences in Integration Strategies

We may be seeing the emergence of a set of global "best practices" with regard to the effective integration of firms in an M&A. For example, practices such as performance-related pay, formal planning systems, cost control, and a high level of investment in training have been found across nationalities.[57] However, preferences for certain integration practices in different cultures also exist. For example, among U.S., British, and French acquirers of Western European targets, the French exercised higher formal control consistent with high uncertainty avoidance in French culture. Conversely, U.S. firms were more likely to rely on informal communication.[58] French firms are also more likely to rely on centralizing power at headquarters consistent with French cultures' higher power distance.[59] Differences in integration approach also exist with regard to employment terms, openness of communications, formal versus on-the-job training, performance appraisal, and career development, which are consistent with the cultural and institutional context of the acquirer (see Chapter 2). Despite some consistency in HR practices, there remains the possibility that acquirers may be culturally disposed toward the way they approach integration and targets may be culturally disposed to the way they respond to integration.[60]

International Joint Ventures and Collaborative Alliances

International collaborative alliances help organizations do things they find difficult or impossible to do on their own, such as gain location-specific advantages, overcome legal constraints, or diversify geographically to minimize exposure in risky environments. The types of collaborations engaged in by MNEs vary according to their degree of ownership and control. For example, licenses, management and sales contracts, and franchises do not involve equity ownership, and the level of control over foreign operations is relatively low. The terms of the relationship are largely spelled out in the contractual agreement between the parties. While HR issues do arise in these types of relationships, the level of HR involvement is much higher in equity-based collaborations, such as international joint ventures.

International joint ventures (IJVs) are perhaps the most popular type of international collaborative arrangement.[61] Equity joint ventures occur when at least one of the collaborating companies takes an ownership position in the others.[62] The resulting legally and economically distinct organizational entity is under the joint control of its parent firms. While the majority of IJVs involve only two parent firms, they can consist of almost any combination of partners as long as at least one of the partners is foreign.

Reasons for IJVs

Joint ventures are not just a mechanism for cross-border entry but are formed by organizations with all levels of international experience. The reasons typically given for forming an IJV or collaborative alliance are the following:

- Gain and transfer technical and administrative knowledge
- Host government insistence
- Gain local knowledge
- Gain rapid market entry, expand market
- Capture increased economies of scale
- Obtain raw materials
- Spread risk
- Improve competitive advantage in the face of global competition
- Support company strategies for internationalization[63]

Joint ventures are usually formed to achieve a specific object, as in the case of the Boeing 787 Dreamliner venture, which is a joint effort among numerous companies from eight countries. However, they may operate indefinitely as objectives are redefined. In M&As, discussed previously, the central issue is integrating an existing firm into the parent. However, in IJVs the challenge is to create a new entity with all its related structures, culture, and practices. Unless all the parties in the JV are satisfied with the new entity and its performance, the arrangement may break down.

Reasons for IJV Failure

As with M&As, the failure rate of IJVs is high, up to 70% by some estimates.[64] The main tensions in IJVs stem from five factors: the relative importance of the JV to partners, divergent objectives, control problems, comparative contributions and appropriations, and differences in culture.

Relative Importance

It is not uncommon for one company to give more management attention to the JV than does the other. If things go wrong, the active partner blames the less active partner for its lack of attention, and the less active partner blames the more active partner for making poor decisions. For example, Elders IXL Ltd of Australia surrendered its 50% stake in a JV to grow pineapple in China to its Chinese Partner and wrote off its one million dollar investment after three years of losses.[65]

Divergent Objectives

Companies may come together to form the JV because of complimentary objectives, but over time their objectives may diverge. For example, in 1994 British Aerospace (BAe) shocked Honda by selling its controlling interest in Rover, which it owned jointly with Honda, to BMW. BAe had decided that the automobile industry was no longer part of its strategic plan.[66]

Control Problems

Sharing assets with another organization can raise issues over control. For example, Sover SPA of Italy alleged that its Chinese partner sold pirated copies of the JVs product (sunglasses) in China and that this constituted a violation of its partnership. However, major decisions required unanimous approval of the board, so Sover found itself in a difficult position.[67] And in a proposed JV between Merrill Lynch and the Japanese firm UFI, one of the key issues was if the person in charge of employees was going to be Japanese or American.[68]

Comparative Contributions and Appropriations

The ability of the partners to contribute assets, technology, or capital to the JV may change over time. And the balance of power in a JV can be affected by the teaching and learning in the alliance. For example, a company that is good at learning can access and internalize its partner's capabilities and becomes less dependent on its partner as the alliance evolves. A U.S. producer of industrial coatings was forced to sell out to its Japanese partner after it had learned the production process skills supplied by the U.S. organization. Since the Japanese partner controlled the relationships with customers the U.S. partner had no choice.[69]

Culture Issues

Both the country culture and the organizational culture of the partners can differ with regard to how the JV is managed and how its success is evaluated. For example, U.S. companies tend to focus on short-term profit and market share while Korean firms tend to view longer-term factors, such as building strategic capabilities and research and development opportunities as more important. European companies often consider more of a balance between profitability and social objectives, and Chinese state-owned enterprises will be concerned with maximizing employment ahead of efficiency and profit.[70] And in contrast to M&As where organizational cultures are integrated, in IJVs the distinct cultures of the partners remain. For example, the highly publicized breakup of AT&T and Olivetti was blamed on differences in culture and management style. "I don't think we or Olivetti spent enough time understanding behavior patterns. We knew that culture was different, but we never really penetrated. We would get angry and they would get upset," said Robert Kravner, an AT&T senior executive.[71] Whether or not cultural differences become dysfunctional of course depends on the ability of the partners to deal with the contradictions that will be present in most alliances.

HRM in IJVs

In IJVs, a number of important issues are related to expertise, policies, and practices in human resource management. An overview of the HR strategy in an alliance is presented in Box 5.6.

Box 5.6 The HR Alliance Strategy Plan

HR issues that may impact partner selection:

- Desired competencies that a partner should possess.
- Need for venture HR support from the partner.
- Assessment of HR skills and reputation of potential partners.
- Assessment of the organizational culture of potential partners.

Venture HR issues that need to be resolved in negotiations:

- Management philosophy, notably concerning HRM.
- Staffing: sourcing and criteria.
- Compensation and performance management.
- Who will provide HR with service support.

Desired negotiation outcomes and possible bargaining trade-offs

Specific HR activities that must be implemented early and resources are required:

- Negotiation stage:
  o negotiation team selection, and
  o negotiation training.
- Startup stage:
  o staffing decisions, and
  o alliance management training.

Estimated timelines for HR actions and allocation of responsibility

Measurements to evaluate the quality of HR support:

- Recruitment target.
- Training delivered.
- Skill/knowledge transferred.

Source: Evans et al. (2002, p. 214).

As shown in Box 5.6, the HRM function has a role to play in all phases of the IJV, including partner selection, negotiating the arrangement, implementing the agreement, and management of the venture.[72] Early involvement of HR in strategy discussions allows an integration of the HR strategy with the business logic and long-term objectives of the alliance.

Partner Selection

Two main HR issues arise at this stage. They are the extent to which each partner's HRM competencies are expected to contribute to the alliance and the degree to which the HRM policies and procedures of the partners will be linked to the alliance. When the expected contribution of the partner to the JV is high and the venture is unlikely to be autonomous, it is important to conduct the same type of cultural assessment as you would for an M&A (discussed previously).[73] Differences in HRM policies and procedures are not necessarily a negative factor and in fact may be one of the motivating factors for forming an alliance. However, recognizing and making plans to address these issues is an important factor in alliance success.[74]

Negotiating the Arrangement

HR can make an operational contribution to the JV by helping to prepare the organization for the negotiation with potential partners. This involves selecting the most appropriate negotiating team for the type of alliance and providing appropriate negotiation training. Different types of alliances require a different mix of entrepreneurial, analytical, and political skills in the negotiation team.[75] Cross-border negotiations require negotiators to restructure their thinking to be effective with potential partners from different cultures.[76] However, organizations tend to underestimate the level of preparation required for these types of complex negotiations.[77]

In addition, HR can influence JV negotiations with regard to both control and senior appointments. While control is often interpreted as the percentage of equity ownership of the venture, it may be a fallacy to assume that equity control means management control. Effective representation on the venture management team and influence over knowledge flows may have more real influence than majority ownership. This type of influence is bound up in key appointments both to the board and senior management of the JV. In most joint ventures, senior managers have far more strategic and operational influence than the board, which may meet very infrequently.[78]

Implementing the Agreement

The implementation phase of the JV involves establishing the vision and mission strategy and structure of the new organization.[79] The entire portfolio of HR policies and procedures needs to be created. Appropriate HR policies and procedures may vary substantially according to the cultural and institutional context of the JV (see Chapter 2), and they must reflect the partnership objectives and the needs of the parent. The key is aligning the policies and procedures with the parent so they support rather than hinder the joint venture. For example, when Ford entered into a broad cooperative agreement in Japan, it recognized the importance of collaboration and made the question, "What have you done to support Ford's alliance strategy?" a part of performance appraisal for a large part of the organization.[80] Because joint ventures are inherently unstable, HR policies and practices must help create trust and an ongoing capacity to cooperate.[81]

Managing the Venture

While the whole range of HR activities requires attention at this stage, the most critical aspect may be staffing. Problems created by poor staffing—repairing the damage done by bad decisions made by individuals unable to cope with the challenges of managing a joint venture—may be difficult or impossible to fix. Differences in the quality of individuals assigned to the joint venture by the different partners is an early warning signal that there may be a lack of commitment on the part of one of the partners to the venture's success, or it may indicate a lack of understanding of the skills required. In either case, once an appointment is made it is difficult to undo. Staffing should reflect a balance of the interests of both partners.[82] In addition to the initial HR decisions made during this stage of the JV process, perhaps the most important aspect of HR management is the process of learning from each other and transferring this knowledge to the JV. Learning and adjustment are the keys to the success of the alliance.[83]

Strategic Alliance Learning

While some alliances are created specifically with learning as their objective, all alliances require learning how to work with partners.[84] This type of learning is difficult because it must occur in a complex context of competition and cultural differences. However, as noted previously, it is required for alliance success, and differences in the ability to learn can result in an uneven return for alliance partners. One of the objectives of HR in a strategic alliance is therefore to help create a climate that encourages organizational learning and to put in place policies and procedures that guide this activity.[85] One way of understanding this is to look at the obstacles that HR can help to overcome with regard to organizational learning. Table 5.1 outlines the obstacles to organizational learning in JVs and strategic alliances.

Table 5.1 Obstacles to Organizational Learning in International Strategic Alliances

HR Activities	HR Practices
HR planning	• Strategic intent not communicated
	• Short-term and static planning horizon
	• Low priority of learning activities
	• Lack of involvement by the HR department

(Continued)

Table 5.1 (Continued)

HR Activities	HR Practices
Staffing	• Insufficient lead time for staffing decisions
	• Resource-poor staffing strategy
	• Low quality of staff assigned to the JV
	• Staffing dependence on the partner
Training and development	• Lack of cross-cultural competence
	• Unidirectional training programs
	• Career structure not conducive to learning
	• Poor culture for transfer of learning
Appraisal and rewards	• Appraisal focused on short-term goals
	• No encouragement of learning
	• Limited incentives for transfer of know-how
	• Rewards not tied to global strategy
Organizational design and control	• Responsibility for learning not clear
	• Fragmentation of the learning process
	• Control over the HR department given away
	• No insight into partner's HR strategy

Source: Adapted from Pucik (1988).

Effective organizational learning can be fostered by designing policies and procedures to combat these obstacles. Organizations have many tools to manage the process of learning, but trust between partners is critical because it allows them to concentrate on mutual learning rather than on monitoring and control.

Chapter Summary

International joint ventures, mergers and acquisitions, and other types of international alliances create unique but increasingly common circumstances for global HRM. While many mergers are advertised as mergers of equals, after the agreement is signed one partner typically dominates. International M&As occur for both strategic and tactical reasons, but only a small percentage achieve their desired results. There are many reasons that M&As fail, but people-related aspects are prominent in the reasons given for M&A failure. The retention of key talent, selecting the right management team, resolving cultural issues, and communication are key factors in M&A success. An important element of HR involvement in the M&A process is participation in the due diligence process by conducting a cultural assessment and a human capital audit early on. While what happens before the deal is signed is important, it is increasingly clear that the success of these ventures is largely related to the ability to integrate across boundaries. A key element in the integration process is reducing employee anxiety, lack of trust, and other negative feelings through effective communication. While there may be an emerging best practice with regard to post-merger integration, cultural differences in the preference for particular approaches persist.

International collaborative alliances, such as joint ventures, present their own set of HR challenges. The reasons for entering into an IJV are very similar to an M&A. However, in the IJV the challenge is in creating a new entity with all its related structures, culture, and practices instead of integrating one firm with another. The main tensions in IJVs are the relative importance of the JV to the partners, their divergent objectives, control issues, differences in contributions to the JV, and differences in culture. In IJVs, the whole range of HR activities requires attention, but two issues stand out. These are staffing and the creation of an environment in which the partners can learn from each other in the context of competition and cultural differences.

Questions for Discussion

1. Why are people and cultural issues the reasons most often given for M&A failure?

2. Compare and contrast the HR issues associated with different post-merger integration strategies.

3. Discuss the importance of communication in international M&As.

4. What are the essential elements of a cultural assessment and a human capital audit? When should they be conducted? Why?

5. From an HRM perspective, what are the key differences between an international M&A and an IJV?

Notes

1. Net cross-border M&As are sales of companies in the host economy to foreign transnational corporations excluding sales of foreign affiliates in the host economy.
2. http://www.unctad.org/en/docs/webdiaeia20111_en.pdf.
3. Goulet & Schweiger (2006).
4. Marks & Mirvis (2010); Schweiger & Lippert (2005).
5. Evans, Pucik, & Barsoux (2002).
6. Creswell (2001).
7. Evans, Pucik, & Barsoux (2002).
8. Kühlmann & Dowling (2005).
9. Pucik, Björkman, Evans, & Stahl (2011).
10. See KPMG (1999).
11. Dobbs, Goedhart, & Suonio (2006). http://people.stern.nyu.edu/igiddy/articles/better_mergers.pdf.

12. Shimizu, Hitt, Vaidyanath, & Pisano (2004).
13. Cartwright & Cooper (1996).
14. Barkema, Bell, & Pennings (1996).
15. Stahl (2008); Stahl, Pucik, Evans, & Mendenhall (2004); Pucik, Björkman, Evans, & Stahl (2011).
16. Stahl (2008).
17. Evans, Pucik, & Barsoux (2002).
18. Marks & Mirvis (2010).
19. Killing (2003).
20. Pucik, Björkman, Evans, & Stahl (2011).
21. Pucik, Björkman, Evans, & Stahl (2011).
22. Evans, Pucik, & Barsoux (2002).
23. Evans, Pucik, & Barsoux (2002).
24. KPMG (1999); Kay & Shelton (2000).
25. KPMG (1999).
26. Schuler, Jackson & Luo, 2004.
27. Evans, Pucik, & Barsoux (2002).
28. Adapted from Evans, Pucik, & Barsoux (2002); Deal & Kennedy (1982).
29. http://www.usnews.com/usnews/biztech/articles/060626/26best.htm.
30. Krishnan, Miller, & Judge (1997).
31. Marks & Mirvis (1998); van Odenhoven & de Boer (1995).
32. Goulet & Schweiger (2006).
33. Thomas (2008).
34. Pucik & Evans (2004); Pucik, Björkman, Evans, & Stahl (2011).
35. Harding & Rouse (2007).
36. Napier (1989).
37. Jemison & Sitkin (1986b).
38. Evans, Pucik, & Barsoux (2002).
39. Cisco's connections: The tech giant has mastered the art of acquisitions. (2006, June 26) *U.S. News & World Report*.
40. Haspeslagh & Jemison (1991).
41. Birkinshaw, Bresman, & Håkanson (2000).
42. Schweiger & DeNisi (1991); Schweiger & Goulet (2005).
43. Schweiger & DeNisi (1991); Sinetar (1981).
44. Vaara (2003).
45. Gertsen, Söderberg, & Torp (1998).
46. Goulet & Schweiger (2006).
47. For example see Empson (2000).
48. Kay & Shelton (2000).
49. Krug & Hegarty (1997).
50. Mäkelä, Björkman, & Ehrnrooth (2010).
51. Michaels, Handfield-Jones, & Axelrod (2001).
52. Pucik, Björkman, Evans, & Stahl (2011).
53. Goulet & Schweiger (2006).
54. Blake & Mouton (1984); Leroy & Ramanantsoa (1997).
55. For an example of this process see Vaara, Tienari, & Säntti (2003).
56. Donnelly, Morris, & Donnelly (2005).
57. Faulkner, Pitkethly, & Child (2002).

58. Calori, Lubatkin, & Very (1994).
59. Lubatkin, Calori, Very, & Veiga (1998).
60. Goulet & Schweiger (2006).
61. Schuler & Tarique (2006).
62. Daniels, Radebaugh, & Sullivan (2011).
63. Schuler, Jackson, & Luo (2004).
64. Schuler, Jackson, & Luo (2004).
65. Daniels, Radebaugh, & Sullivan (2011).
66. Serapio Jr. & Cascio (1996).
67. Serapio Jr. & Cascio (1996).
68. Daniels, Radebaugh, & Sullivan (2011).
69. Bleeke & Ernst (1995).
70. See Napier & Thomas (2004); Thomas (2008).
71. Serapio & Cascio (1996).
72. Similar four stage models with various stage names have been presented. For example, see Schuler (2001).
73. Evans, Pucik, & Barsoux (2002).
74. Ariño & Reuer (2004).
75. Lorange & Roos (1990).
76. Thomas (2008).
77. Weiss (1993).
78. Evans, Pucik, & Barsoux (2002).
79. Schuler & Tarique (2006).
80. Evans, Pucik, & Barsoux (2002).
81. Child & Faulkner (1998).
82. See Pucik (1988).
83. Doz & Hamel (1998).
84. Barkema, Shenkar, Vermeulen, & Bell (1997).
85. Pucik (1988).

Global Staffing

LEARNING OBJECTIVES

After reading this chapter you should be able to

- describe the four types of staffing strategy,
- describe the reasons why an organization might choose to fill a position with an expatriate,
- outline the criteria used to select expatriates,
- describe important differences in staffing across countries, and
- discuss the issues associated with implementing global staffing and talent management programs.

A Manager for Russia

Ben Cohen, cofounder of Ben & Jerry's, had been interested in starting a venture in Russia since he first visited there in 1986. Now Jeff Furman, a longtime friend of Ben's and in charge of partnership opportunities, was searching for an American to head up Ben & Jerry's anticipated joint venture in Karelia, Russia. Karelia was a beautiful resort region near the Finnish border and was the sister state of Vermont, where Ben & Jerry's started and is still home to its headquarters. Jeff had interviewed numerous business school graduates who spoke Russian, but none of them seemed to fit with Ben & Jerry's culture of social responsibility. So Jeff posted the job internally. Responding to the ad, Dave Morse, a production supervisor who had worked for Ben & Jerry's for five years, encouraged Jeff and Ben to reconsider the type of person they were looking for. Dave had reached the limit of his potential in production and had read about Russia and its history, and he was ready for an adventure. He argued that it was more difficult to learn how to make super premium ice cream than anything else the job would require. Anyone else would take at least a year to learn the basics and still would not have Dave's knowledge of the industry, sources of equipment and raw materials, in addition to his technical knowledge of ice cream production. Even though he had no overseas experience, could not speak Russian, and had no formal business training, Dave's energy and can-do attitude impressed Jeff. He was selected to be the first manager of the Russian joint venture.[1]

Introduction

Finding and keeping the people they need to be competitive is a challenge for all organizations. And as organizations cross borders and cultures, the task becomes more critical as well as more difficult. Two trends make this activity even more complex today than it was for Ben and Jerry's when they were first becoming international. First, as discussed in the opening chapter, the number and character of permanent migrants is changing the composition of the workforce in many countries. As boundaries to migration become more permeable, migration resulting from economic, political, and social factors increases. Following World War II, the dominant migration pattern was low-skilled workers from less developed to more developed countries. While economic factors continue to be a major influence on migration, today's migrant (in part because of skills-related immigration systems[2] and the globalization of some professional labor markets[3]) is much more likely to be highly skilled.[4] Second, regardless of economic swings, the demand for skilled workers is outstripping supply. This ranges from finding skilled expatriates to help organizations expand into emerging markets, to accessing short-term or temporary talent for specific projects, to cadres of highly mobile elite managers to build global networks and facilitate knowledge transfer.[5] In fact, shortages on international management talent have been shown to be a significant constraint on implementation of global strategies.[6] Thus, MNEs are now often competing for the same global talent pool.[7]

Approaches to Global Staffing

Increasingly, global organizations are recognizing the influence that matching staffing strategy with organizational strategy has on the performance of the organization.[8] For the multinational enterprise, staffing decisions typically revolve around choices among parent country nationals (PCNs), host country nationals (HCNs), and to a lesser extent, third country nationals (TCNs) for filling key positions in their headquarters and subsidiary operations.[9] Managerial attitudes towards staffing with these three categories of employee have resulted in the classification of staffing strategies as ethnocentric, polycentric, geocentric, and regiocentric.[10] In an *ethnocentric* strategy, key decision-making positions at both headquarters and in the foreign subsidiary are filled by PCNs. In a *polycentric* strategy, subsidiaries are more autonomous, and key managers are usually HCNs. A *geocentric* strategy reflects a more global approach to staffing and is reflected in a mix of PCNs, HCNs, and TCNs both at headquarters and in subsidiaries, with a focus on the unique requirements of each situation. And in a *regiocentric* strategy, the staffing of the foreign subsidiary reflects the geographic strategy and structure of the MNE. For example, the organization might be subdivided into regions within which a great deal of mobility occurs, but mobility outside the region would be limited. While these approaches to staffing strategy may reflect the preferences of management, in many cases organizations may have a somewhat ad hoc policy toward their use of PCNs, HCNs, and TCNs. Also, actual staffing patterns may be based on a variety of contingency factors discussed ahead.[11] Regardless, a number of advantages and disadvantages of staffing with particular employee types have been identified and are presented in Table 6.1.

Staffing Contingencies

While management attitudes may reflect the general strategies outlined previously, it seems that many firms do not have a clearly stated and uniform global staffing policy. It was once thought that the staffing patterns of international organizations followed a pattern consistent with their stage of internationalization.[12] The use of PCNs in overseas posts would predominate in the early stages of internationalization, with the use of HCNs increasing as the technology of the firm was disseminated among foreign subsidiaries. However, more recently other factors not related to the stage of internationalization have been shown to be more important to actual staffing patterns.[13] These include the country of origin of the MNE, the size and task complexity of its foreign

Table 6.1   The Advantages and Disadvantages of Using PCN, HCN, and TCN

	Advantages	Disadvantages
PCN (parent-country national)	• Familiarity with the home office's goals, objectives, policies and practices • Technical and managerial competence • Effective liaison and communication with home-office personnel • Easier exercise of control over the subsidiary's operation	• Difficulties in adapting to the foreign language and the socioeconomic, political, cultural, and legal environment • Excessive cost of selecting, training, and maintaining expatriate managers and their families abroad • The host countries' insistence on localizing operations and on promoting local nationals in top positions at foreign subsidiaries • Family adjustment problems, especially concerning the unemployed partners of managers

	Advantages	Disadvantages
HCN (host-country national)	• Familiarity with the socioeconomic, political, and legal environment and with business practices in the host country • Lower cost incurrent in hiring HCN as compared to PCN and TCN • Provides opportunities for advancement and promotion to local nationals, and consequently, increases their commitment and motivation • Responds effectively to the host country's demands for localization of the subsidiary's operation	• Difficulties in exercising effective control over the subsidiary's operation • Communication difficulties in dealing with home-office personnel • Lack of opportunities for the home country's nationals to gain international and cross-cultural experience
TCN (third-country national)	• Perhaps the best compromise between securing needed technical and managerial expertise and adapting to a foreign socioeconomic and cultural environment • TCN are usually career international business managers • TCN are less expensive to maintain than PCN • TCN may be better informed about the host environment than PCN	• Host countries' sensitivity with respect to nationals of specific countries • Local nationals are impeded in their efforts to upgrade their own ranks and assume responsible positions in the multinational subsidiaries

Source: Borg & Harzing (1995, p. 186)

affiliates, their performance and strategic importance for the MNE, and the cultural and institutional distance of an affiliate from headquarters.

Individual staffing decisions reflect the overall staffing strategy of the firm, whether or not this strategy is made explicit. And much of what we know about staffing strategy comes from understanding why a company will send a PCN to the foreign operation rather than fill the job locally. An important early study of why organizations might fill an overseas position with a PCN suggested that individuals would be transferred internationally for one of three reasons: to *fill a technical requirement*, to *develop the individual*, or to *develop the organization*.[14] These three basic reasons for sending an expatriate reflect either demand driven (filling a position) or learning driven (developing the individual or organization) motives on the part of the organization.[15]

Filling a position because of the need for a specific technical requirement seems to be the key reason for staffing with a PCN.[16] The 2012 Global Relocation Trends Survey Report reported that for 55% of expatriate assignments the objective was to fill a managerial or technical skills gap. However, the country of origin of the firm seems to be influential as well. For example, Japanese firms tend to use more PCNs in their foreign operations than do their U.S. or European counterparts.[17] This may be because Japanese firms rely more heavily on the use of expatriates as a means of management control.[18] In contrast, New Zealand firms are more likely to report that the reason for sending expatriates on assignment is for development of the organization or the individual. And for Korean firms, the reason most often given for staffing with a local national instead of an expatriate is the lack of local knowledge.[19] Further, we have evidence that suggests that the importance of the different reasons for staffing with expatriates differ between subsidiaries in MNEs from different home countries and between subsidiaries in different host regions. Filling positions is more important for subsidiaries of U.S. and British MNEs located in the Latin American and the Far Eastern region. In contrast, management development is more important for German, Swiss, and Dutch MNEs and tends to occur more in the Anglo-Saxon region than in the Far Eastern region. Transfers for organizational development appear to be most important for German and Japanese MNEs in host-countries that are culturally distant from headquarters.[20] Thus, these practices suggest an implicit staffing strategy among firms of different national origins.

A number of other factors also relate to the use of PCNs (expatriates), including the task complexity found in the foreign operation and the cultural distance of the foreign operations from headquarters. For example, subsidiaries with more complex operations are more likely to be staffed with expatriates.[21] And as the cultural distance between headquarters and the foreign subsidiary increases so does the tendency to use expatriates. However, this tendency decreases over time.[22] This same effect is also evident with regard to differences among institutions in home and host countries. Firms rely more heavily on expatriates for staffing subsidiaries in institutionally distant environments. This seems to be because of the need and perceived ease of transferring management practices and firm specific capabilities through the use of PCNs.[23] And of course there is more of a need for knowledge transfer in technology and knowledge-intensive industries.[24] These facts may account for the increased use of expatriates by firms[25] as they respond to the need to compete in a knowledge-based economy.

While it might be desirable for the staffing strategy of organizations to match their firm-level management strategy, the evidence that firms actually do this is far from compelling. One study has found that the use of *developmental* versus *technical requirements* type of assignments differed based on the firm-level management strategy. Firms with a global strategy made greater use of a developmental approach to the use of expatriates, had a higher number of senior managers with overseas experience, and had a stronger focus on leadership development.[26]

Expatriate Roles

The complexity of the global environment in which multinational organizations operate gives rise to the need for continuous environmental scanning and information exchange as well as the need for seamless coordination and control of geographically dispersed operations.[27] The top reason for sending expatriates remains filling positions for which no local skills are available. However, more recently the increasing strategic importance of using these assignments as a means of organizational development has been recognized.[28] The role expectations that organizations have for expatriates reflect these organizational needs and might vary considerably in the extent to which they emphasize coordination and control or boundary spanning.

Expatriates as Agents of Control

Control means ensuring that employee behavior conforms to the expectations of the organization. Expatriates can act as agents of control either directly or indirectly. Their assignments may contain formal authority to implement policies and procedures that are mandated from headquarters and are internally consistent throughout the subsidiaries of the organization. Their responsibilities can also include direct surveillance of subsidiaries to ensure that subsidiary activities are consistent with headquarters mandates, norms, and expectations. Alternatively, they may exert control indirectly through a more informal mechanism, such as transferring corporate values and beliefs throughout the subsidiaries of the organization, sometimes likened to honey bees pollinating flowers.[29]

Another control role available to expatriates is as the disseminator of knowledge from the parent to the subsidiary. This knowledge can be in the form of technical expertise but might also involve work practices in a variety of areas, such as occupational health and safety or quality control. The adoption of uniform practices throughout the organization can be viewed as a form of control. Also, expatriates can establish interpersonal linkages with individuals in the various organizational units with which they have contact. These networks of relationships (like the web of a spider) can also serve as a means of informal control through establishing specific channels of information exchange.[30]

Expatriates as Boundary Spanners

Expatriates, because of their position in the organization, occupy roles that span both internal and external boundaries.[31] They exist on the boundary between headquarters and the subsidiary and also on the boundary between the home and host country cultures. Boundary spanning roles involve not only information exchange across organizational units but also roles such as bicultural interpreter and national advocate that have long been thought to be important to the success of the multinational organization.[32] Expatriates often identify their roles as involving such boundary-spanning activities as representing the organization to customers and the public, transferring information across strategic units, and establishing interpersonal bonds with host nations.[33] These activities are obviously beneficial to the organization, but boundary-spanning behavior can also have benefits to the individual, including higher job satisfaction and more power in their own organizations.[34] Expatriate boundary spanners can also act as culture brokers to connect groups and resources throughout the organization or as *language nodes* upon return to headquarters by bridging different language groups within the organization.[35]

Inpatriates

A variation on the expatriate role occurs when individuals are transferred not from the home country to a foreign subsidiary but from foreign locations to headquarters. This type of role (called *inpatriate*) involves transfers of both HCNs and TCNs and indicates a particular staffing strategy. The expectation is that inpatriates will transfer knowledge about the local subsidiary to headquarters while also learning headquarters routines and procedures that can be transferred back to the foreign subsidiary.[36] There are four key circumstances in which *inpatriation* appears as part of an organization's staffing strategy.[37]

- Desire to create a global core competency, a diversity strategy perspective, or a multicultural frame of reference in the top management team
- Need to develop emerging markets which are recognized as being difficult assignments for expatriates, which reduces the available talent pool
- Desire to increase the capability of the organization to *think globally but act locally*, which can be achieved by involving inpatriates in decision making
- Desire to provide career opportunities for high potential employees of host countries

All of these might be seen as a more strategic approach to management development in the global business environment as discussed ahead in Chapter 7. The number of inpatriates is small as compared to expatriates, but there seems to be a trend toward this activity in some industries.[38] However, despite the potentially strategic role of inpatriates, they typically hold only a peripheral status in multinationals and have a rather low level of social influence and credibility. This makes it difficult for them to highlight their unique role and their potential contribution to the MNE and creates substantial barriers to sharing and transferring knowledge. Therefore, inpatriate assignments are probably most valuable in organizational cultures that truly value diversity, are open to accepting knowledge originating in subsidiaries, and create adequate support and integration mechanisms for inpatriates.[39]

The expectations that the organization has for the employees it transfers internationally can involve any combination of these roles. These role expectations, along with the expectations of local employees, influence the entire process of global staffing, beginning with recruitment and selection.

Global Recruitment and Selection

Recruitment is the process of assembling a pool of potentially qualified applicants for a specific job, while *selection* is the process of evaluating and deciding among these candidates. These staffing issues are much more complex in a global environment, with two factors being distinctively different from staffing in a purely domestic context. The first is that individuals must be recruited and selected to take up assignments in foreign locations. The second is that recruitment and selection processes and procedures vary because of the different cultural and institutional context that exists in the different countries in which the multinational firm operates. In the following, we first discuss recruitment and selection for foreign assignments and then present a comparison of these activities across countries.

Recruiting and Selection for Foreign Assignments

The first key challenge for staffing foreign assignments is the supply side issue of availability of individuals to fill the pool of potentially qualified applicants. The availability of potential foreign assignees is limited by the following five factors. The first of these is shortage of experienced and competent individuals on a global basis.[40] Demand for individuals with the managerial and/or technical skills required in these managerial roles is outstripping supply at an increasing pace, creating what has been called a *war for global talent.* And because most expatriates are sourced internally[41] managers may be reluctant to release their best employees, creating competition within the firm for these individuals. The second factor is the increasing prevalence of dual-career couples. Individuals targeted for overseas assignments are no longer limited to male sole breadwinners whose spouses are willing and able to follow them on their assignment. The willingness of the spouse to relocate has always been a key factor in employee's acceptance of overseas assignments. However, families have become less willing to endure the disruptions to the spouse's career (and children's education, etc.) that an overseas assignment poses[42], resulting in a worldwide problem for multinationals. A third and related factor is the increased participation of women in the workforce. Interestingly, despite the shortage of management talent, the number of women on overseas assignment remains relatively low (discussed in more detail ahead in Chapter 9). There is an apparent lack of willingness on the part of management to recruit women for overseas assignments based on the mistaken beliefs that they are not interested in taking assignments, or if they are, cannot perform effectively once posted abroad. By ignoring the increasingly large percentage of women in the workforce, management thus significantly restricts the size of the applicant pool.[43] The fourth factor that limits the size of the pool of potential applicants has to do with repatriation and career issues (see Chapter 9). Employees typically look to overseas assignments as a way to enhance their career.[44] But because firms typically do not have programs that effectively integrate the overseas assignment into individuals' career progression, employees are increasingly less willing to accept these postings. A final factor affecting recruitment for overseas assignments is the general weakness of global talent management systems. There is little evidence that global organizations practice talent management in a coordinated and efficient way, with many firms unaware of where their best talent is located or unable to identify their high performers.[45] Thus the pool of potential applicants for an overseas posting is limited by a number of factors, including restrictions imposed by the labor market, by other organizational factors, and by individuals themselves.

Selecting Expatriates

Given that firms send expatriates on assignment primarily to fill a managerial or technical need that they cannot staff with a local employee, it is not surprising that technical competency (as in the Ben & Jerry's case that opened this chapter) has traditionally been and continues to be the primary decision criterion used by organizations to select employees for these assignments.[46] Other criteria that can have an important influence on employee's performance on overseas assignments seem to be generally neglected. This overemphasis on technical competence as a selection criterion may result because selection based on technical competence presents a lower perceived risk of adverse consequences to the selecting manager.[47] It is easier to defend a selection decision based on past performance, which is relatively easy to measure as compared to more subjective criteria.

Effective Expatriates: Beyond Technical Competence

Organizations are of course concerned with selecting individuals for overseas assignments who can perform effectively. However, whether an overseas assignment is viewed as a success or failure depends in part on the definition of success. Effectiveness of a global assignment can include direct measures of performance, such as accomplishment of the assigned task and developing productive relationships with host nationals, and also more indirect indicators, such as job satisfaction, organizational commitment, and intention to remain on assignment.[48]

While accomplishing the assigned task is of course the key objective of both the organization and the employee, the most common (and the most studied) measure of expatriate effectiveness (failure) has been the failure to remain on the overseas assignment the agreed upon length of time. This measure is attractive not only because it is easy to assess but also because organizations are concerned with the expense that turnover of expatriates creates.[49] However, the exact rate of premature return from overseas assignments is difficult to pinpoint. Many firms do not keep track of this statistic, and academic research has reported widely varying figures, often based on outdated studies.[50] The 2010 Global Relocation Trends Survey Report reported that 7% of expatriates returned early and 7% of families returned early leaving expatriates behind.[51] The inadequacy of premature return as a measure of effectiveness is obvious. Expatriates who stay on assignment but behave inappropriately or perform inadequately are conceivably more of a failure than those who return early. Conversely, staying on assignment the agreed-upon length of time is not a guarantee that tasks have been accomplished, relationships formed, or personal development achieved. Finally, even though the term of the assignment has been met, the failure to reintegrate into the sponsoring organization[52] or to capitalize on the skills gained overseas[53] can also be regarded as a failure.

Two facets of expatriate performance have a long history of being considered. These are task-based and relationship-based (or contextual) aspects of performance. The first of these involves the accomplishment of goals, meeting objectives, which of course can be established from a variety of sources. The second involves establishing and maintaining relationships and effectively interacting with coworkers, supervisors, and so on. While both goal accomplishment and relationship development are important, they predominantly account for the firm's view on performance. From employees' perspectives, the development of a skill set that can transfer to other aspects of their careers may be equally important,[54] and the transfer of knowledge and skills to the employer is another desirable outcome of expatriation.[55] Other aspects of performance unique to the expatriate experience may also need to be considered, such as handling emergencies or crisis situations, handling work stress, solving problems creatively, and so on.[56] And maintaining effective family relationships as well as performance in the work domain is another important consideration.[57]

Based on these ideas about effectiveness on a foreign assignment, a number of other selection criteria can be suggested. These include personality characteristics and individual skills and abilities that are related to cross-cultural effectiveness. While the idea of an international type of person based on certain traits is probably not well founded, there are certain personality traits that relate to one or more dimensions of effectiveness in international assignments. In particular, four of the big five personality characteristics (*extraversion, emotional stability, agreeableness*, and *conscientiousness*) have been shown to be predictive of one dimension or another of expatriate job performance.[58] With regard to individual skills and abilities, there is a consensus on which skills are important to overseas success only in the broadest sense. These skills can be categorized into four types, each of which have been found to be important to various aspects of expatriate effectiveness.[59] *Information skills* relate to paying attention to and appreciating cultural differences between oneself and others in culture and background and include empathy, tolerance of uncertainty, and open-mindedness. *Interpersonal skills* involve interacting with culturally different others and in foreign cultural contexts and includes sociability, flexibility, and communication skills (including language fluency). *Action skills* involve being able to select behavior that is appropriate to a particular cross-cultural or international context and involve behavioral flexibility, self-monitoring, and self-regulation. Finally, *analytic skills* reflect the ability to accurately assess and use information gained from intercultural experience to perform effectively and includes such skills as mindfulness, attribution ability, and cultural metacognition.

Practical Selection Considerations

Despite evidence that criteria other than technical skills are important to some aspects of expatriate performance, they are, as mentioned previously, typically neglected. One of the key issues is the inability of organizations to assess them. As desirable as it may be to assess personality traits as a criterion, the tests to assess these traits are rarely convincingly validated, and most have been developed in the United States, making them potentially culture specific.[60] A similar situation exists for measuring skills and abilities. While a huge number and variety of skills and abilities measures exist, their ability to predict performance is not well established.[61] Another important consideration is that selection processes tend to focus on the employee. However, the willingness of the spouse and family to relocate and their ability to adjust to the foreign environment (discussed in Chapter 9) are equally important considerations that are often overlooked.[62] This willingness and the appropriateness of a particular candidate can also be influenced by the destination of the expatriate assignment. In the most recent Global Relocation Trends Survey Report (2012), organizations were asked which countries presented the most challenging difficulties for expatriates. The most difficult were China (16%), Brazil (9%), India (8%), Russia (6%), and the United States (4%). Challenges range from cultural differences to immigration, to temporary housing, and so on. For example, while many countries have policies that facilitate employment-related immigration, work permits are often available only to the expatriate and not the trailing spouse, which can reduce greatly the attractiveness of assignments for dual career couples.

Selection Process

Despite efforts to make the process of expatriate selection systematic, many expatriate selection decisions probably contain a good deal of subjectivity and serendipity. As demonstrated in the case that open this chapter, Dave Morse happened to be in the right place at the right time and to have the right attitude to be selected as the manager for Ben & Jerry's new Russian joint venture. A way of categorizing these selection systems is to think of them along the two dimensions of informal/formal and open/closed. As shown in Figure 6.1, this results in four selection system types. Actual

Figure 6.1 Typology of Selection Processes

	Formal	Informal
Open	• Clearly defined criteria • Clearly defined measures • Training for selectors • Open advertising of vacancy (internal/external) • Panel discussions	• Less defined criteria • Less defined measures • Limited training for selectors • No panel discussions • Open advertising of vacancy • Recommendations
Closed	• Clearly defined criteria • Clearly defined measures • Training for selectors • Panel discussions • Nominations only (networking/reputation)	• Selectors' individual preferences determine criteria and measures • No panel discussions • Nominations only (networking/reputation)

Source: Harris & Brewster (1999).

selection processes might take any of these forms depending on characteristic of the organization (size, industry, level of internationalization, and so on) and on the type of expatriate assignment. Formal-open systems would seem to be the most desirable because of their clearly defined criteria and measures, open advertising, and so on, but the most prevalent is probably the informal-closed system in which the selectors' individual preferences determine the criteria, and measures and nominations are by reputation and networking.[63]

Comparative Recruitment and Selection

As organizations globalize, they must consider how to implement staffing practices on a worldwide scale. Staffing decisions for expatriates are typically made at corporate headquarters.[64] Policies championed at headquarters also inform and guide staffing decisions about the local workforce in the various subsidiaries of the MNE. However, these decisions must also reflect local labor market conditions and must consider the extent to which corporate staffing practices will travel well across MNE locations.

Recruitment activities can be classified in numerous ways. A potentially useful classification system for comparisons across cultures is the extent to which the recruitment source is formal and/or active. Formal sources include such activities as job postings in newspapers and job fairs, while informal sources are ones that use friends and relatives as sources. Active processes are those in which the firm initiates the contact with applicants, such as the use of search firms, while passive processes refer to job postings in newspapers or the Internet.[65] The prevalence of recruitment methods are not determined solely by organizational preference. The institutional context in a country is equally important. For example, many organizations from Central and Eastern Europe tend to use informal recruitment channels, as labor market mechanisms in these countries are not yet well developed. Further, the labor market size in these countries is relatively small (especially at the level of top managerial positions), thus allowing informal networks to play a much larger role than in larger and more developed labor markets.[66] It has also been suggested that countries where equal employment opportunity laws exist and are strictly enforced tend to have more formal and structured recruitment processes.[67] Organizations can also differ in the extent to which they tend to fill positions by internal candidates (as in the case of Japan, for example) or external hires (as in the United States).[68] The extent to which different recruitment forms are dominant can also vary in particular cultural contexts. For example, the cultural value of individualism is positively related to the extent to which organizations use (formal and passive) website recruiting.[69] Recruitment channels and methods that are informal and network based tend to be more prevalent in cultures that are high on uncertainty avoidance and collectivism and that give preference to ascribed rather than achieved status. In contrast, formal channels and methods tend to be more widespread in cultures that are high on universalism and performance orientation.[70]

While organizations from around the world rank a person's ability to perform the technical requirements of a job as the top selection criterion, organizations from particular countries may have unique requirements. For example, having the right connections (e.g., from school, family friends, in government) is very important in Mexico. In Japan and Taiwan, it is the person's ability to get along with people already working in the organization that matters. The message that organizations send in trying to generate a pool of potentially qualified applicants reflects the importance of particular criteria. The message sent by Ernest Shackleton (see Box 6.1) certainly reflected the desire to attract a certain type of person for his polar expedition.

Box 6.1   Would You Be Attracted By This Ad?

MEN WANTED
for hazardous journey, small wages,
bitter cold, constant danger, safe
return doubtful, honor and recognition
in case of success.
Ernest Shackleton—4 Burlington st

This ad appeared in a London newspaper in 1907 and was effective enough to attract the men from whom Shackleton selected the 28 who would mount his famous expedition to the South Pole.

In an analysis of hundreds of newspaper articles in eight European countries, 80% of the ads in equalitarian Scandinavian countries (Sweden, Norway, Denmark) illustrated the value attached to interpersonal skills needed for collaboration. However, in the more hierarchical cultures of France, Italy, and Spain, only 50% of the ads emphasized interpersonal skills. Instead, in these countries a particular age was emphasized as a job requirement.[71] Specifying age as a job requirement would of course not only be counter to cultural norms but illegal in many countries. Nepotism (i.e., hiring relatives of existing employees) is common in some labor markets but condemned in other countries. Even in countries in which nepotism is banned (or associated with corrupt business practices), many organizations readily use employee referrals (recommendations by existing employees) as a recruiting tool.[72]

The extent to which individuals are attracted to the particular characteristics of a job can also vary across cultures because of differences in why they engage in work, in what they value in their work, and according to their expectations of their relationship to the organization. For example, when asked to divide 100 points across 11 purposes that work serves, approximately 70% was accounted for by three purposes in all cultures: needed income, an interesting and satisfying experience, and contact with people. But respondents from different countries considered each of these purposes differently in importance. For example, the Japanese gave nearly twice as many points to needed income as did respondents from the Netherlands, and Israelis assigned the most points to an interesting and satisfying experience.[73]

In evaluating the goals that people hope to achieve from work, this same research project uncovered some differences across cultures as shown in Table 6.2.

However, it is important to note that the most important goal across cultures was interesting work (work that you really like). Respondents in four countries ranked this goal as most important, with the remaining countries ranking it second or third. The importance of interesting work as a work goal across cultures has a number of implications, not the least of which is for recruitment and selection.

The messages that organizations send when trying to generate a pool of potentially qualified applicants imply what the organization promises and what it expects from employees in return. As discussed in Chapter 2, this understanding of the exchange relationship between the individual and the organization is called the *psychological contract.* Cultural differences exist in the extent to what social cues are important in defining the psychological contract, the extent to which the contract is shared among organizations, and the specific characteristics of the contract.[74] For example, people in France, China, Norway, and Canada describe their relationships to organizations in different terms that are consistent with the national culture. In Canada, this relationship is described in terms of equal power relationships that emphasize short-term monetary obligations, such as payment for services provided,

Table 6.2 Rank Order of Work Goals Across Seven Countries

Work Goals	Belgium	Britain	Germany	Israel	Japan	Netherlands	USA
Opportunity	7	8	9	5	7	9	5
Interpersonal relations	5	4	4	2	6	3	7
Opportunity for promotion	10	11	10	8	11	11	10
Convenient work hours	9	5	6	7	8	8	9
Variety	6	7	6	11	9	4	6
Interesting work	1	1	3	1	2	2	1
Job security	3	3	2	10	4	7	3
Match between person and job	8	6	5	6	1	6	4
Pay	2	2	1	3	5	5	2
Working conditions	11	9	11	9	10	10	11
Autonomy	4	10	8	4	3	1	8

Source: Adapted from Harpaz (1990).

while at the opposite end of the spectrum, Chinese people describe their relationship to their organization as consisting of an unequal power relationship that emphasizes broad, long-term, socioemotional obligations, such as commitment and loyalty.[75] Thus, culture influences perceptions and interpretation of the messages that organizations send and also determines in part what characteristics of a job individuals find desirable. Recruitment across cultures therefore requires that organizations consider how the mechanisms they use and the messages they send will be received in different cultural contexts.

The evaluation and process of choosing among candidates is also influenced by the national culture context in which it takes place. From a purely descriptive point of view, there seems to be considerable variation in selection procedures around the world. A recent survey of 959 companies in 20 nations captured the similarities and differences in selection procedures.[76] Table 6.3 reports the extent to which companies used a particular technique on a scale of 1= *never* and 5 = *always or almost always.*

In reviewing these findings, the effect of national culture and institutional arrangements on the prevalence of particular selection processes is apparent. For example, graphology (handwriting analysis) is popular only in France and is never used in many countries, and firms in Hong Kong and Singapore are more likely to rely on family connections. We also know that what job candidates perceive as fair may differ across countries. Thus, compared to U.S. college students, French college students assessed personality tests more favorably but thought less favorably of honesty tests (tests that ask about thoughts on theft and experiences related to personal honesty). On the other hand, Americans were more likely to say that personality tests were respectful of privacy.[77] Similarities as the result of globalization are also evident. For example, one to one interviews are now a common practice across all the organizations surveyed. However, only a few years ago this practice was rarely used by Chinese firms. Instead, such factors as a person's home province or the institution from which they got their education were more prevalent as selection criteria.[78]

Thus, the form that recruitment processes take and the message they convey may vary according to cultural norms. While recruiting practices may be influenced by globalization, national culture and institutional factors continue to have an influence. Selection techniques also bear the imprint of contextual factors in the way in which particular techniques are institutionalized. In addition, selection decisions can vary because of the cultural values of the decision maker. Because managers from different cultures perceive the world through different lenses, the way in which they interpret that reality differs.[79] Therefore, culturally different managers can ascribe to the same set of principles but apply them differently.

In summary, global recruitment and selection activities must consider the cultural and institutional context in which this activity is embedded. The processes being used must be evaluated in terms of how individuals in a particular cultural context view why they work, what they value in their work, and the relationship they wish to have with the organization. Global staffing systems therefore have the challenge of not only recruiting and selecting individuals for assignments in foreign countries but also recognizing the cultural and institutional norms for staffing within a variety of national contexts.

Table 6.3 Selection Methods by Country

Method	Australia	Belgium	Canada	France	Germany	Greece	Hong Kong	Ireland	Italy	Netherlands	New Zealand	Portugal	Singapore	South Africa	Spain	Sweden	UK	US	All
Application form	3.39	3.94	3.29	4.09	3.65	2.92	4.75	3.46	4.19	3.35	3.64	3.40	4.67	4.20	3.22	1.19	4.26	4.12	3.53
Education	4.21	3.19	4.31	4.37	4.47	4.32	4.50	4.42	4.08	4.68	4.33	4.91	4.33	4.46	2.43	4.30	4.32	4.47	4.26
Personal references	2.88	2.74	3.00	2.79	3.06	3.44	2.75	3.46	3.04	2.47	3.40	3.14	3.07	3.63	2.91	3.94	3.51	3.18	3.22
Employer references	4.32	2.64	4.05	3.32	2.03	2.30	3.75	4.53	2.69	2.72	4.40	3.14	3.13	4.09	2.43	4.49	4.37	4.02	3.77
Certificate or license	2.52	3.19	3.05	2.25	3.33	2.83	3.88	3.02	2.38	4.23	2.66	4.35	3.47	3.37	3.52	1.89	2.83	2.96	2.95
Family connections	1.30	1.57	1.68	1.56	1.47	1.87	2.00	1.55	1.52	1.50	1.31	1.75	1.80	1.52	1.48	1.22	1.33	1.53	1.46
One-to-one interviews	3.59	4.70	4.35	4.85	4.65	4.92	3.38	3.34	4.93	3.78	4.05	4.77	4.13	4.72	4.70	4.84	3.88	4.78	4.30
Panel interviews	4.08	2.75	3.57	2.06	1.88	2.71	3.63	4.00	1.50	4.30	3.71	3.29	3.47	3.63	2.45	2.82	3.82	3.27	3.36
Questionnaire	2.75	3.73	2.87	2.63	1.74	2.65	2.88	2.98	1.58	3.03	3.45	3.27	2.64	3.44	3.09	3.74	3.41	2.51	3.09
Job trail	2.05	3.05	2.33	2.12	1.56	2.74	1.57	2.71	1.48	3.94	1.59	3.12	2.00	2.06	2.57	1.55	1.87	2.02	2.20
Biodata	1.23	1.52	1.19	1.20	2.77	3.87	1.62	1.19	1.92	1.53	1.35	2.29	1.80	1.41	1.68	1.59	1.23	1.21	1.52
Cognitive ability test	2.39	3.85	2.59	2.29	1.90	2.54	1.83	2.79	1.33	3.76	3.37	3.27	2.83	3.25	3.75	2.86	3.08	2.09	2.98
Physical ability test	1.40	1.04	1.27	1.29	1.00	1.08	1.17	1.15	1.00	1.61	1.12	1.69	1.17	1.26	1.00	1.17	1.18	1.21	1.22

(Continued)

Table 6.3 (Continued)

Method	Australia	Belgium	Canada	France	Germany	Greece	Hong Kong	Ireland	Italy	Netherlands	New Zealand	Portugal	Singapore	South Africa	Spain	Sweden	UK	US	All
Foreign language test	1.11	3.02	1.67	2.79	1.60	2.85	2.83	1.58	1.67	1.62	1.19	2.36	1.00	1.33	3.07	2.18	1.37	1.21	1.75
Work sample	1.89	1.40	1.80	1.50	1.50	1.79	1.83	1.39	1.00	1.32	1.49	1.69	1.67	1.71	2.15	1.22	1.84	1.40	1.59
Personality test	2.56	3.75	2.78	3.42	1.70	3.14	2.50	3.17	1.86	3.29	3.59	3.00	2.67	3.66	4.43	3.68	3.46	1.62	3.21
Honesty test	1.16	1.60	1.52	1.00	1.00	1.85	1.33	1.04	1.00	1.69	1.20	1.92	1.67	1.62	2.21	1.11	1.12	1.09	1.33
Vocational interest test	1.51	1.98	1.76	2.33	1.40	2.29	1.50	1.07	1.00	1.65	1.54	2.62	1.33	1.73	2.33	1.53	1.33	1.15	1.61
Simulation exercise	1.58	2.73	2.58	1.82	1.70	1.85	1.50	1.44	1.57	2.82	1.89	2.57	1.33	2.66	2.15	1.72	2.52	1.82	2.14
Situation judgment test	1.35	2.16	2.30	1.33	1.50	1.15	3.00	1.31	1.00	1.82	1.57	2.23	1.67	1.94	2.33	1.64	1.85	1.71	1.78
Video-based test	1.10	1.33	1.15	1.06	1.00	1.15	1.17	1.00	1.00	1.55	1.07	2.00	1.00	1.30	1.33	1.19	1.18	1.26	1.20
Projective techniques	1.12	1.33	1.33	1.69	1.00	1.00	1.00	1.00	1.00	1.68	1.13	2.60	1.00	1.73	1.69	1.77	1.12	1.03	1.32
Drug tests	1.34	1.08	1.55	1.18	1.18	1.15	1.17	1.32	1.00	1.06	1.13	1.93	1.00	1.58	1.00	1.93	1.35	2.21	1.41
Medical screen	3.34	3.50	2.63	1.76	4.45	2.36	3.67	4.31	2.33	4.18	1.95	4.14	3.33	3.77	3.54	3.26	3.91	2.26	3.18
Graphology	1.07	1.56	1.00	3.26	1.00	1.21	1.00	1.00	1.00	1.24	1.02	1.00	1.00	1.45	1.75	1.27	1.10	1.09	1.25

Source: Adapted from Ryan, McFarland, Baron, & Page (1999).

Note: Scores are mean responses on a 5-point scale anchored by 1 = *never use* and 5 = *always*.

Global Staffing Systems

As indicated in the previous discussion, HR managers in global organizations face numerous challenges as they attempt to manage staffing. Given the differences in labor markets, and cultural and institutional environments around the world, it is understandable that there is often resistance to implementing global systems. However, there are significant advantages to be gained from having HR Systems that can be used across multiple countries. An outline of the obstacles and benefits of such global staffing systems is presented in Table 6.4.

Based on the experiences of six multinational organizations considered leaders in global staffing, one study has suggested a set of best practices related to system acceptability, development, and implementation.[80]

System Acceptability

In order for HR systems to succeed they need to be accepted by employees. Implementing global staffing systems is easier in organizations that are truly global, meaning they have a geocentric staffing policy. In some instances, it is necessary to differentiate staffing practices across countries, but it is important to ensure that differentiation is based on legitimate differences and not just on resistance to change in general. This of course requires developing an in-depth knowledge of the local cultural and institutional context. One way of overcoming resistance is to allow local managers' discretion in staffing as long as it doesn't compromise the integrity of the system.

Table 6.4 Obstacles and Benefits of a Global Staffing System

Obstacles to a Global Staffing System	Benefits of Global Staffing
• Legal requirements across countries/regions • Educational systems across countries/regions • Economic conditions across countries/regions • Ability to acquire and use technology • Labor market variations • Value differences across cultures • Availability of off-the-shelf translated tools • Level of HR experience varies across regions • Role of HR in hiring varies across regions • Familiarity with a tool or practice varies • Misperceptions that something is a cultural difference • Limited local resources for implementation • Beliefs about whether a global system is U.S.-centric or imposed	• Global database of qualified talent • Quick identification of candidates to meet needs of a specific location • Provision of a consistent message about the company to candidates worldwide • Quality of all hires is ensured • Better understanding of country/regional needs by all HR • Global succession planning is enabled • Global HR personnel have access to the latest versions of products/tools • Shared vision of HR globally • Comparisons of staffing results across locations • Global database as an internal benchmark of achievement in different parts of the world

Source: Wiechmann et al. (2003, p. 82).

System Development

A number of best practices with regard to developing global staffing systems have been identified. The first of these involves insuring a broad representation throughout the organization through the use of networking and global teams. It is important to use a global input system that treats all the geographies as equal partners in the development process. Another key development aspect is building flexibility into the system that allows for different methods to accomplish global system requirements through the use of different tools and processes as required. For example, face-to-face interviews are a common global requirement for selection, but details such as who conducts the interview, how prescreening is done, and so on can differ by country.

System Implementation

The best practices for implementing a global staffing system mirror those for any effective systems implementation. First, communication at all levels of the organization is critical, not just with those implementing the system. Second, it is critical to recognize that while technologically sophisticated processes are often at the heart of global staffing efforts they can make things harder. For example, local and cultural differences in the way things are labeled and entered into an automated system can create problems. Third is the need to have geographic representation in the implementation process, and finally is the need to dedicate sufficient resources to the global HR effort.

Many organizations follow a talent pool strategy toward staffing, in which they recruit the best people and place them into positions rather than recruiting specific people for specific positions. This approach is central to the identification and development of high potential employees that are key elements of *global talent management*. While many multinational organizations have systems and mechanisms in place to strategically identify and develop their talent, many more seemingly adopt an ad hoc or haphazard approach. Large organizations, with global HR functions and standardized products and services, are more likely to have global talent management programs, as are firms in the low-tech/low-cost sectors.[81] This trend means that organizations need a global template for talent management that allows local subsidiaries to adapt according to their specific circumstances.[82] Figure 6.2 shows how the coordination of talent management systems leads to different talent alignments.

As shown in Figure 6.2, global standardization with little local differentiation might allow an organization to build a greater talent pool depth, that is, a large pool but one that lacks the diversity needed to adapt to changing environments. Alternatively, a local focus creates opportunities for greater talent diversity but limits the organization's ability to capture economies of scale. Optimally, of course, organizations would be able to balance the talent pool to accommodate both local and global needs (global talent pool alignment). While this balancing act may be difficult to achieve, it is clear that organizations that do not have systems to identify, develop, and effectively manage their talent across their span of global operations are likely to be at a strategic disadvantage compared to those with well-developed systems.

Figure 6.2 Global Talent Management Alignment

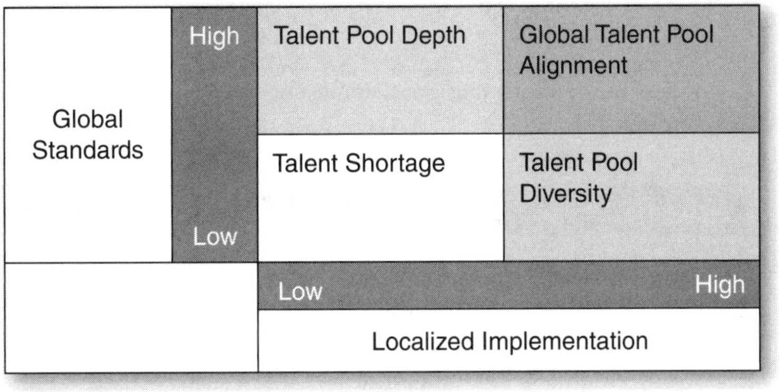

		Talent Pool Depth	Global Talent Pool Alignment
Global Standards	High		
	Low	Talent Shortage	Talent Pool Diversity

Low → High

Localized Implementation

Source: Stahl, Björkman, et al. (2007, p. 24).

Chapter Summary

This chapter examines staffing—the recruitment and selection of the people that organizations need to be effective in a global context. This context means that organizations must be concerned with staffing overseas operations by sending individuals abroad but also with staffing locally. Four staffing strategies—ethnocentric, polycentric, geocentric, and regiocentric—based on managerial attitudes toward staffing with PCNs, HCNs, and TCNs were identified. Much of what is known about global staffing has to do with the decision to fill positions with PCNs versus HCNs. Reasons for staffing with PCNs (expatriates) are dominated by the need to fill a particular managerial or technical requirement. This leads to a bias in selection criteria toward technical skills, while neglecting other factors that have a bearing on expatriate effectiveness. In addition to filling a technical requirement, expatriates perform a number of other roles in the organization, which can be classified as agents of control or boundary spanning. In addition to the issue associated with sending employees on overseas assignments, global organizations must be concerned with variation in staffing practices that exist around the world. These practices reflect underlying cultural and institutional differences with regard to how people perceive their work life and their relationship with their organization. Finally, organizations must find a balance between globally consistent and locally adaptive approaches to global staffing and talent management systems in order to be effective.

Questions for Discussion

1. What are the advantages and disadvantages of staffing with PCNS, HCNs, or TCNs?

2. Discuss the reasons that a firm would adopt a geocentric staffing strategy.

3. In what ways can expatriates be agents of control or boundary spanners for the multinational organization?

4. In what ways are people around the word similar and different in what they want from their work life?

5. Discuss the opposing tensions that must be considered in global staffing and talent management systems.

Notes

1. Material for this vignette was abstracted from the case, "Iceverks-Ben & Jerry's in Russia," by Iris Berdrow and Harry Lane and from the Ben and Jerry's corporate website.
2. Salt & Miller (2006).
3. Clark, Stewart, & Clark (2006).
4. Carr, Inkson, & Thorn (2005).
5. See Farndale, Scullion, & Sparrow (2010) for a discussion.
6. Scullion & Brewster (2001).
7. Michaels, Handfield-Jones, & Axelrod (2001).
8. Taylor, Beechler, & Napier (1996).
9. See Lazarova (2006) for a discussion.
10. Perlmutter (1969); Heenan & Perlmutter (1979).
11. See Harzing (2001c).
12. See Franko (1973).
13. For example, see Beechler & Iaquinto (1994); Boyacigiller (1990).
14. Edstrom & Galbraith (1977).
15. Pucik (1985).
16. See Peterson, Napier, & Won (1995); Scullion (1991).
17. Peterson, Napier, & Won (1995); Beechler (1992).
18. Baliga & Jaeger (1984); Rosenzweig & Nohria (1994).
19. Park, Sun, & David (1993).
20. Harzing (2001a).
21. See Boyacigiller (1990).
22. Gong (2003); Harzing (2001a).
23. Gaur, Delios, & Singh (2007).
24. Delios & Björkman (2000).
25. See Global Relocation Trends Survey Report (2010).
26. Caligiuri & Colakoglu (2007).
27. Vora (2008).
28. Harzing (2001b).
29. Harzing (2001b) refers to the different roles of expatriates as like bears, bees, or spiders.
30. See Schweiger, Atamer, & Calori (2003); Harzing (2001b).
31. Thomas (1994).
32. See Bartlett (1986); Bartlett & Ghoshal (1989).
33. Caligiuri (1997).
34. Au & Fukuda (2002).
35. Marschan-Piekkari, Welch, & Welch (1999).
36. Reiche (2006).

37. Collings & Scullion (2006); See also Reiche (2006).
38. Harvey, Speier, & Novicevic (1999).
39. Reiche (2011).
40. Evans, Pucik, & Barsoux (2002).
41. Collings & Scullion (2006).
42. See Forster (2000); Mayrhofer & Scullion (2002).
43. For example see Adler (1984); Insch, McIntyre, Napier (2008).
44. Stahl, Miller, & Tung (2002).
45. For additional information see Evans, Pucik, & Barsoux (2002).
46. See for example Hays (1971); Anderson (2005).
47. Miller (1975).
49. The precise cost of expatriate turnover depends on a variety of factors, including the level of the expatriate, country of assignment, and how the person is replaced. But in addition to monetary costs, a number of more indirect costs, such as the effect on local business and government relationships, local staff morale, and on the psychological effect on the expatriate can be identified. For an example of ROI of expatriates, see McNulty, De Cieri, & Hutchings (2009).
50. See Harzing (1995a).
51. Global Relocation Trends Survey Report (2010).
52. Black & Gregersen (1991); Harzing (1995a).
53. Inkson, Arthur, Pringle, & Barry (1997).
54. Feldman & Thomas (1991).
55. Downes & Thomas (2000).
56. Mol, Born, Willemsen, & van der Molen (2005).
57. Lazarova, Westman, & Shaffer (2010).
58. See Caligiuri (2000); Mol, Born, Willemsen, & van der Molen (2005).
59. See Thomas & Fitzsimmons (2008).
60. See Torbiörn (1982); Willis (1984).
61. See Thomas (2010).
62. See Harvey (1985).
63. Harris & Brewster (1999).
64. Global Relocation Trends Survey Report (2010).
65. See Ma & Allen (2009).
66. Svetlink & Alas (2006) cited in Nikandrou & Panayotopoulou (2012).
67. Aycan (2005).
68. Nikandrou & Panayotopoulou (2012); Aycan (2005).
69. Puck, Mohr, & Holtbrügge (2006).
70. Aycan (2005).
71. Brewster & Mayrhofer (2008).
72. Vance & Paik (2011).
73. Meaning of Work International Research Team (1987).
74. Thomas, Au, & Ravlin (2003).
75. Thomas, Fitzsimmons, Ravlin, Ekelund, & Barzantny (2010).
76. Ryan, McFarland, Baron, & Page (1999).
77. Steiner & Gilliland (1996).
78. See Huo & Von Glinow (1995); Redding, Norman, & Schlander (1994).
79. See Thomas (2008).
80. Wiechmann, Ryan, & Hemingway (2003).
81. McDonnell, Lamare, Gunnigle, & Lavelle (2010).
82. Evans, Pucik, & Barsoux (2002).

7

Global Human Resource Development

LEARNING OBJECTIVES

After reading this chapter you should be able to

- outline the issues associated with various approaches to training local workforces,
- explain the challenges associated with global management development,
- outline different approaches to identifying and developing high potentials,
- discuss the ways in which the needs for cross-cultural training can be evaluated, and
- identify trends in global training and development.

Training at Systech

Ayesha Gill had grown up learning to do more with less. But the impending cuts to her training budget were really going to test her skill. As training and development manager for Palo Alto-based Systech, she had lobbied long and hard for mandatory cross-cultural training for every employee sent on an overseas assignment. She had never achieved that goal, but at least training was now made available to everyone, including their families, and it was up to the employee to decide. That's how it had been until the financial crisis hit. Now, management was questioning the need for such a broad-based approach to training. Some of the top people even suggested doing away with training altogether. These were typically the ones who had never been overseas, Ayesha mused.

It is no good arguing that training programs shouldn't be cut, she thought. Cuts were coming! And she had always had trouble providing hard data on the effectiveness of training. Employees were sent to so many different cultures, and each person responded differently to different situations and types of training. The best evidence she had was from the returning expatriates themselves. She had heard many stories that began, "If only I had known..."

I have to prioritize, she thought. If I can only provide predeparture training to some employees, who should they be? Or should I cut training for families? I don't like the thought of that. Our newest program is in-country mentoring/coaching after the expatriate has been on the assignment for a few months. We don't have much experience with that program. Maybe that should be the first to go.

Ayesha though back to her childhood. She remembered marveling at how her mother could make a meal, planned for their family of four, stretch to accommodate unexpected guests: As one of the first Indian families to immigrate to Saskatchewan, there were frequent visits from newly arrived immigrants. "How did everyone in the Punjab get our phone number?" she once asked. Mom, I need to know how you did it, she thought.

Introduction

In order to compete effectively in today's dynamic and complex business environment, it is important that organizations develop employees at all levels and in all locations so that they contribute to organizational effectiveness.[1] Global HR development therefore involves the evaluation of human resource development systems in different countries, including their educational and vocational systems, as well as providing for international management development.[2] Much of the focus of HR training and development activities is on the development of global managers and the preparation of individuals for overseas assignments (as discussed in the opening case). However, global HR managers are also concerned with providing training to local employees. The best way of developing and delivering training programs is largely influenced by the characteristics of the workforce in foreign locations, which in turn are a product of diverse local education and vocational training systems.

Comparative Educational Systems

A comprehensive comparison of educational systems around the world is well beyond the scope of this book. However, it is important to have an understanding of the base level of educational achievement in a country in which the organization has or anticipates operations. A fundamental comparison is the level of literacy in that country. The range of literacy rates around the world is very large. Some countries in central Africa have adult literacy rates below 30%, while many parts of the industrialized world have rates approaching 100%.[3]

An index of *workforce potential* in a country is the world education rankings produced by the Organization for Economic Co-operation and Development (OECD) Program for International Student Assessment (PISA), which tests 15 year olds on math, science, and reading.[4] The most recent rankings were led by South Korea followed by Finland, Canada, New Zealand, and Japan. The bottom of the table was anchored by Mexico, Chile, and Turkey. Another indicator of educational attainment in a country is the percentage of individuals having achieved certain educational levels. For example, Table 7.1 shows the percentage of the population holding a postsecondary (college or university) degree in the OECD.

In addition to educational attainment, MNEs need also to consider the prevalent patterns for vocational training in the country. Some countries, Germany is often cited as a prime example, implement a dual-training system in which basic theoretical knowledge is learned at professional schools and colleges but equally substantial training is received in apprenticeships that offer opportunity to gain specific skills through work experience. German organizations take it for granted that they have a role to play in the professional education and skill upgrades of their employees and invest a lot in training and development, with emphasis in training firm-specific skills. For example, large German organizations may have their own training centers, and smaller organizations may set up joint training facilities.[5] In contrast, organizations in the United Kingdom do not consider it their obligation to direct much investment toward training. Also, their training programs often emphasize general skills at the expense of firm-specific skills. The workforce is *upgraded* mainly through downsizing and hiring adequately trained personnel from other companies or by hiring experts with specific skills on a temporary basis.[6]

These patterns of vocational training stem from the larger national context discussed in Chapter 2. Germany is a coordinated market economy, in which organizations operate in an environment characterized by low external mobility, low use of external labor markets, strong emphasis on succession planning, and lower employee poaching. This context allows for large investments in training, establishing close relationships with educational institutions, and strong emphasis on developing company-specific training. In contrast, the United Kingdom is a liberal market economy, in which external labor markets are heavily used and investing in training highly mobile workers does not make as much sense. It is mostly employees themselves who incur the cost for their professional development, and they tend to invest in transferable skills that are seen as routes to employability rather than to a long organizational career.[7]

From an HR development perspective, reference to indicators and trends such as these can form the basis of the needs analysis, which is at the heart of any training and development program. Prospective employee's knowledge and skills in comparison with what is required by the organization should determine the design and implementation of the training and development plan.[8] Individual training programs will vary widely across organizations and in different national contexts. Organizational types as

Table 7.1 Tertiary Education by Country (OECD)

Rank		
# 1	Canada	42%
# 2	United States	37%
# 3	Ireland	36%
# 4	Japan	34%
= 5	Sweden	32%
= 5	Finland	32%
= 7	New Zealand	29%
= 7	Australia	29%
# 9	Norway	28%
= 10	Denmark	27%
= 10	Belgium	27%
# 12	United Kingdom	26%
# 13	Switzerland	25%
= 14	France	23%
= 14	Germany	23%
# 16	Netherlands	22%
# 17	Austria	14%
# 18	Italy	10%
	Weighted average	27.6%

Source: http://www.nationmaster.com/graph/edu_edu_att_ter-education-educational-attainment

well as cultural and institutional contexts influence the extent to which organizations invest in training. For example, firms in low power distance, high future orientation, and high uncertainty avoidance cultures tend to invest more in training than firms in high power distance, low future orientation, or low uncertainty avoidance cultures.

Large high-tech firms tend to invest more in training, probably because of the ability of large firms to invest in training and the shorter product life cycle in the high tech industries.[9] Further, some countries may have explicit legislation regarding employee training. For example, French companies above a certain size are required to invest 1.5% of their payroll in training and development activities.[10] Similar legislation has also been adopted by the Canadian province of Quebec (but not in any of the other Canadian provinces).[11] In another example of legal requirements for training, U.K. organizations have an obligation to provide training that increases health and safety at the workplace.[12]

Regardless of scope, all training programs will involve a needs assessment based on the competencies required for a particular job or set of jobs. Based on the needs assessment, program objectives are set, and content and methods for delivering the training are established. Figure 7.1 shows a simplified diagram of a typical training cycle. As shown in the figure, evaluation should take place at all four stages.[13]

The approaches taken by global organizations to training local workforces range from complete localization, with all training designed and delivered at the subsidiary level, to total integration, with all training directed from headquarters. While there are

Figure 7.1   Basic Training Cycle

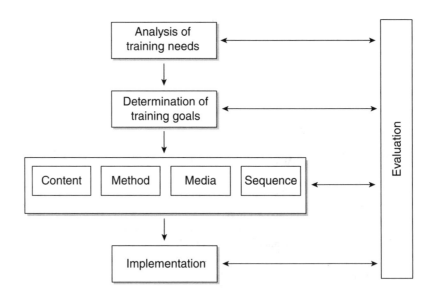

Source: Baumgarten (1995, p. 209).

no general guidelines, training for local workforces in global organizations raises a number of questions about the who, what, where, and how of training that must be answered:[14]

- WHO—Who should deliver training in the foreign subsidiary or joint ventures? Trainers from headquarters? Local trainers? Independent trainers?
- WHAT—What are the effects of language differences? Will there be translation issues? Who should take responsibility for translation, headquarters or local host country specialists?
- WHERE—Where should training programs be developed? If developed at headquarters, will they need to be adapted? Where should they be delivered? Should overseas employees be brought to headquarters or regional training facilities? Can training be developed in various locations and delivered across the organization?
- HOW—How should training be delivered? A key consideration is that training methods need to be based on an understanding of the differences in learning styles that exist in different cultures.[15] Culture differences, and particularly the extent to which power differences are present in and accepted by a society and the extent to which people are comfortable with uncertainty, may impact the relationship and interactions between the instructor and the trainees as well as among trainees. How formal should the training be, and would more didactic (formal approaches such as lectures, presentations, demonstrations) or more experiential (focusing the learning process on the individual such as role plays or simulations) training be more appropriate for a particular group of trainees?[16]

And of course, all these questions must be answered within the confines of a training budget. All global organizations might wish to be like IBM, which has an education department in each of the 170 countries in which it operates and is highly ranked (see Box 7.1) for its outstanding learning programs.[17] However, as shown in the opening case, training and development activities are often one of the first human resource activities to fall under the budget-cutting axe. There are, however, sometimes no-cost training alternatives to which employers can turn. While countries vary significantly in the extent to which government invests in the development of workforce competencies, as discussed previously, many have programs designed to support specific educational goals. The European Union, for example, has set targets for member states based on the recognition that people's skills must be constantly renewed to enable them to meet the challenges of ever-evolving technologies, increasing internationalization, and demographic changes.[18] Another model is that many U.S. states have free training programs targeted at economic development.[19]

Box 7.1 IBM Ranked #1 in Training

IBM has received the #1 ranking in *Training Magazine's* "Top 100" for its outstanding learning programs for the second consecutive year. The publication ranks those companies that understand, embrace, and use training to achieve real business results, support corporate values, and enhance the work lives of

(Continued)

(Continued)

employees. IBM has placed in the top five every year since the inception of the Training Top 100 in 2001 and received the highest honor for 2004 and 2005.

IBM employees spend an estimated 16 million hours each year (about 50 hours per employee) in formal training, online—through online learning activities—or in a traditional classroom. IBM's investments in training prepare employees with the skills they need now and in the future. "Learning is truly core to the DNA of IBM. We are a company focused on innovation, and our executives understand that we need to enable IBMers to grow and to foster the practices that produce business transformation," said IBM chief learning officer Ted Hoff. "Our learning programs are specifically designed to enable IBM to bring increased value to our clients and to provide meaningful learning experiences to all 330,000 IBMers."

Building the expertise of a 21st-century workforce requires a fresh perspective and breakthrough thinking. "A growing discontinuity exists between what business has become and what training has remained," explains Nancy Lewis, vice president, IBM On Demand Learning. "Our on-demand learning strategy allows us to shift the emphasis from 'bringing the worker to the learning' to 'bringing the learning to the work'—an exciting new era of learning that promises to leverage the collective expertise of employees, teams, and organizations throughout its enterprise."

What differentiates IBM as a world-class training organization? Simple—IBM provides learning programs that are aligned to a company's strategy, reflect its values, and drive greater performance and results in every area of the business. "A belief in the value of learning is embedded in the very DNA of IBM. It's not surprising that for the second year running, IBM has captured the top spot in the Training Top 100 ranking," said Richard Ausman, publisher of Training magazine.

Global Management Development

The line between training and management development is not always distinct. However, management development tends to be a longer-term effort focusing on developing current or future managers. The management development process involves assessing the company's strategic needs and implementing programs to develop managers to meet this need. In today's organizations, this involves the development of *globally* competent executives.[20] A starting point for executive management development (often also called leadership development) is mapping the skills, abilities, and characteristics (or competencies) required to be effective in the context of the global organization. Given the variety of environments in which global executives must operate, it is difficult to come up with a generic job description. However, a number of activities associated with the global management context have been identified. These are listed in Box 7.2.

> ### Box 7.2 Global Management Activities[21]
>
> Work with colleagues from different countries
>
> Interact with both internal and external clients from different countries
>
> May need to speak a language other than their mother tongue
>
> Supervise employees who are of different nationalities
>
> Develop strategic business plans on a global basis
>
> Manage a budget on a global basis
>
> Negotiate in other countries and with people from other countries
>
> Manage foreign suppliers or vendors
>
> Manage risk on a global basis

Developing Global Management Competencies

Even a casual look at the job requirements outlined in Box 7.2 suggests numerous distinctive competencies that might require development in global executives. In fact, some multinational organizations have identified as many as 250 such competencies.[22] A number of different typologies of competencies on which management development programs could be based have been proposed.[23] The ability of these typologies to predict success overseas or success as a global leader is not well established, and the range of competencies is quite large. However, they tend to cluster around six broad dimensions as shown in Table 7.2.

These competencies include elements that are relatively stable and difficult to influence, such as traits, as well as those that can be more readily developed. The challenge, of course, is to identify and foster those qualities in individuals that make them better global managers.

While there is little question about the universal value of certain competencies, such as business acumen, for example, the reality of leadership development is much more complex. Research on leadership has long suggested that while some universals exist there are also important differences in what are considered appropriate or desirable traits and behaviors in leaders around the world[24]. For example, U.S. employees and managers value highly transformational and participative leadership styles, but there are many places in the world, especially in Asia, in which it is authoritative, decisive, and forceful leaders that are more effective.[25] Also, across countries managers themselves rate certain skills as more important than others. For example, managing networks is a key competency for navigating the French environment but is not considered critical in Germany, Italy, Korea, or the United Kingdom.[26] Finally, the larger national context is important. For example, managers who operate in countries where the environment is less stable or predictable or in which political connections are just as important as the right organizational strategy (e.g., many countries in Africa) may not benefit as much

Table 7.2 Global Management Competencies

Cross-Cultural Relationship Skills	Traits	Global Business Expertise	Global Organizing Expertise	Cognitive Orientation	Visioning
Close personal relationships	Inquisitiveness	Global business savvy	Team building	Environmental sense-making	Articulating a tangible vision and strategy
Cross-cultural communication skills			Community building	Global mindset	Envisioning
"Emotionally connect" ability	Continual learner	Business acumen	Organizational and global networking	Thinking agility	Entrepreneurial spirit
Inspire, motivate		Total organizational astuteness/savvy	Creating learning systems	Improvisation	Catalyst for cultural change
Conflict management	Accountability	Stakeholder orientation	Strong operational codes	Pattern recognition	Change agentry
Negotiation expertise	Integrity	Results-orientation	Global networking	Cognitive complexity	Catalyst for strategic change
Empowering others	Courage		Strong customer orientation	Cosmopolitanism	
Managing cross-cultural ethical issues	Commitment			Managing uncertainty	
Social literacy	Hardiness			Local vs. global paradoxes	
Cultural literacy	Maturity tenacity Personal literacy Behavioral flexibility				

Source: Based on Mendenhall & Osland (2002, June).

from extensive training about long-term strategic planning as would managers who operate in (relatively) more stable environments (e.g., most developed countries).[27] Reflecting this complexity, the content of management development programs needs to be carefully calibrated, even within the same multinational organization.

Such challenges aside, there is little argument that for organizations to be competitive and to sustain their competiveness, they need to successfully develop managers to lead them into the future. However, because of the potential complexity that is involved in defining and developing all of the required competencies, HR managers often get bogged down in the tools and techniques of training, which can become ends in themselves.[28] There is no doubt that management development is complex. However, the crux of preparing managers for the global business environment is captured very well by the idea that a key requirement is to expand the manager's mind past domestic borders and create a mental map of the world.[29] Development of this type could be achieved by a wide variety of different techniques. But the key to managerial development may lie in the simple principle that people learn most by doing things they have not done before.[30] One strategy that has been proposed along these lines is that global management development should involve travel, teams, training, and transfer.[31] The implication of this idea for global management development is that people develop best through assignments and situations that challenge them. However, challenging assignments come with the risk of failure which must be managed. But at the other extreme, if the risk of failure is minimized and success is guaranteed people never learn to deal with situations that are outside their comfort zone. Therefore, the three basic elements of management development can be categorized as challenging assignments, risk management, and hardship testing.[32] Table 7.3 provides a summary of these elements.

Table 7.3 Management Development Summary

People develop through **CHALLENGING assignments** . . .

this requires **RISK MANAGEMENT (coaching)** so as to avoid failure that the enterprise naturally wishes to avoid . . .

but not so much that success is guaranteed and that people will never learn **to deal with HARDSHIP.**

Assignments:	Risk Management:
• Scope—increase in numbers of people, dollars, and functions to manage (traditional vertical development in responsibility)	• Assessment of the skills, motives, and attitudes of the individual
• Project/task force assignments (integrative negotiating and defining objectives, and working collectively so as to deliver a result meets the often unclear needs of sponsors)	• Clarification of the goals and targets in the new assignment
	• Coaching (supervision or informal)
	• Mentoring

(Continued)

Table 7.3 (Continued)

- Cross-functional assignments (integrative skills)—moving to a job where one has no expertise and learning how to lead, in the sense of getting results through people who have more expertise than oneself
- International assignments (integrative skills)
- Starting from scratch—building something from nothing
- Change projects—fixing or stabilizing a failing operation
- Entrepreneurial projects—being given the go-ahead and resources to test out a project initiative that the person has been fighting for

- Exposure to role models
- Training
- Access to people with experience

Hardship Testing:

- Business failure and mistakes—ideas that fail, deals that fall apart
- Demotions, missed promotions, poor jobs
- Subordinate performance problems—confronting a subordinate with a serious performance problem
- Breaking out of a rut—taking on a new career in response to discontent with the current job
- Personal trauma—crisis such as being fired, divorce, illness, or death

Source: Adapted from McCall (1998); Evans, Pucik, & Barsoux (2002).

Management development must be viewed as a long term process in which each of the elements of challenging assignments, risk management, and hardship testing are balanced. Taking any one of the elements to its extreme risks short-term failure for the sake of longer-term development. Box 7.3 outlines the management development program (Global Leadership Development Program) at Automatic Data Processing (ADP) a world leader in outsourcing solutions.

Box 7.3   Global Leadership Development Program at ADP

Automatic Data Processing, Inc. (NASDAQ: ADP), with nearly $9 billion in revenue and over 585,000 clients, is one of the world's largest providers of business outsourcing solutions. ADP's Global Leadership Development Program (GLDP) is designed to provide high potential individuals with a combination of stretch assignments, development, coaching, and mentoring. Upon successful completion of the program, participants will be positioned to assume a domestic or international leadership role in one of ADP's growing business units.

The GLDP is centered on three key elements: (a) challenging rotational assignments, (b) leadership support, and (c) hands-on coaching and development.

- Challenging rotational assignments—Delegates receive opportunities to rotate across different functions, geographies, business units, and various business situations (e.g., start-up, realignment, sustaining success, and turnaround).

- Leadership support—Delegates are provided with leadership support designed to help them to navigate successfully through the program. This consists of support from senior management, the host manager, an assigned talent manager, and a mentor.
- Hands-on coaching and development—Delegates are assigned a talent manager who provides coaching that focuses on strengths and leadership potential.

Source: Debrah & Rees (2011, p. 388).

The process of global management development begins with identifying those individuals with the potential to become leaders in the organization. Historically, organizations in different parts of the world have managed this process differently. And the way in which individuals are identified as so-called *high potentials* influences the approach to development. Three traditional models have been identified, with a fourth (the multinational model) emerging in recent years.[33] Figure 7.2 shows these four types graphically.

The *elite cohort* approach to management development is typical of many Japanese organizations, although it also exists in some Western firms. Management potential is assessed when future managers are recruited from top universities. These recruits are developed as a cohort by a rotation through different jobs. During this trial period of 7 to 8 years, there are no immediate sanctions for poor performance, but performance and behavior are carefully monitored with regular reports made to a central HR department.

After this trial period, the managers are moved into positions of leadership where the rules of the game change to an up-or-out competition. Outstanding performers are given increasingly challenging opportunities while those who do not perform well are assigned less important roles with almost no chance of getting back in the game. While not impossible, it is difficult for someone not recruited with the cohort to enter the race for the top.

The advantages of this approach are that it assures the development of a highly socialized group of managers whose skills have been carefully honed. However, in the global organization this approach does not allow for the development of local managers. The latter often get frustrated when they realize their future prospects are limited. And even when firms try to engage local managers, the long period of development and cautious appraisal process discourages those who want a relatively early signal that they may have a future with the firm. Because this approach has been successful for Japanese firms, it is not easily changed and may be a disadvantage in the face of a globalized environment.

The *elite political* approach is similar to the elite cohort approach but is a less managed process, which is characteristic of firms in Latin Europe, particularly France. Potential is identified at entry, but individuals are recruited from schools that specialize in grooming an elite for future leadership positions. Competition for entry to these schools is fierce, but the graduates of these grandes écoles are almost guaranteed a top

Figure 7.2 Four Models for Identification and Development of High Potentials

Elite Cohort Approach
The "Japanese" Model

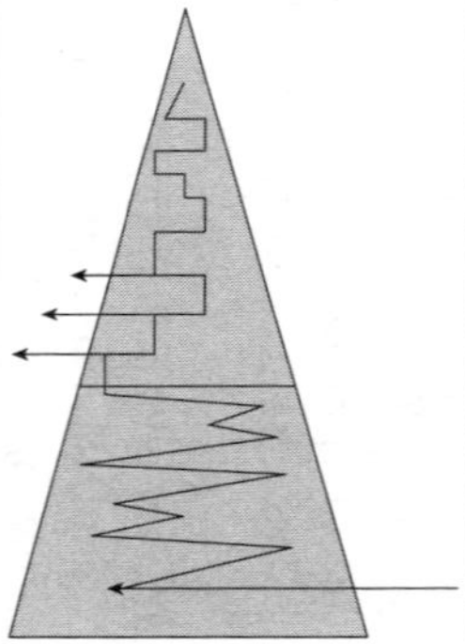

Potential Development—Time-Scheduled Tournament
- Unequal opportunity, good jobs to the best
- Four to 5 years in a job, 7 to 8 years up-or-out
- Comparison with cohort peers
- Multifunctional mobility, technical-functional track for minority

Potential Identification—Managed Elite Trial
- Elite pool or cohort recruitment
- Recruitment for long-term careers
- Job rotation, intensive training
- Regular performance monitoring
- Equal opportunity

Functional Approach
The "Germanic" Model

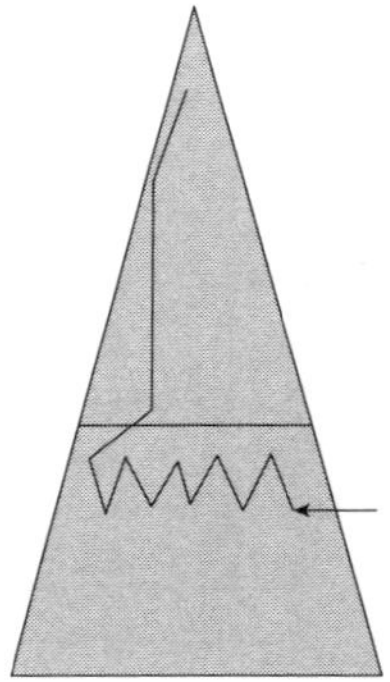

Potential Development—Functional Ladders
- Functional careers, relationships, and communication
- Expertise-based competition
- Multifunctional mobility limited to few elitist recruits, or nonexistent
- Little multifunctional contact below level of division heads and *vorstand* (executive committee)

Potential Identification—Apprenticeship
- Annual recruitment from universities and technical schools
- Two-year-"apprenticeship" trial
  - Job rotation through most functions
  - Intensive training
  - Identification of person's functional potential and talents
- Some elitist recruitment, mostly of PhDs

Elite Political Approach
The "Latin" Model

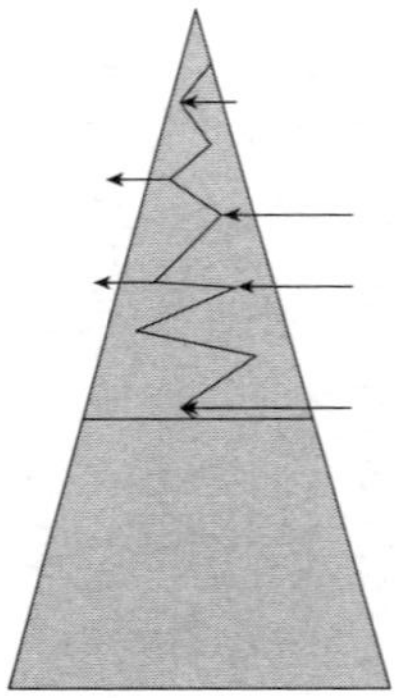

Potential Development—Political Tournament
- High fliers
- Competition and collaboration with peers
- Typically multifunctional mobility
- Political process (visible achievements, get sponsors, coalitions, read signals)
- If stuck, move out-and-on
- The "gamesman"

Potential Identification—Elite Entry, No Trial
- At entry
- Elite pool recruitment (noncohort)
- Predictive qualities
- From schools specialized in selecting and preparing future top managers
  - "grande écoles"
  - MBAs
  - Scientific PhDs

Managed Development Approach
The "Multinational Corporation" Model

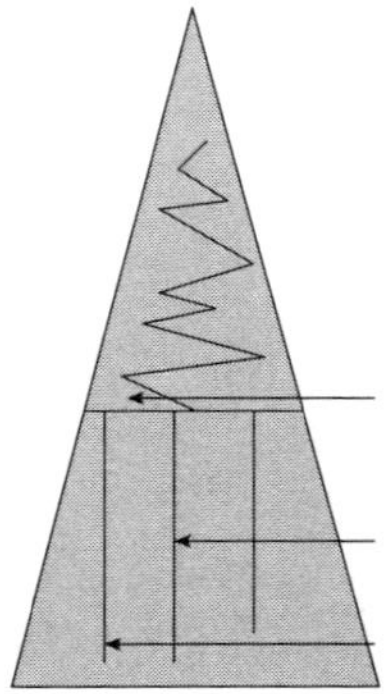

Potential Development—Managed Potential Development
- Careful monitoring of high potentials by management review committees
- Review to match up performance and potential with short- and long-term job and development requirements
- Importance of management development staff (often reporting to GM/CEO)

Potential Identification—Locally Managed Functional Trial
- Little elite recruitment
- Decentralized recruitment for technical or functional jobs
- Five to 7-year trial
- No corporate monitoring
- Problem of internal potential identification via assessments, assessment centers, indicators
- Possible complementary recruitment of high potentials

Source: Evans, Pucik, & Barsoux (2002).

146

leadership position. Top companies recruit exclusively from these schools, and individuals are immediately posted to a position of managerial responsibility.

The competition for promotion is a political process in which managers seek to gain visibility with senior executives who facilitate cross-functional challenges that allow them to develop their skills further. At the same time graduates of less prestigious schools move along functional paths (les métiers). An indicator of progress is how fast one moves from one job to another. While difficulties with regard to developing local managers (similar to the elite cohort model) exist, these are less pronounced because of the existence of the political model across Europe and among Asian firms. The most serious problem is perhaps the creation of a two-tier system involving a functional managerial level and an elite leadership level in the organization.

The *functional* approach to management development can be found throughout the world but is exemplified by German firms. While it is somewhat less elitist in character than the two previous models, it still establishes an elite cohort, but in this case it is based on functional expertise. Potential leaders are recruited from universities and engineering schools and during a trial period are rotated through departments to give them broad exposure to the business and organization. During this trial, the functional area that suits them best is identified. Once assigned to a functional area, the recruit will ascend to higher and higher levels. With the exception of some elite PhDs or individuals recruited to staff roles, they will have little cross-functional experience after this point. Decisions at higher levels of these firms are typically made by management committees representing the various functional areas.

The obvious advantage of this approach is the development of in-depth expertise and attention to detail that has been associated with German engineering firms. However, the resultant need for consensus decision making that emerges as a result may be a disadvantage as the pace of global competition increases. To compensate corporate staff has often been enlarged to bring in outside skills leading to a large headquarters bureaucracy. And local managers who attempt to navigate this process sometimes have difficulty adjusting to the consensual decision-making process.

The early identification of high potentials in all three of these models inevitably leads to a home country bias in the development of top management. As global firms try to internationalize their top-management ranks in response to competing in a global environment, this can prove to be a significant disadvantage. As a result, a model that is more in tune with the needs of the global organization has emerged. This *multinational* approach is characterized by decentralizing the responsibility for functional development to the local subsidiary while maintaining control of leadership development at the corporate level.

In this model, high potentials are not identified at time of entry, and a wide variety of techniques must be employed to identify these individuals. Regional managers, local general managers, expatriates working in the local operation, and even peers can be sources of information leading to the identification of high potentials. However, it is important to remember that local managers are often more concerned with operational issues than with recruiting and developing management talent. And in some firms, there is also the tendency for subsidiaries to hide their best talent. Therefore, it is important that organizations have systems in place that allow for the capture of performance information to identify high potentials and that this information is treated as a corporate resource. Box 7.4 outlines a typical global management development program based on annual performance appraisals.

Box 7.4   Example of a Global Management Development Program

Annual appraisal in all operating units used as a basis for identifying high potentials

Global database updated with this information

Assessment centers for these managers—often held biannually

Workshops using diagnostic instruments (e.g., Myers Briggs, 360 feedback, self-assessment) and one-on-one executive coaching to create individual development plan

Interactive learning, such as case studies, teambuilding, project work

Executive coaching and mentoring from senior management

Follow-up reporting on development plan, periodic international management seminars

---

Source: Adapted from Woodall (2011).

The role of global HR is to act as a guardian of this process in the long-term interests of the organization.

Overseas Experience and Global Management Development

It is commonly believed that traditional training alone cannot constitute the primary tool through which global leadership competencies are acquired. In addition, organizations need to ensure that prospective leaders are exposed to "transformational" experiences (e.g., experiences, interpersonal encounters, decisions, and challenges stemming from global responsibilities) if they are to develop global leadership competencies.[34] To that end, many organizations design management development programs to include the opportunities to work in different countries. In fact, overseas assignments may be one of the best ways of providing the kind of challenging assignments that result in the mental development (global mindset[35]) thought to be important for global managers.[36] During the process of adjustment to a new cultural context, people may develop not only knowledge of another culture and the opportunity to practice different behaviors but also higher-order mental structures and processes because they must be more systematic and careful in processing the cues they get from cultural situations.[37] As individuals deal with new and conflicting information, they must acknowledge the legitimacy of competing perspectives on the same issue and must integrate these multiple perspectives in their minds. For this development to take place, individuals need to be prepared for the international assignment. Therefore, an important initial step in integrating international assignments into the management plan is anticipating and providing training for the international assignment itself.

Training for International Assignments

The widespread belief that the competencies required for success on foreign assignments are not well enough known to design effective training programs is often cited as the main reason that organizations do not make a greater investment in these programs.[38] The most recent Global Relocation Trends Survey Report[39] reported that 81% of firms surveyed provided preassignment cross-cultural training. Only 37% of companies, however, offered cross-cultural training for all assignments. Further, training was mandatory in only 24% of the MNEs that offered it. Some HR directors believe that since expatriate assignments are temporary they do not warrant training expenditures, while others are not convinced that such training programs are effective.[40]

Interestingly, however, when asked to rate the value of cross-cultural preparation for international assignee success, 85% of respondents rated the training as having good or great value. Training for international assignments might involve a range of activities, ranging from formal university programs in international management to cross-cultural coaching and mentoring. However, the most common programs by far are cross-cultural and foreign language training.[41]

Cross-Cultural Training

The general goal of cross-cultural training is to improve the chances of success for the international assignees and their families on the foreign assignment. Success is a somewhat vague term and has often been equated with simply staying on assignment the agreed upon length of time. A broader view of success consists of the following components:

- *Good personal adjustment*, indicated by feelings of contentment and well-being
- Development and maintenance of *good interpersonal relationships with culturally different others*
- The effective *completion of task-related goals*

That is to say, an overseas assignment can be called a success if the expatriate feels happy and satisfied with the situation abroad, is effective in interacting with host nationals, and performs his or her duties and responsibilities in a competent manner. There is broad support for the idea that cross-cultural training has a positive effect on these outcomes related to effectiveness on overseas assignments.[42] Unfortunately, research has often failed to furnish such solid evidence, which may be due primarily to the many methodological challenges of conducting longitudinal studies in which expatriates are studied before training, after training, and during various points of their assignment and are then compared to colleagues who did not receive training.[43]

Despite the general endorsement of cross-cultural training, it is naive to think that all cross-cultural training is the same or is equally effective. Therefore, it is important to distinguish among different training types, such as informational training, area studies, cultural awareness, and intercultural-skills training. Based on social-learning theory, it is possible to evaluate how rigorous different training types are.[44] More rigorous training involves more active mental involvement of the trainee. For example, trainees are more cognitively involved when they must participate as opposed to just observe and are more involved when they physically, as opposed to only verbally, participate in modeling the behaviors taught. And having to rehearse the activity in order to perform correctly involves even more involvement. Based on the modeling and rehearsal processes involved, the level of rigor of common training methods can be arrayed. This is shown graphically in Figure 7.3.

As shown in Figure 7.3, in *factual* training involving books, lectures, and area briefings, trainees are passive receptacles for information. *Analytical* training, such as case studies or cultural assimilators,[45] requires more active engagement, and *experiential* training such as role plays or simulations, involves the highest level of cognitive involvement. All things being equal, the more rigorous training methods give

Figure 7.3   Framework for Selecting Cross-Cultural Training

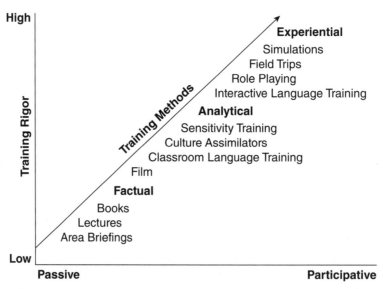

Source: Adapted from Black & Mendenhall (1989).

the best results.[46] However, not all country contexts are the same, and different expatriate assignments have different demands. Therefore, the training needs of individuals will vary according to the characteristics and length of the assignment and the country context.

There are three contextual factors that can help determine how rigorous the training for a particular expatriate assignment should be. They are the degree of novelty of the host culture, the level of interaction required with the host culture, and the novelty of the new assignment.[47]

Culture Novelty

Attending to and retaining various models of appropriate behavior for cultures that are very different to the expatriate's home culture will require more rigorous training. However, individuals with frequent and involved experiences in similar cultures may require somewhat less rigorous training.

Degree of Interaction

The degree of interaction with the host culture involves both the frequency of the interaction and its importance. If the expectation is for few and relatively trivial interactions, the level of training rigor can be lower than for frequent and important interactions.

Job Novelty

The arguments for the effect of job novelty on the need for training rigor are the same as for cultural novelty. While sometimes the novelty of the culture influences how different a job is, there are instances in which the new job overseas is much different than the previous job. Different performance standards, tasks, procedures, resources, legal restrictions, technology, and so on can all contribute to job novelty. Integrating these three factors determines the need for training rigor as shown in Figure 7.4.

As shown in Figure 7.4, the vertical axis represents job novelty, the horizontal axis the degree of interaction with the host culture, and the front to back axis the degree of cultural novelty. Since each of the context dimensions may not have an equal effect on training rigor, the degree of rigor required is represented as a plane, the shape of which is determined by where it intersects each axis. The rational for the model is that as the requirements of the situation become more demanding the cross-cultural training provided should move from more passive to more participative modes. While fact-oriented training might suffice in situations with low job novelty, low cultural novelty, and low interaction requirements, more analytical and experiential elements are required at the other end of the spectrum. Use of rules of thumb, such as this one, depend on adequate time to design and deliver training. However, an often-cited reason for the failure of organizations to deliver cross-cultural training is the lack of adequate time.[48]

Figure 7.4   Integration of Training Contingency Factors

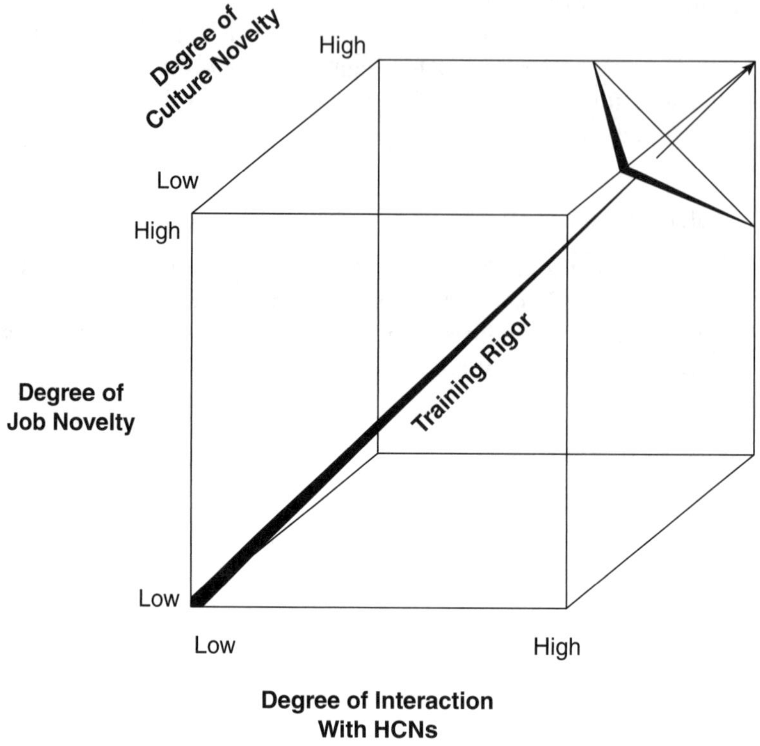

Source: Black & Mendenhall (1989, p. 528).

Foreign Language Training

While English may be becoming the lingua franca of international business,[49] the importance of foreign language training for expatriates and their families cannot be overemphasized. The fact that English dominates business transactions is largely a by-product of Anglo American economic dominance in the twentieth century, and the unwillingness of British and American people to learn languages other than their own.[50] This ethnocentrism is reflected in surveys of overseas executives. When asked if speaking a foreign language was important to their success, executives from Australia, Canada, the United Kingdom, and the United States said it was unimportant, while executives from Europe, Asia, and South America said it was critical.[51] Broad-based research indicates that foreign language skills are a prerequisite for intercultural adjustment and are related to the ability of the expatriate to form accurate expectations of the new cultural environment.[52] In addition, the lack of foreign language skills can have a negative effect on the strategic and operational ability of the manager in that it can limit access to important business information.

One caveat about foreign language training is that it should be viewed as only one component of cross-cultural training. It is important to understand that higher degrees of fluency can lead the second-language user to be perceived as having higher competency in other areas, such as knowledge of cultural norms.[53] For example, cultural blunders by a foreigner who is not competent in the foreign language might be forgiven consistent with his or her level of language fluency. However, the same behavior by a fluent speaker of the language can be perceived negatively, because the person should know better based on his or her level of language fluency.

Training for Family

As discussed in more detail ahead in Chapter 9, one of the main reasons that expatriate assignments do not achieve their desired results is that family members (in particular the accompanying spouse or partner) have difficulty adapting to the foreign cultural environment. The most recent Global Relocation Trends Survey Report[54] indicated that at companies where cross-cultural training was offered, 60% provided it for the entire family, and an additional 27% provided it for the expatriate and spouse, with only 8% providing training for the employee alone. Consistent with the previous discussion, the most common assistance provided to spouses and partners was language training. It is important for organizations to remember that in an international relocation, the expatriate's partner may have the most difficult role, because they have a greater exposure to the host culture and also lack the continuity that membership in the organization provides to the expatriate.[55] Equipping them appropriately by providing training contributes not only to their own adjustment but also to the expatriate's success as well.

Limits of International Assignments as a Development Tool

International assignments are considered a key tool for leadership development,[56] but because many global leadership competencies refer to traits or personality characteristics that are rather difficult to change, they have their limitations as a development tool. For example, a recent study[57] asked three groups of employees (potential expatriates not yet on assignment, current expatriates, and repatriates) to rate themselves on global competencies. While there were no differences in how the groups assessed their personality traits, those who had been on assignment reported having more knowledge compared to potential expatriates. Intriguingly, employees who had been on overseas assignments rated themselves lower on some abilities as compared to their colleagues who had not yet worked internationally. It was not that their abilities had diminished, but rather they were humbled by their international experience. Their assignments had helped them develop an acute sensitivity to the challenges of working in another context and they "knew what they did not know." Thus, it appears that the most valuable developmental aspect of international assignments might be the development of an appreciation for the complexities of transacting business across national borders and the related cognitive complexity that stems from this understanding.

Another important limitation is that organizations often shelter their expatriates by creating cultural bubbles that isolate them from having to engage with local culture. If they are met by a chauffeur at the airport, provided accommodations very similar to what they get at home regardless of the context of the local country, provided with staff that essentially prevents them from figuring out anything on their own, they will be unlikely to experience much change in their mental maps of how things are done differently in different parts of the world.[58] Perhaps having recognized this, forward-thinking organizations have started introducing a very different type of expatriate program: company-sponsored volunteering assignments[59] or service-learning assignments in which participants are sent to developing countries to work in partnerships with local organizations, NGOs, or social entrepreneurs. Research on these types of development assignments is still relatively scant, but early results suggest that they have great potential for developing global leadership competencies, among other benefits for multiple stakeholders.[60]

Training for Nontraditional Assignments

In recent years, short-term and nonstandard international assignments have become a popular alternative to long-term postings (see related discussion in Chapter 9) with 84% of firms in the Global Relocation Survey saying they used them. However, formal training for these employees, in particular for international travelers, who make up a large portion of the international workforce, seems to get little if any attention. Box 7.5 provides an example of the life of the frequent business traveler.

Box 7.5   Senior Executive, Australian Multinational

On average, I would go to Asia for two weeks and come back, go to the United States for two weeks and come back, go to Europe for two weeks and come back. The next time I went to Asia I would probably go to a different part of it. I guess I was away—if you accumulated it—for 8 to 9 months of the year.

Source: Welch & Worm (2006).

HR departments tend to have limited involvement with the international business traveler. Their activities are largely confined to expatriate management and international relocation. However, international business travelers may have significant training needs. In addition to enduring the obvious stress of frequent travel and family separation, these employees often have critical business interactions in a variety of different local contexts on a very regular basis. However, their training seems to be primarily of the on the job variety with little if any involvement of HR. The support of these employees where "the job is the travel and travel is the job" is a current challenge for IHRM.[61]

Trends in Global Training and Development

The future direction of global management development and training is being shaped by the nature of global competition, changes in the makeup of the international workforce, and advances in technology. In addition, the delivery of particular types of programs, such as predeparture training, are under review as more information is gained about their effectiveness. Four trends are particularly important to recognize. These are recognition of the benefits of in-country training for expatriates, the integration of cross-cultural training with diversity training, the training benefits of cross-national teams, and the delivery of training electronically.

In-Country Training

It has long been recognized that a single inoculation of cross-cultural training before an individual takes up an overseas assignment is insufficient. Thus, there is an increasing reluctance to rely on predeparture training alone. In-country training involving individualized coaching or mentoring programs after the employee has had some experience and has a higher learning readiness are increasingly being considered.[62] Such approaches to training have been referred to as sequential[63] or real time,[64] and are consistent with the idea that training is (or should be) a process and not an event.[65]

Cross-Cultural and Diversity Training

Migration patterns coupled with declining birthrates in the industrialized world are creating a workforce that is more diverse than ever before, and this trend is unlikely to abate. As a result, there is a renewed interest in many sectors in diversity training. Since there is much similarity between cross-cultural and diversity training programs, these programs are often carried out in parallel.[66]

Training in Cross-Cultural Teams

The type of development that results from challenging assignments, as discussed previously, is available to many employees through their involvement with multicultural teams. Teams are very prevalent in today's organizations, and their composition is increasingly multicultural. This type of cross-cultural training doesn't require relocation to a foreign environment. However, it does require dealing with cultural differences in group development and processes, which can challenge an individual's patterned way of doing things. To be an effective training vehicle, however, these teams need to be developed in a systematic as opposed to an ad hoc way. Thus, there is a significant opportunity for HR to use multicultural teams as a training and development tool.[67]

Media-Based and Web-Based Training

Another emerging trend is the availability and use of electronic media to deliver training. When asked if their cross-cultural training programs included media-based or web-based alternatives to face-to-face training, 36% of firms surveyed in the latest Global Relocation Survey[68] reported they were available. Of those who provided this alternative, 23% used them as additional premove and postmove support to in-person cross-cultural programs, while 28% used them anywhere anytime. Another 23% used them as a stand-alone alternative to in-person programs, up by 6% from just a year earlier. CD or web-based programs may be particularly valuable for employees on short-term or nonstandard assignments, where firms have difficulty justifying the expense of in-person programs. In some cases, these online training materials are highly suitable to expatriates and their families.[69] In addition, individuals have access to both commercially developed online programs as well as websites and blogs developed by expatriates themselves, which can also be effective training tools. On the other hand, many of the web-based training tools are not very high in terms of interactivity or rigor, which may limit their application in the case of more challenging assignments.

Chapter Summary

The challenge for global organizations is to develop individuals at all levels and in a variety of locations. Global HR has largely been concerned with the training of expatriates for overseas assignments and for the development of global managers. However, it also needs to be concerned with training and development needs of employees in all the locations in which it does business. All training and development is based on needs analysis in which the competencies required for a particular job or set of jobs are considered. For international training and development, this means working with individuals from different cultures and countries and conducting operations on a global basis. A key way of developing these abilities is to provide employees with challenging assignments that expand their thinking beyond domestic borders. An important aspect of global training and development is the identification and development of those employees who have a high potential to become leaders in the organization. The process of identifying and developing these individuals has been managed differently in different parts of the world. While many organizations decentralize the responsibility of functional development to the local subsidiary, leadership development is typically controlled at the corporate level.

One of the best ways to provide the type of challenging assignments that develop managers is a posting overseas. For these assignments to be a successful developmental exercise, these managers must be prepared for the overseas posting. This preparation most often involves cross-cultural and language training. Different types of overseas assignments need different types and levels of cross-cultural training. The level of training required can be determined by the degree of cultural novelty, degree of interaction with local nations and the novelty of the new job. This type of training can range from fact-oriented training to analytical, and finally, experiential types of training. Many firms recognize the importance of training for the spouse and family of the expatriate as well. Challenges for global training and development in the future involve training for short-term and nontraditional assignments, evaluating in-country versus predeparture training, the use of cross-cultural teams, the combination of cross-cultural with diversity training, and the availability of media- and web-based training.

Questions for Discussion

1. Why should the global organization be concerned with the educational system in countries in which it does business?

2. What are the most important competencies for global mangers? Why?

3. Describe ways in which high potential managers can be identified.

4. If cross-cultural training is so effective, why don't all firms make it mandatory?

5. Should fluency in a foreign language be a requirement for global managers? Why or why not?

Notes

1. Thomas, Lazarova, & Inkson (2005).
2. See Metcalfe & Rees (2005).
3. http://www.nationmaster.com/graph/edu_lit_tot_pop-education-literacy-total-population
4. http://www.guardian.co.uk/news/datablog/2010/dec/07/world-education-rankings-maths-science-reading#data.
5. van der Klink & Mulder (1995).
6. van der Klink & Mulder (1995); Mabey & Ramirez (2012).
7. Tregaskis & Heraty (2012).
8. Dessler (2011).
9. Peretz & Rosenblatt (2011).
10. Thomson, Mabey, Storey, Gray, & Iles (2001); van der Klink & Mulder (1995).
11. Pangarkar & Kirkwood (2008).
12. van der Klink & Mulder (1995); For a general discussion of contextual factors, see Mabey & Ramirez (2012); Tregaskis & Heraty (2012).
13. Baumgarten (1995).
14. See Briscoe & Schuler (2004).
15. Yamazaki (2005).
16. Briscoe, Schuler, & Tarique (2012).
17. http://www-304.ibm.com/services/learning/content/ites.wss/us/en?pageType=page&c=a0004380.
18. http://www.kslll.net/EducationAndTraining2010/Default.cfm.
19. Dessler (2011).
20. See Gregersen, Morrison, & Black (1998).
21. Adapted from Caligiuri (2006).
22. Morrison (2000).
23. See for example Connor (2000); Kets de Vries, Vrinaud, & Florent-Treacy (2004); and Mendenhall & Osland (2002).
24. House, Hanges, Javidan, & Gupta (2004).
25. Woodall (2011).
26. Woodall (2011).
27. Jones (1986).
28. Evans, Pucik, & Barsoux (2002).
29. Black & Gregersen (2000).
30. McCall (1998).

31. Gregersen, Morrison, & Black (1998).
32. Evans, Pucik, & Barsoux (2002); McCall (1998).
33. This model is from Evans, Lank, & Farquhar (1989) and the following discussion from Evans, Pucik, & Barsoux (2002).
34. Mendenhall, Osland, Bird, Oddou, & Maznevski (2008).
35. See Levy, Beechler, Taylor, & Boyacigiller (2007).
36. Evans, Pucik, & Björkman (2011).
37. See Tadmor & Tetlock (2006).
38. Baumgarten (1995).
39. Brookfield Global Relocation Services (2012).
40. Mendenhall & Oddou (1985).
41. Caligiuri & Tarique (2006).
42. Morris & Robie (2001).
43. Caligiuri & Tarique (2012).
44. This section based on Black & Mendenhall (1989).
45. The cultural assimilator uses a series of critical incidents that involve some sort of culture clash or misunderstanding. The trainee reads the incident and selects one of several explanations (attributions) and then receives feedback on the appropriateness of his or her choice. Through repeated exposure, trainees learn to make attributions similar to those made by the culture involved.
46. Brislin, MacNab, & Nayani (2008).
47. Based on Tung (1981, 1998); Black & Mendenhall (1989).
48. See for example Enderwick & Hodgson (1993).
49. Naisbitt & Aburdene (1990).
50. Thomas & Inkson (2008).
51. Tung (1998).
52. Puck, Kittler, & Wright (2008); Caligiuri, Phillips, Lazarova, Tarique, & Bürgi (2001).
53. Hui & Cheng (1987).
54. Brookfield Global Relocation Services (2012).
55. Briody & Chrisman (1991).
56. Pucik, Björkman, Evans, & Stahl (2011).
57. Caligiuri & Di Santo (2001).
58. Mendenhall, Osland, Bird, Oddou, & Maznevski (2008).
59. Caligiuri, Mencin, & Jiang (2012).
60. Pless, Maak, & Stahl (2011).
61. See Welch & Worm (2006).
62. Mendenhall & Stahl (2000).
63. Selmer, Torbiorn, & de Leon (1998).
64. Mendenhall & Stahl (2000).
65. Baumgarten (1995).
66. Moore & Rees (2008).
67. For more on cultural differences in teams see Gibson & Zellmer-Bruhn (2001).
68. Brookfield Global Relocation Services (2011).
69. Mendenhall & Stahl (2000).

Global Performance Management and Compensation

LEARNING OBJECTIVES

After reading this chapter you should be able to:

- describe the objectives of a global performance management system,
- explain how and why performance management systems are different in different countries,
- identify the issues in performance appraisal of expatriates,
- explain the influence of national differences on compensation systems, and
- outline best practices in compensation programs for expatriates.

Home on the Bosphorus

It had been three years since Maya Trudeau had seen her old university friend Yasemin Önal. They had both received their MBA from McGill University five years before, and

Maya had jumped at the chance to visit Yasemin in Istanbul. She was only a little surprised when Yasemin had offered to "have my driver pick you up from the airport." She knew that as a country manager for one of the world's largest pharmaceutical companies that her compensation would be pretty good. However, nothing had quite prepared her for the fabulous apartment in the upmarket Bebek neighborhood, with its panoramic view.

Shortly after receiving her degree, Yasemin had been offered the position in Istanbul. At the time she was already a senior product manager, and the opportunity to work in Turkey where she could use the language she learned as a child but never used in Canada was a big attraction. Compensation hadn't really been on the top of her list of issues to discuss, so she was very pleased that Pharmaceutico had a clear policy about salary and benefits for foreign assignments. Her base salary was 120% of what it would be in Canada, health care was taken care of, and she was protected from double taxation in Turkey. The company paid for the apartment, car and driver, and so on and deducted 7% from her salary to cover. And overall, the cost of living in Istanbul was just about the same as Montreal.

"This is like something out of a movie" said Maya looking out at the brightly lit Bebek Mosque and the fishing boats out on the Bosphorus.

"Yes, it does have a great location," said Yasemin. "But it is very short on closet space, and with Duygu, my housekeeper, here it does become a bit claustrophobic at times."

"You have a maid!" replied Maya.

"Well, it sort of goes with being in Istanbul," explained Yasemin. "I'd never get my job done if I didn't have Duygu and Mustafa, my driver who brought you here, to help out. And Duygu makes the best Imam Bayildi[1]—you do like aubergine don't you?"

Introduction

The "care and feeding" of expatriate executives, such as Yasemin, is but one aspect of global performance management and compensation. Global organizations need performance management systems that achieve the best return on the investment made in all their employees, and the global environment requires a consideration of both cultural differences in performance management and institutional differences in compensation practices. Research indicates that organizations with strong performance management systems are much more likely to outperform their competitors both on financial and nonfinancial (e.g., customer satisfaction, employee retention, product, and service quality) indicators of performance.[2] Therefore the design and implementation of effective performance management systems is an extremely important aspect of global HRM.

Performance Management

Performance management is the evaluation and continuous improvement of individual and work group performance. For global organizations, this involves performance management for parent country nationals (PCNs), host country nationals (HCNs), and third-country nationals (TCNs). Performance management systems are increasingly used for identifying organizational talent, leadership development, and succession planning. To be effective, performance management systems must define, facilitate, and encourage performance.[3] While the more complex global context affects their implementation, the goals of these systems are probably universal. And advances in technology and the introduction of HR information systems have allowed for corporate-wide standardization of key elements of the performance management system and for central control in many MNEs.[4]

Performance management systems have both evaluative and developmental components as part of their goals.[5] The *evaluative* aspects of performance management are the following:

- Provide feedback to employees so they will know where they stand
- Develop valid bases for decisions involving pay, promotions, job assignments, retention and termination
- Provide a means of communicating with employees about unsatisfactory performance

The *developmental* aspects of performance management are the following:

- Help employees to improve their performance and develop their professional skills
- Diagnose individual and organizational problems
- Enhance commitment to the organization through discussions about career opportunities, action plans, and needs for training and development
- Motivate employees through recognition of their performance

While the performance management system includes performance management interventions, including goal setting and motivation, the central component of performance management is the performance appraisal process.

Performance Appraisal Process

In order to provide employees effective feedback about their performance against goals, performance appraisal processes need to address the following elements:[6]

How will the evaluation be conducted? The process for conducting the evaluation includes the responsibilities of the employee and the evaluator(s), specific steps, dates, venue, and so on. The specific steps will vary considerably among organizations, but the critical factor is the communication of the process to everyone involved.

Who will conduct the evaluation? While it may seem obvious that all employees need to be aware who is ultimately responsible for evaluating their performance, the complex structures of global organizations make this less than straightforward. For example, expatriate managers may often find themselves reporting to both a headquarters and a local supervisor for various aspects of their role.

When will the evaluation be conducted? Many traditional systems rely on annual performance appraisals (often at the anniversary of employment), but numerous options are available, including quarterly or biennial reviews, end of project evaluations, and so on. Ad hoc (when the supervisor has time) evaluations often seem to substitute for carefully scheduled processes but have the potential of undermining the process.[7]

What will be evaluated? Options for what should be evaluated include traits, behavior, and outcomes. The merits of evaluations based on each of these criteria have long been debated.[8] The decision to use each or all of these criteria depends on the organization's culture, its objectives, its management philosophy, and the extent to which they are perceived as legitimate in the broader sociocultural context.

What are the potential consequences of the evaluation? The effectiveness of performance appraisals in meeting the objectives outlined previously is that the connection between the performance appraisal and outcomes is made clear. Tying rewards to the results of performance reviews makes them more effective for two reasons: (a) when rewards (pay, bonuses, stock options) are involved, all parties are likely to take them seriously; and (b) when significant financial rewards (and continued employment) are on the line, it is more likely that organizations will spend more time developing and training individuals to use their performance management systems properly.[9]

Performance Management in Global Context

The challenges in implementing global performance management systems result from both the differences in cultural and institutional context associated with international operations and the organizational context of the MNE. The fact that multinational firms are single entities that must operate in a number of different national contexts creates numerous issues for effective performance management. And even the purpose of performance appraisal itself may vary across cultures, ranging from determining individual rewards, to developing long-term potential, to maintaining group harmony.[10]

Cultural and Institutional Factors

Cultural and institutional factors can have wide-ranging influence on performance management systems in terms of performance criteria or standards, supervisor subordinate relationships, and the results or consequences of the appraisal.[11] One of the most significant issues in performance evaluation is the "criterion problem," or what constitutes good performance. In global performance management, the problem is heightened because what is considered good performance is culture bound. For example, in individualist cultures, evaluation systems tend to be based on individual employee productivity, timeliness, quality of output, and job-specific knowledge and proficiency. In these cases, performance criteria are objective, quantifiable, and observable. In contrast, in collectivist cultures, the in-group is valued more than individual productivity, and high-performing employees who stand out may disturb group harmony. While work outcomes are important, social and relational criteria, such as trustworthiness, a respectful attitude, awareness of duties and obligations, gratitude, and conformity carry more weight.[12] Even off-the-job behavior can be considered a legitimate criterion in some cultures.[13]

Culture also influences the appropriateness of particular performance appraisal processes and the manner in which feedback is given. For example, the popular multi-source (360 degree) feedback method is only appropriate in low power distance cultures in which high levels of participation is the norm, such as the United States. Self-appraisals are more likely to be used in individualistic than in collectivistic countries.[14] Thus, according to a recent study, in Japan only 10% of employees contributed to their own evaluation, in Spain 61% did, and in the United Kingdom it was 94%.[15] In high power distance cultures, performance appraisal is more likely to be a top-down, unilateral process,[16] which should be initiated by a trusted or expert superior.[17] A directive and autocratic style of delivering feedback is common, while open discussions between supervisor and employee are not expected. Feedback is typically not challenged as it comes from a powerful authority figure.[18] Feedback in collectivist cultures is likely to be indirect, nonconfrontational, subtle, and often delivered to the work group as opposed to individuals.[19] Even positive feedback delivered to individuals in these cultures can be seen as disturbing group harmony.[20]

Institutional factors, such as the legal and labor relations system, operating in a country influence the manner in which performance appraisals are conducted and the extent to which information is shared. In countries where performance appraisals are potentially open to external scrutiny, such as in the United States, they may be very detailed and well documented.[21] In countries with a strong tradition of collective bargaining, such as in Germany, performance management systems have a high level of worker involvement through works councils and similar groups, and the focus is on long-term career, job security, and technical development.[22] And while the strict labor laws in France dictate many aspects of performance management systems, the hierarchical French culture accepts that factors, such as the university a person attended and their position in the organization, will influence performance appraisals.[23]

While it is impossible to outline all of the variation in performance management systems that exist across the world, the preceding discussion should alert us to the importance of designing systems that align with local realities, while serving organizational objectives. Table 8.1 illustrates the performance management systems in three countries with very different cultural and institutional contexts. It is important to note that differences exist across of the dimensions of performance appraisal.

Organizational Factors

Since the overriding goal of performance management strategies is to encourage behavior that helps the organization meet its goals, performance management systems will reflect the industry in which the firm operates as well as firm strategy. For example, organizations in advanced manufacturing industries have performance criteria that are narrow and task related as compared to service organizations. And private-sector firms tend to use more specific and outcome-based criteria than do public-sector

Table 8.1   Some Characteristics of Performance Appraisal Systems in the United States, Saudi Arabia, and Korea

Issue	United States	Saudi Arabia	Korea
Objective	Administrative decisions, employee development	Placement	Develop relationship between supervisor and employee
Done by	Supervisor	Manager several layers up who knows employee well	Mentor and supervisor
Authority of appraiser	Presumed in supervisor role	Reputation (prestige determined by nationality, age, sex, family, tribe, title, education)	Long tenure of supervisor with organization
Style	Supervisor takes the lead, with employee input	Authority of appraiser is important; never say "I don't know"	Supervisor takes the lead, with informal employee input
Frequency	Usually yearly	Yearly	Developmental appraisal monthly for first year, annually thereafter
Assumptions	Objective; appraiser is fair	Subjective appraisal is more important than objective; connections are important	Subjective appraisal is more important than objective; no formal criteria
Feedback	Criticisms are direct; may be in writing	Criticisms more subtle; not likely to be in writing	Criticisms subtle and indirect; may be given verbally
Employee acknowledgement and possible rebuttal	Employee acknowledges receipt; may rebut in writing	Employee acknowledges receipt; may rebut verbally	Employee does not see or sign formal appraisal; would rarely rebut
How praised	Individually	Individually	Entire group
Motivators	Money, upward mobility, career development	Loyalty to supervisor	Money, promotion, loyalty to supervisor

Source: Cascio & Bailey (1995, p. 29).

organizations. Organizations that require innovation and creativity will likely use performance criteria that are broadly defined and process rather than outcome oriented.[24] Finally, large organizations tend to have more formal performance management systems, consistent with a more formal HRM structure overall, as discussed in Chapter 3.

The fact that MNEs operate subsidiaries across a variety of locations creates an additional set of performance management issues for employees whose performance is tied to a local organizational unit. These issues are the importance of firm-level versus subsidiary goals, differences in performance criteria and data across country contexts, and the additional difficulties imposed by time and distance between organizational units.

Firm Versus Subsidiary Goals

Global firms often make strategic decisions based on the overall long-term impact on the organization, as opposed to the short-term effect on a particular subsidiary. For example, as discussed ahead in Chapter 10, a firm might decide to withhold needed investment in a particular subsidiary in order to focus activity and ultimately move production to another market, thus negatively affecting the short-term performance of the subsidiary. Or an organization might establish a joint venture in a particular geographic location simply as a temporary measure, without the intent of supporting it long term. In cases such as these, performance of the affected subsidiary and its management should take into account organizational-level strategy.

Consistency of Criteria and Data

The volatility of the global environment as well as national differences in the availability of data increases the difficulty in specification of performance criteria that apply across the organization. For example, managers of a foreign subsidiary may have less control over profit levels because of exchange rate fluctuations, price controls, and differences in accounting standards, making profit an unfair standard appraisal criterion. In addition, in the global environment subsidiaries are differently affected by issues, such as natural disasters, political and labor unrest, or terrorism, making the use of standard performance criteria based on subsidiary performance questionable. For example, imagine the U.S. manager of a mine in Chile who single handedly averted a strike that would have shut down production for months (considered a major accomplishment by his Chilean colleagues), but who received only an average performance rating based on mine productivity.[25]

Geographic Separation of Organizational Units

A third factor that constrains global performance management is the geographic and time differences among far-flung organizational units that result in low levels of contact between headquarters and subsidiaries. The infrequency of contact among individuals in organizational subunits and headquarters in multinational firms forces these organizations to design performance management systems that rely less on face-to-face interactions.[26] Advances in communications technology are beginning to provide solutions to geographic separation. However, these sophisticated performance management systems are not substitutes for clearly specified roles, processes, and procedures.[27] And these systems often need modification to account for country-specific factors.

In addition to helping to solve problems of geographic separation by allowing appraisal of employees who cannot be observed directly, technology can have a number of other effects on the performance appraisal process. Technology can drive the content of the appraisal system, by focusing attention on those aspects of performance that can be easily captured by the system. For example, it is easier to record the number of calls a customer service representative handles than it is to assess the satisfaction of the customer with the service. However, increasingly affordable web-based systems allow for the ability to gather more information from a variety sources. Finally, technology makes it much easier to provide detailed documentation of performance information about employees.[28]

The preceding factors affect performance management for all employees. However, the multinational enterprise is faced with the additional challenge of assessing the performance of employees sent to a foreign country for both long- and short-term assignments. It is the special situation of performance appraisal for these employees that we discuss next.

Performance Management of Expatriates

Several factors related to the unique role of expatriates (PCNs) in the multinational enterprise affect the ability of organizations to design effective performance management systems for them. In addition to the time and distance associated with managing far-flung overseas assignees, expatriate performance can be viewed through different lenses by host country nationals and home country supervisors,[29] and the tasks they are assigned are dependent on the reason for their overseas posting (as discussed in Chapter 6). These factors result in unique issues associated with the fundamental questions of (a) who conducts the appraisal, (b) what criteria are assessed, (c) when and how often appraisals are conducted, and (d) what format is used?[30]

Who Conducts Expatriate Appraisal

The issue of who conducts the appraisal of expatriates is complicated by the differing expectations that host country stakeholders and the home country management have for expatriates. Based on the expatriates' interpretation of the potentially conflicting communication from these two sources, their behavior may or may not meet the performance expectations of the parent company or host country stakeholders. Therefore, performance appraisal from these different sources runs the risk of offering different judgments of an expatriate's performance.

Because the overseas context varies widely and can be a major determinant of expatriate performance,[31] it is important that appraisers understand the foreign situation and the context in which the expatriate must perform. While host country stakeholders may be better able to take into account the contextual issues surrounding expatriate performance,[32] home country superiors may have a clearer picture of the goals of the expatriate assignment. Often, performance appraisals are conducted by the expatriate's immediate supervisor as opposed to HR professionals, under the assumption that the immediate supervisor is in the best position to evaluate a subordinate's performance.[33] However, as discussed previously, if the expatriate's performance is tied to that of the local subsidiary, the remoteness of a headquarters superior could influence the effectiveness of the evaluation.

Alternatives to immediate supervisor appraisals include peer appraisals, rating committees, self-ratings, subordinate ratings, and multiple (360 degree) rater feedback.[34] Each of these has its advantages and disadvantages, and the extent to which they are considered legitimate in various societies will vary widely. However, many firms recognize the advantage of using more than one rater in assessing expatriate performance in order to get a more balanced view of the performance. One recent survey found that 81% of firms used more than one rater to evaluate expatriates, with 21% of firms using four or more raters.[35] There is some difference among firms with regard to their beliefs about the best way to evaluate expatriate performance. In the 2011 Global Relocation Trends Survey Report, 45% of firms said that a performance review in the host country was best, 26% said that using both home and host country appraisals was the best alternative, while only 9% said that home country reviews were best. Interestingly, 17% reported that they did not know the best appraisal approach.[36]

What Expatriate Performance Criteria are Assessed

Deciding what is to be measured and evaluated in expatriate appraisals is a more complicated issue than in domestic situations. Expatriate assignments differ in what expatriates are expected to accomplish, with some assignments being very technical while others are more strategic. These differences need to be reflected in the performance appraisal criteria used to assess the expatriates, and the development of accurate expatriate performance appraisals may depend on identifying and considering these criteria.[37]

However, certain aspects of performance criteria apply across situations. Generally performance criteria range from objective to subjective but also include specific contextual criteria.[38] Objective criteria that are performance or outcome based (profits, market share, etc.) are generally referred to as *hard* criteria, while relationship or trait-based goals are referred to as *soft* criteria. Hard criteria are typically easier and quicker to collect and interpret and can be more easily defended legally.[39] Hard criteria have the appearance of being more comparable across employees and organizational units, but the complexity of expatriate performance context, as noted previously, can create inconsistent data.

While hard criteria are important to evaluating many aspects of the expatriate role, *soft* or interpersonal factors (for example, how good the expatriate is at establishing relationships with host country national constituents) may be even more important to expatriate performance.[40] In addition, in expatriate settings, objective measurable criteria are often not available.[41] However, the subjective nature of soft criteria makes them susceptible to an almost limitless list of biases.[42] It is important to remember that performance ratings amplify the relationship between the appraiser and the employee. Good relationships tend to produce good appraisal experiences, and bad relationships produce bad ones.[43]

As important to the appraisal of expatriates are *contextual* criteria that deal with factors resulting from the situation in which he/she is performing (for example, how successful the expatriate is in terms of developing a local successor or transferring the corporate culture to a MNE subsidiary that was obtained through a local acquisition). These factors can include a host of environmental factors that influence the subsidiaries of MNEs, which can make comparisons across subunits difficult, and also cultural issues with regard to what is expected of expatriates. Expatriates who meet the expectations of employees are likely to be evaluated more favorably.[44] The challenge for performance management is that it may be very difficult to interpret the effect of some contextual factors, particularly for individuals without experience as expatriates.

When and How Often Should Expatriate Appraisals be Conducted

While the *annual* performance appraisal is enshrined in many international organizations, research indicates that conducting performance appraisals once or even twice a year may be insufficient.[45] Not only is it difficult for raters to recall information over the previous six to twelve months, but the more recent information is likely to be given more weight in the evaluation.[46] Also, frequent performance appraisals are more likely to have a developmental component.[47] In addition to these factors, the international context of the expatriate assignment suggests more frequent appraisals for the following reasons:

- Business and environmental conditions change frequently.
- Determining problems earlier makes them easier to solve.
- Raters can become more familiar with the expatriate, the job, and required performance.
- This can lead to improved development of expatriates.[48]

What Format Should be Used in Expatriate Appraisal

Many organizations develop standardized formats for particular categories of jobs. The use of standard performance appraisal formats is based on maintaining a system that has been validated, has identified baselines, and that will minimize future development costs.[49] This makes sense if the context of employee performance is relatively stable. However, the context of an expatriate assignment is very fluid and can sometimes change quite a lot within a relatively short period. Therefore, standardized formats can rarely capture the complexity of international assignments and should be customized to specific country contexts and expatriate roles.[50] However, research indicates that a majority of firms use the same standardized appraisal forms for expatriate appraisal.[51]

In summary, the expatriate assignment has a number of unique elements that should be considered when designing a performance management system. Despite these unique aspects of expatriate performance management, many firms, regardless of where their overseas subsidiaries are based, treat the performance appraisal of expatriates as extensions of domestic evaluation systems.[52] Appropriately, evaluating expatriate performance is important not only to the expatriate but also for creating competitive advantage for the organization. However, the performance management system for expatriates should be modified to fit the overseas position and the particular country context. In order to accomplish this, it may be necessary to create a development cycle that continuously reevaluates the system and includes input from returned expatriates and/or outside experts who specialize in these areas.[53] In addition, as discussed in later chapters, organizations are introducing new forms of global mobility such as short-term/project work or commuter assignments (whereby the employee is a resident of one country but works in another, spending the majority of their working week in their work country and their weekends in their country of official residence). These new assignment types make it difficult to isolate the international and the domestic aspects of the job, which in turn can make it more difficult to assess individual performance.[54]

As stated at the outset, to be effective, performance management systems must define, facilitate, and encourage a clear understanding of the performance of members that is consistent with organizational goals. It is equally important that such shared understanding be translated into relevant and clear performance objectives with tangible measurements, building commitment to the goals and dealing with the numerous tensions related to the structure of the performance objectives and measures (e.g., financial vs. nonfinancial targets, short-term vs. long-term goals, unit level vs. corporate level objectives, incremental vs. breakthrough activities).[55] Performance management is integral to other aspects of global HRM, such as training and development, as discussed in Chapter 7, and international mobility and careers, as discussed in Chapter 9. However, one of the key linkages with the evaluative component of performance management is the relationship to organizational rewards. Therefore, the remainder of this chapter is concerned with compensation in a global business environment.

Compensation in a Global Context

Compensation refers to all forms of pay to employees, as a result of their employment, and consists of direct financial payments (wages, salaries, incentives, commissions, and bonuses) and indirect financial payments (benefits, such as employer-paid insurance and vacations).[56] Direct financial payments can be based on either time (hourly, weekly, monthly, etc.) or performance (commissions, incentives), or a combination of both. Time-based pay is still the foundation of most organizations' pay plans, but the mix of time-related versus performance-related pay as well as other aspects of total compensation varies greatly around the world. Economic, institutional, organizational, and cultural aspects of the global environment all have an influence on compensation systems.

National Variation in Compensation Systems

There are a very large number of factors that affect differences in compensation systems around the world. However, the factors that affect global compensation practices can be reduced to a small number of broad categories. These include culture, social contracts, labor relations, ownership structures, management autonomy, and local communities of practice.[57]

Culture

As discussed in Chapter 2, societal-level culture influences HRM policies and practices to the extent that members of society see the practice as important or beneficial. Therefore, we would expect preferences for compensation policies and practices to be consistent with culturally-based values. For example, hierarchical compensation systems would be prevalent in high power difference countries, fixed salary programs in high uncertainty avoidance cultures, individual-based pay for performance systems in individualistic cultures, differential pay policies that allow inequalities in pay in more masculine cultures, social benefits in more feminine cultures, and so on.[58] Research has also suggested that culture congruence may result in higher organizational performance. Thus, high use of merit-based awards was associated with superior performance in masculine cultures and inferior performance in feminine cultures.[59] While practices that fit with cultural norms in most cases may be more effective, national variation in compensation systems is the result of the interaction of culture with other factors, as discussed ahead.

Social Contract

With respect to compensation systems, the social contract refers to the expectations and obligations of all relevant parties (government, unions, employees, employers, and business organizations) with regard to compensation. Differences among countries resulting from a general agreement among all parties as to what is appropriate can be seen in the extent to which compensation frameworks are centralized and influenced by social legislation. For example, the United States, Canada, and the United Kingdom have highly decentralized compensation systems with minimal government intervention, while Sweden, Denmark, and Belgium have highly centralized, national wage systems.[60] And France and Germany have highly regulated social welfare systems that have a direct bearing on compensation systems.[61] There is wide variation in the proportion of social insurance expenditures (health insurance, retirement and disability pensions, pay for sick leave, unemployment insurance, etc.) as a percentage of total compensation around the world. For example, these expenditures represented one third of pay in Sweden, about 24% in the United States, and in Asian countries social insurance is less than 20%.[62] A very significant component for organizations in some countries, such as the United States, is health insurance. Different social contracts also influence the extent to which wage inequality is present and accepted in a society. For example, in the United States the top 10% earn about 4.5 times as much as the bottom 10%, whereas in the Nordic countries the ratio is only about 2.25.[63]

Labor Relations

Related to the overarching social contract is the labor relations system and the presence of collective bargaining. Trade union involvement reduces the freedom that organizations have to unilaterally establish compensation systems (see Chapter 10 for national differences in trade union membership). The influence of collective bargaining is an important consideration in the existence of differences in compensation systems. In Belgium, for example, employee compensation is established through a collective agreement with employees (through employee boards) regardless of union membership,[64] and while labor law in Germany mandates that employees are given 24 vacation days per year, the norm is to provide 30 vacation days as a result of collective bargaining agreements that extend beyond the confines of the firms where they were negotiated.[65] And of course labor relations influence compensation rates and income inequality, especially in the lower end of the income distribution.[66] For example, in 2010 the average hourly compensation costs in manufacturing was US$1.90 per hour in the Philippines to US$57.53 per hour in Norway.[67]

Ownership Structures

Financial and ownership structures differ around the world, and these differences can affect compensation structures. For example, ownership and access to capital in the United Sates is very dispersed, while at the opposite end of the continuum, the economic structure in South Korea depends on a small number of huge family dominated *chaebol* with strong reliance on government funding.[68] In countries with highly concentrated ownership structures, compensation programs that have incentives linked to an increase in the value of shares make little sense.[69] Another good example of the influence of ownership structure is provided by Chinese private sector enterprises, which are more likely to have performance-based compensation programs than their state-owned counterparts.[70] Ownership structures also influence the appeal of stock option plans, equity participation or equity compensation programs, and profit sharing, with clear differences in the occurrence and character of financial participation practices in companies located in different countries.[71]

Management Autonomy

The degree of discretion that managers have in designing the compensation system is inversely related to the extent to which the compensation system is centralized. While legislation and unions restrict managerial autonomy, so do corporate policies. For example, compensation decisions aligned with the corporate strategy of a parent organizations may or may not be the same as those that would be implemented by subsidiary management if they had authority. This is a much larger issue if these compensation decisions are inconsistent with institutional or sociocultural aspects of the local environment.[72]

Common Practices

Organizations, in their compensation practices as well as with other HRM structures and practices, are influenced by the extent to which these practices are seen to be legitimate and acceptable in a society. Organizations are influenced to be similar to each other not only because of regulations requiring particular practices but also by mimicking other successful organizations and by adopting the best practices (norms) for compensation as established by professional organizations, consultants, and the like.[73] For example, if an organization is overgenerous in compensating its executives, it may lose social support and its reputation may suffer,[74] or the use of incentive systems based on stock options may be used not only to align the interests of management with that of the organization, but also to gain legitimacy by imitating the practices of other firms in the same sector.

Performance-Based Pay in Global Context

Pay for performance plans reward certain behaviors or their results on an individual or collective level. The various types of pay for performance plans are categorized in Table 8.2 according to whether they are fixed versus variable and individual versus collective.

As shown, pay for performance can be a fixed part of salary, such as merit pay based on supervisor evaluations or skill-based competency pay. Alternatively, it can be variable and based on measures of productivity, efficiency, or performance of individuals or a collective. It can be paid in a variety of ways such as bonuses, shares, or stock options.[75] As popular as these programs are and as logical as linking pay to performance seems to be, many of these programs don't seem to work. Only

Table 8.2 Types of Pay for Performance

	Individual	Collective
Fixed	• Merit pay	
	• Skill- or competency-based pay	
	• Promotion	
Variable	• Payment by results	• Performance-related pay
	• Piece-rate pay	• Financial participation
	• Commissions	• Gain sharing, goal sharing, and profit sharing
	• Bonuses	• Ownership
	• Individual incentives	• Group incentives

Source: Salimäki & Heneman (2008 p. 159).

a small minority of workers says they are personally motivated by their company's incentive plan.[76]

The challenges of designing pay for performance systems center on two basic issues, effectiveness and acceptance.[77] To be *effective*, performance-based pay must reward those behaviors and outcomes that are related to the strategy of the firm. As discussed previously in this chapter, that means determining correct reward criteria that can be measured in a valid way. To be *accepted*, performance-based pay must be consistent with the institutional and organizational framework in which it exists and also must serve to motivate employees. Not everyone reacts to rewards in the same way, and not all rewards are appropriate for all situations. Failure to recognize the motivational basis for incentive pay plans in a global context may be an important reason for their lack of success.

In summary, it is particularly difficult to design global pay for performance systems that employees will accept and that will reward behaviors and/or performance that are consistent with the strategy of the organization. The wide variation that is found in both institutional and cultural contexts may encourage the adoption of local practices with little regard for how they align strategically. An alternative is that MNE executives focus on creating the right organizational culture, including a common mindset among all employees, no matter where they are located in order to achieve strategic organizational priorities worldwide. They can do this by adopting a *strategic flexibility approach* to compensation, whereby compensation packages consist of three related components: core, crafted, and choice. The *core* section includes compensation forms that signal the corporate global mindset (i.e., whatever is of strategic importance to the MNE). The *crafted* set of compensation elements should reflect conditions at the national business unit (i.e., offer compensation deemed desirable by local employees that is culturally influenced and mandated by law). The *choice* components allow individual employees to select among various forms of total compensation that are important to them and meet their individual needs (e.g., education leave vs. dental insurance), thus providing customization at the individual level. Such an approach allows MNEs to achieve both global integration and local responsiveness with regard to compensation practices.[78]

Compensation of Expatriates and Other International Assignees

A problem particular to global compensation programs is designing effective systems that effectively reward individuals sent on international assignment. As discussed ahead in Chapter 9, the length of these assignments may vary from the traditional expatriate assignment of three to five years, and overseas assignees can be either parent country nationals or third-country nationals. The factors that influence compensation of international assignees include their nationality, their family situation (number and ages of children, work situation of their spouse), differences in exchange rates and rates of inflation, cost-of-living differences, host country laws regarding compensation and benefits, and taxes.

Approaches to and Components of Expatriate Compensation

MNEs use one of three main approaches to expatriate compensation. These are the *host country, global,* and *home country* approaches.[79] Each has its positive and negative aspects with regard to the goals of expatriate compensation, as shown in Table 8.3.

The intention of the *host country* approach is to fit expatriate compensation into the local salary structure. This approach is cost-effective and creates a sense of equity with local nationals. However, it is limited in its ability to attract individuals to international assignments except in cases where the local salary is attractive on a comparative basis or when individuals have a personal interest in living in the country. Worldwide variation and inconsistencies in compensation structures limit the effectiveness of this approach.

The *global* approach bases compensation on an international scale that is applied to expatriates regardless of country of origin.[80] While most appropriate in cases where expatriates move to more than one foreign country and lose contact with home country pay structures, it carries a high cost and can create problems upon return home.[81]

By far, the most common approach to expatriate compensation is the *home country* approach (also called *balance sheet* approach) in which the central idea is to provide the expatriate equivalent purchasing power in the host country in order to maintain an

Table 8.3   Influence of Compensation Approaches on Objectives

Objectives of an International Compensation System	Approach		
	Host Country	Home Country	Global
1. To attract personnel for the international service	−	+	+
2. To be cost-effective	+	−	−
3. To be fair			
with respect to local employees,	+	−	−
with respect to other expatriates from a different nationality in the same location	+	−	+
with respect to other expatriates in another location	−	+	+
4. To facilitate reentry	−	+	−
5. To support the company's international strategy	0	0	0

Source: Adapted from Bonache (2006, p. 161).

Note: + = positive impact, − = negative impact, 0 = irrelevant.

equivalent standard of living to that of his or her home country. This system applies home country scales and deductions and then adjusts through allowances (cost-of-living differential, housing allowances, etc.) to arrive at a net disposable income that should maintain the expatriate's standard of living.[82] According to the 2012 Global Relocation Trends Survey Report, 67% of firms used a home-based approach, with incentives and/or allowances, and 22% used a traditional home-based balance sheet approach. In contrast, only 3% used a host-based approach.[83] The advantage of the home-based approach is that expatriates are equally treated around the world and are kept in line with home country structures so they can more easily be reintegrated. However, inequality among expatriates of different nationalities on the same assignment and with local nationals is a drawback. Recent studies have highlighted the negative impact of the perceived unfairness (on behalf of local nationals) of the pay inequalities between expatriates and local employees, which can affect expatriate adjustment and ultimately, performance.[84] Further, the balance sheet approach is expensive, with expatriates costing two to five times as much as their counterparts at home.[85]

The specific components of an expatriate's compensation can vary widely. However, they fall into four main categories. These are base salary, foreign-service premium, allowances, and benefits.

Base Salary

For employees posted overseas, base pay is the pay they would receive for performing the same job at home or the pay they would receive for the job in the host country (depending on the general compensation approach). Base pay serves as the benchmark for other forms of discretionary compensation, such as merit pay, bonuses, and incentives, and can vary substantially depending on where a company's headquarters is located. However, an example of logistical challenges faced by MNEs is protecting expatriates' net salaries from variations in tax rates. For example, the U.S. maximum marginal tax rate is 31%, compared to 45% in Spain, 53% in Germany and 65% in Japan. Thus to maintain the same base salary, U.S. expatriates must receive higher gross salaries in these host locations.[86]

Foreign Service Inducements

There are four types of foreign service inducements, with each having a different goal.[87] *Foreign service premiums* are given to encourage employees to accept assignments in a foreign country. Foreign service premiums vary depending on base salary and typically range from 10% to 30% of base. *Mobility premiums* are lump-sum bonuses made to employees for their willingness to relocate between international posts. *Hardship premiums* are lump-sum cash bonuses paid for the adversity encountered in living in locations where living conditions are difficult, unhealthy, or where physical hardships are extreme. The rate for selected countries is shown in Table 8.4. The fourth type of foreign service inducement is awarded for working in situations where there is threat of physical harm due to civil disobedience, civil war, terrorism, and war. Depending on the level of danger, differentials range from 5% to 35% of base salary.

Table 8.4 Hardship Differential (Selected Locations) Percentage of Base Compensation

Country (City)	Rate
Afghanistan (Kabul)	35%
Azerbaijan (Baku)	20%
Belize (Belize City)	15%
Brazil (Rio de Janeiro)	10%
Cameroon (Yaoundé)	25%
China (Beijing)	15%
Korea (Pusan)	5%
Ghana (Accra)	20%
Greece (Athens)	5%
India (Mumbai)	20%
Iraq (Bagdad)	35%
Malaysia (Kuala Lampur)	10%
Mexico (Monterrey)	5%
Nigeria (Lagos)	25%
Pakistan (Islamabad)	25%
Russia (Moscow)	15%
Saudi Arabia (Jeddah)	20%
South Africa (Johannesburg)	10%
Turkey (Istanbul)	10%
Vietnam (Hanoi)	20%

Source: U.S. Department of State, Bureau of Administration (2011).

Allowances

Allowances are discretionary payments made to employees to promote a sense of well-being in them and their families, to maintain their standard of living, and to protect their purchasing power.[88] They can include cost-of-living allowances; exchange rate protection; housing allowance; home-leave allowance; rest, relaxation, and rehabilitation allowance; education allowance for children; relocation allowance; and spouse support allowance.

Cost-of-living allowances (COLAs) are the most widely used discretionary allowance and compensate expatriates for differences in living expense between the home and host country. (As of 2008–2009, as many as 93% of long-term assignees received a COLA.)[89] COLAs are calculated based on the cost of a typical market basket of goods and services in different locations. The indexes shown in Table 8.5 are based on expatriate spending across 13 broad categories.

Because of price volatility and different spending patterns among expatriates from different countries, calculating comparative cost-of-living indexes can be complicated and need to be updated regularly. A number of global relocation organizations provide

Table 8.5 Cost-of-Living Comparisons

City	Index
Tokyo, Japan	126.03
Oslo, Norway	123.74
London, United Kingdom	118.23
Moscow, Russia	113.41
Paris, France	112.38
Vienna, Austria	109.68
Rome, Italy	107.29
Hong Kong, China	103.43
New York, United States	100.00
Berlin, Germany	98.18
Singapore	94.60
Vancouver, Canada	93.48
Athens, Greece	86.59
Auckland, New Zealand	80.71
Mexico City, Mexico	76.13
Kuala Lumpur, Malaysia	71.82
New Delhi, India	71.40
Shanghai, China	68.48
Johannesburg, South Africa	64.51
Islamabad, Pakistan	58.33

Note: Based on expatriate spending patterns across a market basket of 13 categories of goods (2010).

cost-of-living calculations. In addition to COLAs, *exchange rate protection* is offered by an increasing number (80% according to the most recent Global Relocation Trends Survey Report) of organizations because of the volatility in the foreign exchange markets. Firms who offer this allowance use a variety of methods with most (46%) making periodic adjustments for rate fluctuations. For example, if the exchange rate changes more than 10% within three months, an adjustment might be made. Others used a split-pay method where some pay is made in the home country currency, while a minority used a combination of methods.[90]

Housing allowances are provided in order that employees can maintain their home country living standards or in some cases receive accommodation that is equivalent to local employees and peers. Housing issues are typically dealt with on a case-by-case basis. These allowances are either paid on an actual or assessed basis. Alternative to allowances, such as company-provided housing, fixed-housing allowances, or a deduction of a fixed percentage of income with actual costs paid for by the firm are also common. And, the *home-leave allowance* and *rest, relaxation, and rehabilitation allowance* are designed to allow expatriates to make trips home to maintain business or family ties. For those in hardship or danger areas, they may need time away to recover from the rigors of the environment. Home-leave allowance is typically restricted to trips home, but some firms allow its use for foreign travel. These benefits typically apply to both the expatriate and family members.[91] Another family issue involves *education allowances for children* that are provided by a significant percentage of MNEs[92] and cover costs such as tuition, books, fees, supplies, room and board, and uniforms. The level of education support provided is dependent of the adequacy of local schools, transportation issues, and so on. The ability of the children of expatriates to keep pace with their contemporaries in the home country is an important issue for many expatriate families.

Relocation allowances cover the costs of moving and storage of household goods and can also cover the costs of temporary housing while searching for permanent accommodation. In addition, it is often necessary (because of differences in electric current) or more cost-effective to buy new electrical appliances in the foreign location. Finally, travel expenses for the expatriate and family to the new location are covered in this category. The increase in dual-career couples has created the need to add *spouse assistance* to many expatriate compensation plans. Spousal careers are often disrupted and income lost as a result of overseas assignments. While the provision of this allowance is not common, for most MNEs the need for career support of spouses is growing (see Chapter 9).

Benefits

The ability to transport pension plans, medical coverage, and social security programs between countries is very limited, and national practices vary considerably. Some countries do not allow individuals to opt out of local plans even if they are on temporary assignment. While PCNs are typically well looked after by their MNE employers, the issues for TCNs are more complicated because of the inability to transfer benefits and their lack of a "home country" base. The basic decisions for MNEs regarding global benefits plans are: Should home country plans be maintained? What are the tax implications of this decision? Must or should the expatriate enroll in local benefits programs? Is making up any difference in local versus home benefits an option? What options for social security benefits are available or best for the expatriate?

Global Tax Issues

The nature of expatriate assignments makes many expatriates subject to tax regimes in more than one jurisdiction. Countries differ in the determination of tax obligations in that some countries tax the income of residents while others, such as the United States, tax their citizens, regardless of where they reside. Tax treaties or conventions between governments allow certain credits, deductions, exemptions, and reduced foreign tax rates. However, depending on tax rates, expatriates may be obligated for more tax than at home, and in some cases, double taxation cannot be avoided. Other than a laissez fare (the MNE does not provide assistance with tax issues) or ad hoc (every case is handled individually, and no common policy exists) methods there are two basic approaches to expatriate tax issues, *tax equalization* and *tax protection*.

Tax equalization programs provide that expatriates neither gain nor lose as a result of taxation while on assignment. MNEs withhold taxes in an amount approximate to what the expatriate would pay at home (commonly referred to as "hypothetical tax") and the company pays the actual taxes owed in both the home and host country. If the overall tax obligation is higher than the tax obligation had the expatriate stayed in his or her home country, the employer covers the difference. If the tax obligation is lower, the employer collects the difference. This approach is by far the most common among MNEs.[93] Under *tax protection* plans, employees pay their taxes based on the home and host country tax laws. As with the tax equalization approach, if their overall tax obligation exceeds the taxes they would have owed in their home country, the employer reimburses them for the excess amount. In contrast to tax equalization, employees with lower tax obligations get to pocket the resulting tax benefit. Thus employees are "protected" against higher taxes The complexity of global tax issues requires a significant amount of country-specific expertise and makes this issue a likely candidate for outsourcing.

Compensation in Short-Term Assignments

Compensation programs for short-term international assignments involve considerably fewer elements than expatriate compensation. However, the occurrence of these assignments is increasing. While less expensive than expatriate assignments, shorter assignments present additional areas of expense that require attention. Commuter assignments, where employees remain on assignment six weeks or less, are often treated like business travel. Therefore, the issues involve reimbursement for accommodation, transportation, and subsistence. One source of guidance for appropriate travel allowances are rates that are published by the governments of many countries.[94] For intermediate-term assignments of greater than six weeks but less than a permanent transfer, the compensation mix will need to shift to include more elements associated with expatriate compensation. However, firms have very little experience with these types of assignments, and best practices have yet to be established. It is likely that the particular compensation program in these circumstances will depend a good deal on the employee, the goal of the assignment, and the relationship that the employee has with the organization.

Chapter Summary

This chapter examines performance management and compensation in a global context. Performance management involves the evaluation and continuous improvement of individuals and has both evaluative and developmental components. Central to performance management systems is the performance appraisal process. Both institutional and cultural factors influence the implantation of performance management systems on a global basis. In addition, the fact that MNEs operate in a variety of locations creates an additional set of performance management issues, such as differences in firm versus subsidiary goals, consistency of criteria and data, and the geographic separation of organizational units. The unique role of expatriate managers affects the ability of organizations to design an effective performance management system for them. Key issues are who conducts the performance appraisal, what criteria are assessed, and how should the appraisal be conducted.

One of the key linkages between performance management and other aspects of global HRM is the relationship to organizational rewards in the form of compensation systems. National compensation systems are influenced by such factors as the social contract, labor relations, ownership structures, and the degree of management autonomy. Also, the institutional and cultural context influences the extent to which compensation systems are seen to be legitimate and acceptable in society. This influence is particularly apparent with regard to performance-based pay. As in performance management, the compensation of expatriates presents an additional set of issues. Approaches to expatriate compensation are host country, global, and home country models with the latter being the most popular. Expatriate compensation systems need to be cost-effective but at the same time attract individuals to international assignments and appropriately reward these employees. Myriad factors are involved in expatriate compensation, but benefits and tax issues are potentially the most difficult to manage.

Questions for Discussion

1. Compare and contrast the evaluative and development components of performance management systems.

2. Explain the effect of cultural and institutional factors of performance management.

3. Outline the key issues in the performance evaluation of expatriates.

4. Describe the key factors affecting compensation practices in various countries.

5. Compare the advantages and disadvantages of the main approaches to expatriate compensation.

Notes

1. Imam bayildi (translated from Turkish as the imam [priest] fainted, presumably because the dish was so good) consists of braised aubergine (eggplant) stuffed with onion, garlic, and tomatoes, then simmered in olive oil.
2. Bernthal, Rogers, & Smith (2003).
3. Cascio (2006).
4. Boselie, Farndale, & Paauwe (2012).
5. Beer (1981).
6. Varma & Budhwar (2011).
7. Varma & Budhwar (2011).
8. See DeNisi (1996) for a discussion.
9. Cascio (2006).
10. Varma, Budhwar, & DeNisi (2008); Varma & Budhwar (2011).
11. Varma & Budhwar (2011).
12. Aycan (2005).
13. Seddon (1987).
14. Cascio (2012).
15. Boselie, Farndale, & Paauwe (2012).
16. Fletcher & Perry (2001).
17. Huo & Von Glinow (1995).
18. Mendonca & Kanungo (1996).
19. Fletcher & Perry (2001); Bailey, Chen, & Dou (1997).
20. Triandis (1994).
21. Murphy & DeNisi (2008).
22. Festing & Barzantny (2008).
23. Festing & Barzantny (2008).
24. Aycan (2005).
25. Oddou & Mendenhall (2000).
26. See Pucik (1985).
27. See Varma & Budhwar (2011).
28. Murphy & DeNisi (2008).
29. Toh & DeNisi (2007).
30. See Claus & Briscoe (2009) for a discussion.
31. See Chapter 9 this volume.
32. See Murphy and Cleveland (1991) for an in depth discussion of performance appraisal issues.
33. Dessler (2011).
34. Dessler (2011).
35. Gregersen, Hite, & Black (1996).
36. Global Relocation Trends Survey Report (2011).
37. Caligiuri (2006).

38. Dessler (2011).
39. Bernardin & Cascio (1984).
40. Thomas & Lazarova (2008).
41. Gregersen, Hite, & Black (1996).
42. For a discussion of reducing bias in performance appraisal see Wilson & Jones (2008).
43. Simmons (2003) *Training & Development, 7* (9), 47–53.
44. See Thomas & Ravlin (1995).
45. Cardy & Dobbins (1994).
46. Dessler (2011).
47. Murphy & Cleveland (1991).
48. Gregersen, Hite, & Black (1996).
49. Dessler (2011).
50. Oddou & Mendenhall (2000).
51. Gregersen, Hite, & Black (1996).
52. Shih, Chiang, & Kim (2005).
53. Oddou & Mendenhall (2000).
54. Fenwick (2004).
55. Evans, Pucik, & Björkman (2011).
56. Dessler (2011).
57. Adapted from Milkovich & Newman (2008).
58. Schuler & Rogovsky (1998); Gomez-Mejia & Welbourne (1991).
59. Newman and Nollen (1996).
60. Freeman & Katz (1994).
61. Marín (2008).
62. BLS News Release USDL-11-1778: International comparison of hourly compensation costs in manufacturing, 2010; available at http://www.bls.gov/news.release/pdf/ichcc .pdf.
63. Vernon (2011).
64. Milkovich & Newman (2008).
65. Festing, Engle, Dowling, & Sahakiants (2012).
66. Vernon (2011).
67. BLS News Release USDL-11-1778: International comparison of hourly compensation costs in manufacturing, 2010; available at http://www.bls.gov/news.release/pdf/ichcc .pdf.
68. Steers, Shin, & Ungson (1989).
69. Milkovich & Newman (2008).
70. Zhou & Martocchio (2001).
71. Pendleton & Poutsma (2012).
72. Roth & O'Donnell (1996).
73. See DiMaggio & Powell (1983).
74. Gomez-Mejia & Wiseman (1997).
75. Dessler (2011); Salimäki & Heneman (2008).
76. *Compensation & Benefits Review* (2003, June).
77. Salimäki & Heneman (2008).
78. Milkovich & Bloom (1998).
79. See Bonache (2006) for a discussion of these three approaches.
80. Freeman & Kane (1995).
81. See also O'Reilly (1996).

82. Bonache (2006).
83. Global Relocation Trends Survey Report (2012).
84. Toh & DeNisi (2003, 2007).
85. Reynolds (1997).
86. Bonache & Stripe (2012).
87. Burnett & Von Glinow (2011).
88. Burnett & Von Glinow (2011).
89. OCR Worldwide (2008, 2009); cited in Bonache & Stripe (2012).
90. Global Relocation Trends Survey Report (2011).
91. Burnett & Von Glinow (2011).
92. Burnett & Von Glinow (2011).
93. Latta & Danielson (2003).
94. Meyskens, Von Glinow, Werther, & Clarke (2009).

International Mobility and Global Careers

LEARNING OBJECTIVES

After reading this chapter you should be able to

- describe the impact of a global assignment on an individual's career,
- outline the types of global mobility assignments,
- discuss the factors associated with adjusting to a foreign environment,
- describe the special issue associated with women expatriates and dual-career couples, and
- outline the elements of an effective global mobility program.

The Cantonese Lunch

Well that was three hours of my life I can never get back, thought Mike Faraday as he walked toward the Tsim Sha Tsui MTR Station from the Golden Pearl Seafood Restaurant where he had just attended his first "Cantonese Lunch." It had sounded like a good idea when he read on the expat website about the opportunity to learn Cantonese while having lunch at a different Hong Kong Restaurant each week. The food had been fabulous—that is, when he could snag some of it using his novice chopstick skills. An amazing variety of dishes had whizzed around in front of him on the turntable (which he had learned to call a "lazy Susan" as a kid in the United States) in the centre of the table of ten. He knew that the other "spouses" of expatriate managers were most likely to be wives. However, he was surprised at how quickly the language lesson had been dispensed with. Despite the organizer's protest that they should introduce Cantonese words, the conversation quickly turned to where to buy favorite foods from "back home" and how to deal with the Filipina maid.

As he changed to the Island Line at Admiralty, he reflected on the decision of his wife Meredith to take the job as senior vice president for Asia for Financebank. It had hardly required any discussion at all, he remembered. He had just lost his job as a securities trader in the Wall Street meltdown, and Meredith, unlike many of her colleagues, was not only going to survive the banking crisis, she would be one of the most senior women in the firm. The opportunity was just too good to pass up, and within a month they were in Hong Kong.

Mike got off the train at Sheung Wan; the heat and humidity pressed down on him unmercifully as he began the hike up to their apartment in the midlevels. We've been here four months now. Meredith is so busy I rarely see her and I still haven't any idea what I'm doing here. This trailing spouse business isn't as much fun as I thought it might be. I hope there is still some vodka in the fridge!

Introduction

A period of time living and working in a foreign country can be exciting but also challenging for the individual, for his or her family, and also for the employer. Whether or not an overseas work experience has a positive effect on an employee's career, benefits his or her family, and also achieves the desired organizational outcomes depends on a wide variety of factors. These include the characteristics of the overseas work, organizational differences, and also factors associated with the employee and his or her family.[1] In addition, how a person views his or her career is an important consideration. The way in which people view their career has been changing from an upward progression of job experiences to a more subjective sense of where one is going in one's work life.[2] The characteristics of a career in the age of globalization require that we consider global mobility from the perspective of both the individual and the organization.[3]

Global Careers

Traditionally a global career involved one or several long-term expatriate assignments, each of which might last several years and included relocation of the expatriate's family. There was a fairly standard expatriation support package in terms of relocation assistance and compensation. The typical expatriate was male, married, with his family joining him on his posting. These assignments were not truly integrated into most employees' career progression, the returnees were often rather dissatisfied with their positions upon returning home because these positions rarely offered the opportunity to use their newly acquired international management skills. This led to higher than expected turnover among expatriates.[4]

Because of large-scale changes in economic activity as well as migration trends, more companies are now doing business in more different countries, some of which were previously inaccessible.[5] Therefore, additional globally mobile people are needed. Many organizations are reconsidering long-term expatriation to solve this need, because of the cost involved, and are experimenting with other more flexible mobility types, such as the short-term assignments, commuting, frequent travelers, and virtual assignments.[6] Organizations are also introducing more mobility across organizational units, including mobility from host locations to the head office (called inpatriates, see Chapter 6).[7] In addition, we are seeing an increase in individually initiated mobility (self-initiated assignments) as the global market place puts greater value on international experience and as restrictions on mobility and migration are lifted or eased around the world.[8] Finally in some cases, a global career may not even include international mobility. For example, some employees have international responsibilities without relocating, as they interact with clients or partners internationally and work on global projects in virtual teams.[9]

Global Assignment Types

Despite changes in the international business environment, traditional expatriation continues to be the dominant type of global mobility. While there have been noticeable changes in the ratio of long-term and short-term expatriate postings, long-term expatriate positions remain strategically important for MNEs as they are a key way of transferring expertise and controlling and coordinating their networks of subsidiaries.

Traditional Long-Term Expatriation

As discussed in Chapter 6, the key reasons for corporate expatriation include filling a skills gap and organizational and managerial development. Traditionally, expatriate postings have lasted for at least a year, but 3 to 5 years has been a much more common assignment duration. Expatriates have been well supported logistically before and during their assignments, and many earn significantly more during assignment than in their domestic positions, receiving standard expatriate supplements, such as housing allowances and cost-of-living adjustments.[10]

Advances in transportation and technology combined with increasing costs of managing *traditional* assignments (especially in conditions of economic downturn, such as the 2008 global financial crisis) led to speculation that long-term assignments would decline. However, these predictions have proven to be largely unfounded. While exact percentages differ year by year, the majority of companies do not report a reduction of traditional assignments, nor do they expect that a reduction is imminent.[11] In 2012, 64% of MNEs reported an increase in their expatriate population in the preceding year. For another 25% of MNEs, the expatriate population stayed the same. Further, only 9% of organizations expected a decrease in expatriate assignments, whereas 63% expected an increase.[12]

According to the 2010 Global Relocation Trends Survey Report, 65% of expatriate assignments are between 1 and 4 years, and according to the Economist Intelligence Unit, 70% of assignments are between 1 and 5 years. However, there are signs suggesting that what is understood as *long-term* may be changing, with a clear tendency toward shortening assignment length.[13] Other changes include a reduction in expatriate benefits[14] along with a change in the demographic profile of expatriates.[15] In addition, MNEs have introduced a portfolio of alternate types of international assignments that are shorter in duration (often involving considerable travel and rarely including family relocation)[16] as a means of satisfying some of their global mobility needs.[17]

Table 9.1 shows the current profile of expatriates according to the 2012 Global Relocation Trends Survey Report.[18] As shown, most expatriates are still male (80%), but the number of female assignments has been rising steadily (from less than 5% in in 1984[19] to 20% at present). The majority is aged 30 to 49 years (65% in 2012 compared to 72% in 2010 and 68% in 2008), but recent data have indicated an increase in the number of expatriates aged 20 to 29. Most are married, but that percentage has been declining steadily, from 70% in 2000 to 60% in 2012. Perhaps not surprising is that male expatriates are much more likely to be married or attached (70% of all male

Table 9.1   The International Assignee Population

- Sixty-four percent of respondents believed the number of international assignees increased in 2011, the biggest increase since the 2008 report and much higher than the historical average of 45%; 63% expected the number to increase in 2012, higher than the historical average of 58%.
- Twenty-one percent of all employees had previous international assignee experience, which is significantly higher than 12% in the 2011 report; 11% of current international assignees were new hires, 3% higher than last year.
- Twenty percent of international assignees were female; the historical average is 16%.
- Thirteen percent of international assignees were 20 to 29 years old; 31% 30 to 39 years old; 34% were 40 to 49 years old; and 19% were 50 to 59 years old, the same as in the 2011 report, which was second highest in the history of this report.
- Sixty percent of international assignees were married, compared to a historical average of 67%.
- Only 43% of international assignees had children accompanying them during the assignment, an all-time low and 4% lower than the 47% in the 2011 report.
- The percentage of single male assignees, 25%, increased by 7% over the 2011 report.

(Continued)

Table 9.1 (Continued)

- Spouses and partners accompanied 81% of international assignees; this percentage is the same as the historical average. Thirty-eight percent of single-status assignments were long term (1 year or more) and 62% were short term (3 to 12 months). This compares to 39% and 61% respectively in 2011.
- Forty-nine percent of spouses and partners were employed before an assignment but not during; 6% were employed during an assignment, but not before; 12% were employed both before and during the assignment.

Source: 2012 Global Relocation Trends Survey report, published by Brookfield Global Relocation Services, LLC.

assignees) than their female counterparts (42% of all female assignees). The majority of married expatriates are accompanied by their spouse (81% in 2012) and children (43%). The 2012 Global Relocation Trends Survey Report also notes that the percentage of expatriates accompanied by children has been declining slowly over time (the historical average is 56%).[20]

Alternate Forms of Corporate Global Assignments

Short-Term Assignments

Definitions of short-term assignments vary, but they typically last from 3 months to a year and rarely involve relocation of family members. These postings typically involve project work, skill/technology transfer, or problem solving but are sometimes simply a shorter term posting. The employee salary, pension, and social security as well as career aspects are handled in the home country.

Commuter Assignments

A commuter assignment involves a person living in one country but doing most of his or her work in another, which involves regular travel between home and host destination, usually weekly or biweekly.[21] These assignments typically involve weekdays working abroad and returning home for the weekend.

International Business Travelers

International business travelers are employees who take multiple short international business trips to various international locations. While international commuting is more structured, there is no regular rhythm to international business travel.[22] The most common reasons for these assignments are knowledge transfer, negotiations, meetings, conferences, or discussions. Trips may last for up to 3 weeks and may involve multiple countries.[23]

Flexpatriates[24] *and Other Arrangements*

Flexpatriate is a catch-all term sometimes used to indicate employees with domestically-based jobs but who also travel extensively and work in alternating locations (i.e., frequent travelers, commuters, and short-term assignments).[25] Another type of work that has been added to the group of global experiences is *virtual work*. Most frequently this refers to being actively engaged in cross-border virtual teams, but it can mean any domestic job with substantial international responsibilities. These assignments do not involve relocation, nor do they involve extensive (or even any) international travel. Employees work from their home office but have to collaborate with (or sometimes manage) colleagues from different national locations, across (several) time zones, languages, and cultural barriers.

Self-Initiated Global Mobility

Another category of global mobility involves individuals who give themselves an overseas assignment for personal or professional development. They simply go to a foreign country without a preset contract or posting in search of better professional opportunities, or they move because of personal reasons and find a job as a consequence. Their move is not supported nor orchestrated by anyone else. These self-initiated expatriates are not migrants, as they intend this "assignment" to be temporary. The skills they gain are for their own benefit but may ultimately be used to advantage by an organization when they return.[26]

Adjustment to the Foreign Culture

An important consideration in global assignments is the ability of the individual to adjust, not only to their new job but also to the new and often very different cultural environment. Adjustment is a condition consisting of a person's relationship with their environment in which their needs are satisfied and the ability to meet physical and social demands exists.[27] Adjustment can include psychological and emotional well-being and satisfaction as well as the ability to fit in, to acquire culturally appropriate skills, and to interact effectively in the host culture.[28] In addition to this general adjustment, expatriates must adjust to new work roles and family role demands.[29]

The challenges faced by individuals in adjusting to a new cultural context are complex, and different individuals might employ very different coping mechanisms. However, it has been suggested that for many people adjusting to a new cultural context progresses through a cycle of adjustment that follows a U-shaped pattern,[30] which is extended to a W shape when repatriation is considered.[31] This adjustment cycle is presented in Figure 9.1.

According to the model shown in Figure 9.1, expatriates (and their family members) progress through the four phases of honeymoon, culture shock, adjustment, and finally mastery. In the *honeymoon* stage, everything is new and interesting, and the environment intrigues the expatriate and family in much the same way as if they were a tourists. There is a sense of adventure and excitement. At the *culture shock* stage, individuals become frustrated and confused because the environment is not providing

Figure 9.1   The U-Curve of Cross-Cultural Adjustment

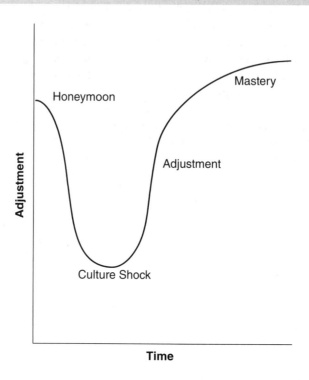

familiar cues. The realities of everyday life have become apparent, and the novelty has worn off. At the *adjustment* stage, the expatriate and family begin to understand cultural differences, learn the ways to get things done, and begin to settle into the rhythm of daily living in the foreign country. Eventually, people can achieve the *mastery* stage and become able to function in the new culture almost as well as at home. Not all individuals achieve mastery in their new culture. Some return home early, whereas others complete their assignment but without really adjusting. While this model is useful as a guide to possible phases of adjustment, neither the various phases nor the time parameters have been supported by research.[32] In addition, different patterns of adjustment have been found for work and nonwork environments and for expatriates and their spouses.[33] And of course the model does not explain how and why people adjust.

Predictors of Adjustment

Family Considerations

The strongest predictor of expatriate adjustment is the extent to which their partner adjusts.[34] And the partner, particularly if he or she is not working, often has a more difficult time making the transition to the new environment than the expatriate.[35] There are several reasons for this. First, while the expatriate may have a work environment that is somewhat similar to that in the parent country, with a social network of host nationals and other expatriates, other family members are completely immersed in the new surroundings in their day-to-day life, with more limited opportunities to establish a social network. Contributing to the problem is that the partner may have given up a career in support of the expatriate's move, creating issues around self-worth and identity. In moving, children may lose friends and ties to the community that may be critical to their identity formulation, thus affecting their feelings of security and well-being and creating stress.[36] And, just when the partner needs the expatriate to help with adjustment issues at home, he or she is faced with the challenges of a new job, often with long hours and extensive travel requirements.

According to the 2012 Global Relocation Trends Survey Report, when asked of the most critical family challenges on assignment, MNEs highlight adjustment (94%) and spouse or partner resistance to relocation (88%). Spouse or partner dissatisfaction during the assignment and other family concerns were given as causes of 38% of assignment failures. Further, the two most common reasons for assignment refusal were family concerns and spousal careers.[37] It is important to note that these overall results may not apply equally across contexts. For example, Japanese expatriates are less likely to list inability of the spouse to adjust as a factor because of the role and status of the spouse in Japanese society.[38] And Chinese expatriates in Hong Kong are generally not permitted to bring their spouse or children along.[39]

With the increased number of women taking global assignments, it is now more probable that the trailing spouse will be male. However, expatriate enclaves, social support networks, and the like have been established around the fact that most accompanying partners were female. As shown in the case that opened this chapter, this can make male trailing spouses feel uncomfortable or disinterested in the activities of these groups,[40] and appropriate support activities for them may be difficult to find.[41] Research indicates that while 70% of female accompanying partners feel included in socializing that takes place with other global assignees, less than 40% of male accompanying partners feel that way.[42] Some male trailing spouses feel uncomfortable when put in a position that does not allow them to contribute to the household income. And male accompanying partners report being perceived as atypical by others in the host country, which can cause them to reexamine their identity, even if they themselves have no gender-role concerns.[43]

Individual Factors

In an effort to provide appropriate expatriate selection and training recommendations, numerous individual factors related to adjustment have been studied. This search for an *expatriate type* of person has been inconclusive. Some personality characteristics, such as openness to new experience, seem to be important predictors, but others do not.[44] And there is no consensus with regard to which of the many skills, such as adaptability or relational ability, are most important.[45] We do know that certain demographic characteristics, such as age, tenure, and education level, are positively related to adjustment, but the reasons for this relationship are unclear.[46] However, as indicators of life stage, career stage, or family situation, and in combination with organizational and environmental factors, these individual differences can be useful in understanding adjustment. It may be possible to create a profile of an individual based on their characteristics and match that profile to the specific overseas assignment to understand and predict adjustment issues.

Both ability in the foreign language and previous international experience would seem to be logical predictors of adjustment. It turns out however that this intuitively appealing idea does not hold up in all situations. It seems clear that the individuals highly fluent in the foreign language are more likely to interact with host nationals[47] and in some cases are better adjusted.[48] However, it is probably not fluency in the foreign language itself, but the willingness to interact with and seek support from local nationals (helped along by language fluency) that is the critical factor in adjustment.[49]

Another consideration is previous overseas experience that individuals may have. Some research has found that the amount of previous overseas experience helps with adjustment,[50] but other research indicates it can have a negative effect on job attitudes.[51] It is probably the quality of the overseas experience as opposed to the quantity that is important. In order for previous experience in another culture to have a positive effect that carries over to a new situation, individuals must undergo self-development in the way they think about and act toward other cultures.[52] This development requires a significant amount of engagement with the foreign culture.[53] For some people, this could occur in a small amount of time in another culture, but others may never really engage despite having spent a long time overseas. For both language fluency and previous international experience, the effect on adjustment is likely influenced by organizational and environmental factors, such as how different the foreign culture is, the organizational level of the expatriate, and the amount of interaction with locals that is required by the assignment.[54]

Job and Organizational Factors

It is important to remember that an overseas assignment involves taking on a new job or role in the organization as well as a move to a foreign location. Organizational roles are the set of behaviors associated with a particular position. An expatriate role is defined by both the expectations of the home organization as well as the local context. In addition to the conflicting signals sent by the home and host organizations, the expatriate role is characterized by lack of clarity with regard to appropriate behavior and new behavior required by the local context. Role ambiguity, role novelty, and role conflict have a negative effect on the ability of expatriates to adjust and on their job satisfaction.[55] Expatriates who effectively adjust to their new role are more likely to remain on assignment the agreed upon length of time,[56] and the amount of discretion expatriates have in conducting their role is important to helping them adjust.[57] Allowing individuals freedom to adjust their work role to the situation and to their preferred way of behaving is an important element in expatriate adjustment.

Another important organizational factor related to adjustment is the level of the individual in the organization. The organizational level of individuals influences the type of strategies available to them to deal with the effects of taking on a new role.[58] However, it is not entirely clear how organizational level affects adjustment. For example, expatriates at higher levels tend to have higher job satisfaction and are more likely to remain on assignment. However, they also often have more difficulty in certain aspects of adjustment, perhaps because their assignments are more challenging.[59]

Yet another organizational factor related to expatriate adjustment is the organizational support provided to expatriates. It is tempting to think that more organizational support is simply better. The level of support activities, such as visits to and communications with the parent company, has indeed been shown to have a positive effect on some aspects of adjustment.[60] And the overall level of company assistance has been shown to be related to job satisfaction as well.[61] However, the effect of the level and type of organizational support is more complicated. For example, male accompanying partners may need a very different type of support compared to female accompanying partners.[62] In short, organizational support requirements are related to the needs and expectations of each employee and their situation. Thus the effectiveness of a particular support program depends a great deal on the employee and his or her specific situation and relationship with the organization.[63]

Adjustment and Other Challenges in Alternate Assignment Types

Alternate assignment types, such as commuter assignments, frequent travelers, virtual assignments and the like, although typically motivated by cost savings to the organization, would seem to solve many of the problems associated with the typical expatriate assignment, such as expatriate adjustment, family relocation, dual-career couples, and so on. However, neither managers nor researchers have enough experience with these kinds of assignments to know with any sense of certainty if they offer an improvement over traditional expatriation.[64] While many of the challenges of expatriation associated with relocation are eliminated, these global road warriors face a whole new set of challenges. They are frequently absent from home and family, which can have negative effects on their relationship with their partner and with children. For example, familial separation is often associated with stress and higher divorce rates as well as higher incidence of alcoholism.[65] Additionally, their work roles often have domestic aspects that cannot be neglected while they travel. And of course, all the negative aspects of frequent travel, such as waiting at airports, lack of sleep and exercise, poor diet, time zone differences, and so on can take a heavy toll.[66] Even the idea that adjustment issues are minimized might be challenged. In these types of mobility assignments, the employee is often confronted with multiple foreign environments to which he or she is expected to adapt. Adapting one's perspective and behavior on each occasion may be a very different skill set from that required of the traditional expatriate.[67] And it is unlikely that shorter assignments, with limited involvement in different cultural contexts, will be particularly helpful in terms of developing an international perspective, which is a key positive outcome of traditional overseas postings.[68]

Unlike expatriation, alternate assignment types are rarely supported by the organization, and HR departments are less consistently involved in managing them. For example, despite having to work with employees from different cultures, these assignees are rarely offered any form of cross-cultural training.[69] They are typically offered limited destination services, may have to stay in hotels for extended periods of time, and the financial terms and taxation-related terms of their assignments may be decided at hoc, and so on.[70] Perhaps because of their newness, few MNEs have developed formal policies for alternate assignments. Indeed, while most organizations (96% as of the latest data available) have policies in place for long-term assignments and short-term assignments (86%), alternate assignment types get much less attention, with about a third of MNEs having policies on commuter assignments and only 25% having policies on extended international business travel in 2012. And policies on virtual teamwork are the exception rather than the rule (3%–7% in 2012).[71] Performance management of these assignments is also an emerging challenge given their often simultaneous responsibilities in multiple MNE locations. It appears that while organizations embrace the flexibility such assignments provide, they are not entirely clear about their real value or cost.[72]

Women on Overseas Assignments

Almost twenty years ago predictions were that the number of women expatriates would increase because of a shortage of qualified men, legal and social pressure for equal opportunity, the increasing familiarity with women in management positions, and the increasing ability (because of changing company attitudes) of women to self-select for an overseas assignment.[73] However, while the proportion of women has been rising, it seems to have plateaued around 20%.[74] This is in contrast to the percentage of women in management positions, which is reported at between 25% to 45%.[75] The low percentage of women on overseas assignment seems to have little to do with their performance. Women perform as well as their male counterparts even in environments considered unfriendly to female managers.[76] And in some cases, their uniqueness may actually be an advantage.[77] The reasons for the low percentage of female expatriates fall into four categories: *perceptions* regarding their willingness to accept an overseas assignment, work family balance issues, host country national attitudes, and organizational factors.

The perception that women are unwilling to take up international postings is fairly common.[78] It is also often disputed.[79] There is no clear evidence in support of either position. What we do know is that women have a similar desire to have an international career compared to their male counterparts.[80] Their willingness to accept a foreign assignment is influenced by a number of factors. For example, the location (specifically the level of development of the country and political risk), the perceived benefits of the assignment to personal growth, career advancement, and security all seem to have an effect on women's willingness to accept an overseas assignment.

Family factors form another set of considerations. For example, women with children and in dual-career relationships are *perceived* to be less likely to accept global assignments. Family issues are also considered to be a bigger challenge for female expatriates. While work-life balance issues are equally relevant to men and women, societal norms often cast women as the primary care givers for children, and thus female expatriates may feel pressure to take on a greater share of the work associated with children's relocation, education, and so on. And male trailing spouses are typically more concerned with continuing their careers in the host country than are their female counterparts.[81] However, it may be that the importance of career can outweigh gender-based family issues. A recent study found that the more important a woman's career role was to her, the more likely she was to accept an international assignment. In contrast, there was no relationship between the importance she attaches to her roles as partner and parent and her willingness for assignment.[82]

Another core issue for female expatriates is the extent to which women actually face greater difficulty overseas than men. While it is true that negative attitudes toward women expatriates, discrimination against them and preferences for dealing with male executives, do exist in some countries,[83] women expatriates seem to find ways to overcome these issues over time.[84] Overcoming this resistance may have its costs, with women in countries with low female workforce participation and a low percentage of women managers reporting being less adjusted to the nonwork aspects of their life.[85] But research has shown that, even in culturally tough countries, the longer female expatriates spend on assignment the less likely they are to think that local prejudices inhibit their effectiveness. While women can overcome the additional challenges associated with an overseas assignment, the *perception* of these additional difficulties may nevertheless influence decisions by both organizations and potential assignees.[86]

Finally, women may have low expectations of their opportunity for being selected and therefore fail to actively pursue opportunities for overseas placement.[87] There are two factors that may be relevant here: the quality of the relationship between female subordinates and predominantly male supervisors and negative attitudes of senior managers with regard to the participation of women on international assignment. First, individual characteristics, such as gender, age, race, educational background, and so on can be related to the quality of the relationship between a subordinate and his or her supervisor. It is certainly possible that this informal relationship is important in selecting overseas assignees and that women are disadvantaged as a result.[88] Second, senior managers in the home country are often responsible for selecting overseas assignees. And surveys of these managers continue to show that they mistakenly believe that women are not interested in international assignments, will not be accepted by local nationals, or are not as qualified as their male counterparts. Supervisors are also more likely to think that women in dual-career relationships are less likely to accept a foreign posting. It may be that these senior management attitudes are the factor that is the most resistant to change.

Impact of Overseas Assignments

Overseas assignments have important outcomes for the expatriate, for his or her family, and for the organization. The effect of an overseas assignment on the longer-term career of managers may depend in part on how a person views his or her career. Reports are common that instead of moving up the career ladder, expatriates are often neglected upon their return, put in a holding pattern, and not valued for their international experience by their firms.[89] However, expatriates also report high levels of personal enrichment and skills development, which they can leverage in a new role anywhere. This is consistent with a view of career as more of a subjective sense of where one is going in one's work life as opposed to an upward progression of roles, which has been called the *boundaryless career*.[90] Individuals may recognize that overseas assignments may not have a positive effect on their advancement in their firm but may undertake them in the anticipation of the personal and professional development they afford.[91] In fact, many individuals seek overseas experiences on their own for personal enrichment, but almost as a by-product, develop the kinds of skills they can use to further their career.[92]

While the failure of family members to adjust to the foreign environment is a key factor in the failure of expatriates to remain on assignment the agreed upon length of time, families who do adjust to the overseas experience can gain huge benefits. If expatriation occurs during the critical developmental stages, expatriate children's maturity can be enhanced, as they develop an international perspective.[93] Many of these children may become what have been called *third-culture kids* (exposed to more than one culture for a significant period of time) who develop differently and exhibit different characteristics than their single-culture peers. In particular, in addition to foreign language skills and preference for international careers, they have a greater open mindedness, respect and tolerance toward other cultures, as well as flexibility with regard to their own cultural identity.[94] Clearly, for some families, a global assignment can have far reaching implications.

From an organizational standpoint, all overseas assignments require a substantial investment, which includes direct costs, such as increased compensation, relocation expenses, and so on, and also indirect costs, such as the cost of premature return, underperformance, and the opportunity cost of not using a local national.[95] However, knowing if an adequate return on this investment (ROI) is achieved is difficult. In the most recent Global Relocation Trends Survey Report, 89% of firms rated their ROI on expatriate assignments (defined as accomplishing the assignment objectives at the expected cost) as good or very good. However, only 8% actually made an effort to measure ROI, reflecting the difficulty in actually calculating the costs and benefits of an expatriate assignment.[96] In particular, benefits to the firm, such as knowledge and skills transfer, management development, and developing relationships with host nationals that have potentially positive long-term benefits to the firm, are particularly difficult to quantify.

Organizations historically report a 13% average annual turnover rate for expatriates. The majority of these employees leave after returning home (24% leave within a year of returning and 26% leave the following year).[97] While the overall turnover rates among returned expatriates (repatriates) is not unusually high compared to general turnover, repatriates are a unique group in that their assignment usually equips them with specialized knowledge, skills, and abilities, such as country-specific knowledge, interpersonal skills, job-related management skills, knowledge of business networks, and general management knowledge, that can create competitive advantages for their organization.[98] To actually gain the benefits from this knowledge, it must be effectively transferred to the organization. However, much of this knowledge is contained within the person and difficult to codify (*tacit*) and thus harder to transfer. Skills and abilities developed overseas are also, of course, within the individual. Therefore, the knowledge, skills, and abilities of repatriates can only be leveraged to the organization's benefit if they are retained following the overseas experience.[99] Losing expatriates before the firm capitalizes on its substantial investment in them is an important issue in the process of bringing expatriates home—repatriation.[100]

Repatriation

Returning home from a long period abroad involves an adjustment similar to the initial transfer but differs from other types of geographic-related job transfers. In a traditional repatriation situation, the individual is returning to his or her home country after a period of absence of 2 to 5 years (or longer for German or Japanese expatriates).[101] During this time, the individual, the country, and the organization have undergone gradual changes largely independent of each other. However, the expatriate is very likely confronted with these changes simultaneously upon return. And the repatriation experience is qualitatively different in that most repatriates (80% by some estimates)[102] are returning home from an assignment in a country of which they had little or no prior experience. Therefore, their knowledge and expectations about moving *home* are likely very different to the initial move to a foreign country. Also, the same sorts of things that help expatriates adjust to their expatriate assignment can in turn inhibit repatriation.[103] For example, the improved housing conditions that most expatriates experience might help them cope while on assignment, but the drop in housing conditions on repatriation has a negative effect.

The factors that make the transition back to the home country and the sociocultural environment so difficult include both job-related and family issues. Job-related issues involve concerns about career, adjustment to the new work role, and compensation and status changes. Family issues include the adjustment of the family to the home environment, including reestablishing social networks, and the effect on the partner's career.

Career Concerns

Perhaps the most important reentry issue is the uncertainty about their career that many expatriates face. Only a minority of repatriates have clearly assigned duties upon return, and there seems to be a trend away from post-assignment job guarantees.[104] Typically, the repatriate's role back home is at best a lateral move that does not take advantage of their development on assignment. Given that many expatriates take up the overseas assignment with the expectation of career advancement upon return, these unmet expectations are clearly a source of concern with regard to adjustment. In addition, many expatriates will experience the *out of sight, out of mind* effect as a result of being absent from the home office environment where constant exposure to informal communication and mentors is possible. Lack of information can increase anxiety about the type of reentry position that is available, about details of the repatriation process, and generally what to expect upon return. Career concerns can also be heighted by organizational changes at home. Organizational reorganization creates anxiety for all employees, but this effect can be even more stressful for the repatriate who is already wondering how he or she will fit back into the organizational structure.[105] Inadequate career advancement upon repatriation is related to perceptions of underemployment among repatriates, which in turn leads to higher turnover intentions.[106] We now know that lack of career-related support is linked to repatriate intentions to leave their companies, such that career prospects after repatriation are positively related to retaining repatriates 2 and 4 years after their assignments have ended.[107]

Work Role Adjustment

The role that expatriates assume upon return is highly variable. Many are put in *holding patterns* until an appropriate job is found, and some are promoted, but in all cases their role back home has different characteristics from their job overseas. In their overseas post, expatriates often have a very high level of overall responsibility in challenging jobs with a high level of status. They may have even adjusted their behavior to be more consistent with what was expected of them overseas. Some of the behavior that was appropriate in their expatriate role may not conform to home office expectations. The mismatch between the expectations that returnees have about their role and what is expected of them by the organization is a significant cause of stress.[108]

Many employees develop what is called *an international employee identity* during their assignments. They think of themselves as international employees and identify strongly with their international assignment experience. If they perceive that their situation (job autonomy, job responsibility, compensation, status, and promotional opportunity) compares negatively to that of their peers who have not been on international assignments, they develop a sense of conflict, tension, and misfit between their sense of self and their current organizational roles. This identity strain is in turn related to turnover.[109]

Compensation and Status Changes

In many cases, an expatriate assignment is a promotion carrying with it greater responsibility and autonomy and even a prominent role in the local community. On return, the expatriates resume their position in the organization, resulting in a loss of this status and autonomy. Decisions that were the responsibility of the expatriate while on overseas assignment must now be cleared with a superior or taken to a committee. While most expatriates report being financially better off after their overseas assignment, their overall compensation is usually lower in absolute terms. [110] Many expatriates are able to increase their savings while on assignment. However, they lose such factors as cost-of-living allowances (COLA) and other perks upon return. Often the absence of these financial considerations has a negative influence on the ability of the expatriate and his or her family to reintegrate into the home environment. [111]

Family Adjustment

The experience of living overseas can distance the expatriate's family both socially and psychologically from their friends and family back home. Many people can recall returning from a particularly exciting or interesting holiday only to find when they try to recount the experience their friends have little if any interest. Returning from many years in a foreign country only enhances this effect. Without a frame of reference, friends and family are unlikely to understand the significant influence that life in a foreign environment has had. [112] This, along with economic factors, can often make the home environment, which they may have glamorized while overseas, dull and unexciting by comparison. Expatriates often return from a very tight-knit community of fellow expatriates to a home environment in which everyone seems consumed by their own lives, which makes reestablishing social networks difficult. [113] Children may also have a difficult time reintegrating into peer groups and the education system. [114] Although not well studied, it seems likely that being out of touch with home country changes in fashion, music, slang, sports, and the like will make it difficult for children to reestablish their own social networks.

Partner's Career

The ability of the trailing partner to reenter the workforce upon return is affected by the trailing partner's occupation, length of time abroad, unemployment levels in the home country, and individual factors, such as age and gender. [115] Even with the rise in dual-career couples, we know surprisingly little about this issue. According to the Global Relocation Trends Survey Reports, about a third of firms provided some sort of career assistance to spouses, but it is not clear if this extended to repatriation. [116]

The impact of these factors on repatriation adjustment is influenced by the magnitude of the change from the host to the home country and the length of time spent abroad. [117] Also, the severity of the effect of these factors is influenced by the availability of a number of repatriation support practices. Table 9.2 shows the percentage of expatriates reporting the availability if each practice.

Although the types of support practices vary widely, it seems fairly clear that an integrated set of practices is required for successful repatriation. In fact global mobility programs require organizational action well before individuals are sent abroad.

Table 9.2   Availability of Repatriation Support Practices

Practice	Availability (%)
Continuous communications with the home office	49.6
Communications with the home office about the details of the repatriation process	42.4
Career planning sessions	41.9
Guarantee/agreement outlining the type of position expatriates will be placed in upon repatriation	33.6
Lifestyle assistance and counseling on changes likely to occur in expatriates' lifestyles upon return	33.6
Predeparture briefings on what to expect during repatriation	31.1
Visible signs that the company values international experience	25.2
Financial counseling and financial/tax assistance	9.8
Mentoring programs while on assignment	8.9
Reorientation program about the changes in the company	8.1
Repatriation training seminars on the emotional response following repatriation	8.1
Mean availability (average across all practices)	26.6

Source: Lazarova & Cerdin (2007).

Designing a Global Mobility Program

Recent mobility surveys indicate that about 70% of MNEs have a formal repatriation policy. And in about 20% to 25% of MNEs, repatriation issues are addressed prior to departure for the expatriate assignment as an indication that they recognize the importance of integrating the expatriate assignment into an overall career plan.[118] If organizations are to capitalize on the knowledge and competencies gained by expatriate managers, they need global mobility programs that are not only systematic but also aligned to the strategy of the organization. The following outlines four key areas that need to be considered in designing a global mobility program.

Ensure Strategic Alignment

The initial step in designing a global mobility program is understanding how the expatriation/repatriation program fits with the staffing strategy of the organization. For example, if the organization is shifting its strategy from ethnocentric to geocentric, programs must be designed for third-country nationals and inpatriates as well as for the more traditional expatriates. Understanding the overall strategy of the firm allows time for these programs to be developed in advance as opposed to as a response to problems.

Understand Different Geographic and Role Demands

The strategic market(s) in which the firm operates is a key consideration in designing a global mobility program. The support requirements for an organization that operates in a few relatively similar host countries are dramatically different to that of an organization that relocates employees to dozens of culturally different locations around the world. Also, each assignment is likely to vary on the degree of intercultural interaction required. And as noted previously, expatriate roles vary with regard to the extent to which they contain a developmental component. These factors influence the appropriateness of specific support activities.

Define Expatriation-Repatriation Cycles

Consistent with the staffing strategy of the firm, the most likely mix of assignment types, including their sequence and duration, needs to be determined. Determining this mix provides the organization and the employee with a road map of the type, length, and possible countries of assignments that would be likely and how this would relate to career development. Of course it is not possible to be specific about every assignment, but establishing expectations prior to an initial assignment assists both the organization and the employee. For example, if an employee knows that he or she will likely be required to undertake an overseas assignment for developmental purpose in order to advance to senior management, this will be factored into his or her implicit contract with the organization.

Develop Support Practices

In order to meet the strategic objectives of an expatriate assignment, support practices need to be developed for the expatriate and family before, during, and after the assignment. While these practices will need to be customized to fit the specific circumstances of each international assignment, the best practices that have been identified center around improving career support, greater opportunity to use the international experience, guarantees of post-assignment positions, greater choices of post-assignment positions, greater recognition during and after assignment, logistical help, and repatriation support for the family. Best practices also include support during the assignment in the form of improved communication with the home office, mentoring, and repatriation discussions while the employee is still posted abroad.

Monitor Programs

Given the lack of experience with many of the support practices, each must be carefully monitored to insure the desired effects are being achieved. For example, given the shift to a more boundaryless career perspective by employees, programs designed to encourage long-term loyalty may succeed only in improving short-term retention.[119] Organizations must consider the career aspirations of their employees as well as how global mobility fits with the organizations strategic staffing plan. Continuing assessment and external benchmarking of the results of global mobility programs is required.

Beyond Repatriate Retention

While retaining expatriates after they return is an important consideration, it is not the only organizational goal related to these employees. What is desirable for organizations may not always be desirable for individuals, and meeting individual needs does not always accomplish organizational goals. For example, retention in itself does not equal success for either party. Consider the frustrated repatriate who is put in a holding pattern and never uses the knowledge or skills obtained abroad—not only is he or she unhappy, but the organization is not actually gaining the benefit of its investment in the overseas assignment. Even if an organization handles repatriation well, some individuals with overseas experience may receive competitive offers from other employers and leave. On the other hand, not all turnover is dysfunctional. Sometimes both parties are better off by severing the employment relationship. This is not to suggest that MNEs should not improve how they currently handle repatriation or that they should minimize the support they provide to returnees. However, in addition to being concerned about retention, MNEs must consider knowledge and skills transfer and building and maintaining networks that are beneficial to the organization. And instead of becoming frustrated with inadequate support and/or slower than expected career progress, repatriates should focus on developing new skills, competencies, and knowledge and become more proactive in managing their own careers.[120]

Chapter Summary

This chapter examines global mobility issues both from the perspective of the employee and the employer. Employers are interested in deploying individuals according to their global staffing strategy to positions where they can perform effectively. Employees are also interested in accomplishing the job at hand but typically take on a foreign assignment with the goal of advancing their career. A changing perspective on what constitutes a career is an important consideration in how both the individual and the organization view a global assignment. A key factor in the success of an overseas assignment is the extent to which the employee and his or her family adjust to the overseas environment. Individual, job, and organizational factors all contribute to the ability of expatriates and their families to adjust. In addition to traditional expatriate postings, many organizations, often in order to reduce costs, employ different mobility options, such as short-term assignments, commuter assignments, and flexpatriate assignments. Each of these mobility types has its own advantages and disadvantages for both the employee and the organization. While most employees on overseas assignment are men, a significant percentage is female. Along with the increase in dual career couples, this presents additional challenges to organizations to provide appropriate support for international assignees. In order for firms to capitalize on the knowledge and experience gain by employees on overseas assignments they must be retained in the organization. The difficulty in retaining returned expatriates has focused the attention of organizations on designing global mobility programs that meet both the organizations staffing goals and the career goals of employees.

Questions for Discussion

1. What are the advantages and disadvantages of the different types of global assignments?

2. Why is family adjustment the reason most often given for expatriates failing to meet the terms of the global assignment?

3. Are women just as effective in global assignments as men? Why or why not?

4. Are global assignments good for your career? Why or why not?

5. Why is repatriation adjustment often more difficult than the initial adjustment to the foreign country?

Notes

1. Shaffer, Kraimer, Chen, & Bolino (2012); Takeuchi (2010).
2. Schein (1996); Briscoe and Hall (2006).
3. Thomas, Lazarova, & Inkson (2005).
4. GMAC, NTFC, SHRM Global Forum (2004); Reiche & Harzing (2011).
5. World Trade Organization (2012).
6. Shaffer, Kraimer, Chen, & Bolino (2012).
7. Reiche (2006, 2011).
8. Inkson, Arthur, Pringle, & Barry (1997).
9. See Peiperl & Jonsen (2007) for a discussion.
10 Dowling, Festing, Engle, & Gröschl (2009); Briscoe, Schuler, & Tarique (2012); GMAC, NTFC, & SHRM Global Forum (2004); Global Relocation Trends Survey Report (2012).
11. Global Relocation Trends Survey Report (2010, 2011, 2012).
12. Global Relocation Trends Survey Report (2012).
13. Economist Intelligence Unit (2010).
14. Global Relocation Trends Survey Report (2012).
15. GMAC, NTFC, & SHRM Global Forum (2004); Global Relocation Trends Survey Report (2010, 2011, 2012).
16. Shaffer, Kraimer, Chen, & Bolino (2012); Briscoe, Schuler, & Tarique (2012); Mayrhofer, Reichel, & Sparrow (2012).
17. Global Relocation Trends Survey Report (2012); Economist Intelligence Unit (2010).
18. Global Relocation Trends Survey Report (2012).
19. Adler (1984).

20. Global Relocation Trends Survey Report (2012).
21. Mayrhofer, Reichel, & Sparrow (2012).
22. Mayrhofer, Reichel, & Sparrow (2012).
23. Shaffer, Kraimer, Chen, & Bolino (2012).
24. Shaffer, Kraimer, Chen, & Bolino (2012).
25. Mayerhofer, Hartmann, Michelitsch-Riedl, & Kollinger (2004).
26. For more on self-initiated overseas experience, see Inkson, Arthur, Pringle, & Barry (1997) and Suutari & Brewster (2000).
27. English (1958).
28. Ward & Kennedy (1993).
29. Lazarova, Westman, & Shaffer (2010).
30. Lysgaard (1955).
31. Gullahorn & Gullahorn (1963).
32. Church (1982).
33. See Briody & Chrisman (1991); Nicholson & Imaizumi (1993).
34. Bhaskar-Shrinivas, Harrison, Shaffer, & Luk (2005); Hechanova, Beehr, & Christiansen (2003); Takeuchi, Yun, & Tesluk (2002).
35. Shaffer & Harrison (2001); Cole (2011).
36. De Leon & McPartlin (1995).
37. Global Relocation Trends Survey Report (2012).
38. See Tung (1981).
39. Selmer, Ebrahimi, & Mingtao (2002).
40. See Harris (2004); Punnett, Crocker, & Stevens (1992).
41. Cole (2012); Linehan & Walsh (2001).
42. Moore (2002).
43. For additional discussion see Cole (2012); Punnett (1997); Punnett, Crocker, & Stevens (1992); Harris (2004); and Linehan & Walsh (2000); Harris (2006).
44. See Mol, Born, Willemsen, & van der Molen (2005).
45. See Thomas & Fitzsimmons (2008).
46. Thomas (1998).
47. Church (1982).
48. Thomas & Fitzsimmons (2008).
49. See Benson (1978); Thomas (2008).
50. See for example Naumann 1993); Takeuchi & Hannon (1996).
51. Black & Gregersen (1992)
52. See Thomas & Inkson (2008).
53. Tadmor & Tetlock (2006)
54. See Taylor & Napier (1996).
55. See Thomas (1998).
56. Black (1990b)
57. Thomas (1998)
58. See Feldman & Brett (1983).
59. For example see Gregersen & Black (1990); Takeuchi & Hannon (1996).
60. See Black (1990b).
61. See Stroh, Dennis, & Cramer (1994).
62. See Elron & Kark (2000); Moore (2002).
63. See Guzzo, Noonan, & Elron (1994) for a discussion.

64. Meyskens, Von Glinow, Werther, & Clarke (2009); Mayrhofer, Reichel, & Sparrow (2012).
65. Shaffer, Kraimer, Chen, & Bolino (2012).
66. Mayerhofer, Hartmann, Michelitsch-Riedl, & Kollinger (2004); Welch, Welch, & Worm (2007); Starr & Currie (2009).
67. See Thomas & Fitzsimmons (2008) for a discussion of cross-cultural skills.
68. Thomas (2008).
69. Global Relocation Trends Survey Report (2012).
70. Mayerhofer, Hartmann, Michelitsch-Riedl, & Kollinger (2004); Welch, Welch, & Worm (2007).
71. Global Relocation Trends Survey Report (2010, 2011, 2012).
72. Mayrhofer, Reichel, & Sparrow (2012).
73. Antal & Izraeli (1993).
74. Global Relocation Trends Survey Report (2010, 2011, 2012).
75. Caligiuri & Lazarova (2002).
76. Caligiuri & Tung (1999); Sinangil & Ones (2003).
77. For example see Taylor & Napier (1996).
78. Stroh, Varma, & Valy-Durbin (2000).
79. Adler (1984); Stroh, Varma, & Valy-Durbin (2000).
80. Adler (1984); Lowe, Downes, & Kroeck (1999).
81. Punnett (1997).
82. van der Velde, Bossink, & Jansen (2005).
83. See Thomas (2008).
84. Napier & Taylor (2002).
85. See Caligiuri & Tung (1999); Napier & Taylor (2002).
86. Stroh, Varma, & Valy-Durbin (2000).
87. Chusmir & Frontczak (1990).
88. Varma & Stroh (2001).
89. For example see Feldman & Thomas (1992); Stahl & Cerdin (2004).
90. See Arthur & Rousseau (1996).
91. Stahl, Miller, & Tung (2002)
92. Inkson, Arthur, Pringle, & Barry (2000)
93. De Leon and McPartlin (1995); see also Weeks, Weeks, & Willis-Muller (2009).
94. See Selmer & Lam (2004).
95. McNulty & Tharenou (2004).
96. Global Relocation Trends Survey Report (2010).
97. Global Relocation Trends Survey Report (2012).
98. Fink, Meierewert, & Rohr (2005).
99. See Lazarova & Tarique (2005) for a discussion of knowledge transfer upon repatriation.
100. Lazarova & Cerdin (2007).
101. See Black & Gregersen (1991); Peterson, Napier, & Won (1995).
102. Black & Gregersen (1991).
103. See Poe (2000).
104. Global Relocation Trends Survey Report (2010).
105. Lazarova & Cerdin (2007).
106. Kraimer, Shaffer, & Bolino (2009).
107. Reiche, Kraimer, & Harzing (2011).
108. For a discussion see Torbiörn (1985) and also Black & Gregersen (1991).

109. Kraimer, Shaffer, Harrison, & Ren (2012).

110. Napier & Peterson (1991).

111. Harvey (1989).

112. See Harvey (1982) for additional information on this topic.

113. See De Cieri, Dowling, & Taylor (1991).

114. Enloe & Lewin (1987).

115. Black & Gregersen (1991).

116. Global Relocation Trends Survey Report (2010, 2012).

117. Harvey & Novicevic (2006).

118. Global Relocation Trends Survey Report (2010, 2011, 2012).

119. Global Relocation Trends Survey Report (2010, 2011, 2012).

120. Lazarova & Cerdin (2007); Yan, Zhu, & Hall (2002).

10

International Employee Representation and Corporate Social Responsibility

LEARNING OBJECTIVES

After reading this chapter you should be able to

- compare and contrast the elements of a national labor relations systems,
- explain the relationship between MNEs and organized labor around the world,
- discuss how different institutional environments relate to different forms of corporate social responsibility (CSR),
- compare the various guidelines for ethical decision making, and
- discuss the elements and usefulness of corporate codes of conduct.

Social Dumping Within the EU[1]

Jan de Vries, director of HR at Digital Device Corporation's (DDC) Rotterdam production facility, stared in disbelief at the email he had just received from DDC's headquarters in San Jose, California. It seemed that the company had decided to make the production facility in Limerick, Ireland, its lead operation in Europe. Two production lines in the Rotterdam plant were to be shut down, making several hundred employees redundant, while the Limerick facility would be greatly expanded. In addition, once the transition was complete, his own responsibilities would be handled from the Limerick facility, and it was suggested that he should take early retirement.

DDC was a leading manufacturer of signal processing devices. Increased competition from Asia had caused it to restructure worldwide with the goal of reducing manufacturing costs. Two days previous, all employees at the Limerick facility had attended a video presentation in which the CEO of DDC had (based on an EU grant) described DDCs intention to invest almost €75 million in the plant, resulting in the gain of hundreds of jobs. However, in return for the additional investment, DDC wanted employees at the Limerick plant to take a 12% pay reduction. The following day, each employee received a letter saying that DDC was not convinced that Limerick was the best location for their European headquarters and that the question of location was still open. Attached to the letter was a ballot asking for acceptance of the pay cut. Only a dozen employees voted no.

Jan de Vries wasn't sure about the labor laws in Ireland, but he felt sure the company's action was a clear violation of the Works Councils Act in the Netherlands and similar EU legislation that required consultation on such matters. This will all be settled in court, he thought to himself. But how long will that take and what will be the end result? Can our local works council actually win in a battle with a large multinational company like DDC?

Introduction

Different economic, political, legal, and sociocultural environments have resulted in very different industrial relations systems around the world. However, global organizations, such as DDC in the opening vignette, must increasingly consider the increased profile of international employee representation. Major campaigns by international trade union federations bolstered by regional regulation such as in the EU are increasing the level of cross-border communication on labor relations issues. And multinational organizations, whether motivated by demonstrating social responsibility or to legitimize strategic initiatives, are sometimes finding that coordinated labor relations efforts work to their benefit.[2] Furthermore, global labor issues are at the heart of many of the pressures for multinational organizations to respond to the broader needs of the societies in which they operate.

International Industrial Relations

Contemporary international employment relations has at its core the trade union movement that evolved in many countries during the industrial revolution. Trade unions (called labor unions in the United States) have as their origins the large number of workers drawn into the workforce by the industrial revolution, taking up unfamiliar roles in industrial firms. These unskilled and semiskilled workers lacked individual bargaining power with their employer and thus banded together to improve the conditions of their employment. While similar to the guilds of medieval Europe in some ways, these unions lacked the control over the artisanship of a craft because of the changing nature of work.

In general, a trade union, through its leadership, bargains with the employer on behalf of union members and negotiates contracts regarding wages and working conditions. Some unions may provide benefits to members, such as unemployment insurance, professional training, or legal advice. In addition, unions can try to further their goals through industrial action (strikes and resistance to lockouts) and by promoting favorable legislation.[3]

National Industrial Relations Systems

National industrial relations[4] systems are a reflection of the society in which they operate. In fact, they can be thought of as subsystem of society not unlike political or economic systems.[5] A system of industrial relations consists of *actors, rules, environmental context,* and *ideology,* which is represented graphically in Figure 10.1.

The actors are organizations, employees, and government who maintain relations with each other through three tightly interconnected contexts. The technological features of the work situation (technological context), the market opportunities or limitations (economic context), and the relative power distribution between actors (political context) are dynamic forces that result in the interactions among actors. The products of this interaction are the substantive and procedural rules regarding labor relations that occupy the center of Figure 10.1. Finally, the system includes an ideology that helps to bind the system together as an entity. This framework identifies a general equilibrium model of industrial relations that exists within a nation. However, the precise structure of the industrial relations system in different countries is distinctive because of its historical development.

National Variation in Industrial Relations Systems

Several types of unions are common today, with their prevalence varying in different parts of the world. *Industry unions* represent all levels of employees in an industry (typical in Belgium, Canada, Finland, Norway, Sweden, the United States, and Germany). In contrast *craft unions* are based on occupation and represent employees across industries (e.g., Australia, Denmark, Great Britain, Norway, Sweden, and the United States) as do *conglomerate unions* (the Netherlands and the United States).

Figure 10.1 Industrial Relations System

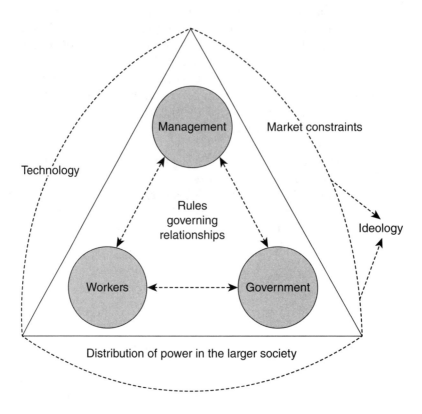

Source: Bomers (1976, p. 5); de Nijs (1995, p. 281)

General unions may be open to membership of almost everyone in a country (e.g., Australia, Denmark, Great Britain) while *enterprise unions*, such as those that exist in Japan, limit their membership to employees of a single firm. Other more restrictive categories of unions exist, including *professional unions* (Australia, Denmark, Finland, Great Britain, the Netherlands, Sweden, Germany), and unions limited to *public sector* employees (e.g., Great Britain).[6]

Studies of industrial relations across countries have also pointed out that there are some systematic differences in industrial relation approaches in different institutional contexts. Thus, in *liberal market economies* market participants have a lot of autonomy when they bargain with other labor market participants, while *coordinated market economies* are characterized by dense networks of institutions, sustained by laws, customs, and values, which constrain individual actors to broader collective priorities.[7] In many countries, unions and management are considered to be adversaries (e.g., the United States), while in others (e.g., the Netherlands) they are consulted in decision making through works councils, and in some (e.g., Germany) they are represented on supervisory boards and other decision-making bodies and employers must obtain their agreement on major strategic decisions.[8]

The union structure in a society is the result of several factors, including the mode of technology and industrial development at critical stages in union development, the way in which unions are regulated by government, ideological differences within the trade union movement, the influence of religion on trade unions, and management strategies for industrial relations in large organizations.[9] For example, the new skills of the industrial revolution led to craft and professional unions, while mass production favored industrial and general unions. White-collar employees tend to see their interests as different from those of other workers and hence prefer separate unions, and as their numbers increased, so have their unions. Some union movements, while influenced by these factors, are still divided on ethical or religious grounds. Also, as the public sector has grown, its union representation has tended to reflect its unique status in society. Finally, management's endorsement of a particular union structure, such as the enterprise union in Japan, is influential. As can be seen from this discussion, every national industrial relation system is unique as it is a result of a distinctive historical evolution. Therefore a deep understanding of the labor relations system in a given country requires an appreciation of the way in which the labor movement has developed over time within the country.

While unions continue to be influential around the world, trade union membership as a percentage of the workforce (union density) has been in decline in the industrialized world for some time. Table 10.1 shows the union density in the Organization for Economic Cooperation and Development (OECD) in 2008 and also indicates the peak of union participation.

Table 10.1   Trade Union Density in OECD Countries 2008

Peak Trade Union Density Since 1960

Country	Density 2008	Peak Density	Date of Peak
Australia	18.6	50.2	1976
Austria	28.9	67.9	1960‡
Belgium	51.9	55.7	1995
Canada	27.1	35.9	1984
Chile	13.6	20.1	1991
Czech Republic	20.2	46.3	1995‡
Denmark	67.6	80.8	1983

(Continued)

Table 10.1 (Continued)

Peak Trade Union Density Since 1960

Country	Density 2008	Peak Density	Date of Peak
Finland	67.5	80.7	1993
France	7.2	22.1	1973
Germany	19.1	36.0	1991
Greece	24.0	37.6	1992
Hungary	16.8	49.1	1995‡
Iceland	86.4*	94.3	2004
Ireland	32.3	54.8	1978
Italy	33.4	50.4	1978
Japan	18.2	35.2	1969
Korea	10.3	18.6	1989
Luxembourg	37.4	53.0	1984
Mexico	17.4**	24.3	1992‡
Netherlands	18.9	40.0	1960‡
New Zealand	20.8	69.1	1980
Norway	53.3	60.8	1961
Poland	15.8	56.3	1992
Portugal	20.4	60.8	1978
Slovak Republic	16.8	64.2	1994
Spain	14.3	18.0	1993
Sweden	68.3	83.9	1993
Switzerland	18.3	36.1	1960‡
Turkey	5.8	23.0	1987
United Kingdom	27.1	50.0	1981
United States	11.9	30.9	1960‡
OECD Average	17.8	33.9	1979

Source: OECD (2011).

 * 2007

** 2005

 ‡ First year data available

In 2008, the average (employee weighted) union density in the OECD countries was 17.8%, down from a high of 33.9% in 1979. The highest level of union membership was in Iceland with 86.4 (2007 data), followed by Sweden at 68.3%, and Denmark at 67.8%. The lowest union membership was in Turkey at 5.8% followed by France at 7.7%. It is important to recognize that union density tells only part of the story, as in some countries unions may represent the majority of workers even though only a small percentage are members (e.g., Austria, Germany, France, the Netherlands), while in other countries they only represent their actual members (e.g., Canada, the United States).[10] Even so, union representation appears to be in decline.[11]

Much of the numerical decline can be attributed to economic factors, such as reduced public sector employment, heightened competition, and a reduction in the percentage of employment accounted for by manufacturing industries. However, a dramatic rise or fall in trade union membership is often linked to systematic changes in governance or major legislative changes in countries or regions.[12] For example, a huge increase in unionization rates accompanied the end of the apartheid era in South Africa, and a large decrease followed the introduction of the Employment Contracts Act in New Zealand.

The diverse strategies of labor, management, and the state are all related to variations in union density. For example, in the low union density in the United States is likely because of the limited extent of collective bargaining in the public sector and among white-collar workers. In contrast, the depth of collective bargaining and union security combined with favorable public policy explains Sweden's high union density.[13]

Industrial Relations Policies in MNEs

Because of the significant variation in industrial relations systems that exit around the world, multinational organizations often rely heavily on local subsidiaries for labor relations policy and practice. International HRM departments within multinational organizations can typically be classified according to the following approaches:

Hands off—Responsibility for labor relations is left entirely in the hands of the local subsidiary.

Monitor—Primary responsibility remains in the hands of the local subsidiary, but headquarters' HRM monitors the situation and tries to prevent problems by asking probing questions of the local managers.

Guide and advise—This is a step beyond monitoring. HR managers from headquarters provide ongoing advice and guidance to subsidiary managers on labor relations issues while leaving control with local staff.

Strategic planning—In this case, international labor relations issues are incorporated into the MNE's strategy. Local subsidiaries remain in control but follow this global strategy.

Limits with exceptions—Subsidiaries are allowed freedom of action within narrowly defined limits. Approval from headquarters is required for deviations from these guidelines.

Headquarters management—All labor relations policies and practices are directed from headquarters.[14]

The extent to which MNE headquarters exercises control over labor relations in the subsidiary depends on a number of factors including (a) the location of firm headquarters and the importance of its international operations, (b) the characteristics and degree of integration of subsidiaries, and (c) the experience of the MNE in industrial relations and the attitude of its managers towards unions.[15]

U.S. headquartered firms tend to exercise greater control over labor relations in their subsidiaries than do their European counterparts. This may be the result of more ethnocentric management approaches in the United States and/or than U.S. firms, because of a large domestic market, largely see foreign subsidiaries as extensions of domestic operations. In contrast, European firms may see international operations as a more integral part of their overall business. Also, European firms have a long history of dealing with industrial unions as compared to the United States, where firm-level industrial relations are more prevalent. Also, union avoidance seems to be a fairly common attitude among U.S. managers.[16]

A key factor in determining the extent to which headquarters exercises control over labor relations in subsidiaries is the extent to which the activities of subsidiaries are integrated. The development of an integrated network among subsidiaries requires a high level of coordination and control, not only of investment and production policies but also for the transfer of technology. The combination of the need for consistency in technology transfer, the importance of the integrated subsidiary to overall operations, and the high degree of labor mobility that this causes encourages the involvement of headquarters in labor relations.[17] Other subsidiaries characteristics are influential as well. Not surprisingly, for example, subsidiaries that are formed through greenfield activities tend to be more influenced by headquarters than those acquired from an established indigenous organization. In these cases, organizations are likely to replicate policies and practices that have worked well elsewhere. And, there tends to be more headquarters involvement in labor relations for younger, strategically important, and poorly performing subsidiaries or those highly dependent on headquarters.[18]

The previous discussion outlined the variation in labor relations policies and procedures that exist in MNEs. However, it is not just the multinationality of the organization that is important but also the strategy of the particular multinational in combination with the labor relations systems in the countries in which it operates that must be considered. In the following, we examine some of the ways in which the multinational upsets the balance in a labor relations system and also how trade unions influence the strategy of the multinational enterprise.

MNEs and the Labor Relations System

The multinational enterprise upsets the balance of the system shown in Figure 10.1 because (a) the decision-making process and strategy of the multinational lies outside national boundaries, making it difficult for local actors to know about or understand it, and (b) the multinational has the capability to reorganize its factors of production internationally.[19] It is not bound by the constraints of a single national labor relations system and thus has far more leverage than any enterprise that operates strictly within national boundaries. This raises a number of concerns for trade unions as discussed ahead. MNEs cause concern for trade unions in at least the following three areas.[20]

Ability to relocate factors of production. Multinationals can find alternate sources of supply to reduce exposure to an unfavorable labor relations climate. Multiple sources of supply can be used to reduce vulnerability to industrial action, and production can be temporarily shifted between subsidiaries in various countries in the case that it occurs. According to the International Confederation of Free Trade Unions, it is the "ever present threat of relocation to countries with low wages, low standards and a low degree of organization" that puts MNEs in a strong position to put pressure on trade unions and their workers as well as on their governments to accept whatever they are proposing.[21] Another advantage of having production facilities in a variety of locations is the ability to stage an *investment strike*, in which the multinational withholds needed investment in order to make operations in multiple facilities obsolete.

Remote location of authority. The decision-making structure of the multinational is not tied to location, and the exact locus of power may be difficult for unions to decipher. Local management may claim that they are simply following orders from headquarters, while at the same time headquarters may claim that local management is entirely responsible for the issue at hand. Contributing to this issue is that the exact strategy of the multinational is difficult for unions to understand. And because of obscure financial reporting, internal transfers among subsidiaries, and so on, it may even be difficult to know exactly what activities are carried out by the organization in what countries. This severely limits the union's bargaining position because they find it difficult to determine if a particular subsidiary can meet bargaining demands.

Significant resources. The broad financial resources of the multinational can limit union's bargaining power. Large multinationals can absorb losses as a result of industrial action in one location, and as indicated previously, compensate with operations in another location. The ability of unions to have an economic impact on these organizations is therefore limited. In addition to financial resources, large MNEs have significant expertise in industrial relations at their disposal, which may be far superior to the knowledge held by local unions.

Despite the many advantages that accrue to the multinational enterprise because of its border-spanning activities, trade unions are a significant consideration in the formation and implementation of is strategy. In fact, the characteristics of the labor relations system have become a key consideration in making strategic location decisions.[22]

Influence of Trade Unions on the MNE

The concerns that organized labor has about MNEs are similar to those held by host governments. And while labor does not have the enforcement tools of government, it can still influence the strategy of the MNE. From the perspective of the multinational enterprise, organized labor limits strategic choice by preventing the optimum degree of global integration, constraining the ability of multinationals to vary employment levels, and by affecting wage rates.[23]

Barriers to global integration. Plans to increase efficiency by rationalizing and integrating operations can be prevented or delayed in countries, under pressure from national unions that have enacted restrictive legislation. For example, in some European countries in order to carry out redundancy plans, MNEs must demonstrate substantial losses resulting from structural conditions that make the proposed changes necessary. As shown in the opening vignette, unilateral action by MNEs can sometimes create serious repercussions. As a result, some MNEs have bought labor peace by committing not to integrate their operations to the most efficient degree.[24]

Constraints on employment levels. The inability to adjust staffing levels at will can have broad implications, especially in countries where reductions in staffing levels are particularly difficult. For example, a strike at one General Motors plant in the United States prevented GM's Mexican operations from getting the parts it needed. However, Mexican labor law prevented GM from laying off workers, thus adding to the pressure on GM to settle.[25]

Influencing wage rates. Labor costs, while decreasing in comparison to other costs, still play a major role in determining organizational competitiveness. The influence of labor negotiations on wage rates within different countries can significantly limit the strategic options available to firms.

In this way labor unions may exert influence more by quietly limiting strategic decisions than by open conflict where they often are at a disadvantage to the superior power of the MNE. The MNE, while delegating much of its labor relations activity to the local subsidiary, must take labor relations into account when making strategic decisions, especially those involving integration, rationalization and divestment.

Trade Union Response to MNEs

Despite the fact that multinationals are not uniformly antiunion, they have generally been regarded as a threat to the bargaining power of labor.[26] The response of trade unions to try to restore a balance of power in the labor relations system has taken two basic forms. First is the exchange of information and coordination of activities through the formation of international trade secretariats. Second is lobbying for favorable national legislation and trying to influence multinationals through international organizations.[27]

Coordination and international trade secretariats. Perhaps the most common way in which trade unions try to counter the MNEs' bargaining power is through sharing information on the MNEs policies and activities. In addition, labor groups in one country may support their counterparts in other countries by such activities as refusing to work overtime to supply a market served by striking workers, sending aid to workers in other countries, or disrupting work in their own country.

More formal coordination, primarily information exchange, occurs through international trade secretariats. International trade secretariats represent workers in a specific industry, such as the International Confederation of Free Trade Unions (ICFTU), the World Federation of Trade Unions (WFTU), and the World Confederation of Labor (WCL). These organizations engage in a number of information exchange activities (research, conferences, company councils, union-management discussions, etc.) with a long-term goal of achieving transnational collective bargaining in the industry they represent.[28]

Influencing through transnational organizations and regulation. Another way in which organized labor can influence MNEs is by lobbying national governments directly. Trade unions in the United States and Europe have been engaged in this activity for many years. However, the conflicting economic interest of both governments and unions has limited the effectiveness of this strategy.[29] It is important to recognize that countries are in competition with each other for the economic benefits that the MNE can bring. Unions, through trade union federations, have had more success exerting influence over multinationals through transnational organizations. such as the International Labor Organization (ILO), the United Nations Council on Trade and Development (UNCTAD) and the OECD.

The ILO was formed following World War I and is the international organization responsible for drawing up and overseeing international labor standards. It is the only *tripartite* United Nations agency that brings together representatives of governments, employers, and workers to jointly shape policies and programs promoting humane labor conditions. The goals of the ILO are to promote rights at work, encourage decent employment opportunities, enhance social protection, and strengthen dialogue on work-related issues.[30] The ILO adopted a code of conduct for multinationals, which was in turn influential in the OECD guidelines for multinational enterprises. The OECD guidelines were updated in 2011 for the fifth time since they were first adopted in 1976. Box 10.1 presents the general policies section of the guidelines.

Box 10.1   OECD Guidelines for Multinational Enterprises

General Policies
    Enterprises should take fully into account established policies in the countries in which they operate, and consider the views of other stakeholders. In this regard:

A. Enterprises should

    1. Contribute to economic, environmental, and social progress with a view to achieving sustainable development.

    2. Respect the internationally recognized human rights of those affected by their activities.

(Continued)

(Continued)

3. Encourage local capacity building through close cooperation with the local community, including business interests, as well as developing the enterprise's activities in domestic and foreign markets, consistent with the need for sound commercial practice.

4. Encourage human capital formation, in particular by creating employment opportunities and facilitating training opportunities for employees.

5. Refrain from seeking or accepting exemptions not contemplated in the statutory or regulatory framework related to human rights, environmental, health, safety, labor, taxation, financial incentives, or other issues.

6. Support and uphold good corporate governance principles and develop and apply good corporate governance practices, including throughout enterprise groups.

7. Develop and apply effective self-regulatory practices and management systems that foster a relationship of confidence and mutual trust between enterprises and the societies in which they operate.

8. Promote awareness of and compliance by workers employed by multinational enterprises with respect to company policies through appropriate dissemination of these policies, including through training programs.

9. Refrain from discriminatory or disciplinary action against workers who make bona fide reports to management, or as appropriate, to the competent public authorities on practices that contravene the law, the Guidelines, or the enterprise's policies.

10. Carry out risk-based due diligence, for example, by incorporating it into their enterprise risk-management systems, to identify, prevent, and mitigate actual and potential adverse impacts as described in Paragraphs 11 and 12 and account for how these impacts are addressed. The nature and extent of due diligence depends on the circumstances of a particular situation.

11. Avoid causing or contributing to adverse impacts on matters covered by the Guidelines, through their own activities, and address such impacts when they occur.

12. Seek to prevent or mitigate an adverse impact where they have not contributed to that impact when the impact is nevertheless directly linked to their operations, products, or services by a business relationship. This

is not intended to shift responsibility from the entity, causing an adverse impact to the enterprise with which it has a business relationship.

13. In addition to addressing adverse impacts in relation to matters covered by the Guidelines, encourage, where practicable, business partners, including suppliers and sub-contractors, to apply principles of responsible business conduct compatible with the Guidelines.

14. Engage with relevant stakeholders in order to provide meaningful opportunities for their views to be taken into account in relation to planning and decision making for projects or other activities that may significantly impact local communities.

15. Abstain from any improper involvement in local political activities.

B. Enterprises are encouraged to

1. Support, as appropriate to their circumstances, cooperative efforts in the appropriate fora to promote Internet Freedom through respect of freedom of expression, assembly, and association online.

2. Engage in or support, where appropriate, private or multi-stakeholder initiatives and social dialogue on responsible supply chain management while ensuring that these initiatives take due account of their social and economic effects on developing countries and of existing internationally recognised standards.

Source: OECD (2011).

As shown in Box 10.1, the OECD guidelines are wide ranging, and we will return to them in our discussion on CSR ahead. As significant as the establishment of these guidelines has been, it is important to note that compliance with them is entirely voluntary. Because of the voluntary nature of this and other codes of conduct, European trade unions have lobbied the European Union, which can make rules with the force of law, such as the European Social Charter of the Council of Europe and later the Charter of Fundamental Rights of the European Union.[31]

Overall, organized labor has met with only limited success in influencing national and international bodies to regulate MNEs. Additionally, several factors hamper the ability of unions to cooperate internationally. These include that unions in different countries have different goals, different union structures and collective bargaining methods, and operate in very different legal environments with regard to labor relations.[32] The goal of transnational collective bargaining may in fact be too ambitious, and unions might better focus their activities on strengthening national union involvement though company-based bargaining, supporting research on the vulnerability of selected multinationals (such as Wal-Mart)[33] and consolidating the activities of international trade secretariats.[34] Related to this change in focus to interunion cooperation is the advent of the European works councils and the prospect that they might open the door to cross-national negotiations.

European works councils. A works council is a firm-level organization representing workers, which functions as a complement to national labor negotiations. Works councils exist under different names in a variety of forms in a number of European countries. In 1994, the European Union passed a directive on establishing European Works Councils (EWCs)—with functions similar to the function of the local works councils but which operate at the European Union level. The EWC Directive applies to companies with at least 1,000 employees within the EU and at least 150 employees in each of at least two member states. EWCs affect about 60% of the workers in the EU. EWCs were created to give representatives of workers from all European countries in big multinational companies a direct line of communication to top management.[35] They also ensure that workers in different countries receive the same information about transnational policies and plans (see the vignette that opened this chapter). They give workers' representatives in unions and national works councils the opportunity to consult with each other and to develop a common European response to employers' transnational plans, which management must then consider before those plans are implemented.[36] While there is some speculation that EWCs could become instruments for collective bargaining at the European level, so far this does not seem to be the case. Most sectors seem to use the EWCs as a means to gain information to be used in domestic negotiations rather than across countries.[37]

The effectiveness of EWCs on management decision making has been traced to six factors which relate to the company's business operations and the organization and policy approaches of the parties involved.[38] Three sets of structural factors are expected to facilitate or constrain the effectiveness of EWCs. These are

1. Business alignment—the focus and integration of the firm's business activities

2. Management structure—the characteristics of the European management structure if any

3. Industrial relations structure—the existence of an industrial relations

Three additional sets of factors relate to the parties involved. These are

1. Management policy—the levels and functions of management that are routinely involved in the EWC (minimalist compliance versus enthusiastic embrace)

2. Employee organization—the extent to which the employees involved are a cohesive unit and are able to draw on trade union resources to support its activity

3. EWC interaction—open constructive and ongoing versus adversarial interaction between management and employees

In general it has been found that while EWCs affect the *process* of decision making on industrial-relations issues; it is less common for the *outcomes* of decisions to be affected.[39]

MNE Interest in Employee Representation

The growth both in number and significance of multinational enterprises has created the need for a countervailing force to restore balance to the labor relations system. International employee representation in the form of EWCs or the like is thus likely to increase in significance. However, the MNE need not see international employee representation as its adversary. In fact, there are two reasons why MNEs might want to embrace, even take the initiative in establishing international employee representation. These result from a concern for maintaining employee cooperation and commitment and a concern for social responsibility.[40]

Given the intensive competition for scarce human resources (as discussed previously), management has to reconcile two potentially conflicting pressures. On the one hand there is pressure to reduce costs (often through restructuring) and on the other to promote the conditions that result in security, teamwork, and innovation among employees. Employee representation that legitimates management decisions can help to ensure the kind of cooperation and commitment necessary to implement organizational structures that give management the flexibility it needs while also providing security for workers.

In addition to the usefulness of employee representation for maintaining internal legitimacy is the increasing concern that organizations have for their image in the larger society. The negotiation of global frameworks that require employee representation is an important way in which MNEs can demonstrate their CSR. The broader issue of international CSR is discussed ahead.

Corporate Social Responsibility

The concept of CSR is not understood in exactly the same way around the world.[41] However, the EU defines social responsibility as a concept whereby companies integrate social and environmental concerns into their business operations and into their interaction with their stakeholders on a voluntary basis.[42] This social performance by firms can be thought of as occurring on a continuum from narrow self-interest to broader social interests resulting in three stages of development:

Social obligation—in which responsibility is limited to compliance with local laws attending to shareholder interests

Social responsibility—in which the firm reacts to the needs of all organizational stakeholders including employees, customers, and suppliers

Social responsiveness— in which the firm is proactive in determining the needs of external social interests including the environment[43]

Whether reactive or proactive, CSR is often considered to be acting beyond legal obligations to ensure that the interests of stakeholders and the wider environment are considered.

National Differences

National differences in the conceptualization and motives for CSR can be traced to differing institutional environments (discussed in Chapter 2). Institutional factors influence the nature of firms, the organization of the market, and coordination and control systems among actors[44] resulting in a continuum from *liberal market economies*, in which competitive markets dominate interactions, to *coordinated market economies*, in which organizations interact more directly with the institutional environment. These different institutional environments give rise to two distinct approaches to CSR—*explicit* and *implicit*.[45] A comparison of these two approaches to CSR is presented in Table 10.2.

Explicit CSR refers to corporate policies that speak to responsibility for some societal interest and typically involve voluntary programs by organizations that address issues perceived as being the social responsibility of the company. These often combine social and business interests, such as the response of U.S. firms to working conditions in Asian supply chains. Explicit CSR, while it may reflect governmental or broader institutional views, is at the discretion of the organization. In contrast, *implicit* CSR consists of mandatory or customary requirements for organizations to address stakeholder issues within the wider framework of formal and informal institutions of society. Representative business associations, as opposed to individual firms, are directly involved in the definition and legitimization of these activities. Explicit approaches to

Table 10.2 Explicit and Implicit CSR Compared

Explicit CSR	Implicit CSR
Describes corporate activities that assume responsibility for the interests of society	Describes corporations' role within the wider formal and informal institutions for society's interests and concerns
Consists of voluntary corporate policies, programs, and strategies	Consists of values, norms, and rules that result in (often codified and mandatory) requirements for corporations
Incentives and opportunities are motivated by the perceived expectations of different stakeholders of the corporation	Motivated by the societal consensus on the legitimate expectations of the roles and contributions of all major groups in society, including corporations

Source: Matten & Moon (2008).

CSR are typical of U.S. organizations, while implicit approaches are more consistent with the European (and to some extent Asian) context. For example, explicit CSR practices with regard to customers and community stakeholders have been found to be more prevalent in the U.S. than in China.[46] However, there may be a worldwide trend toward more explicit CSR, especially in larger firms, as local governments and industry associations change their focus and as locally important CSR issues (such as genetic engineering in Europe) emerge.[47]

Organizational Differences

Some research suggests that CSR positioning reflects the overall strategic orientation of the MNE. For example, while all MNEs place importance on global CSR issues, such as preservation of the environment, only multidomestic and transnational MNEs place significant importance on local CSR issues, such as creating employment in developing countries.[48] Also, CSR initiatives may be driven primarily by pressures in the environment or by values embraced inside the organization. Both may be important and reinforce each other. For example, one study found that both trade intensity and management commitment to ethics contributed to higher corporate social performance and these effects were greater when both were present. However, there was no difference between MNEs and local firms in their corporate responsibility performance.[49]

Global HR and CSR

Controversy regarding the proper role of business in society[50] has in the past fueled debate about the necessity of CSR activities. Today, however, whether or not management sees value in CSR activities may be largely irrelevant as there is a rapidly growing interest in the social dimension of business. The pressures for a greater concern for the environment, work practices, and human rights come from increased regulation by a diverse set of international institution such as the UN and OECD, from consumers who are increasingly making purchases in accordance with CSR criteria, and from financial markets where a growing number of investors are looking for socially responsible investments.[51] CSR involves many dimensions that affect almost all facets of an organization. Table 10.3 presents a list of the variety of issues that have been included under the CSR concept.

While labor issues are often at the core of the ethical questions that arise under this umbrella concept, many of the issues seem unconnected. However, HR is often at the forefront in all manner of CSR activities. There are at least four reasons for this.[52]

First, of course, many CSR principles are directly related to employees as a key stakeholder group. Issues of discrimination, working conditions, health and safety, harassment, pay, child labor, forced-labor freedom of association, and collective bargaining are all prominent among CSR issues.

Second, the social and ethical dimensions of CSR involve people and their relationships, which relates to the values of the organization. The link between an

Table 10.3   Issues Covered by CSR

• Environmental	• Concern for human rights
• Fair trade	• Philanthropic history
• Organic produce	• Cooperative principles
• Not tested on animals	• Support for education
• Community involvement	• Participates in local business initiatives
• Cause-related marketing	• Supports national business initiatives
• Charitable giving	• Commitment to reporting
• Religious foundation	• Employees schemes
• Support for social cause	• Refusal to trade in certain markets

Source: Howard and Willmott (2001).

organization's values (its culture) and the resources of the company is often made through HR decisions. CSR can be driven from the top, by the values of leaders, or from the bottom by employees who have direct knowledge of the influence of their work. In any case, HR plays a critical role. Recognition of this linkage is reflected in the fact that HR departments are second only to legal departments in developing corporate codes of conduct (discussed ahead).[53]

Third, CSR often requires a significant change in the philosophy and behavior of organizational units. HR is well positioned to act as a change agent through its roles in organizational socialization, training and development, and the management of reward systems. Some organizations use appraisal and pay systems to encourage socially responsible behavior by making bonus payments partly dependent on health and safety and environmental and employee satisfaction outcomes.[54]

Finally, CSR is becoming central to the perception that an organization is a good employer. A poor reputation in this regard can have an adverse effect on recruitment and retention of staff in an increasingly competitive labor market. And employees need to understand the point of CSR initiatives for them to be effective. HR is a central player in communicating with and engaging employees and is therefore a focal point for CSR activities.

The pressures for business to respond to the greater needs of society have existed for centuries. The specific issues may have shifted, and the intensity of these pressures may have grown but at the core of these issues is a concern for the ethical dimension of decisions and actions of organizations. Nowhere are these issues more apparent than in international organizations that operate in countries with very different values, attitudes, and beliefs about appropriate behavior.

Ethical Global HR Decisions

CSR and business ethics are distinct concepts in that business ethics involves who does or should benefit from particular decisions, while CSR refers to the broader integration of social and environmental concerns into business operations. Increasingly, however, a focus on CSR requires organizations around the world to recognize the ethical dimension involved in their decisions. Although they generally agree that sound ethics is good for business, they are very skeptical in their views about the existence of unethical practices in their industry.[55]

The decisions that international managers make cross cultural as well as geographic boundaries. In crossing these boundaries, the consensus about what is morally correct erodes in the face of differing values and norms. For example, discrimination in employment against women that is reprehensible in one culture is a normal expression of gender-based roles in another. The study of ethical decision making in organizations has resulted in both normative and prescriptive approaches (what you should do) and in descriptive approaches (what is actually done). However, managers and organizations are reluctant to have their *ethics* directly observed or measured. Therefore, we know much more about what should be done than we do about what organizations and managers actually do. The following outlines some common normative frameworks or moral philosophies for ethical decision making.

Moral Philosophies

A moral philosophy is a set of principles used to decide what is right or wrong.[56] Organizations and managers can be guided by one of several moral philosophies when making decisions or designing a policy that presents an ethical dilemma. The main categories of moral philosophies that are relevant to global HR decisions are (a) teleology or consequential models, (b) deontology or rule-based models, and (c) cultural relativism.

Consequential Models

Consequential models focus on the outcomes or consequences of a decision to determine if the decision is ethical. A key precept of this principle as a guide for decision making is utilitarianism.[57] Utilitarianism is the moral doctrine that we should always act to produce the greatest possible balance of good over harm for everyone affected by our decision.[58] Selecting a decision that considers the interests and maximizes the utility for all individuals and groups affected by a decision is in reality extremely difficult. It becomes even more difficult when those stakeholders affected by a decision have culturally different values and attitudes. Sometimes it is suggested that general rules (religious norms, for example) if followed, will maximize the benefits to all and can be used as a shortcut to the complexity of evaluating the utility of each decision or policy. These models are guided by the belief that some types of behavior (e.g., refraining from excess profits) will always maximize the utility of everyone involved.

Deontological or Rule-Based Models

Deontological principles hold that human beings have certain fundamental rights and that a sense of duty to uphold these rights is the basis of ethical decision making rather than a concern for consequences.[59] One of the best known of these rule-based approaches is the categorical imperative of Immanuel Kant (1724–1804). Essentially, the categorical imperative asserts that individuals have the right to be treated as an entity unto themselves and not simply as a means to an end. Unlike utilitarianism, deontology argues that some behaviors exist that are never moral even though they maximize utility. An obvious difficulty with rule-based normative approaches to decision making is achieving wide consensus on which rules (whose values) to base fundamental rights.[60] Despite this difficulty, a number of transnational corporate codes have been constructed that attempt to specify a set of universal guides for international managers.[61] The OECD guidelines shown in Box 10.1 are an example. It might be possible to gain universal acceptance for such a set of fundamental rights if they protect something of great importance in all cultures, if they are under continuous threat, and if all cultures can absorb the cost of protecting them.[62] However, some research suggests that national culture affects the preference of individuals for consequential versus rule-based principles in ethical decision making. For example, consequential principles are preferred in China, but ruled-based approaches are preferred in the United States, Mexico, and to some extent, Korea. More important, perhaps, is that managers in different cultures can subscribe to the same moral philosophy but still choose to behave in ways that are very different.[63] This is the problem of cultural relativism.

Cultural Relativism

In cultural relativism, moral concepts are legitimate only to the extent that they reflect the habits and attitudes of a given culture.[64] Ethical standards are specific to a particular culture, and any cross-cultural comparison is meaningless. What is considered unethical in one culture might be quite acceptable in another even though the same moral principle is being adhered to. Cultural relativism implies that one should not impose one's own ethical or moral standards on others and that international decisions should be evaluated in the context of differences in legal, political, and cultural systems. However, it also leaves open the opportunity to attribute a wide range of behavior to cultural norms. The use of child labor in Myanmar and China[65] and discrimination against women in Japan and Saudi Arabia[66] are just two examples of conduct that is attributed to cultural relativism. To adopt the concept of cultural relativism in its entirety declares global business decisions an arena where anything goes.[67] For cultural relativism to hold up as a useful model for global business decisions, we must declare that even the most hideous or reprehensible acts are not objectively wrong but depend on how a culture defines *wrong*. However, most of us can imagine acts that we cannot defend in terms of variation in cultural practice.

Corporate Codes of Conduct

The problems associated with ethical relativism become clear to HR managers when faced with the common dilemma of an employment practice that is viewed as wrong in the home country but acceptable in the host country. The occurrence of these situations has caused many multinationals to develop written codes of conduct. While there are sources (mostly trade or employment legislation) that mandate that certain issues are addressed by businesses,[68] corporate codes of conduct are largely voluntary initiatives. Often developed in response to a particular crisis in their supply chain, these codes have been widely criticized as "corporate gloss" and public relations exercises with a goal of preempting accusations of unacceptable practices.[69] Indeed, a PricewaterhouseCoopers survey found that nearly 30% of CEOs regard CSR mainly as a PR issue.[70] Interestingly, a recent study showed that the process of establishing an MNE code of conduct involved negotiations with an international union federation or works council in less than 20% of the cases, with U.S. MNEs being much less likely to conduct such negotiations compared to their Nordic and German counterparts.[71]

Even when they are well-intentioned, a number of issues have been raised about corporate codes of conduct. These include failure to translate the code in languages other than that of headquarters (often English), the lack of availability of the code throughout the organization, and failure to monitor and enforce the code. Even the monitoring of codes by large accounting firms has come into question in the wake of conflicts of interest brought to light by the Enron crisis. While many organizations file CSR reports, only a minority includes any hard data about what CSR has accomplished, even in cases where it would have been relatively easy to obtain.[72]

In addition, there are significant differences in the content of these codes, according to a review of 215 codes of conduct conducted by the ILO. The most frequently addressed issues were occupational health and safety (75%), followed by discrimination in hiring or terms and conditions of employment (66%). Approximately 45% of the codes reviewed contained clauses relating to the elimination of child labor or refusing to work with companies that employ children, and 25% spoke to forced labor. Issues around wage levels appeared in about 40% of codes. Interestingly, only about 15% of codes dealt with freedom of association and collective bargaining. The selectivity in the areas covered by these codes is probably the result of the concern for particular issues by the firm, the extent to which various stakeholders are involved in the process of the creation of the code, and the degree to which a particular policy or practice is acceptable to the firm.[73]

A recent development is an international standard for Social Accountability (SA8000) along the lines of the ISO 9000 quality standard. SA8000 is based on the principles of international human rights norms as described in ILO conventions, the UN Convention on the Rights of the Child and the Universal Declaration of Human Rights. It measures the performance of companies in eight key areas: child labor, forced labor, health and safety, free association and collective bargaining, discrimination, disciplinary practices, working hours, and compensation. SA8000 also provides for a social accountability management system to demonstrate ongoing conformance with the standard.[74]

Issues of MNE social accountability are likely to remain to the forefront given the trend for governments to withdraw more and more from economic activities, with businesses left to fill in the gaps and play a major role in providing services that were once the domain of the state. Some have argued that MNEs have risen in prominence in a way that has diminished national political institutions.[75] This makes it necessary that they become more socially accountable. But there is also the opinion that CSR activities in many MNEs are mostly financially driven, with the utmost objectives to uphold the reputation of corporate brands. As to whether investment in CSR pays off, researchers have produced somewhat conflicting accounts. Some studies suggest negative financial outcomes, but more studies appear to find positive outcomes in terms of increased corporate reputation and improved financial returns, with some differences across industries.[76]

CSR and the Global Supply Chain

A major challenge facing MNEs results from global supply chains and the conditions of workers in countries in which its downstream suppliers operate. These challenges are particularly acute in textiles, footwear, and agriculture where very large percentages of production are outsourced to independent companies in foreign countries. These suppliers are often located in the developing world where working conditions are well below that of the firm's home country. For MNEs, the challenge is not only navigating the legal, cultural, and political context on its own behalf but recognizing that the overseas supplier faces its own local pressures. Responding to this challenge requires MNEs to seek creative solutions to the ethical dilemmas these situations create. For example, Levi Strauss discovered that the issue of two of its Bangladesh suppliers employing workers under the minimum working age of 15 was not as simple as it first seemed. In Bangladesh it is not uncommon for children this young to be the sole support for the family. Rather than just instruct its suppliers to fire the underage workers or terminate their contracts, Levi Strauss negotiated an agreement in which the factories agreed to pay the underage workers their salaries and benefits while they attended school and then offer them full-time jobs when they reached legal working age.[77] It is important to note that Levi Strauss discovered the underage workers in an assessment of their suppliers' compliance with what the company calls their Terms of Engagement. These guidelines specify the requirements by which all of their contract factories and licensees must abide—including ethical standards, legal requirements, environmental requirements, and community involvement. They also set out employment standards and specifically address issues of child labor, forced labor, disciplinary practices, working hours, wages and benefits, freedom of association, discrimination, and health and safety.[78] Similar creative solutions have been found by IKEA for suppliers of carpets in India, even though carpets make up a very small percent of IKEA's sales, and it would have been very easy to sidestep the issue.[79] Sometimes, however, there are few short-term alternatives to just leaving the market and advocating for change as shown in Box 10.2.

Box 10.2   Government-Approved Child Labor

My 9-year-old son's list of daily tasks is pretty brief. Make your bed. Feed the dog. Do your homework. Pick up after yourself. Simple stuff.

If we lived in Uzbekistan, it could be a different story. Each fall, the Uzbekistan government closes schools and forces more than one million children to work in the country's cotton fields. This is child labor, driven not by poverty but by government policy. And why? It earns the government more than $1 billion annually. If you're a citizen of the developed world, it may seem like a distant problem. But remember what's happening in Uzbekistan…and think about what happens with cotton once harvested. It's often made into clothing—like khakis, shirts, and jeans.

That brief list of products should tell you why Levi Strauss & Co. cares about what's happening in Uzbekistan: We don't want cotton textiles made with child labor used in our products. That's why we've prohibited the use of cotton from Uzbekistan since 2008, when credible sources brought this issue to our attention. We were the first U.S. apparel brand and/or retailer to prohibit the use of Uzbek cotton in its supply chain, and we're proud that others have joined us. But the fact is prohibiting the use of Uzbek cotton in our products is difficult to verify. As a commodity, cotton is challenging to trace as it moves from farm to textile mill to garment factory. We're working closely with experts in supply chain traceability to address this challenge. It's important to us as a company, to those of us who work here, and to our customers.

My uncle was a cotton farmer in West Texas. It's difficult, backbreaking work— for an adult. From my perspective, forcing children to do this kind of hard labor is cruel, especially when you're depriving them of an education in the process.

Our hope at Levi Strauss & Co. is that, with mounting international awareness and advocacy, we will see real change by the Uzbek government to end the practice of forced child labor in Uzbekistan.

As my son grows, his daily chores will change. Still, he and I can both be thankful that his tasks will never be anything like those currently faced by the children in the cotton fields of Uzbekistan.

Source: Cory Warren, Editor. LS&Co. Unzipped, http://www.levistrauss.com/blogs/government-apprived-child-labor.

Global HR has a significant role to play in shaping and implementing policies relating to the broader social interests of the organization. Whether acting as the champion of employee interests, as guardian of the corporate culture, or as organizational change agent, global HR is a central player in the ethical behavior of the organization. In a global context, this behavior should be guided by respect for the core human values that establish the moral threshold for business decisions, combined with a respect for local traditions and a belief that context matters in determining an appropriate course of action.[80] This approach will often lead to creative solutions to ethical dilemmas in international business operations that transcend the simple enforcement of corporate codes of conduct.

Chapter Summary

This chapter discusses the related topics of international employee representation and CSR. Contemporary international employment relations is based in the industrial relations systems that exist in the various societies in which MNEs operate. These systems are composed of organizations, employees, and government that maintain a balanced relationship with each within the society. However, the transnational capabilities of the MNE, such as the ability to relocate factors of production, their remote location of authority, and their significant resources, upset the balance of these systems. In order to try to reestablish this balance, organized labor exchanges information and coordinates activities through trade secretariats as well as lobbying for favorable national legislation. In addition, international organizations such as the OECD have established guidelines for multinational organizations with regard to labor relations as well as broader issues of social responsibility. Global HRM plays a crucial role in both the formulation and implementation of policies and procedures with regard to CSR. At the core of many CSR activities is the ethical dimension of business decisions. A common ethical dilemma that often confronts multinationals occurs when practices considered proper in a foreign location are unacceptable at home. Global HR has a key role to play in finding creative solutions to these difficult problems.

Questions for Discussion

1. Describe how the MNE upsets the balance of national labor relations systems.

2. Why is there a decline in union density around the world? What is the likely cause of dramatic rises and falls in unionization?

3. Describe the ways in which a MNE might organize its international industrial relations.

4. What is a works council and why might MNEs be interested in them?

5. Describe and give examples of the key ethical dilemma(s) that confronts most MNEs.

Notes

1. This case is fictional but based on an incident that occurred with Hyster Co. as reported in the *Wall Street Journal*, Nov 30, 1983.
2. Sisson, Arrowsmith, & Marginson (2003).
3. Croucher & Cotton (2009).
4. While recognizing newer terms, such as *employment relations*, we use the more traditional term *industrial relations* here.

5. Dunlop (1958).
6. Poole (1986).
7. Hyman (2004).
8. Rogers & Streeck (1995); Hannon (2011).
9. Clegg (1976).
10. Briscoe, Schuler, & Tarique (2011); Schmitt & Mitukiewicz (2012).
11. Schmitt & Mitukiewicz (2012); Croucher & Rizov (2012).
12. ILO Press Release, November 4, 1997.
13. Poole (1986).
14. Briscoe & Schuler (2004).
15. Hamill (1984); Enderwick (1984); Rosenzweig & Nohria (1994).
16. Kochan, McKersie, & Cappelli (1984).
17. Hamill (1984).
18. Hamill (1984).
19. de Nijs (1995).
20. Bean (1985); International Confederation of Free Trade Unions (2004) http://www.icftu .org/pubs/globalisation/EN/report.pdf.
21. International Confederation of Free Trade Unions (2004).
22. Cooke and Noble (1998); Radulescu and Robson (2013).
23. Prahalad & Doz (1999).
24. Prahalad & Doz (1999).
25. Templin, N. (1996, March 20). *Wall Street Journal.*
26. de Nijs (1995).
27. See Kosterlitz (1998).
28. See Neuhaus (1982).
29. de Nijs (1995).
30. http://www.ilo.org/global/lang--en/index.htm.
31. See Addison & Siebert (1994) and http://www.europarl.europa.eu/charter/pdf/text_en.pdf.
32. Daniels, Radebaugh, & Sullivan (2011).
33. See *Wal-Mart: The high cost of low price.* http://www.imdb.com/title/tt0473107/.
34. Enderwick (1982).
35. European Trade Union Confederation, http://www.etuc.org/r/57.
36. See Sisson (2006) for a discussion of various forms of employee representation.
37. Hancke (2000).
38. Maginson, Hall, Hoffmann, & Müller (2004).
39. Maginson, Hall, Hoffmann, & Müller (2004).
40. Sisson (2006).
41. Matten & Moon (2008).
42. Cooke (2011).
43. See Sethi (1975) for a discussion of social responsiveness.
44. Whitley (1999).
45. Matten & Moon (2008).
46. Lo, Egri, & Ralston (2008).
47. Lo, Egri, & Ralston (2008).
48. Husted & Allen (2006).
49. Muller & Kolk (2010).
50. For example, see Friedman (2002) for a discussion.
51. Fuentes-Gracía, Núñez-Tabales, & Veroz-Herrandón (2008).

52. This discussion is based on Lam & Khare (2010).
53. Sachdev (2006).
54. Maitland (2003).
55. Brenner & Molander (1977).
56. Ferrell & Fraedrich (1994).
57. Mill (1863).
58. Shaw (1996).
59. Borchert & Stewart (1986).
60. Donaldson (1989).
61. See Frederick (1991) for more on this topic.
62. Donaldson (1989).
63. Phatak & Habib (1998).
64. Donaldson (1989).
65. Beaver (1995).
66. Mayer & Cava (1993).
67. Donaldson (1989).
68. Sachdev (2011).
69. Klein (2000).
70. Sachdev (2006).
71. Sachdev (2011).
72. Sachdev (2006).
73. Diller (2008).
74. http://www.sa-intl.org/index.cfm?fuseaction=Page.ViewPage&PageID=937.
75. Sachdev (2011).
76. Baird, Geylani, & Roberts (2012); Aguinis & Glavas (2012).
77. http://www.levistrauss.com/sites/default/files/librarydocument/2010/4/Case_Study_Child_Labor_Bangladesh.pdf.
78. http://www.levistrauss.com/sustainability/people/worker-rights.
79. Luce (2004).
80. Donaldson (1996).

11

Emerging Issues in Global HRM

LEARNING OBJECTIVES

After reading this chapter you should be able to

- describe the changes in the global business environment that will affect HRM,
- discuss the importance of relating HRM activities to firm performance,
- discuss the role of the HRM function and HR professionals in the future,
- describe the changes that are likely in global talent management, and
- outline the challenges associated with global mobility in the future.

Tension in Indonesia

Ian McKinstry general manager of global human resources for Sydney-based AusBank, had been enjoying watching Australia demolish Italy in the Rugby World Cup, when a news bulletin caused him to switch to Sky News Australia. The screen was filled with images of water cannons spraying rioters and protestors beating an unconscious police officer. Most disturbing for Ian was the travel advisory from the Australian government that Australian citizens should consider leaving Indonesia. AusBank had 150 employees in Indonesia, and this was his cue to initiate the bank's crisis management plan.

The riots began over an apparent misunderstanding over the fate of the tomb of Habib Hasan bin Muhammad Al Hadad, a revered 18th-century Arab cleric known to Indonesians as Mbah Priok. Shortly after dawn, members of the public order branch of the police, called Satpol, arrived to evict squatters and remove illegal buildings on the land surrounding the tomb. But residents of Tanjung Priok port, where the tomb is located, believed the police and city officials were there to tear it down and attacked them. The violence spread rapidly, and ethnic Chinese businesses quickly became the new targets of the rioters. While ethnic Chinese make up only about 3% of Indonesia's population, they control a substantial part of the economic wealth of the country. Some Prebunis (native Indonesians) felt that this economic power was a result of a close association with and patronage from the previous Suharto government, and thus ethnic Chinese were often scapegoats regardless of the issue.

Ian's first call was to Bill Witherspoon at Brave Heart Security, with whom AusBank had contracted for global security. Bill had already contacted his Jakarta office, and plans were being made to move all expatriates and their families to foreign hotels where they would be more secure and could be evacuated more easily if it came to that. But that's only about 15 employees, thought Ian. What about the rest of the staff? We don't have an automatic protocol for local nationals. Should I offer emergency assistance to them, especially the ethnic Chinese? The cost of that would be huge, and what would be the reaction if I only provided security to some local employees and not others.

Ian turned back to the television; the final score of the rugby was Australia 32 to Italy 6, but there were fires burning on the streets of Jakarta. Maybe this will all just blow over, he hoped.

Introduction

The issues associated with having HRM policies and procedures that apply to all employee types in every location in which a global firm operates is highlighted in the previous vignette. Integrating local, regional, and global HR policies and procedures is only one of the challenges that are presented by the complexity, interconnectedness, growing diversity, and discontinuous change that are the characteristics of the global business environment.[1] In this chapter we discuss the changing environment of global business and the challenges this presents for global HRM.

Changing Environment of Global HRM

From a wide range of global business environment issues, we focus on five trends that present challenges for global HRM in the future. These are the uneven economic development that is occurring around the globe, the influence that transition/emerging economies have as they grow in importance on the global stage, the exponential rate of change in information and communications technology, the increased pressure on and concern for the natural environment, and finally, the changes in the profile of global organizations.

Uneven Economic Development

Economic development within nations affects the availability of wage-earning jobs. In developing countries, working hours are longer, part-time employment is high, and many people work several part-time jobs because of limited full-time employment. Additionally, few developing countries provide the type of social safety net enjoyed in the industrialized world, and workers are often subject to a variety of abuses on the job, including discrimination based on gender and the employment of children.

According to the World Bank, almost half the world lives on less than US$1,000 per year, and at least 80% live on less than US$3,650 per year with the bottom of the pyramid anchored by the Democratic Republic of the Congo at US$231 GNP per capita. This compares to a 2011 GNP per capita of US$98,102 for Norway, US$60,642 for Australia, US$56,927 for Sweden, and US$48,442 for the United States.[2] In addition, non-income dimensions of global inequality are on the rise[3] and include inequalities in health, access to education, employment, gender, and so on, which, apart from making poverty even more devastating, also lead to greater marginalization within society. MNEs create many of the jobs on which the domestic economies of developing countries are based and can therefore influence work lives in these countries.

Uneven economic development is the second (after political issues) greatest influence on worldwide migration as economic migrants cross boundaries between developing and developed countries.[4] These immigrants increase the diversity of the workforce and add to the managerial complexity of the firms that employ them. Additionally, policies that favor the migration of skilled workers raise issues about the so-called *brain drain* from less developed countries.[5] Although the majority of economic migrants are men, there is a trend toward the migration of more women.[6] Another trend that is important to consider is what might be called reverse migration. Traditional economic migration involves a permanent move from a developing to a developed country. However, because of economic liberalization, a significant number of migrants are choosing to return to their country of origin. This reverse migration has most often been seen with Chinese and Indian migrants, and involves the high-tech sector or, more broadly, on professional employees.[7] Reverse migration can also occur as business conditions in a country shift from attractive to unattractive. For example, many Eastern Europeans who migrated to their more advanced EU neighbours after the EU enlargement in early 2000s are returning home as the post 2008 global financial crisis worsened conditions in the EU.[8] These migration patterns might be thought of as a continuous *brain circulation* rather than brain drain[9].

Difference in the cost of labor between the developed and developing world is also influencing the migration of *jobs* to countries where labor is cheap and abundant. In addition to direct labor cost savings, this outsourcing of jobs can provide access to skills not available in the local labor pool. Although the first jobs to migrate are typically low-skilled manufacturing jobs, the trend is toward the migration of service and medium-skill jobs, such as those in call centers and payment processing centers. The final stage of job migration occurs when highly skilled professional and knowledge jobs are outsourced.[10] Job migration, in combination with the growing need for knowledge workers, will increase the demand for people with higher levels of education worldwide, increase the average age of workers (particularly in the developed world), and increase the numbers of women in the workforce (particularly in developing countries).

Developing countries continue to experience an increase in employment, which had slowed following the financial crisis of 2008/2009. However, the labor markets in most countries have not recovered from the global crisis, which has led to an increase in poverty and inequality even in the advanced economies. An annual global survey shows a heightened sense of socioeconomic insecurity in most parts of the world with 54% of the countries reporting an increase in the score of the Social Unrest Index in 2011 compared to 2010.[11] Contributing to social unrest is the increased fragmentation in religious ideology, ranging from the conservative Christian movement in the United States to influence of radical Islam around the globe.[12] As shown in the case that opened this chapter, social unrest influenced by income disparity can create an environment for global business that is even more dynamic and uncertain than ever.

Influence of Economies in Transition

The dramatic rise in the influence of developing and transition economies can perhaps be traced to the fall of the Berlin Wall on November 9, 1989.[13] This event left democratic, consensual, free market oriented governance as the most viable alternative in the modern world. By the early 1990s, a country that was not a democracy or democratizing society and held on to a highly regulated centrally planned economy was on the wrong side of history. The fall of state socialism had a ripple effect that was felt in the huge populations of China and India. With the help of the leveling effect of the Internet, an additional three billion people from largely closed economies were increasingly free to join the free market game. By 2000, as a result of the collapse of communism in the Soviet Union, India's shift in economic perspective and China's move to market capitalism (of course in China within the context of a communist government[14]) another 1.5 billion workers entered the global economic labor force. You can't add this many people to the world economy without having a huge effect, especially with the increase coming from societies with rich educational heritages. The whole relationship between geography and talent has changed. As Microsoft chairman Bill Gates has been reported as saying, "Thirty years ago if you had a choice between being born a genius on the outskirts of Bombay or Shanghai or being born an average person in Poughkeepsie, you would take Poughkeepsie, because your chances of thriving and living a decent life there, even with average talent, were greater. Now, I would rather be a genius in China than an average guy born in Poughkeepsie."[15] Talent has begun to outweigh geography.

Fundamental to economic transition is the replacement of one set of institutions that govern economic activity by another. As transition economies grow in importance on the global stage, HR managers will be confronted with the need to understand the legacy of state socialism that influences both organizations and their members outlined in Chapter 2.[16] Although organization members in transition economies are heavily affected by the external influences of the market, the new institutions that are acceptable in their own society will inevitably contain some vestiges of state socialism. Characteristics of organizations in this institutional context created a psychological contract between employees and the firm that differed dramatically from the Western capitalist model. Employees under state socialism were encouraged to perceive their relationship with the organization in long-term socio-emotional terms that included commitment and loyalty, consistent with the collective interest. The socialist legacy includes a high valuation of social security, general suspicion of organizations, a preference for direct management styles, and a more central (although declining) role of unions.[17]

In addition, two issues with regard to organization members in these countries should be noted. First, although managers in transition economies often have exceptional educational backgrounds, their exposure to Western-style business education is highly variable.[18] There has been a boom in management education in transition economies,[19] but there is also cause to be pessimistic about the ability to deliver management education in societies where there is so much to learn and still political and social resistance to a market economy.[20] Second, the cultural characteristics of individuals in these economies is likely to reflect hierarchical and collectivist value orientations that have been reinforced by the socialist system. For example, paternalistic management in these societies may have evolved because society fostered it. Although the leveling influence of globalization is increasingly present and there are many changes in legislation, formal administrative procedures and macroeconomic policies, business practices, and social values change a lot more slowly.[21] One commentator has aptly pointed out that new post socialist structures are built "not *on* the ruins but *with* the ruins of communism."[22]

Information and Communications Technology

The rapid growth of information and communication technologies and innovation in digital systems represent a revolution that has fundamentally changed the way people think, behave, communicate, work, and earn their livelihood. This *digital revolution* has created new ways to produce knowledge, educate people, disseminate information, conduct economic and business practices, engage politically, and run governments.[23] Box 11. 1 shows some key statistics regarding the exponential growth of key elements in the digital landscape.

Box 11.1   Key Statistics—Digital Revolution

Internet

- By the end of 2011, 2.3 billion people (1/3 of the world population) were online.
- In developing countries, the number of Internet users doubled between 2007 and 2011.
- By the end of 2011, 70% of households in developed countries had Internet access as compared to 20% in the developing world.
- Differences in Internet bandwidth are dramatically different around the world with a user in Europe averaging 25 times more international Internet capacity than a user in Africa.

(Continued)

(Continued)

Mobile Cellular

- Total mobile cellular subscriptions reached almost 6 billion by the end of 2011, or about 86% global penetration.
- By the end of 2011, there were 105 countries with more mobile cellular subscriptions than inhabitants (including African countries such as Botswana, Gabon, and Namibia).
- Growth in mobile cellular is being driven by developing countries, accounting for 80% of the new subscriptions in 2011.

Broadband (Wired and Mobile)

- By the end of 2011, there were more than 1 billion mobile broadband subscriptions and 590 million wired broadband subscriptions worldwide.
- Mobile broadband is the most dynamic information and technology service with a 40% growth rate in 2011.
- Mobile broadband penetration is about 51% in the developed world but only 8% in developing countries.
- Wired broadband growth in developed countries has slowed to about 5% (2011), whereas developing countries grew at 18% in 2011.
- In 2011, 30 million wired broadband subscriptions were added in China (half the new subscriptions worldwide).

Source: ITU World Telecommunications/ICT Indicators Database (2012).

The digital revolution has created the platform for a free flow of information, ideas, and knowledge across the globe. The Internet has become a global resource that is important to both the developed world as a business and social tool and the developing world as a passport to a more level playing field as well as economic, social, and educational development. A particularly impressive example was the effect of Facebook and other social networking sites during the Egyptian revolution in 2011.[24]

However, as the statistics in Box 11.1 point out, there remains a *digital divide* that separates those who are connected to the digital revolution in information and communications technology and those who have no access to the benefits of the new technologies. Information and communications technology services continue to be more affordable in developed as opposed to developing countries, but the cost of technology is decreasing (down 18% from 2008–2010) with the steepest drop of 52.2% in fixed broadband prices in developing countries.[25] As the cost of technology decreases, the developing world is making steady progress in coming online. And as the world's online population becomes more culturally diverse, the Internet will lose its U.S.-centric flavor and may over time be as generalized and invisible as today's electrical networks. The influence of the flow of high-quality and inexpensive information will be felt by firms both in the organization of work and in consumer behavior, as well as by societies as they adjust to this influence.

The ability to take advantage of knowledge provided by the digital revolution can be a strategic advantage for organizations[26] and a source of power for individuals in global organizations.[27] MNEs will increasingly rely on people as opposed to organizational structures in order to thrive in a knowledge-based competitive environment. Information technology can become an equalizer in terms of access to knowledge and may also have an effect on work opportunities. For example, because of strong cultural norms, having a career and a family was impossible for Japanese women until some women began setting up Internet-intensive home businesses.[28] On the downside, the constant connection to work that is available through electronic media is having a profound influence on how individuals view and manage their relationship to their organization and on navigating the boundaries between their personal and professional lives.[29]

Another example of how the Internet is reshaping decades-old patterns of interaction involves the advent of the massive open online courses, (MOOCs). They allow access to previously inaccessible education, which can be hugely beneficial to both individuals and organizations. In less than 2 years since its founding, Coursera, a for-profit MOOC provider boasted more than 1.7 million students. Elite U.S. universities such as Princeton, Brown, Columbia, and Duke have partnered with Coursera to offer specially designed free, noncredit classes. These classes are very different from open courseware and are designed in a way that encourages real time peer-to-peer collaboration. At present, it is predominantly U.S. universities that offer such classes, but by some estimates the majority of students who take them come from outside the United States.[30] While details regarding the business model (including delivery, grading approaches, certification, etc.) are still being worked out, few doubt that these developments will have major implications for education and professional training and development.

In order to get the benefit from information and communications technology, the business practices associated with the new technology have to change as well. Because of changing work methods, such as virtual global teams, the most in demand jobs 10 years from now may not even exist today. What's next is difficult to predict. The possible long-term impact of such changes is only beginning to be analysed, but it is clear that the revolution in information and communications technology is only beginning.[31]

Concern for the Natural Environment

The unprecedented economic growth and prosperity that occurred during the 20th century has been accompanied by extreme damage to the natural environment on which it was based.[32] A recent study commissioned by the United Nations (involving 1,360 experts) concluded that in the second half of the 20th century, humans have changed the earth's ecosystems more rapidly and extensively than any time in human history. And 60% of the world's ecosystems were found to be degraded or used unsustainably.[33]

The world's population growth combined with global economic development is placing increasing demands on the resources we all share, which some authors[34] call the *global commons*. Obviously such natural resources as air and water are shared by everyone, but the global commons can also include such things as the atmosphere, space, and even (as discussed previously) the Internet.[35] The self-interest of nations and individuals also affects the land on which the world's food is grown. For example, some reports suggest that a significant portion of the world's farmland is threatened by erosion, nutrient depletion, and increased salinity. The impacts of global organizations on other aspects of the natural environment are perhaps more direct.[36] For example, despite the widespread use of electronic communication, global paper use continues to rise, and paper production requires vast amounts of timber. The approaches to dealing with the stress being placed on the natural environment by development are tremendously variable across countries and are potentially a result of the influence of national culture. Although it is rarely studied, some evidence suggests that culture is an important influence on a nation's performance regarding environmental sustainability. For example, the national-level cultural values of power distance and masculinity have been shown to be negatively related to country-level scores on the Environmental Sustainability Index of the World Economic Forum.[37] It is now obvious that activities in one part of the world affect organizations and individuals in other regions, and we are increasingly aware that the earth is a finite natural resource that must be shared by everyone. However, it is becoming apparent that national governments are ill equipped to address global environmental issues alone,[38] and large MNEs are more powerful than some governments. Therefore, there will be increasing pressure on the international organizations of the future to be environmentally responsible. Four trends toward more sustainable development are apparent:[39]

- Tensions between economic growth and environmental protection will continue to rise.
- Developing nations will not be able to imitate the consumption patterns of the developed world.
- Lifestyles in developed nations will need to change.
- Maximization of profits will need to be replaced by the expansion of opportunities.

Organizations involved in global business will be expected to explicitly consider their role in preserving the natural environment. Thus, the final environmental trend involves the vested interest we all have in protecting the natural environment and the fact that this influences the role organizations fulfill in society. Global organizations will increasingly find themselves engaged with the different values, attitudes, and assumptions about the natural environment that exist throughout the world.

Changing Organizational Context of Global HRM

Future challenges for HRM are shaped in part by how the organization as a whole responds to the complex and dynamic global environment. Several key trends are apparent and include changes in who are the global organizations and where and how they are doing business.[40] Influenced by globalization, the characteristics of organizations involved in global business are changing. Global organizations now include more small- and medium-sized enterprises and firms from small and developing economies. Because of the interconnectedness demanded by global operations, the influence of these new players on the international stage is broader than just their own strategies, structures, and management philosophies.[41] One way in which organizations are adapting to the emerging global business environment is by adapting their organizational structures, including the formation of more loosely coupled organizational forms and strategic alliances with these emerging players. These more complex structures will require the ability to manage the transfer of knowledge across organizational units embedded in different country contexts.[42]

Increasingly inexpensive communications technology makes the delegation of decision making and flatter organizations possible. However, hierarchical structures may continue to be prevalent in many cases because they provide a sense of identity, status, and belonging that can influence productivity.[43] A continuing issue for global organizations, regardless of the specific form they take, will be establishing and maintaining legitimacy in the wide range of environments in which they must operate.[44]

Global HRM Challenges

These five trends regarding the future environment of global business provide the background against which global HRM must function in the future. While the context in which global organizations operate has numerous implications for global HRM, four categories of challenges are of particular importance. These are the relationship of HRM to firm performance, sustainable HRM, global talent management, and global mobility and careers.

HRM and Firm Performance

As people become an increasingly important part of the competitive advantage of firms, it will become even more important to understand and demonstrate the linkage between global HRM and firm performance (often referred to as *strategic IHRM*). There are currently more questions than answers regarding this relationship. The most fundamental of these questions is the level of specificity at which HRM is evaluated.[45] HRM can be considered at a variety of levels as shown in Box 11.2.

Box 11.2   Levels of HRM

HRM philosophy—overall beliefs about HRM in the organization (e.g., promotion from within)

HRM strategy—defined strategic focus of HRM (e.g., quality, efficiency, innovation)

HRM systems—bundles of HRM practices (e.g., high-performance work systems)

HRM practices—actual HRM activities (e.g., formal performance appraisal)

HRM techniques—forms or web-based tools (e.g., behavioral-based performance appraisal form)

Source: Paauwe & Farndale (2012).

The level of specificity is important, especially when considering HRM in a global context. In addition, the specification of firm performance can be highly variable, ranging from profit or market value to productivity and quality outcomes, which are of course subject to numerous non-HR interventions. The most common approach to understanding the relationship between HRM and firm performance is to suggest that HRM activities lead to identifiable employee outcomes that in turn lead to firm performance. And consistent with the changing context for global business, firm performance is often addressed to a broader range of stakeholders. *Strategic* performance addresses the priorities of shareholders, directors, and so on, while *societal* performance considers outcomes related to broader groups of stakeholders, including employees, governments, and the broader society. *Professional* performance considers the functional integration of HR within the organization.[46]

A key idea at the systems level of HRM is that in order to achieve high performance, organizations must adopt certain bundles of *high-performance workplace practices*.[47] It is suggested that different strategic orientations and different environments call for the adoption of different bundles. However, the focus has mostly been on the immediate organizational environment and has not included a discussion of the international dimensions of HRM. Recent research has found that even given similar investment in high-performance work practices, organizational performance across countries varied. These differences in performance were attributed to differences in national economic cycles and on the efficacy of national business systems. Also, adopting collaborative HR practices has been shown to increase performance to a different degree in different countries, in that collaborative HR practices get more positive results in countries where they are better supported by the institutional context. In contrast, adopting practices that clash with the institutional context can lead to decreased firm performance.[48] The evidence available to date has concluded that at the systems level, HRM practices are weakly related to firm performance[49] and that high-performance work systems generally increase return on assets and reduce turnover.[50]

However, much more attention to the specifics of these relationships, including differences in the institutional context, will be required in the future.

A special case in which the significance of HRM to organizational performance has been made more clearly is in cross-border alliances. While HRM is important at all phases of mergers and acquisitions and international joint ventures, performance in these cross-border alliances relies heavily on the effectiveness of the integration stage. The need for sociocultural integration (creating a shared identity, positive attitudes, and trust) to the success of cross-border alliances focuses attention on HR strategies to achieve this.[51] And the HRM strategy with regard to structural integration focuses on keeping key employees' routines in place.[52] Because of the importance of integrating both people and processes, the strategic role of HRM is obvious. And because of the increased consolidation in many industries and the search for competitive advantage through increasing cross-boarder acquisition activity, global HRM's increased strategic role in these complex ventures is a future certainty.[53]

The elevation of global HRM to the level of strategic partner with other centers of expertise in the global organization raises several questions about the organization of the HRM function.[54] For example, how do HR professionals at the corporate level most effectively interact with their counterparts at the local level, and how are the boundaries managed? And how do national characteristics influence the status of HR in the organization? HR functions in Western organizations are typically regarded as more strategically oriented—than are their counterparts in India and China. This may result from the fact that HR has a more established history and is more deeply embedded in these Western countries.[55] The traditional transactional aspects of HR have not disappeared but are increasingly automated or outsourced. Other aspects of HR are increasingly under pressure to demonstrate their contribution to organizational objectives.

Despite the rhetoric that HR has become a strategic partner in organizations, some recent evidence illustrates that the configuration of the HRM departments and the people who lead them has changed little in the last fifteen years. While we see some evidence of increased formalization of HRM strategies and of HRM being represented in upper management, there is also evidence of HR's decreasing involvement in corporate strategy. And the people who are leading HR departments have changed little in terms of educational background or HR experience but are considerably more likely to be female (which some have associated with a declining credibility of the HR profession).[56] As the role of the global HR department evolves in the future, it will be affected by a wide range of factors, including national culture, changes in legal and regulatory systems, the history and status of HR in the organization, the sharing of best practices, and also the competencies of HR professionals.[57]

The competencies required for HR professionals in the future were documented in a recent series of studies.[58] These included response to environmental changes, such as computer and technology literacy, a broad knowledge of HR functions, and an ability to anticipate internal and external changes, but also factors related to the strategic role of HR, such as the ability to demonstrate financial impact of HR policies and practices and a focus on the quality of HR services. Most important perhaps is the need for HR professionals to define a global HR vision and communicate this by educating and influencing line managers; that is, exhibiting leadership for the HR function. Of course, the precise nature of the role of the HR professional is evolving, but it is clear that it will include working across levels and geographies to design and implement HR policies and procedures that have an identifiable impact on the performance of the overall organization.

Human Resource Management and Sustainability[59]

Sustainability is an important goal for many organizations and has two major components: environmental sustainability and social sustainability (efforts to eradicate poverty, inequality, assist disadvantaged communities, help diminish outbreaks of malaria, AIDS, etc.). Many organizations have realized that commitment to sustainability can increase profit margins by cutting costs and even increasing revenues. Further, investors recognize promoting sustainability is a proxy for good management. And attracting and retaining top talent is related to the extent to which sustainability is supported in the organization around the world.

Global HR departments have a central role in achieving sustainability goals in MNEs because these practices must be woven into the fabric of the organization by creating an organizational culture for which sustainability is a core component. Global HR can introduce a diverse portfolio of sustainability initiatives that begin with recruitment (i.e., clearly signaling the organizational values and aiming to attract individuals passionate about sustainability) and also involve redesigning work practices in ways that diminish the environmental footprint of the organization, giving employees guidance on how to act on their interest in promoting social and environmental responsibility, monitoring employee attitudes, and encouraging employees (through introducing key performance indicators related to sustainability and through compensation) to engage in sustainable practices. Many sustainability initiatives do not involve a large financial investment. For example, simple practices in which sustainability champions engage are facilitating carpooling, rewarding biking or walking to work, rewarding participation in volunteering days, giving time off for charity work, requesting that employees make double-sided copies of documents, donating used technology to local charities, using energy-efficient lighting systems and equipment, powering down computers during longer periods of inactivity, recycling office supplies, and using water-preserving water fixtures. Global HR departments can encourage such initiatives worldwide through communication and engagement. Indeed, in view of the fact that recognition is often the first step to addressing sustainability issues, one of the key tasks of global HR departments is to incorporate sustainability in organization-wide training and in leadership development programs. HR managers can also lead in designing *green* jobs (jobs that involve reducing pollution or waste, reducing energy use and use of limited natural resources, protecting wildlife and ecosystems, lowering carbon emissions, and developing alternative energy sources).

Box 11.3   Sustainability at SAP[60]

SAP is the world's third-largest provider of enterprise application software with operations in more than 130 countries. SAP is also an MNE that has pioneered many sustainability initiatives. For example, the company has launched a global network of sustainability champions, consisting of 125 champions worldwide, with all major locations in the United States, Canada, Germany, and the Asia Pacific represented in the network. These champions develop ideas for participation in various activities that are shared throughout the organization through online social networks at regular two-week intervals. There are four core areas of focus: energy reduction, travel (business and commuting), paper reduction, and social sustainability (micro credits, health, and diversity). SAP's goal is to achieve significant behavioral changes, a process that involves reexamining their perceptions, decision making, attitudes, and motivation towards a more sustainable organization. Further, SAP has stated that they seek to provide local answers to global issues. They analyze data on printing, commuting, and energy consumption, thus creating transparency on the respective realities in each location and region. These data are then analyzed to identify what remedies need to be introduced in which geography.

The role of global HR departments in sustainability has largely been in implementation rather than strategy formulation, echoing the discussion that becoming strategic partners is one of the key challenges for HR departments. While the business results of engaging in sustainable initiatives are still being evaluated, initial research has been quite positive. It has pointed to outcomes, such as improved employee morale, more efficient business processes, stronger public image, increased employee loyalty, increased brand recognition, attraction of top talent, and improved retention. Clearly, sustainability is an important issue that will increasingly influence the work of global HR departments in the future.

Global Talent Management

Numerous challenges for global HR stem from the fact that the demand for skilled workers is outstripping supply, labor markets around the world are rapidly changing, and the management competencies required in a global business environment are changing. Shortages of talent are an important driver of global talent management systems, but these shortages are not uniform across the world because of variation in immigration and education systems and government regulations regarding labor mobility.[61] In addition, the talent shortage is more severe in some industries than in others. In the future, organizations will need to have a global framework for talent management but one that also allows local subsidiaries to adapt to their specific circumstances.[62]

The development of global leaders tops the priority list of HR in the global organization.[63] The future managers and leaders who will be able to deal with the many additional layers of complexity that globalization brings to their jobs and who operate effectively within the complexity of the various trends in the cultures of the world will be different. They will be true global leaders, able to function effectively in a multinational context. They will have competencies that allow them to compete in an increasingly competitive and multicultural world.[64] Exactly what these competencies are and how they can be best developed is a matter of some debate. What seems to be clear, however, is that a key element is the cognitive development of managers so that they are capable of making sense of the complex environment in which they must operate.[65] Called variously global mindset, cultural intelligence, cognitive complexity, or multicultural personality,[66] this ability seems to be best developed through experience either on international assignment or through global projects.[67] However, some personality characteristics may predispose individuals toward developing this ability.[68] Therefore, in the future, global talent management systems may need to include assessments of the propensity to development needed abilities as well as programs of rotational postings and multinational team assignments.

A recent recognition in the development of management talent is that this process may be nonlinear.[69] The outcomes of the many daily experiences that contribute to management development may not be directly proportional to the experiences themselves. Certain intercultural experiences might trigger either a functional or dysfunctional competency development that is completely out of proportion to the event that triggered it. Small events such as a brief encounter with someone from another culture could create substantial insight if it forced individuals to confront and resolve fundamental differences in beliefs, while numerous overseas assignments might have little benefit in the absence of such cognitive development.[70] To the extent that global leadership development involves more than just compiling a portfolio of competencies, global HR needs to better understand this nonlinear process and find ways to facilitate the type of experiences that result in positive development.

The future of global talent management is focused on senior management development, succession planning, and developing a cadre of international managers.[71] A recent study from McKinsey suggested that the creation of globally consistent talent evaluation processes, the management of cultural diversity, and the mobility of global leaders were significantly related to financial performance, measured by profit per employee. Companies that were better in developing global talent were more likely to have top managers and promotion systems that actively encouraged their employees to gain international experience and provided incentives for managers to share their talent with other organizational units.[72]

A key consideration for organizations is the need to establish the effectiveness of an organization's global talent management system. To the extent that global talent management systems are effective and difficult for competitors to imitate, they can be a source of competitive advantage. What global HR managers need to establish is the causal linkage that explains how the attraction, development, and retention of key talent affects HR outcomes, and in turn, how these outcomes relate to indicators of organizational performance.[73]

Global Mobility and Careers

The character of global staffing is becoming increasingly complex as assignments to emerging markets, with their increased challenges, become more prevalent and as organizations are increasingly concerned with focusing on reducing costs associated with international assignments.[74] While it is unclear that a focus on reducing costs is a rational approach, given the strategic demands of global organizations, it remains a key area of concern.[75] Further complicating the picture is an increasing shortage of international management talent coupled with the importance of these individuals for implementing global strategy.[76] Constraints of the supply side of globally mobile managers include the underutilization of women,[77] dual-career issues,[78] and problems with repatriation.[79] However, as discussed in Chapter 9, few organizations expect a reduction in the use of traditional overseas assignments in the near future. Thus, global HRM must face up to the challenge of increasing the pool of talented managers willing to relocate, while at the same time containing costs. This may prove to be a difficult balancing act.

Increasingly, global mobility needs are being filled by a range of alternative types of international assignments. The increased use of these assignment types raises a number of issues for global HRM. First, while organizations typically have well-developed policies for traditional expatriates covering such things as organization support, compensation, reparation agreements, and the like, there is not the equivalent for alternative assignments. Employees attracted to these types of assignments may be quite different to traditional expatriates in terms of their motivation and thus have very different needs for support and so on. General policies for working overseas are unlikely to be effective, and a good deal of customization may be required. This is particularly true as the growth of emerging markets changes the demographic makeup of assignees. Individuals of different nationalities may be assigned within and across regions, including reverse assignments.[80]

The changing nature of the global assignee has raised new questions about what constitutes a career. The way individuals view their careers has shifted from a progression up the career ladder to a more subjective sense of what one does during one's work life. An issue that HR managers are increasingly facing is managing a multigenerational workforce, with each generation embracing a different notion of what is a career and what are the characteristics of a good career. The challenge to organizations is how to meet the expectations of distinct, generational groups. Different national contexts have produced different levels of generational differences across countries.[81] Therefore, solutions to managing a multigenerational workforce (such as baby boomers, generation X, and generation Y in the United States) that work in one country may be largely ineffective in another. And the evidence is mixed on whether younger generations around the world value similar aspects of careers. The implication for global HR managers is that no matter where their organization operates, they are likely to have to pay increasing attention to managing multigenerational workforces, including their differing interests in global mobility.

Another aspect of global mobility is that the kinds of knowledge and competencies required of global managers can be developed by means other than company-sponsored international assignments.[82] International experience, such as living in a foreign country as a child, develops learning and information-processing skills that can be usefully employed in organizations.[83] In the future, many employees will come to organizations with the kind of international experience and personal development that was previously associated with only an elite cadre of international executives. Global HR will need to find ways to leverage the skills of these internationally experienced employees or risk losing them to organizations more capable of absorbing their knowledge.

Another aspect of global mobility does not involve leaving one's own country. As a result of technology, many organizations are dealing with the need for talent around the world through the use of geographically distributed (virtual) teams. These teams change the nature of work by allowing members who are separated by time, geography, and organizational unit to collaborate. The ability of these teams to provide effective solutions to organizational issues depends on overcoming the additional barriers presented by the discontinuity between group members and electronic intermediation.[84] Global virtual teams seem to perform best when they have some sort of formal coordination mechanism, appropriate participation norms, and a strong group identity. Global HR's role in this type of mobility will include developing training for the skills to effectively use the technology and collaborate in this way, supporting the development and use of virtual teams and also in integrating this form of work into other HR routines and practices.[85]

A final aspect of the challenges to global mobility responds to the increasing complexity of global organizations. A key challenge for global HR will be integrating global, regional, and local policies and procedures. Recently, the idea that HR management needs to consider the idea of justice in formulating its policies has emerged.[86] HR policies and procedures should be fair to all categories of employees in all locations. For example, the compensation disparities that have traditionally existed between expatriates and local employees performing similar work will likely be unsustainable as the definition of what is an international assignment changes.[87] In addition, variation in employment rights and opportunities that exist around the world will potentially play a larger role in the formulation of HRM policies and procedures.

Related to the changing nature of global business organizations is what has been referred to as a decline in social capital. As organizations are more loosely coupled and individuals more mobile, the strong links with the organization and the sense of community decline.[88] Achieving the strategically necessary transfer of knowledge in highly interdependent but geographically dispersed organizations requires social capital (mutual trust, common goals, etc.). Building social capital in organizations as a way to encourage cooperative and proactive behaviors may be one of the most important challenges for global HRM in the future.[89] However, exactly how to accomplish this is very much on the drawing board.[90]

While the future is always uncertain, it seems fairly clear that global organizations will need to develop an in-depth understanding of new forms of working internationally and also adjust HR activities, policies, and procedures appropriately. Global HR will also need to come to grips with a more diverse international workforce in terms of what this means for knowledge sharing, strategy, and organizational change. And finally, global HR will need to effectively manage new employee groups, such as individuals who have self-initiated overseas experiences and are ready to take on international assignments early in their careers.[91]

Chapter Summary

This chapter highlights some of the challenges that global HR will face in the future as a result of the increased complexity, interconnectedness, growing diversity, and rapid change that is the result of globalization of business. The changing environment for global HRM is influenced by uneven economic development around the world that influences the characteristics of the global workforce, the increased influence of emerging and transition economies, the exponential growth and change in information and communications technology, and a deepening concern for the natural environment. In addition, global HRM is influenced by broader organizational response to changes in the external environment. Taken together, these five trends create numerous challenges for the future of global HRM.

Four broad categories of challenges for global HRM are apparent. The first involves demonstrating the link between global HRM and firm performance. As HRM is elevated to the level of strategic partner with other centers of expertise in the organization, it must demonstrate through its organization, activities, and the professionalism of its members the value added that HRM provides. Second, global HR seems ideally positioned to take the lead in the important issue of sustainable business practices, which is a growing concern for organizations and indeed for the broader society. Third, the demand for skilled workers combined with the changing demographics of the world's workforce will create numerous challenges under the heading of global talent management. Linked to the previous global HR issue, organizations will need to establish the effectiveness of their global talent management systems. Finally, changing needs, locations, and types of international assignments combined with an increasing focus on cost reduction are reshaping global mobility. Adding to this challenge is the changing nature of careers and the need to create policies and procedures that are fair across employee categories, countries, and regions. Thus, while not short on challenges, global HRM promises to be exciting, interesting, and an increasingly important aspect of international business in the future.

Questions for Discussion

1. What are the major aspects of globalization that affect HRM?

2. What is meant by the digital revolution, and what impact will it have on global business operations?

3. What are the key changes that are occurring in the world's workforce?

4. Discuss the future of different types of international assignments.

5. What implications does being fair to all employee categories have for global HRM?

Notes

1. See Parker (2005) for a discussion of globalization.
2. World Bank (2012).
3. ILO (2012).
4. Parker (2005).
5. Carr, Inkson, & Thorn (2005).
6. Parker (2005).
7. Chacko (2007); Tung (2008); Tung & Lazarova (2006).
8. Dougherty (2008).
9. Saxenian (2005).
10. See Rivoli (2009) for an interesting discussion of this process.
11. ILO (2012).
12. Taylor & Napier (2005).
13. This discussion is taken from Friedman (2005).
14. Wong (2010).
15. Friedman (2005).
16. Napier & Thomas (2004).
17. Martin (2006).
18. Napier & Thomas (2004).
19. Child & Tse (2001).
20. Puffer (1996).
21. Martin (2006).
22. Stark (1997), cited in Martin (2006, p. 1354).
23. World Summit on Information Society http://www.itu.int/wsis/index.html.
24. Sutter (2011).
25. ITU World Telecommunications/ICT Indicators database (2012).
26. Senge (1990).
27. Parker (2005).
28. Guth (2000).
29. See for example Perlow (2012).
30. Pappano (2012).
31. Friedman (2005).
32. Hoffman & Bansal (2011).
33. Millennium Ecosystem Assessment (2005).
34. Buck (1998).
35. Henderson (1999).
36. Parker (2005).
37. Park, Russell, & Lee (2007).
38. French (2003).
39. Parker (2005).
40. Taylor & Napier (2005).
41. See Parker (2005) for a discussion.
42. Bartlett & Ghoshal (1989).
43. Leavitt (2005).
44. See Kostova & Zaheer (1999) for a broader discussion.
45. Wright & Gardner (2003).

46. Paauwe (2004).
47. Huselid (1995).
48. See Gooderham & Nordhaug (2011) for a discussion; see also Rizov & Croucher (2009).
49. Wright & Gardner (2003).
50. Combs, Yongmei, Hall, & Ketchen (2006).
51. Stahl (2008).
52. Inkpen, Sundaram, & Rockwood (2000).
53. See Schuler & Tarique (2007) for a broader discussion.
54. This discussion is based on Stiles (2012).
55. Björkman, Budhwar, Smale, & Sumelius (2008).
56. Lazarova, Mayrhofer, & Brewster (2013).
57. Paauwe & Farndale (2012).
58. Towers Perrin (1992).
59. This section is written based on two SHRM reports on HR and sustainability: SHRM (2007); & SHRM, BSR, & Aurosoorya (2011).
60. For more on sustainability at SAP see http://www.sapsustainabilityreport.com/.
61. Cascio (2012).
62. Evans, Pucik, & Barsoux, (2002).
63. Scullion & Starkey (2000).
64. Suutari (2002).
65. Bartlett & Ghoshal (1989); Gupta & Govindarajan (2002).
66. See Thomas (2010) for a review of these concepts.
67. Osland, Bird, & Mendenhall (2012).
68. Caligiuri & Di Santo (2001).
69. Lichtenstein & Mendenhall (2002).
70. See Tadmor, Galinsky, & Maddux (2012).
71. See Scullion & Starkey (2000) for a discussion.
72. Guthridge & Komm (2008); Guthridge, Komm, & Lawson (2008).
73. Schuler & Tarique (2012).
74. Collings & Scullion (2012).
75. See Bonache & Stirpe (2012) for a more detailed discussion of compensation issues.
76. Scullion & Starkey (2000).
77. Linehan & Scullion (2008).
78. Harvey (1997).
79. Lazarova & Cerdin (2007).
80. Mayrhofer, Reichel, & Sparrow (2012).
81. Unite et al. (2012).
82. Inkson, Arthur, Pringle, & Barry (1997).
83. See Caligiuri & Tarique (2012).
84. See Thomas (2008).
85. See Jonsen, Maznevski, & Davison (2012).
86. Ferris, Hochwarter, Buckley, Harrell-Cook, & Fink (1999).
87. Bonache & Stirpe (2012).
88. Fukuyama (1995).
89. See Kostova & Roth (2003).
90. Taylor & Napier (2005).
91. Mayrhofer, Reichel, & Sparrow (2012).

Appendix

GLOBE Country Scores

Country	Assertiveness	Institutional Collectivism	In-Group Collectivism	Future Orientation	Gender Egalitarianism	Humane Orientation	Performance Orientation	Power Distance	Uncertainty Avoidance
				Regression Predicted Scores for Societal Cultural Values Scales					
Albania	4.39	4.30	4.98	5.17	4.04	5.16	5.47	3.47	5.17
Argentina	3.18	5.29	6.07	5.73	4.89	5.50	6.28	2.30	4.62
Australia	3.83	4.47	5.82	5.21	5.02	5.60	5.99	2.77	3.99
Austria	2.85	4.78	5.32	5.15	4.83	5.68	6.12	2.52	3.65
Bolivia	3.68	5.03	5.91	5.56	4.65	5.11	5.98	3.31	4.64
Brazil	3.06	5.57	5.17	5.60	4.91	5.52	5.98	2.59	5.00
Canada (English-speaking)	4.15	4.20	5.94	5.34	5.04	5.58	6.13	2.73	3.73
China	5.52	4.52	5.12	4.70	3.73	5.34	5.72	3.01	5.34
Colombia	3.45	5.27	5.99	5.52	4.85	5.43	6.15	2.21	4.92
Costa Rica	4.04	5.14	5.94	5.10	4.59	5.08	5.78	2.66	4.58
Denmark	3.59	4.41	5.71	4.49	5.20	5.59	5.82	2.96	4.01
Ecuador	3.57	5.19	5.81	5.62	4.42	5.13	5.95	2.36	4.95
Egypt	3.22	4.72	5.39	5.60	3.34	5.13	5.71	3.20	5.24
El Salvador	3.67	5.60	6.28	5.89	4.66	5.38	6.37	2.76	5.27
England	3.76	4.39	5.66	5.15	5.20	5.52	6.03	2.82	4.17

	Regression Predicted Scores for Societal Cultural Values Scales								
Country	Assertiveness	Institutional Collectivism	In-Group Collectivism	Future Orientation	Gender Egalitarianism	Humane Orientation	Performance Orientation	Power Distance	Uncertainty Avoidance
Finland	3.91	4.34	5.60	5.24	4.47	5.80	6.23	2.46	4.04
France	3.57	5.27	5.88	5.35	4.71	5.91	6.10	2.96	4.65
Georgia	4.29	3.79	5.58	5.45	3.83	5.48	5.63	2.86	5.23
Germany (former East)	3.24	4.86	5.38	5.36	4.97	5.56	6.24	2.74	4.02
Germany (former West)	3.21	5.07	5.46	5.06	5.06	5.63	6.27	2.66	3.38
Greece	3.05	5.41	5.47	5.17	4.84	5.28	5.79	2.57	5.16
Guatemala	3.65	5.16	5.95	5.78	4.49	5.24	5.96	2.49	4.85
Hong Kong	4.80	4.35	5.11	5.52	4.27	5.38	5.71	3.00	4.52
Hungary	3.42	4.57	5.58	5.74	4.65	5.48	5.97	2.59	4.74
India	4.65	4.59	5.22	5.43	4.40	5.20	5.87	2.58	4.58
Indonesia	4.50	4.96	5.46	5.48	3.71	5.06	5.54	2.38	5.04
Ireland	4.00	4.55	5.72	5.18	5.07	5.45	5.99	2.66	3.94
Israel	3.74	4.25	5.69	5.17	4.66	5.51	5.71	2.72	4.34
Italy	3.87	5.20	5.76	6.01	4.88	5.57	6.11	2.51	4.52
Japan	5.84	4.01	5.44	5.42	4.41	5.53	5.37	2.76	4.40
Kazakhstan	3.88	4.16	5.62	5.22	4.85	5.66	5.57	3.19	4.52
Kuwait	3.61	5.04	5.32	5.62	3.50	5.06	5.89	3.02	4.65
Malaysia	4.73	4.78	5.77	5.84	3.72	5.43	5.96	2.75	4.81
Mexico	3.67	4.77	5.78	5.74	4.57	5.10	6.00	2.75	5.18
Morocco	3.68	5.34	6.03	6.33	4.07	5.73	6.12	3.30	5.77
Namibia	3.76	4.26	6.13	6.30	4.20	5.47	6.52	2.59	5.19
Netherlands	3.13	4.76	5.39	5.24	5.10	5.41	5.71	2.61	3.34
New Zealand	3.52	4.31	6.54	5.90	4.32	4.85	6.24	3.56	4.17
Nigeria	3.14	4.86	5.31	5.80	4.16	5.71	5.99	2.66	5.45

(Continued)

(Continued)

	Regression Predicted Scores for Societal Cultural Values Scales								
Country	Assertiveness	Institutional Collectivism	In-Group Collectivism	Future Orientation	Gender Egalitarianism	Humane Orientation	Performance Orientation	Power Distance	Uncertainty Avoidance
Philippines	4.93	4.55	5.86	5.66	4.36	5.19	6.00	2.54	4.92
Poland	3.95	4.24	5.69	5.17	4.53	5.32	6.06	3.19	4.75
Portugal	3.61	5.40	5.97	5.50	5.12	5.40	6.41	2.45	4.50
Qatar	3.72	5.10	5.55	5.92	3.49	5.31	5.94	3.18	4.82
Russia	2.90	4.01	5.90	5.60	4.34	5.62	5.68	2.73	5.26
Singapore	4.28	4.42	5.46	5.46	4.43	5.66	5.70	2.84	4.08
Slovenia	4.61	4.36	5.71	5.43	4.78	5.31	6.41	2.50	5.03
South Africa (Black sample)	3.97	4.46	5.14	5.25	4.43	5.23	5.09	3.80	4.92
South Africa (White sample)	3.65	4.36	5.82	5.59	4.54	5.53	6.13	2.67	4.65
South Korea	3.69	3.84	5.50	5.83	4.23	5.61	5.41	2.39	4.74
Spain	4.01	5.25	5.82	5.66	4.82	5.63	5.85	2.23	4.80
Sweden	3.49	3.91	6.25	4.96	5.19	5.72	6.01	2.49	3.45
Switzerland	3.31	4.87	5.16	4.93	5.01	5.63	6.00	2.54	3.20
Switzerland French-speaking	3.83	4.42	5.54	4.89	4.77	5.68	6.17	2.80	3.84
Taiwan	2.91	4.95	5.30	4.94	3.88	5.15	5.58	2.77	5.14
Thailand	3.43	5.08	5.73	6.26	4.12	5.05	5.76	2.74	5.71
Turkey	2.68	5.18	5.63	5.71	4.46	5.40	5.34	2.52	4.61
United States	4.36	4.20	5.79	5.34	5.03	5.51	6.14	2.88	3.99
Venezuela	3.34	5.28	5.92	5.61	4.70	5.24	6.11	2.43	5.19
Zambia	4.24	4.55	5.64	5.76	4.27	5.37	6.08	2.37	4.45
Zimbabwe	4.60	4.84	5.74	6.01	4.40	5.20	6.33	2.65	4.68

Source: House et al. (2004).

Note: Corrected for response bias.

Cases

Case 1

Footwear International

R. William Blake

John Carlson frowned as he studied the translation of the front page story from the afternoon's edition of the Meillat, a fundamentalist newspaper with close ties to an opposition political party. The story, titled "Footwear's Unpardonable Audacity," suggested that the company was knowingly insulting Islam by including the name of Allah in a design used on the insoles of sandals it was manufacturing. To compound the problem, the paper had run a photograph of one of the offending sandals on the front page. As a result student groups were calling for public demonstrations against Footwear the next day. As Managing Director of Footwear Bangladesh Carlson knew he would have to act quickly to defuse a potentially explosive situation.

Footwear International

Footwear International is a multinational manufacturer and marketer of footwear. Operations span the globe and include more than 83 companies in 70 countries. These include shoe factories, tanneries, engineering plants producing shoe machinery and moulds, product development studios, hosiery factories, quality control laboratories and approximately 6300 retail stores and 50,000 independent retailers.

Footwear employs more than 67,000 people and produces and sells in excess of 270,000,000 pairs of shoes every year. Head office acts as a service center and is staffed with specialists drawn from all over the world. These specialists, in areas such as marketing, retailing, product development, communications, store design, electronic data processing and business administration, travel for much of the year to share their expertise with the various companies. Training and technical education, offered through company run colleges and the training facility at headquarters, provide the latest skills to employees from around the world.

Although Footwear requires standardization in technology and the design of facilities it also encourages a high degree of decentralization and autonomy in its operations. The companies are virtually self-governing, which means their allegiance belongs to the countries in which they operate. Each is answerable to a board of directors which includes representatives from the local business community. The concept of "partnership" at the local level has made the company welcome internationally and has allowed it to operate successfully in countries where other multinationals have been unable to survive.

Bangladesh

With a population approaching 110,000,000 in an area of 143,998 square kilometres (Figure 1),Bangladesh is the most densely populated country in the world. It is also among the most impoverished with a 1987 per capita Gross National Product of $160 US and a high reliance on foreign aid. Over 40% of the Gross Domestic Product is generated by agriculture and more than 60% of its economically active population works in the agriculture sector. Although the land in Bangladesh is fertile, the country has a tropical monsoon climate and suffers from the ravages of periodic cyclones. In 1988 the country experienced the worst floods in recorded history.

The population of Bangladesh is 85% Moslem and Islam was made the official state religion in 1988. Approximately 95% of the population speaks Bengali with most of the remainder speaking tribal dialects.

Bangladesh has had a turbulent history in the 20th century. Most of the country was part of the British ruled East Bengal until 1947. In that year it joined with Assam to become East Pakistan, a province of the newly created country of Pakistan. East Pakistan was separated from the four provinces of West Pakistan by 1600 kilometres of Indian territory and, although the East was more populous, the national capital was established in West Pakistan. Over the following years widespread discontent built in the East whose people felt that they received a disproportionately small amount of development funding and were under-represented in government.

Following a period of unrest starting in 1969 the Awami League, the leading political party in East Pakistan, won an overwhelming victory in local elections held in 1970. The victory promised to give the league, which was pro independence, control in the National Assembly. To prevent that happening the national government suspended the convening of the Assembly indefinitely. On March 26th, 1971, the Awami League proclaimed the independence of the Peoples republic of Bangladesh and civil war quickly followed. In the ensuing conflict hundreds of thousands of refugees fled to safety across the border in India. In December India, which supported the independence of Bangladesh, declared war and twelve days later Pakistan surrendered. Bangladesh had won its independence and the capital of the new country was established at Dhaka. In the years immediately following independence industrial output declined in major industries as the result of the departure of many of the largely non-Bengali financier and managerial class.

Source: Previously published in *International Management Behavior* (2000), edited by H. Lane, J. J. DiStefano, and Maznevski (pp. 165-172). Blackwell Business. Reprinted with permission.

Throughout the subsequent years political stability proved elusive for Bangladesh. Although elections were held, stability was threatened by the terrorist tactics resorted to by opposition groups from both political extremes. Coups and counter coups, assassinations and suspension of civil liberties became regular occurrences.

Since 1983 Bangladesh had been ruled by the self proclaimed President General H.M. Ershad. Despite demonstrations in 1987, that led to a state of emergency being declared, Ershad managed to retain power in elections held the following year. The country remains politically volatile, however. Dozens of political parties continually manoeuvre for position and alliances and coalitions are the order of the day. The principal opposition party is the Awami League, an alliance of eight political parties. Many of the parties are closely linked with so called "opposition newspapers" which promote their political positions. Strikes and demonstrations are frequent and often result from co-operation among opposition political parties, student groups and unions.

Footwear Bangladesh

Footwear became active in what was then East Bengal in the 1930's. In 1962 the first major investment took place with the construction of a footwear manufacturing facility at Tongi, an industrial town located 30 kilometres north of Dhaka. During the following years the company expanded its presence in both conventional and unconventional ways. In 1971 the then Managing Director became a freedom fighter while continuing to oversee operations. He subsequently became the only foreigner to be decorated by the government with the "Bir Protik" in recognition of both his and the company's contribution to the independence of Bangladesh.

In 1985 Footwear Bangladesh went public and two years later spearheaded the largest private sector foreign investment in the country, a tannery and footwear factory at Dhamrai. The new tannery produced leather for local Footwear needs and the export market while the factory produced a variety of footwear for the local market.

By 1988 Footwear Bangladesh employed 1800 employees and sold through 81 stores and 54 agencies. The company introduced approximately 300 new products a year to the market using their in house design and development capability. Footwear managers were particularly proud of the capability of the personnel in these departments, all of whom were Bangladeshi.

Annual sales in excess of 10,000,000 pairs of footwear gave the company 15% of the national market in 1988. Revenues exceeded $30 million US and after tax profit was approximately $1 million. Financially, the company was considered a medium contributor within the Footwear organization. With a population approaching 110,000,000, and per capita consumption of one pair of shoes every two years, Bangladesh was perceived as offering Footwear enormous potential for growth both through consumer education and competitive pressure.

The Managing Director of Footwear Bangladesh was John Carlson, one of only four foreigners working for the company. The others were the managers of production, marketing and sales. All had extensive and varied experience within the Footwear organization.

The Incident

On Thursday, June 22nd 1989, John Carlson was shown a copy of that day's **Meillat**, a well known opposition newspaper with pro Libyan leanings. Under the headline "Footwear's Unpardonable Audacity," the writer suggested that the design on the insole of one model of sandal produced by the company included the Arabic spelling of the word "Allah" (Figure 2). The story went on to suggest that Footwear was under Jewish ownership and to link the alleged offense with the gunning down of many people in Palestine by Jews. The story highlighted the fact that the design was on the insole of the sandal and, therefore, next to the foot, a sign of great disrespect to Moslems.

Carlson immediately contacted the supervisor of the design department and asked for any information he could provide on the design on the sandals. He already knew that they were from a mediumpriced line of women's footwear known as "Chappels" which had the design on the insole changed often as a marketing feature. Following his investigation the supervisor reported that the design had been based on a set of Chinese temple bells that the designer had purchased in the local market. Pleased by the appearance of the bells she had used them as the basis for a stylized design which she submitted to her supervisor for consideration and approval (Figure 3).

All of the employees in the development and marketing department were Moslems. The supervisor reported that the woman who had produced the offending design was a devout Bengali Moslem who spoke and read no Arabic. The same was true of almost all of the employees in the department. The supervisor confirmed to Carlson that numerous people in the department had seen the new design prior to its approval and no one had seen any problem or raised any objection to it. Following the conversation Carlson compared the design to the word Allah which he had arranged to have written in Arabic (Figure 4).

Carlson was perplexed by the article and its timing. The sandals in question were not new to the market and had not been subject to prior complaints. As he reread the translation of the **Meillat** article he wondered why the Jewish reference had been made when the family that owned Footwear International were Christian. He also wondered if the fact that students from the university had taken the sandals to the paper was significant.

As the day progressed the situation got worse. Carlson was shown a translation of a proclamation that had been circulated by two youth groups calling for demonstrations against Footwear to be held the next day (Figure 5). The proclamation linked Footwear, Salman Rushdie and the Jewish community and, ominously, stated that "even at the cost of our lives we have to protest against this conspiracy." More bad news followed. Calls had been made for charges to be laid against Carlson and four others under a section of the criminal code that forbade "deliberate and malicious acts intended to outrage feelings of any class by insulting its religion or religious believers" (Figure 6). A short time later Carlson received a copy of a statement that had been filed by a local lawyer, although no warrants were immediately forthcoming (Figure 7).

While he was reviewing the situation Carlson was interrupted by his secretary. In an excited voice she informed him that the Prime Minister was being quoted as calling the sandal incident an "unforgivable crime." The seriousness of the incident seemed to be escalating rapidly and Carlson wondered what he should do to try to minimize the damage.

Figure 1   Bangladesh

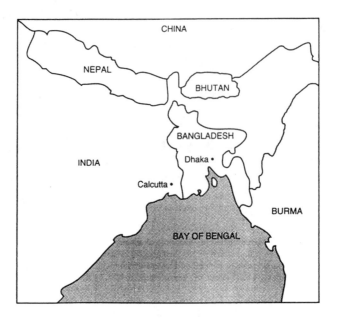

Figure 2   Translation of the **Meillat** Story1

UNPARDONABLE AUDACITY OF FOOTWEAR

In Bangladesh a Sandal with Allah as Footwear trade mark in Arabic designed in calligraphy has been marketed although last year Islam was made the State Religion in Bangladesh. The Sandal in black and white contains Allah in black. Prima facie it appears it has been designed and the Alif "the first letter in Arabic" has been jointly written. Excluding Alif it reads LILLAH. In Bangladesh after the Salman Rushdies2 Satanic Verses which has brought unprecendented demonstration and innumerable strikes (Hartels). This International shoe manufacturing organization under Jewish ownership with the design of Allah has made religious offence. Where for sanctity of Islam one million people of Afganistan have sacrificed their lives and wherein occupied Palestine many people have been gunned down by Jews for sanctity of Islam in this country the word Allah under this guise has been put under feet.

Last night a group of students from Dhaka university came to **Meillat** office with a couple of pairs of Sandal. The management staff of Footwear was not available over telephone. This sandal has got two straps made of foam.

1. The translation is identical to that which Carlson was given to work with.

2. Salman Rushdie was the author of the controversial book, "The Satanic Verses." The author had been sentenced to death, in absentia, by Ayatollah Khomenei, the leader of Iran, for crimes against Islam.

Figure 3 The Temple Bells and the Design Used on the Sandal

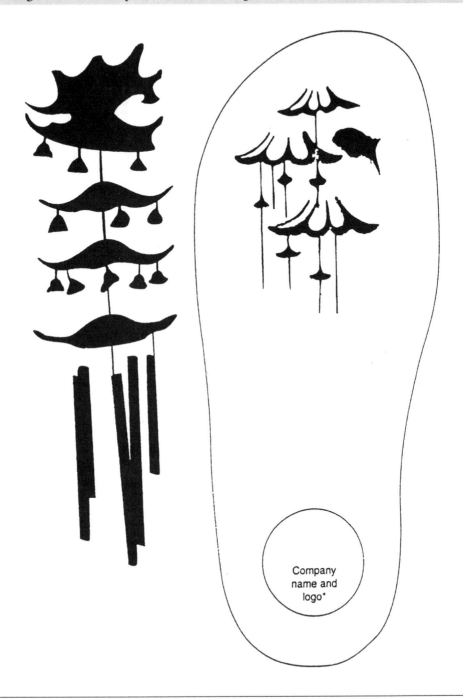

Source: Redrawn from a facsimile sent to headquarters by John Carlson.

Figure 4 The Arabic Spelling of Allah

Source: Redrawn from a facsimile sent to headquarters by John Carlson.

Figure 5 Translation of the Student Groups Proclamation[1]

The audacity through the use of the name "Allah" in a sandal

Let Rushdies Jewish Footwear Company be prohibited in Bangladesh.

Dear people who believe in one God It is announced in the holy Quran Allahs name is above everything but shoe manufacturing Jewish Footwear Shoe Company has used the name Allah and shown disrespect of unprecedented nature and also unpardonable audacity. After the failure of Rushdies efforts to destroy the beliefs of Moslems in the Quran, Islam and the prophet (SM) who is the writer of Satanic verses the Jewish People have started offending the Moslems. This time it is a fight against Allah. In fact Daud Haider, Salman Rushdie Viking Penguin and Footwear Shoe Company all are supported and financed by Jewish community. Therefore no compromise with them. Even at the cost of our lives we have to protest against this conspiracy.

For this procession and demonstration will be held on 23rd. June Friday after Jumma prayer from Baitul Mukarram Mosque south gate. Please join this procession and announce we will not pardon Footwear Shoe Companys audacity. Footwear Shoe Company has to be prohibited, don't buy Jewish products and Footwear shoes. Be aware Rushdies partner.

Issued by Bangladesh Islamie Jubashibir (Youth Student Forum) and Bangladesh Islamic Satrashbir (Student Forum)

1. The translation is identical to that which Carlson was given to work with.

Figure 6 Section 295 of the Criminal Code

[295-A. *Deliberate and malicious acts intended to outrage religious feelings of any class by insulting its religion or religious believers.* Whoever, with deliberate and malicious intention of outraging the religious feelings of any class of [the citizens . . . .], by words, either spoken or written, or by visible representations insults or attempts to insult the religion or religious beliefs of that class, shall be punished with imprisonment. . . .

. . . In order to bring a matter under S. 295-A it is not the mere matter of discourse or the written expression but also the manner of it which has to be looked to. In other words the expressions should be such as are bound to be regarded by any reasonable man as grossly offensive and provocative and maliciously and deliberately intended to outrage the feelings of any class of citizens. . . . If the injurious act was done voluntarily without a lawful excuse, malice may be presumed.

Figure 7 The Statement of the Plaintiff

The plaintiff most respectfully states that:

1) The plaintiff is a lawyer, and a Bangladeshi Citizen and his religion is Islam. He is basically a devout Moslem. According to Islamic tradition he regularly performs his daily work.

2) The first accused of this . . . is the Managing Director of Footwear Shoe Company, the second accused is the Production Manager of the said company, the third accused is the Marketing Manager, the fourth accused is the Calligrapher of the said company and last accused is the Sales Manager of the said company. The said company is an international organization having shoe business in different countries.

3) The accused persons deliberately wanted to outrage the religion of Muslims by engraving the calligraphy of "Allah" in Arabic on a sandal thereby to offend the Religion of majority this Muslim Country. By marketing this sandal with the calligraphy of "Allah" they have offended the religious feelings of millions of Muslims. It is the solemn religious duty and responsibility of every devout Muslim to protect the sanctity of "Allah." The plaintiff first saw the sandal with this calligraphy on 22nd June 1989 at Elephant road shop.

The accused persons collectively and deliberately wanted this calligraphy under the feet thereby to offend the religion of mine and many other Muslims and have committed a crime under provisions of section 295A of the Penal Code. At the time of hearing the evidence will be provided. Therefore under the provisions of section 295A of the Penal Code the accused persons be issued with warrant of arrest and be brought to court for justice.
The names of the Witnesses

1)

2)

3)

Source: Blake, R. W. (2000). Footwear international. In H. W. Lane, J. J. DiStefano, & M. L. Maxnevski (Eds.), *International management behavior: Text, readings and cases* (4th ed. pp. 165–172). Malden, MA: Blackwell.

Case 2

Computex Corporation

Martin Hilb

Goteborg, May 30, 1985

Mr Peter Jones

Vice President—Europe

Computex Corporation

San Francisco

USA

The writers of this letter are the headcount of the Sales Department of Computex Sweden, AS, except for the Sales Manager.

We have decided to bring to your attention a problem, which, unsolved, probably will lead to a situation where the majority among us will leave the company within a rather short period of time. None of us want to be in this situation, and we are approaching you purely as an attempt to save the team for the benefit of ourselves as well as Computex Corporation.

We consider ourselves an experienced, professional, and sales-oriented group of people. Computex Corporation is a company that we are proud to work for. The majority among us have been employed for several years. Consequently, a great number of key customers in different areas of Sweden see us as representatives of Computex Corporation. It is correct to say that the many excellent contacts we have made have been established over years; many of them are friends of ours.

These traits give a very short background because we have never met you. What kind of problem forces us to such a serious step as to contact you?

Problems arise as a result of character traits and behavior of our General Manager, Mr Miller.

First, we are more and more convinced that we are tools that he is utilizing in order to "climb the ladder." In meetings with us individually, or as a group, he gives visions about the future, how he values us, how he wants to delegate and involve us in business, the importance of cooperation and communication, etc. When it comes to the point, these phrases turn out to be only words.

Mr Miller loses his temper almost daily, and his outbursts and reactions are not equivalent to the possible error. His mood and views can change almost from hour to hour. This fact causes a situation where we feel uncertain when facing him, and consequently are reluctant to do so. Regarding human relationships, his behavior is not acceptable, especially for a manager.

The extent of the experience of this varies within the group due to our location. Some of us are seldom in the office.

Second, we have experienced clearly that he has various means of suppressing and discouraging people within the organization.

The new "victim" now is our Sales Manager, Mr Johansson. Because he is our boss, it is obvious that we regret such a situation, which to a considerable extent influences our working conditions.

There are also other victims among us. It is indeed very difficult to carry through what is stated in our job descriptions.

We feel terribly sorry and wonder how it can be possible for one person almost to ruin a whole organization.

If this group consisted of people less mature, many of us would have left Computex Corporation already. So far, only one has left the company due to the above reasons.

From September 1, two new Sales Representatives are joining the company. We regret very much that new employees get their first contact with the company under the present circumstances. An immediate action is therefore required.

It is not our objective to get rid of Mr Miller as General Manager. Without going into details, we are thankful for what he has done to the company from a business point of view. If he could control his mood, show some respect for his colleagues, keep words, and stick to plans, we believe that we can succeed under his leadership.

We are fully aware of the seriousness of contacting you, and we have been in doubt whether or not to contact you directly before talking to Mr Miller.

After serious discussions and considerations, we have reached the conclusion that a problem of this nature unfortunately cannot be solved without some sort of action from the superior. If possible, direct confrontation must be avoided. It can only make things worse.

We are hoping for a positive solution.

Six of Your Sales Representatives in Sweden

Peter Jones let out a long sigh as he gazed over the letter from Sweden. "What do I do now?" he thought, and began to reflect on the problem, He wondered who was right and who was wrong in this squabble, and he questioned whether he would ever get all the information necessary to make a wise decision. He didn't know much about the Swedes, and was unsure whether this was strictly a work problem or a "cross-cultural" problem. "How can I tease those two issues apart?" he asked himself, as he locked his office and made his way down the hallway to the elevator.

As Peter pulled out of the parking garage and on to the street, he began to devise a plan to deal with the problem. "This will be a test of my conflict management skills," he thought, "no doubt about it!" As he merged into the freeway traffic from the on-ramp and began his commute home, he began to wish that he had never sent Miller to Sweden in the first place. "But would Gonzalez or Harris have done any better? Would I have done any better?" Few answers seemed to come to him as he plodded along in the bumper-to-bumper traffic on Interstate 440.

Source: Hilb, M. (2012). Computex corporation. In G. K. Stahl, M. E. Mendenhall, & G. R. Oddou (Eds.), *Readings and cases in international human resource management and organizational behavior* (5th ed., pp. 185–187). New York, NY: Routledge.

Case 3

Common Bond Values at the New Zealand Office of AT&T

Deborah Shepherd

Una Diver, Human Resources, AT&T GIS, New Zealand

How would the "down-to-earth," practical Kiwis working in the New Zealand offices respond to these types of ideas? The reason Una Diver, from Human Resources in AT&T GIS NZ, was contemplating these issues was that in a couple of days, she would be hosting Kim Rose, a visiting Australian AT&T trainer. Rose was coming to New Zealand to introduce and implement a host of ideas from Corporate Office in America. Specifically during this visit he was going to facilitate workshops on the values called "*Our Common Bond*" and the new "*Vision and Direction*" workshops that everyone in AT&T GIS throughout the world were required to attend. This included both employees and everyone in a management position although interesting at AT&T the terms managers and employees had been replaced with the terms "coaches" and "associates" respectively.

This was May 1994. As Una pondered on the upcoming workshops, she also reflected on her brief time with the company since joining in October 1993. Una had joined when AT&T GIS was still called NCR as the Human Resource assistant. In the 8 months until the following May she had witnessed and been part of a huge number of changes as NCR was integrated into the AT&T stable of businesses.

Development of a Values Set at AT&T

In answering some of these critical questions, it was decided that there was a need for a shared value set that would guide behaviour, decision-making, internal and external interactions and essentially govern the way AT&T people conducted business with both their internal and external customers. As a result of the many organisational changes, Bob Allen perceived a sense of confusion around what the company stood for amongst associates and was concerned that people in AT&T were struggling to adjust. He had hearing through his network that some associates had concerns about the company. He then began reflecting on the question: "If everyone is working fairly independently in their customer-focused teams (CFTs) then what is the glue that holds the company together?" In response to this, and other similar questions, Allen and members from the US Quality Council began work on what he called "The Common Bond."

However, recognising the importance of getting people's input, Bob Allen didn't develop AT&T's values alone. He encouraged and received plenty of assistance. From meetings that spawned the original ideas, through surveys and then focus groups, hundreds of associates, mainly Americans, helped produce what later became "*Our Common Bond*" — a set of five values for AT&T world-wide.

The process began with senior executives out-lining seven values upon which associates from many different offices were asked to comment. It was associates who suggested that one of the original values, citizenship, not be a separate value. Similarly, while many associates acknowledged the importance of shareowners receiving a competitive return on investment, they successfully argued that if AT&T people behaved in accordance with all of the other values, benefits to the shareholders would accrue automatically. Both of these changes were accepted.

It was Bob Allen's intention that the values would reflect what critical success elements for AT&T, what differentiates AT&T from its competitors, what would make AT&T a superior place to work, and a set of statements that AT&T people around the globe would embrace. By the end of the process, 16 groups of associates at all job levels, from 8 states and 4 countries (the United States, the Netherlands, the United Kingdom, and Singapore), representing all parts of the business, had voiced their views in focus groups. Following these discussions, the list of values was reduced to the "final five" and the last alteration was to change the title from "The Common Bond" to "Our Common Bond."

"Our Common Bond"

The following values and brief description now make up "Our Common Bond":

Respect for Individuals

"We treat each other with respect and dignity, valuing individual and cultural differences. We communicate frequently and with candor, listening to each other regardless of level or position."

Dedication to Helping Customers

"We truly care for each customer. We build enduring relationships by understanding and anticipating our customers' needs and by serving them better each time than the time before."

Highest Standards of Integrity

"We are honest and ethical in all our business dealings, starting with how we treat each other. We keep our promises and admit our mistakes. Our personal conduct ensures that AT&T's name is always worthy of trust."

Innovation

"We believe innovation is the engine that will keep us vital and growing. Our culture embraces creativity, seeks different perspectives and risks pursuing new opportunities."

Teamwork

"We encourage and reward both individual and team achievements. We freely join with colleagues across organizational boundaries to advance the interests of customers and shareowners."

During the workshop in which the values were introduced and their meaning and implications discussed, every AT&T member was given a foldout business/information card that included the values and summaries as above. Under the heading "*Our Common Bond*" is the following statement: "*We commit to these values to guide our decisions and behavior.*"

After the five value descriptions the concluding statement is: "By living these values, AT&T aspires to set a standard of excellence world-wide that will reward our shareowners, our customers, and all AT&T people."

Responses to the Values

Una recalls the first time she saw the values and their descriptions. There was no way that you could disagree with their intention, there was no doubt that the values were admirable and worth pursuing but Una wondered whether the values might be "too idealistic to make practical and be of use in the everyday workplace?" Particularly she questioned how New Zealand associates would cope with the very American style of the values and the idea of having them written down and displayed to the public.

Prior to launching the value set to associates across the entire company, sixty senior officers from Corporate devoted a full day to understanding the values and the connections between the values and behaviour and desired business results. These officers engaged in a lively discussion of corporate versus business unit and division values. Should there be a single value set for *all* AT&T people who represent an extremely diverse group of people around the world, or should different groups of people develop or continue to endorse the values that are meaningful to them? One side argued the need for a common bond across all of AT&T, the other argued to maintain other values that some people had worked long and hard to embrace and personally commit to their group's values.

It was Bob Allen who made the final call. He stated that "while we must respect and honour the work already done on values by AT&T people in their business units and divisions, *"Our Common Bond"* must become the core, the corporation's 'glue.'" Bob Allen believed that with these values, "we preserve the best of our past and define the framework for our future success."

Now, almost one year since the values were introduced to NZ, along with many other directives from America, Una considers if Bob Allen was right in his decision. Una could only reflect on the implications for the NZ office, but certainly she had experienced some resistance and difficulty implementing US directives amongst the strong-minded and independent NZ associates. "Are HR coaches in other countries experiencing similar resistance?" wondered Una.

Values Workshops

The values were introduced to every associate of AT&T via training sessions by specially trained facilitators for this role from within AT&T. Each workshop discussed the five values in detail, including what behaviours reflected the spirit of each value and which behaviours violated the underlying meaning and intention of each value. Issues such as harassment, acknowledging and valuing diversity in the workplace, managing change, giving and receiving feedback and personal development were addressed during these sessions. In New Zealand Kim Rose and Una Diver facilitated these workshops during the first six months of 1994. All NZ associates attended a two-day workshop that not only addressed *"Our Common Bond"* values but also included sessions on Opportunity and Change, and Vision and Direction.

Interestingly, the people least committed to these sessions were senior management personnel, the senior coaches. During one workshop, one of the NZ quality council members was never seated for more than 15 minutes without leaving to take or make telephone calls on a cellular phone. Another was required to give part of a seminar and, seemingly, from nonchalance and a lack of preparation, read straight from the manual and seemed totally disinterested and, perhaps, even cynical about the material. Yet another coach was part of a discussion group during the workshop and said something derogatory to one of the other discussants. When the offended individual chastised the manager by saying that the remark was "a common bond violation" the manager replied with "tell someone who cares."

Kim Rose saw many incidents that indicated that it was frequently more difficult getting people in senior positions to adopt the values and align their behaviour to them than people further down the organisational hierarchy. Rose pondered that "perhaps the values were more threatening for senior people if associates under them could challenge their behaviour."

The 1994 "Values Fest"

Una's concerns about how applicable the American "way" of operating for the NZ division were heightened again in recent times as the latest Corporate Office initiative landed on her desk. This time it was for a Common Bond celebration called a "Values

Fest." A directive came from Dayton, Ohio outlining the "Values Fest" to be held on the 7th of November. As usual, the material only arrived on her desk a few days before the actual required action date—the celebration day. The timeframe and her imme- diate and strong reservations about the content of the directive forced her to make a decision at short notice. The manuals instructed her to show a video, to get associates to complete a quiz and some written exercises, to get involved in discussion groups on the values, to make a "call to action" in relation to each of the five values outlined in the Common Bond, and to get people to sign a Common Bond poster as a celebration of the values. All of this would have taken half a day. Una knew that such sessions just would not go down very well with the NZ associates because they would see it as both a waste of time and, more importantly, that the content and style was just not relevant to them in the New Zealand office. Instead, she chose the 45 minute option for compa- nies that "did not have sufficient time for the full agenda and who could give Corporate Office a serious reason for adopting this option." Una felt she had a very definite reason. She describes her decision for the short version as "a cultural decision." The material and session exercises and activities outlined in the manual from the United States were not appropriate for AT&T's New Zealand associates. It appeared to Una that following the 45 minutes of formality, everyone gathered around for refreshments and food and seemed to thoroughly enjoy themselves.

Appropriateness of American Directives for the NZ Division

This Common Bond Celebration again raised the issue of how and when does the NZ office need to adapt Corporate directives to suit the NZ working style. Following the celebrations, Una believed that she had made the right decision to alter the American format and use the shortest possible version for the NZ organisation. As the Human Resources manager she knew she had to make a judgement decision and she decided in this case that if all of the material was taken and used literally from the documentation she received, "it would go down like a lead balloon."

The telephone rings in the Human Resources reception area. Enough daydreaming thinks Una. She chuckles her notorious laugh that has helped her and others keep these issues in perspective. It is time to get back to work and deal with the mounting 'in-tray' of work. She knows the company will get through the difficult times and that change is now just an inevitable and constant part of life. Although that makes her HR role difficult at times, there is no denying that this is a dynamic, well-known, ambitious and successful company which makes her life at AT&T interesting, rewarding and above all challenging.

Source: Shepherd, D. (2003). Common bond values at the New Zealand office of AT&T. In D. C. Thomas (Ed.), *Readings and cases in international management* (pp. 92–100). Thousand Oaks, CA: Sage.

Case 4

Peter Hanson: Building a World-Class Product Development Centre for Hi Tech Systems in China

Ingmar Björkman

Introduction

Peter Hanson, the Head of the Product Development Centre (PDC) of Hi Tech Systems in Shanghai had been in China for five months. He was the first person in the Product Development Centre when he arrived in Shanghai in April 2000. Thinking back at the period he had spent in China so far, he felt that things had gone quite well. The PDC was now up and running and today, on September 12, 2000, Peter welcomed its sixteenth employee.

Nonetheless, Peter still had a number of concerns. The PDC was still rather small and it was possible for him to interact with and influence all employees. As the PDC would grow significantly over the next year, he wanted to make sure to create a healthy and positive atmosphere and orientation towards work. His vision was to create a world-class PDC in Shanghai, but how to do that in a country that mainly was a recipient of technological know-how from abroad, and what measures should be taken to convince other parts of Hi Tech Systems to engage in joint development projects with his PDC? And even if he managed to develop the competencies needed to build a world-class PDC through careful recruitment and selection as well as good investments in training and development, how were they to retain the employees in a market where job hopping was common, money apparently an important reason why people switched jobs, and well-educated people had ample opportunities in other companies? Basically, his question was: would lessons on now to manage human resources obtained in North America and Europe apply also on the People's Republic of China?

Product Development in Hi Tech Systems

Hi Tech Systems was established in Stockholm, Sweden, in 1976. By the late 1980s, it had become known as one of Europe's most innovative firms in its industry. The growth continued in the 1990s, with firm profitability remaining healthy. The company is currently one of the three largest firms in its industry. Hi Tech Systems' global manufacturing comprises six production facilitates in five different countries on three different continents. Approximately 45 percent of sales come from Europe, but Japan, China and, in particular, the United States have become important markets.

Product development is seen as key to the success of Hi Tech Systems. Almost 20 percent of Hi Tech Systems' employees are working in research and development. Hi Tech Systems has Product Development Centres (PDCs) in Sweden, the UK, the US, Japan, Hong Kong (China) and, most recently, mainland China. There is a global PDC management group headed by Johan Lind that consists of all the PDC heads, which convenes once a month. Johan Lind reports to the head of global product development in Hi Tech Systems, Anders Jonsson.

The responsibility for product development programs resides with the global business lines and the "platforms" (such as Japanese user interface). Research programs within the business lines that lead to actual products also draw on the work being done within the platforms. In each PDC, people work on projects related to both Hi Tech Systems business lines and platforms.

A full-grown PDC has some 400–500 employees, a variety of competencies, and is expected to have the capability needed to develop an entire new product. There are several reasons why the company has established a whole portfolio of PDCs. First, different areas differ in terms of technologies and standards relevant for the business. Therefore, it makes sense to locate research and development activities in locations where the technologies reside. Second, by dispersing PDCs to different parts of the world, the company can move product creation activities in response to environmental and market changes. Third, it enables Hi Tech Systems to draw on human resources not available in one location. Hi Tech Systems has traditionally done most of its product creation in Sweden, but as a result of growth there are not enough engineering students in the whole country to satisfy its needs. Fourth, products need to be local-adapted and this is easier to carry out locally than in a distant PDC.

In a typical research program, most of the work on the key components of a new product is done within one single "core" PDC. Within each project, there is a fairly clear distribution of responsibilities across the PDCs involved. Other 'peripheral' PDCs are typically involved in developing locally adapted variances of the product. Most of the work has typically already been done in the core PDC before the other PDCs get involved (although, in order to ensure that the necessary local adaptations of the final product can be made at a later stage, people from each of the geographical regions are involved in steering groups during the conceptualization stage). The knowledge transfer mostly takes place through people from the PDCs who visit the core PDC for 1–3 months to work with the product development people before they return to their own units. At the point when the project has been established in the peripheral PDCs, the focal project leader reports to the global head of the focal product development project and to the head of their own PDC. Heavy emphasis is put on establishing and following up project milestones.

Hi Tech Systems in China

The People's Republic of China started opening up to the outside world in 1979. In 1992, the Hi Tech Systems group established a representative office in Shanghai and, in 1995, a first joint venture was established. By the beginning of 2000, Hi Tech Systems already had four joint ventures and wholly owned subsidiaries in China. Hi Tech Systems had become a significant player in the rapidly growing Chinese market, where it was competing with other Western, Japanese, and also increasingly strong local competitors. China had become one of Hi Tech Systems' most important markets. Most of the products sold in China were produced in the firm's local factories.

However, Hi Tech Systems had so far no Product Development Centre in China. Towards the end of the 1990s, there was growing consensus that this neglect had to be rectified. A decision to establish a PDC in Shanghai was made by Hi Tech Systems' management board in January 2000. Peter Hanson was chosen to head the PDC.

Peter Hanson

Peter Hanson was born in California in 1962. After graduating from college with a major in management, his first job was with a major US industrial firm. As a part of his job, in 1989–90 he spent 6 months in Hong Kong. During his assignment in Hong Kong, he fell in love with Asia and China. Since that moment he knew that he was going to return to Asia. Peter also met his future wife, who moved with him to the US. In 19991–93, Peter did an MBA and then started to work in a small start-up company. In late 1997, Peter was persuaded by one of his previous colleagues to join Hi Tech Systems. When joining Hi Tech Systems, Peter was appointed operations manager. After some months, he was asked to head the engineering unit of the new Product Development Centre that was built up in Philadelphia. Peter accepted the job, which meant that he would be responsible for the largest unit of the PDC. Peter and his new boss, Curtis O'Neill, soon became very close, with Peter acting as the second in charge of the PDC. Peter recalls,

> I learnt a lot from Curtis. He was very people-oriented. He would make sure that you get an opportunity to get into an environment where you either learn or you don't. He gave people lots of challenges, lots of learning opportunities, where they could prove themselves. He would also quite directly point to areas of improvement. He also underlined the importance of networking, how to build networks of people that you can draw on.

One of the things that Peter learned soon after joining Hi Tech Systems was the importance of having good personal contacts within the company. The Hi Tech Systems global product development worked, to a significant extent, through informal contacts across units and it was crucial to be well connected. His choice of the five product line managers in his department reflected this view. While people in the Philadelphia unit expected and pressured him to choose local people for the positions, he selected three expatriates and only two local employees:

> People thought I was taking promotions away from Philadelphia. I had my own views in mind—we needed to be connected to the other centers. If you're well connected people trust you to do a good job within a research program, and it is also easier to get technical help if needed. I then used lots of interviews with the candidates to convince people about their capabilities and to get some buy-in from the other managers. I also made sure to tell people that the objective was to fill the positions with local people in two-three years. In fact, the line managers had as an explicit objective to develop a local replacement of themselves.

During the next 18 months, Peter visited Sweden several times. He often took part in the global PDC group meetings as O'Neill's stand-in. The global PDC management also knew that he was interested in returning to Asia, something Peter had mentioned from the outset in his performance management discussions.

Establishing the Product Development Centre

During the summer of 1999, the global PDC management group decided that a feasibility study on the possible creation of a PDC in the People's Republic of China should be carried out. In October 1999, Peter was asked to become involved in the project. His task was to examine the data and write a report on whether or not a PDC should be established and, if so, where in China it should be located. By that time, Peter also knew that he would be the preferred candidate as head of the PDC (if approved). In January 2000, the HI Tech Systems global management board approved the establishment of a PDC in Shanghai. One of the advantages of Shanghai was that the PDC would be able to use the existing Hi Tech Systems organization in the city. It would be easier to learn from the experiences of Hi Tech Systems' largest Chinese production and its China headquarters, both of which were located in Shanghai. In February, Peter went to China on a pre-visit mainly to meet with people in the Hi Tech Systems organization.

When it became clear that the PDC would be established, Peter started to look for people. There was no established policy for people management within the global product creation organization, but Peter was told to draw on the HR department at the Hi Tech Systems group in China for support. He thought he would initially need approximately ten positions for expatriates, and it would be of crucial importance to find suitable people for the key positions:

> It was networking all the way—the social networks were very important! There were many people who knew that I would do it and some of them contacted me. I contacted and spoke to lots of people in all parts of the Hi Tech Systems organization. I wanted the candidates to have experience in launching Hi Tech Systems products in China. They should know the Chinese environment and culture. This meant that there were only a very small number of

people who fulfilled my criteria. And they had to commit to staying at least two or even three years, which is not usual in Hi Tech Systems. Towards the end of the period they start hunting for another job anyhow.

Peter finally identified four people that he wanted: one Swede, and three persons from the People's Republic of China who had studied and worked for several years abroad (two in the United States one in Sweden). One of them he already knew in advance, the others he had identified through his networking activities. All the Chinese had a strong educational background, with degrees from top Chinese universities before leaving the country for overseas graduate studies. Everybody had at least some experience in leading their own teams:

> I talked a lot to them. Have they thought about living in China? Were they (the Chinese) conscious about the challenges involved in going back to China? For instance, people may be jealous of them making much more money, travelling abroad and having much higher positions than they themselves had? Have they realized that it's going to be a start-up operation, and that it may be difficult to get things started and people on board?

To persuade the people he wanted to accept relocating to China, Peter tried to create a positive and challenging vision for the PDC. To date, Hi Tech Systems had probably not done enough to meet the needs of the Chinese-speaking countries. Did they want to become a part of the process of creating a world-class PDC in China? The PDC would become responsible for the Chinese user interface platform—did they want to participate in the challenge of its development? Being restricted by the company's expatriate compensation policy, which was built on a standardized job grading system, he was able to offer competitive but not exceptional salaries. He finally managed to persuade all four candidates to accept a job in his PDC. They all knew each other from their previous jobs. During the late spring of 2000, he found some additional people in the global Hi Tech Systems organization who also agreed to taking up jobs in Shanghai:

> A part of my strategy was to get people from different Product Development Centers. By having these people in my organization we are able to easily reach into the other PDCs, which is particularly important in the beginning as we are dependent on doing parts of larger projects in collaboration with other centers. If we have good people who have credibility from each of the other PDCs, we will be recognized and seen as trustworthy.

But Peter did not see technical competence as the only important criterion. In his view:

> 80 percent is attitude. It doesn't matter what you can do, if you lack drive. With drive you can always fill in the gaps . . . Perhaps it has something to do with my own background. I have had to manage without an engineering education in an organization and industry that are extremely technology-intensive.

The PDC was to report to the Global PDC management and to the Hi Tech Systems China country management. As agreed upon with the Global PDC management group,

PDC Shanghai would be responsible for product creation in the Chinese language area, including mainland China, Hong Kong, Singapore, and Taiwan. In the beginning, it would mostly do limited parts of larger products in collaboration with other global PDCs, working, for example, on software and on Chinese-specific applications. The long-term vision was eventually to have the competencies to be able to build new products in China.

The Start of the Product Development Centre

Peter and his family finally arrived in Shanghai on April 12, 2000. The next employee arrived from overseas in May, and by September the unit had 16 employees, half of whom had been recruited from abroad. Peter's estimate was that, long term, 15–20 percent of the employees would be from overseas but that it would take 3–4 years to decrease the proportion of expatriates to that level:

> When you build a home, first you build the foundations. You need to make sure that the foundations are in place—the recruitment process, human resources management, finance. Then you need key managers to build the organization around.

In the recruitment of local employees, the PDC was collaborating closely with Hi Tech Systems' human resources (HR) department. After job descriptions and job grade levels had been determined by the PDC, the HR department would announce the position using both advertisements and the Hi Tech System home page, receive CVs, do a first screening of the candidates, and arrange for interviews and assessment of the applicants. The interviews were done by a minimum of two PDC managers, who also acted as observers in the assessment centers organized by the HR department. For the assessment of applicants in China, Hi Tech Systems used "The Space Shuttle." The Space Shuttle was a game where the applicants worked together in a group with the objective of reaching an agreement on how to build a space shuttle. By observing the applicants involved in a problem-solving situation where they also interacted with each other, the observers could draw their own conclusions about the applicants. Recruitment and selection of local employees largely resembled practices used elsewhere in the global Hi Tech Systems organization.

Some other Western firms had apparently made larger adjustments in their selection practices in China. For instance, Peter had heard that Shell had changed its selection practices based on an in-depth study of its existing Chinese managers and entry-level management trainees. Traditionally Shell focused on analytical and problem-solving abilities. However, when, for example, applicants were asked to identify the strengths and weakness of the Chinese educational system and then say what they would do to remedy deficiencies if they were the Minister of Education, if there were any responses at all they tended to be uniformly bland. It was also found that the kind of "Who would you throw out of the airplane?" question commonly used in the West also tended to engender a "learned helplessness effect" on the part of Chinese university graduates, who have excelled at clearly defined tasks in a familiar environment and who had "learnt" to respond to the unfamiliar by simple freezing. Shell's system identified the Chinese education system as the chief culprit. The educational system is hierarchical, extremely competitive and almost exclusively based on examination of rote learning. Problem-oriented interaction among strangers is unnatural and problematic for most Chinese. Therefore, to evaluate the decision-making skills, communication skills, analytical problem-solving abilities, and leadership capabilities of the applicants based on hypothetical cases solved in assessment situations may be very difficult. As a result, Shell's study recommended the use of real case studies rather than hypothetical questions.[1]

Competence development would probably be key to the success of the PDC, both in terms of localizing its operations and in producing good results. By mid-September, the new employees had mostly worked on small projects, such as setting up the IT system. A couple of people had also been sent to Hong Kong to work in the field with experienced engineers for 3 weeks. Formal training would be important, and the PDC would need to collaborate with Hi Tech Systems' HR unit on the course program offered to the PDC employees. To what extent should the Chinese employees receive the same content and delivery as Hi Tech Systems employees elsewhere? In China, the Confucian- and communist-influenced Chinese educational system in which the learner is a mostly passive receiver who is obedient to instructor tends to create linear rather than lateral thinking and precedent-based problem-solving where the focus in on getting the "right" answer.

Nonetheless, hands-on on-the-job coaching would be even more important for the development of the new employees. Most of the responsibility for coaching would obviously be on the experienced Hi Tech Systems employees but also important would be to bring in people from other PDCs for visits in Shanghai. Coaching on the part of the expatriates would be extremely important, Peter thought. He had already been discussing it at length with the managers that he had hired, but he was not sure whether or not that was enough, especially not when the unit would grow over the next couple of years. He certainly would not be able to coach all expatriates by himself.

In Hi Tech Systems' globally standardized performance management system, all employees should carry out performance management discussions with their superiors. Within this system, individual objectives are established and followed up. According to company policy, the individual's objectives must be specific and, if possible, measurable; key activities for how to reach the objectives shall be specified; criteria for how to evaluate the performance agreed upon; and finally, development plans decided upon. Peter's aim was that every new employee would do their first performance management discussion within a month after they joined the organization. All Hi Tech Systems superiors in China were trained in how to use the system but there was still a question of how the "Western" system would be implemented in the Chinese culture characterized by respect for hierarchy, face, and harmonious personal relationships.

Peter had also given the question of the relationship between employee competence development and career progress quite a lot of thought. In Hi Tech Systems worldwide, people achieved high status by having excellent technological knowledge and skills rather than having made a successful career as a manager. However:

In China especially the young people expect to get a new title every year; otherwise they had better start looking for another company. The speed of expected career progression clearly differs from the West. To develop the level of competence required for the next career step will be a challenge. Can they achieve it once a year? I think very few will.

The compensation of employees would follow the Hi Tech Systems policies. Managers and team leaders were compensated based on both business and individual performance. High-level executives and senior managers had a large business performance component in their bonus system, while the compensation of lower-level employees was mostly based on their individual performance. In the Shanghai PDC, individual performance would be evaluated based on 4–5 objectives. Peter required that the objectives had to be measurable on a ten-point scale. For instance, a manager's performance could be evaluated based on the manager's ability to fill positions in his/ her group, employee satisfaction (as measured in company-wide surveys), employee turnover, the team's ability to stay within the budget, and some measure of quality (to be determined in discussions between the person and Peter). Each person's performance was evaluated every 6 months, and bonuses paid accordingly. The target bonus was 10 percent of the person's base salary, with 20 percent as maximum. People working on a specific development project were evaluated not every 6 months but the evaluation rather followed the milestones of the project. The bonus element was also somewhat larger for people working on projects than for other PDC members.

Peter believed that the compensation system would work well in China. Having clear objectives and rewards linked with their fulfillment would help send a clear message to the employees: your performance equals what you deliver—not the personal connections, or "*guanxi*," that you have! Nonetheless, at least in the start-up phase of the PDC it might be somewhat difficult to establish feasible objectives for the employees. Additionally, there had been reports from other foreign firms that there was a tendency among local employees to set objectives so that they would be reached by the subordinates.

Looking Towards the Future

Analyzing the start-up phase of PDC, Peter found that many things had gone quite smoothly. For instance, the two Chinese "returnees" who had joined PDC so far (the third was still in Sweden but would relocate next month) seemed to do well. Although China had changed a lot since they left the country some 10 years ago, their interaction with the local employees seemed to go well.

Managing the growth would certainly be a challenge in the next couple of years, Peter thought. For instance, local employees would have to be taught to manage themselves and to take responsibility—behaviors not automatically understood and accepted in the Chinese environment. While the Hi Tech Systems culture was non-hierarchical and meritocratic, the Chinese culture is hierarchical, and the "face" of superiors could be at stake if subordinates made their own initiatives rather than waiting for orders from their superiors. Furthermore, since the communist regime from

1949, the Chinese have been discouraged from engaging in competitive and entrepreneurial behavior. The Chinese proverb "the early bird gets shot" aptly illustrates the reluctance on the part of Chinese employees to engage in the kind of innovative behavior that Peter wanted to see in the PDC. On the order hand, Peter had seen several Chinese changing their behavior significantly abroad. What should they do to promote this behavior also in the Shanghai PDC?

Peter was also looking for somebody to work closely with Hi Tech Systems' HR function. This person would work closely with him and the line managers to define future competence needs and how they could be met. "So far I guess I have fulfilled this role, but I'm afraid that neither me nor line managers will have time enough to pay sufficient attention to this issue in the future."

Finally, Peter was concerned about retention. "I have also been told by [a human resources expert] that a 1 renminbi salary difference may make a person switch job." Peter believed that money would not be key to retaining the employees, though. To create a positive, family-like atmosphere might help. Peter had started a tradition of everyone in his unit meeting for a snack on Monday mornings. He also made a conscious effort to spend time talking to people in the department. Furthermore, he had invited people out for lunch and dinner. To maintain a positive relationship between the foreign and local employees, he tried to coach the expatriates not to mention how much money they made, how they lived, and how cheap they found most things to be in Shanghai (say "reasonable" instead, was his advice). All this had apparently contributed to there starting to circulate rumors that "things are done a bit differently in PDC." He was now thinking of whether to involve the employees' families in some way. Formal team-building exercises should probably also be done.

There were so many things to do . . . Peter looked out of his window in one of the many new multistory buildings in the Pudong area of Shanghai—where should he start?

Note

1. The Economist Intelligence Unit (1998, September 28) *China on the Couch*, 3–4.

Source: Björkman, I. (2012). Peter Hanson: Building a world-class product development centre for hi tech systems in China. In G. K. Stahl, M. E. Mendenhall, & G. R. Oddou (Eds.), *Readings and cases in international human resource management and organizational behavior* (5th ed., pp. 62–70). New York, NY: Routledge.

Case 5

Lenovo-IBM: Bridging Cultures, Languages, and Time Zones

Kathrin Köster and Günter K. Stahl

(A) An Audacious Deal

> *"Cultural integration is still one of the biggest challenges . . . We face the combined effect of different corporate cultures and the difference between the cultures of the East and the West."*

> Orr and King, 2007[1]

On Tuesday, December 20, 2005, the public learned of the departure of Steve Ward, the CEO of Lenovo. He had lasted just eight months in the position before he was replaced by William Amelio, a former Dell executive.[2] The move came as China's Lenovo, despite its difficult start, seemed poised to become the world's leading PC maker.

Just 23 months prior, on December 8, 2004, Yang Yuanqing, who was then Lenovo's CEO, announced his intention to purchase IBM's PC division for US $1.75 billion—an unprecedented move for a company based in an emerging market (for a timeline of the deal, see Appendix A1). The radical deal would transform Lenovo from a company that sold exclusively in China into a major global player. Furthermore, IBM's PC division accounted for three times the sales that Lenovo earned, so the announcement seemed less like a merger and more like David was trying to swallow Goliath.

The Long March from Legend to Lenovo

Prior to 2004, Lenovo had been known as Legend, a company established by Liu Chuanzhi, a graduate from Xi'an Military Communications Engineering College. In 1984, he and a few colleagues spun off Legend from the state-owned Chinese Academy of Sciences, which provided seed money of US $25,000 that the young entrepreneurs used to set up shop in a ramshackle building in "Swindler's Alley," Beijing's electronics black market. Very quickly, Liu Chuanzhi realized that differentiation through innovation was the only way forward. The Legend brand thus developed an add-on card that allowed Chinese applications to run on English-language operating systems; it capitulated China into the PC age. For this innovation, Legend received one of China's highest honors, a National Science Technology Progress Award.

In contrast with its main competitor, Great Wall, Legend was not well connected to or protected by government authorities. For example, the company was refused a license to manufacture in China. But with innovation as its watchword, Legend came up with the idea of entering into a joint venture in Hong Kong, in which capacity it would also build motherboards and PCs and thereby outmaneuver its better-connected Chinese rivals. It was not until 1990 that Liu Chuanzhi could realize his dream to build PCs in his home country, though.

In 1994, Legend went public to raise capital in Hong Kong and thus be able to compete with foreign computer manufacturers, whose products had been flooding the Chinese markets since the beginning of the 1990s. Before its competitors, Legend introduced a Pentium PC in China; this first-mover advantage contributed greatly to its status as the leading PC maker in the Chinese market.

Although Legend diversified into a few non-core businesses, such as IT services, the PC business remained the center of its operations. During the mid-1990s, a young manager, Yang Yuanqing, stood out for his work in this division. An unusually bright engineer with a strong desire for clarity and precision, Yang had been promoted at a very young age. A forceful personality and firm believer in discipline and centralized decision-making, the young Yang Yuanqing prompted descriptions such as acutely intelligent, touch and decisive[3] as well as autocratic in his leadership and abrasive. Yet Yang also proved a visionary, with a sharp eye for promising innovations and new business opportunities. In retrospect, observers noted that his arrival at the company was a true turning point in Legend's history (Appendix A2 provides a description of Yang Yuanqing).

With Liu, Yang shared the conviction that to achieve ambitious goals, Legend needed to attract China's best and brightest and then imbue them with the Legend spirit. Newcomers had to "fit the mold," and the company went to great lengths to instill the right mindset, values, and work ethic.

Legend's vice president Du Jianhua described the desired corporate culture, as well as required changes in management practices and individual behavior, using the "1-2-3-4-5 formula:"[4]

1. Adopt one common culture and vision that all Legend employees and managers share.

2. Require dual attitudes from employees. That is, Legend employees were expected to treat customers with the utmost respect and care, in line with the motto, "the customer is the emperor," and go the extra mile to meet customers' needs. Legend's definition of "customers" included internal customers, suppliers, dealers, and distributors, so employees also were warned not to offend or exploit these members of the extended Legend family. The second employee characteristic the company prioritized was frugality. Every employee needed to be aware that Legend was a profit-maximizing organization, with the motto "Save money, save energy, save time."

3. Concentrate on three fundamental leadership tasks: build the management team, determine the strategy, and lead the troops. These tasks, reflecting the philosophy of Sunzi, constituted not only the capabilities that leaders needed to possess but also the recommended approach to managing people. Thus, management was to instill the discipline and obedience in the rank-and-file staff and ensure employees strictly adhered to company rules and policies. Only in case of an emergency or crisis that might cause severe damage to the company could employees act according to their own judgment.

4. Adhere to four commandments: (1) don't abuse your position to line your own pockets; (s) don't accept bribes; (3) don't take any second job outside the company; and (4) don't discuss your salary with anybody in the company. These rules defined minimum requirements; employees also were expected to meet additional standards of conduct. In a management meeting in August 1997, Yang described the ideal Legend employee as follows: accurate, careful, and meticulous when it comes to details; able to analyze the root causes of problems and come up with practical solutions; able to effectively communicate and cooperate with others; and marked by relentless self-discipline. At Legend, such military-like discipline as strictly enforced and backed by stiff penalties for misbehavior. Only under pressure and with clear rules and accountabilities, Yang was convinced, would employees perform and thrive. Employees had to clock in and out; if they came late to a meeting, they had to stand for one minute behind their chair. If they were seen outside the office building without a plausible explanation, they had to accept a pay deduction.

5. Consider five changes. As the twentieth century drew to a close, Legend's top management perceived a need to move away from hierarchical control toward a more participative style of leadership that encouraged people to take ownership and responsibility for their performance. Strict lines of authority and top-down control, Yang and Liu came to realize, would prevent Legend from responding to market needs and trends and achieving international significance. Thus the company faced the significant challenge of delegating responsibility broadly and promoting an entrepreneurial spirit, as well as leadership at all levels. Five changes in behavior and skills would be needed to implement Legend's new management model, which Yang introduced in 1998. Specifically, managers were expected to:

   i. work toward meeting goals and objectives rather than blindly following a supervisor's instructions;

   ii. develop from a people-oriented into a task-oriented manager;

   iii. do what needs to be done to respond to the needs of the customer;

   iv. think in terms of numbers and specify concrete, quantifiable objectives to be achieved; and

   v. become more inquisitive and open-minded.

These management principles and rules aimed to impart a greater performance orientation and cultivate a culture of accountability throughout the company. They also were designed to reflect the company's core values: customer service, innovative and entrepreneurial spirit, accuracy and truth-seeking, trustworthiness, and integrity.

To instill these values, Legend's top managers decided to adopt Western-style performance management and human resource (HR) practices. It was among the first Chinese companies to introduce a stock option program for managers. It also implemented a forced ranking, or "rank and yank," system that required managers to identify the top and bottom 10% of performers, similar to the appraisal system introduced by Jack Welch at General Electric. This prompted some observers to conclude that Legend was not a "typical" Asian company.[5]

In 2001, when Yang was appointed CEO and Liu took on the chairman role, Legend also began globalizing. Yang and Liu had become convinced that growth opportunities in China were limited by the increasingly fierce competition in the Chinese market. To pursue opportunities outside China, they established a new vision for Legend, names, to join the *Fortune* 500 and become the first global Chinese player. But the name Legend was already copyright-protected outside of China, so the company renamed itself Lenovo—"Le" from Legend and "novo" to indicate a new start. Also, in 2004, Lenovo announced its decision to become the worldwide partner of the International Olympic Committee, as the computer equipment provider for the 2006 Winter Olympics in Turin, Italy, and the 2008 Beijing Olympic Games.

The IBM Opportunity: Acquiring an American Icon

IBM, an icon of corporate America, was founded in 1911 as The Computer-Tabulating-Recording Company. After its geographical expansion into Europe, South America, Asia, and Australia, the company took the new name International Business Machines, or IBM, under the leadership of Sir Thomas J. Watson Sr., the head of the organization from 1915 to 1956. A self-made man with no higher-level education, he reportedly stated: "The trouble with every one of us is that we don't think enough. We don't get paid for working with our feet; we get paid for working with our heads" (Forbes, 1948).[6] The slogan "THINK" was thus a mantra for IBM; it was also the motto above the door of the IBM schoolhouse where all new hires, usually fresh from college, had to undergo 12 weeks of education and orientation.[7]

The beliefs of Sir Watson not only prompted the company's innovativeness but also had long-term impacts on the attitudes and behaviors of its workforce. Watson emphasized impeccable customer service and insisted on dark-suited, white-shirted, alcohol-abstinent salesmen. With fervor, he instilled company pride and loyalty through job security for every worker, company sports teams, family outings, and a company band. Employees received comprehensive benefits and were convinced of their own superior knowledge and skills.[8]

IBM also prided itself on shaping the entire computer industry. With the advent of high-performing integrated circuits, "Big Blue"—a corporate nickname that recognized IBM's army of blues-suited salesmen and blue logo—could launch the System/360 processors that enabled it to lead the market with high profit margins and few competitive threats for decades. This position changed with the rise of UNIX and the age of personal computing, though. In 1986, IBM developed the first laptop, which weighed

12 pounds; by 1992, it was promoting the ThinkPad, the first notebook computer with 10.4-inch color display that used Thin Film transistor technology.

Despite its pioneering entries into the PC market, IBM did not make its PC business a top priority and surrendered control of its highest-value components, namely, the operating system and the microprocessor, to Microsoft and Intel, respectively. Critics widely attributed IBM's decline in the late 1980s and early 1990s to its failure to protect its technological lead; it became a follower rather than an innovator.[9] The once-dominant giant came close to collapse when its mainframe computer business, the primary growth engine of the 1970s and 1980s, ground to a halt.

But the CEO in what were arguably IBM's darkest hours brought the company back from the brink. When he took over in 1993, Luis Gerstner recognized that IBM's cherished values—customer service, excellence, and respect—had become a sort of rigor mortis, which turned them from strengths to liabilities. "Superior customer service" had come to mean servicing machines on the customer's premises; "excellence had mutated into an obsession with perfectionism. The numerous required checks, approvals, and validations nearly paralyzed the decision-making process. Even the belief in respect for the individual had turned into an entitlement, such that employees could reap rich benefits without earning them.[10]

Under Gerstner's leadership, the company was recentralized and structured around processes. He introduced global customer relationship management, a complex web of processes, roles, and IT tools that affected tens of thousands of employees. It took IBM nearly a decade to remake itself into a comprehensive software, hardware, and services provider, but Big Blue's successful strategic repositioning increased the "we feeling" and strengthened what has been described as an almost cult-like culture.[11]

Thus, when Sam Palmisano took over as CEO in 2002, his challenge was to come up with a mandate for the next stage in the company's transformation. His primary aim was to get different parts of the company to work together so IBM could offer a bundle of "integrated solutions"—hardware, software, services, financing—at a single price. A set of shared values supported the change in a strategy and ensured consistency across the globe:

1. Dedication to every client's success.

2. Innovation that matters—for our company and for the world.

3. Trust and personal responsibility in all relationships.[12]

These core values provided the basis for IBM's management system and a crucial orientation frame for its diverse workforce, which serves clients in more than 170 countries.

Along with these changes to the company's orientations and values, in 2004, it made another sharp break with its history: IBM would sell off its PC business. The move would affect 10,000 IBMers working in the PC business, which was part of the company's Personal Systems Group. Although this division contributed 13 percent of the company's overall turnover of US $96.3 billion in 2004, it also incurred losses from the PC business.[13]

The Great Leap Forward

When IBM announced its interest in selling its PC division, Lenovo jumped at the chance; for Lenovo, the IBM deal was a giant leap forward. It gave Lenovo access to the computer giant's technology and expertise, a foothold into the lucrative US and European markets, and worldwide brand recognition.

As a well-established brand worth an estimated US $53 billion,[14] IBM was globally present and enjoyed a reputation for high quality, innovation, and reliability. As part of the deal, Lenovo obtained the right to use the IBM brand name for five years. This agreement would help maintain customer loyalty and avoid the risk that customers would notice any major changes. IBM also committed to continuing to provide service for its PCs and laptops, a move aimed to dispel customers' service concerns. Moreover, Lenovo hoped to benefit from IBM's long experience in global marketing and sales. Lenovo's own sales channels were limited to China, where it maintained excellent relations with major distributors, mainly due to the organization's transparent rules and procedures. But IBM had sales, support, and delivery operations all around the world.

In addition, IBMs huge sales volume would help lower the company's component costs. In the PC industry, 70-80 percent of total revenues go to components, so economies of scale are key contributors to keeping costs low. Lenovo expected to realize annual savings of US $200 million just through larger purchasing volumes. The "new Lenovo" thus could tackle price-sensitive markets, such as India, and appeal more to small- and medium-sized enterprises around the world. Lenovo estimated that these markets offered growth opportunities of about US $1 billion.[15] Finally, Lenovo extended its product portfolio overnight, immediately offering a broad range of products and services to diverse customers.

The deal also seemed to make sense for IBM. Since its reinvention in the 1990s, IBM had been moving constantly toward becoming a software and integrated services provider. In 1993, revenues from the hardware business represented more than half of IBM's total revenues; by 2004, they were less than one-third.[16] With this strategic reorientation, the low-margin hardware business lost importance. In addition, IBM's PC division continued to be a source of ongoing profit drains. From 2001 to mid-2004, the unit accumulated losses of US $965 million, which imposed a major burden to the overall organization.[17] The Lenovo deal promised to stop this profit drain and pave the way into the lucrative Chinese market. Lenovo's well-developed distribution network provided inroads into China, especially those leading to new corporate customers of IBM's software and service solutions. Lenovo's existing relationships with regulatory bodies and potential corporate customers, as well as its well-established brand name, could help IBM gain footing and expand quickly into mainland China.

Thus, Lenovo-IBM would obtain a competitive advantage that its closest competitors, Hewlett-Packard and Dell, could not match. As one Lenovo executive recalled: "On paper this was pretty much a match made in heaven."[18] The challenge was to make it work in practice.

Appendix A1: Timeline for the Lenovo-IBM Merger

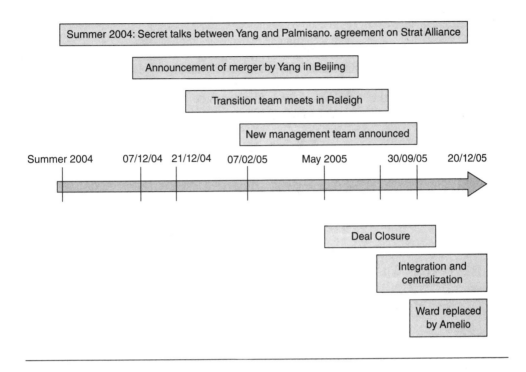

Appendix A2: Yang Yuanqing: A Portrait

Yang's colleagues thought himself both strict with others and immodest about himself. For sure, he was honest and straightforward to the point of being blunt. Sometimes people were afraid to enter his office. Yang would eventually have to learn a more co-operative management style but for the moment there was no time.

—Shan Feng and Janet Elfring, *The Legend Behind Lenovo,* unofficial corporate history

As chairman Yang centralized decision-making authority—in himself. He took full control of strategy, procurement, manufacturing, and marketing, which meant he was breaking virtually every management philosophy rule in the book. Yet it worked, perhaps because, as Yang himself recalled, "I could make quick decisions because I could look through all the functions. I knew the supply chain very well. I knew which components were in short supply. I knew when new [micro]processors were available. We could change our products, change our prices, respond quickly."

This agility combined with a willingness to make long-term investments. In 1997, Legend became the first Chinese company to implement an enterprise resource planning system provided by SAP, the German software company. Yang was determined to give his company a technology platform that at least equaled those of its global rivals. Thus, by the late 1990s, Legend was the best-selling PC brand in China. In 1999, it took 20 percent of the Chinese market. The combination of operational efficiency with PCs that had been designed specifically for the Chinese market proved difficult for its competitors to match.

In 2001, the distribution side of the business became Digital China, managed by Guo Wei, another young protégé of Liu. Yang became chief executive of the PC arm.

Sources

Sull, Donald N. (2005). *Made in China: What Western Managers Can Learn From Trailblazing Chinese Entrepreneurs*, Cambridge, MA: Harvard Business School Press.

Feng, Shan and Elfring, Janet. (2000). *The Legend Behind Lenovo: The Chinese IT Company that Dares to Succeed*, Hong Kong: Asia Publishing.

(B) Integration Challenges

Post-Merger Integration

While the synergies between Lenovo and IBM looked great on paper, the roadblocks to making Lenovo-IBM the PC industry's world leader remained formidable. Not only would the process need to merge two companies with vastly different business models and cultures across 12 time zones, but the combined company needed to stay constantly competitive in the fast-paced PC industry. Michael Dell, the chairman of Lenovo's main rival, asserted: "It won't work."[19] Most observers agreed.

But Lenovo's top executives vowed to prove these skeptics wrong. Their vision for the new Lenovo was to create a computer powerhouse that would combine the best of both worlds and thereby reinvent the entire global PC industry. As Lenovo executives stated, "What Lenovo brings to the table is the best from East and West. From the original Lenovo we have the understanding of emerging markets, excellent efficiency and a focus on long-term strategy. From IBM we have deep insights into worldwide-markets and best practices from Western companies."[20]

This best-of-both-worlds integration approach could work if the combination represented a partnership rather than a takeover. Lenovo's CEO repeatedly stressed his perception of the IBM deal as a "marriage of equals," based on trust, respect, and compromise. Yang demonstrated his willingness to compromise right from the start: he stepped down as CEO to make way for IBM's Steve Ward, while he became chairman. Yang also accepted Ward's proposal to locate the new headquarters in New York, rather than establishing dual headquarters in the US and China. Lenovo's new global headquarters took up the top floor of a nondescript office building outside the city; the IBM PC division's staff mainly continued to work out of their existing site in Raleigh, North Carolina.

Despite the seeming friendliness of the deal, cross-border problems soon emerged. Simple geographical distance was a major barrier: the flight from Beijing to New York took 13 hours and crossed 12 time zones. Without any direct flights from Beijing to North Carolina, that trip took an additional few hours. Making the trip, in either direction, for a day of meetings or workshops was not possible, and any gathering or information exchange had to be planned weeks in advance to make the trip worthwhile. The thousands of miles separating the company's main locations made exchanging information about best practices incredibly difficult. The regular business hours of New York and Beijing overlap only for three to four hours each day; if the company needed to include European colleagues, the operation became nearly impossible—or required employees to arrive at the office at very odd hours.

Even as they racked up miles of travel and readjusted alarm clocks, the management teams on both sides continued to view the deal as an opportunity to learn. They displayed a genuine and remarkable willingness to set aside their own egos and make decisions in the best interest of the combined company. As one former IBM executive recalled: "Where the Chinese approach worked best, we borrowed it, and where the IBM approach worked best, we borrowed that. Or maybe an outside approach. The point was to do the right thing . . . because the fundamental mission [was] to be seen as a global corporation, not a Western and not a Chinese company. And wherever we could get ideas or implement tools that advance that idea, we did."

This pragmatic and learning-oriented approach also featured what appeared to be an honest enthusiasm for creating something new and better. Ravi Marwaha, the Indian-Australian in charge of running Lenovo's worldwide sales, admitted, "I spent 36 years in IBM. I could easily have retired. Why am I here? Because it is exciting."[21] Another senior Lenovo executive explained, "We are the first of this kind in the world, and I think people are authentically and genuinely excited about being in a place that is very fresh, and young, and new . . . It is an experiment and something that has never been done before, and there is no company like us in the world."

Such enthusiasm might have been expected from Lenovo, given that it was Lenovo that had acquired IBM's PC business. But the general sense of excitement also seemed shared among the IBM PC executives, who had for years felt like the unpopular stepsister in their former company. That is, IBM considered hardware a peripheral business and thus made few investments in the PC division. With the merger, the PC division became a core business again, if for Lenovo.

This positive attitude spanned various levels of the organization. In the first days of the new Lenovo, people took creative steps to bridge the geographical distance. IBM sent camera teams to Raleigh and Beijing, to enable video greetings to various counterparts around the globe. In the call center in Raleigh, employees filmed themselves throwing their IBM badges in the trash. Frances O'Sullivan, the COO of Lenovo International, initiated a program called the "Trash Bin Project," which encouraged ex-IBMers to submit examples of what they had done in their previous work life but did not want to do in the new Lenovo.[22]

Creating a Structure

The new Lenovo started with three separate business units: China PCs, China Cell Phones, and International Operations (former IBM PC division). In this sense, business continued much as usual for the IBMers, except that project teams formed to support different functions, such as sales, finance, and order management. The project teams consisted of former Lenovo and IBM managers and took the responsibility of preparing the further integration of the functions.

Yang Yuanqing announced a managerial restructuring on September 30, 2005. Top management jobs would be split approximately evenly between the Chinese and Western sides (see Appendix B1 for an overview). One-third of the board members would be from Hong Kong (where Lenovo is registered); another one-third would come from the US and Europe; and the rest would be from China.[23] This restructuring aimed to provide a framework for further integration, but it also was designed in accordance with Lenovo's goal of joining the league of global technology powerhouses, in that it provided a multinational management team spread across national boundaries and several time zones.

The new management structure then led to closer integration in functions such as supply chain management, planning and control, product development, and marketing. In support of its global supply chain, the company applied a unified IT system that enabled it to ship directly to 100 countries, usually with products configured to order.[24] In the wake of this integration, corporate headquarters moved from New York to Raleigh.

But the integration also meant some redundancies, especially in IBM's sales structure. Therefore, layoffs announced in March 2006 affected approximately 1,000 of the company's 21,400 employees. The cuts spread across company offices in the Americas, Asia-Pacific, and EMEA regions.[25]

Ubiquitous Differences

The functions integrated, headquarters moved, and managerial responsibility was being shared. Yet without a common language and shared values, it would be impossible to form a unified, global management team.

A year before the acquisition, Lenovo had launched a major campaign to improve the English-language skills of its managers and employees. Most of the company's senior Chinese executive could speak some English, though not all were able to do so fluently or without sufficient ease to support effective working relationships. Few of the lower-level managers were fluent in English. Of the IBM managers, virtually no one had even rudimentary knowledge of Mandarin. These immense language barriers led to lengthy meetings and frequent misunderstandings. For example, one of the most senior executives did not speak English, so board meetings had to include a translator. Yet the company was determined that English would be its corporate language.

The language barriers seemed obvious from the start; less apparent were the widely divergent preferences regarding communication styles. Especially tricky were conference calls, which offered no visuals to help participants interpret the meanings and nuances of others' verbal comments. Bill Matson, the HR Director of Lenovo, observed:

> IBM leaders would do most of the talking and the Lenovo leaders would do most of the listening. The Chinese, and Asian cultures in general, are much more silent in a conversation. They first think about what they want to say before they say it. And if you think about what you want to say before you say it, and you also translate it from your native language into English . . . you can understand that a 5-second or a 7-second gap in a conversation is not a long time. Yet, to a Western person, 5 seconds silence in a conversation seems like an eternity. So, often times what you would see in meetings is that the Western leaders would be filling in the gap in conversation, and therefore would dominate these discussions, and all too often would not spend as much time as they probably should have seeking out the perspectives and experiences of their Lenovo colleagues.

These differences in communication style were not just frustrating; they affected decision-making and problem-solving quality.

Therefore, the company instituted several programs design to overcome such barriers. The "East Meets West" program taught the company's global executives about the foundations of both Chinese and American cultures. The "Lenovo Expression Workshop" targeted the Chinese managers—typically, pragmatic, hands-on people who were not strong communicators, according to Western standards. One Chinese manager explained, "When Chinese people talk, we start from the background, and then we . . . talk about the present situation and the challenges that we are facing, and then we gather lots of supporting materials, so at the end we say, 'OK, this is our proposal.' I guess this is different from what you call the Western approach: you have an executive summary at the very beginning, basically you tell what you want to tell on the first page." The program coached Chinese executives in Western communication and presentation styles, with the ultimate goal of facilitating mutual understanding and helping the staff members collaborate more effectively.

Beyond these differences, the variance in cultural norms and values became something of an issue; the US and China can be *worlds* apart, both literally and figuratively. In particular, their attitudes toward hierarchy and authority are widely divergent. As one former senior IBM executive observed, "Lenovo was a more hierarchically driven company . . . You didn't challenge authority quite as much, and the leadership was certainly revered . . . in IBM, you are probably a bit more process-oriented, a culture that is a bit more accepting of challenges and bottom-up kind of thinking." Another former IBM manager was surprised to receive, during his first meeting with his Chinese counterpart, gifts of a cell phone and a portable music player. He also noted a significantly greater level of attention to detail by his new Chinese colleagues.[26]

For the American managers, these differences were notable; for the Chinese delegates, they often verged on offensive. For example, Yang and several other Lenovo executives arrived at John F. Kennedy International Airport in New York for their first planning meeting and found no representatives of IBM waiting to greet them. In China, any such high-ranking guests would have found not only counterparts at the airport to greet them but also a limousine to whisk them away to their hotels.

The potential for offense was mitigated somewhat by the commonalities in the corporate cultures—both sides shared strong beliefs in innovation, personal responsibility, and responsiveness to customer needs. Both sides also talked about the need for commitment. However, on this topic, the interpretations were rather different: "In Lenovo, planning before you pledge, performing as you promise, delivering your commitment is really deeply engrained in the culture. And when people sign up for a plan, they execute it. And that was probably not as effectively implemented in the old company [i.e., IBM's PC Division] that we bought."

These ubiquitous differences were not limited to the relationships between the two companies; they also influenced customer relationships. The deal had been tailored to minimize disruptions and offer service as usual to customers, but some refused to work with the new entity. The US State Department, citing fears of spyware in Lenovo computers, altered its use of some 14,000 PCs it had ordered from Lenovo.[27] The bias against the Chinese company also reared its head in some former IBM sites; in Japan, the former IBM staff fiercely resisted the idea of Chinese ownership. The Japanese design team in particular expressed deep concerns about any attempts to change the look or feel of ThinkPad notebooks—a design inspired by a Japanese lunch box that had remained unchanged since 1992.

Leadership

A year into it, the "new" Lenovo could look back on some major achievements: it had launched operations and brand in more than 65 countries, without any major disruptions to deliveries and support. No mass exodus of customers had occurred, as some had predicted. It managed to retain 98% of its employees. And it had gained global market share, including in BRIC countries, making it the world's third-largest PC manufacturer, behind Dell and HP (see Appendix B2 for an overview of global PC market shares).

Then, in December 2005, the skeptics felt a sense of vindication, because something had to be wrong: the American CEO Steve Ward resigned. Why did Ward last only eight months? Some guessed a personality clash with Yang Yuanqing—a man 10 years his junior who embraced a completely different style. Other speculated that Ward had been too accustomed to the "IBM way" and could not adapt to the new culture. Perhaps his departure marked the end of a power struggle between the Lenovo and former IBM executives, won by Yang. No one outside the company's top management team knew the answer for sure, which kept observers buzzing. Whether the IBM deal would help Lenovo become the global market leader in the PC industry remained uncertain, but this incident certainly raised questions about Lenovo's ability to build a strong multinational management team and successfully run a global business.

Appendix B1: "New" Lenovo's Executive Team

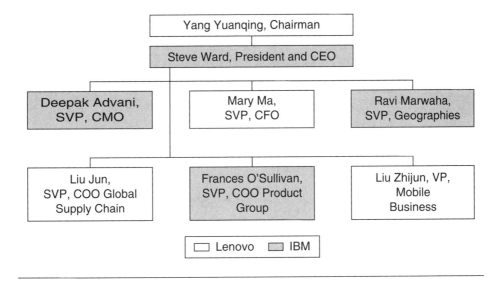

Appendix B2: Lenovo's Maret Share

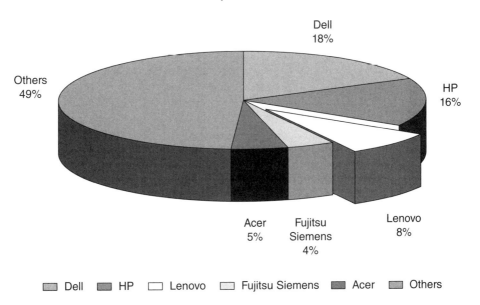

NOTES

1. Orr, G. and Xing, J. (2007). When Chinese Companies, go Global: Interview with Lenovo's Mary Ma. *McKinsey on Finance*, 23 18-22. Available on http://corporatefinance.mckinsey.com/knowledgemanagement/mof.htm.
2. Einhorn, B. (2005). Lenovo's New Boss: from Dell. *Business Week*, December 21, 2005. Available on www.businessweek.com/technology/content/dec2005/tc20051221_376268.htm.
3. Ling, Z. (2006). *The Lenovo Affair: The Growth of China's Computer Giant and its Takeover of IBM-PC*. Singapore: Wiley & So
4. N.N. (2009). Lianxiang qiye wenhua yu guanli sixiang 12345, June 16, 2009. Available on http://oxford.icxo.com/htmlnews/2009/06/16/1389015.htm.
5. London, S. (2005). The Making of a Multinational Part II: Your Rules and My Processes. *Financial Times*, November 10, 2005, p. 13.
6. Bell, L. (1948). Thomas J. Watson, in Forbes, B. (ed.) *America's Fifty Foremost Business Leaders*, New York: Forbes & Son Publishing Company, p. 427.
7. Weeks, J. (2004). *Culture and Leadership at IBM*. INSEAD case 10/2004-5239.
8. Collins, J. & J. Porras (2002). *Built to Last: Successful Habits of Visionary Companies,* New York: HarperCollins.
9. Mills, D. and Friesen, G. (1996). *Broken Promises—An Unconventional View of What Went Wrong at IBM*. Boston, MA: Harvard Business Press.
10. Gerstner, L. V. Jr. (2002). *Who Says Elephants Can't Dance? Inside IBM's Historic Turnaround*. London: HarperCollins.
11. Source: ibid.
12. Palmisano, S. (2004). *IBM Annual Meeting of Stockholders*. Providence: RI, April 27, 2004. Available on www.ibm.com/ibm/sjp/04-27-2004.html.
13. IBM (2004). IBM Annual Report 2004. Available on ftp://ftp.software.ibm.com/annual report/2004/.
14. Wolf, D. (2009). Lenovo: Amelio's Exit a Sign that IBM Integration Hitting the Rocks? Available on http://seekingalpha.com/article/118829-lenovo-amelio-s-exit-a-sign-that-ibm-intetration-hitting-the-rocks.
15. Source: ibid.
16. IBM (2004). IBM and Lenovo: New Leadership in Global PCs. Available on i.i.com.com/cnwk.1d/html/news/all_hands_presentation_final.ppt.
17. Pilzweger, M. (2006). IBM: PC-Sparte seit Jahren im Minus, *PC-Welt*, January 19, 2006. Available on www.pcwelt.de/news/IBM-PC-Sparte-seit-Jaren-im-Minus-18253.html.
18. Quelch, J. and Knoop, C.-I. (2006). *Lenovo: Building a Global Brand*. (Case No. 9-507-014). Boston, MA: Harvard Business School.
19. London, S. (2005). Lenovo: The Making of a Multinational Part I. A Global Power Made in China. *Financial Times*, November 9, 2005.
20. Quelch J. and Knoop C.I. (2007) *Lenovo – Building a Global Brand*, Harvard Business School Case Stud 9-508-703. Boston, MA: HBS Publishing. Available on http://etgstage.hbs.edu/lenovo/index.html, site of quotation: http://etgstage.hbs.edu/lenovo/heaven-brand.html.
21. London, S. (2005). Lenovo: The Making of a Multinational Part I. A Global Power Made in China. *Financial Times*, November 9, 2005.
22. Hamm, S. and S. Wildstrom (2005). Turning Two Tech Teams into One, May 9, 2005, Information Technology Online Extra. Available on www.businessweek.com/print/magazine/content/05_19/b3932116_mz063.htm?chan=gl.

23. Liu, C.. (2007). Lenovo: An Example of Globalization of Chinese Enterprises. *Journal of International Business Studies*, 38, pp. 573-577.

24. Van Duijl, M. (2006). Lenovo: An Example of Chinese Globalization. Lenovo internal presentation delivered June 15, 2006 by EMEA and SVP president. Available on www.oecd .org./dataoecd/60/43/36929454.pdf.

25. Ames, B. (2006). Lenovo to Lay Off 1,000, Move Headquarters to N.C. *Computerworld*, March 16, 2006. Available on www.computerworld.com/s.article/109604/Lenovo_to_lay_ off_1_000_move_headquarters_to_N.C.

26. Tang, Y. (2006). We Are Trying Everyday To Make Lenovo a Global Brand: Interview with Deepak Advani. Available on http://english.peopledaily.com.cn/200606/19/ eng20060619_275249.html.

27. Peng, M. (2009). *Global Business Update 2009*, Mason, OH: South-Western College Publisher.

All interview excerpts were taken from Baumeister, B. (20009), Lenovo's acquisition of IBM's PC Division, unpublished master thesis, WU, Vienna, unless referenced otherwise.

Source: Köster, K., & Stahl, G. (2012). Lenovo-IBM; Bridging cultures, languages, and time zones. In G. K. Stahl, M. E. Mendenhall, & G. R. Oddou (Eds.), *Readings and cases in international human resource management and organizational behavior* (5th ed., pp. 351–365). New York, NY: Routledge.

Case 6

Recruiting a Manager for BRB, Israel

William Roof
Barbara Bakhtari

BRB Inc., a multinational electronics corporation, plans to establish a new subsidiary in Israel. The firm's base is in Los Angeles, California, with a second overseas headquarters in England. The U.S. office staffs and operates six North American divisions and three South American subsidiaries. The U.K. office is responsible for operations in Europe and Asia. The Israeli venture is the company's first business thrust in the turbulent Middle East.

During the past 10 years, BRB's phenomenal growth resulted largely from its ability to enter the market with new, technically advanced products ahead of the competition. The technology mainly responsible for BRB's recent growth is a special type of radar signal processing. With Fourier transforms, BRB's small, lightweight, and inexpensive radar systems outperform the competitions' larger systems in range, resolution, and price. It is this type of lightweight, portable radar technology that has enormous potential for Israel during conflicts with the Arab States.

BRB's human resource functions in the United States and Europe each boast a vice president. John Conners is the Vice President of Human Resources in the United States, and Francis O'Leary is the Vice President of Human Resources in the United Kingdom. Paul Lizfeld, the CEO of BRB, contacted the two vice presidents and told them to recruit a general manager for the Israeli operation. "I don't care who finds him, but he better be right for the job. I cannot afford to replace him in six months. Is that clear!" Lizfeld told them to look independently and then coordinate together to select the right person. They knew that their jobs could be in jeopardy with this task.

The two human resource operations were independent, and each was managed individually. Recruiting processes differed between U.S. and U.K. operations. Each had different organizational structures and corporate cultures. The only link between the two was Lizfeld's strong micromanagement style, which emphasized cost control.

U.S. Operations

John Conners has worked for BRB for the past 20 years. He started with a degree in engineering and worked in the engineering department. After earning his M.B.A. in human resource management from UCLA, he transferred to the human resource department. Management felt that someone with an engineering background could hire the best technical employees for BRB. With BRB's high turnover rate, they felt that someone who could relate to the technical side of the business could better attract and screen the right people for the organization. BRB promoted Conners to vice president three years ago, after he hired the staffs for the subsidiaries in Peru and Brazil. Except for the general managers, they were all correct fits. Conners felt that the problem with the general managers was an inability to work with Lizfeld.

John Conners looked at many different strategies to determine how to begin recruiting for the Israeli position. He wanted to be sure he found the right person for the job. The first step in choosing the ideal candidate was to determine the selection criteria.

Conners defined the task in Israel to include control and management of BRB'S Israeli operations. The GM must work with the Israeli government both directly and indirectly. The political unrest in Israel also requires the GM to conduct sensitive transactions with the Israeli government. This person would also work directly with Lizfeld, taking direction from him and reporting regularly to him.

As with many countries in the Middle East, Israel was in turmoil. Conners actually knew very little about the Israeli culture, but decided to ask different associates who had past dealings with Israel. He knew that the threat of war constantly hung over Israel. The country was also suffering from high inflation rates and troubled economics. Lately, he also learned that the country had become divided over certain political and cultural issues. The person accepting this job needed nerves of steel and extraordinary patience.

Conners decided the selection criteria that would be important for the candidate included technical skill, cultural empathy, a strong sense of politics, language ability, organizational abilities, and an adaptive and supportive family. He also felt that the GM would have to have the following characteristics: persuasiveness, ability to make decisions, resourcefulness, flexibility, and adaptability to new challenges. Now all he needed to do was find a person who had all these attributes.

He decided to begin his search for candidates within the organization. He knew this route had both advantages and disadvantages. Since BRB was still in the beginning stages of internationalization in Israel, a "home country" presence might prove to be very helpful. Lizfeld would appreciate this. The disadvantages would be many. It might be very difficult to find someone willing to relocate in Israel. The increased cost of living and the political unrest make it a tough package to sell. Conners knew of the "Israeli mentality." He also knew he would have to take care in sending someone who might either overpower the Israelis or break under their aggressive business style. Conners knew that Lizfeld wanted to have the home country atmosphere in Israel and planned to be very active in the management of Israeli operations.

The second option Conners had was to recruit from outside the company. The ideal candidate would have both domestic and international experience. Conners could recruit either by contacting an employment agency or by placing an ad in the *Wall Street Journal.* He thought he could find a person with the right qualifications, but he also knew it would be difficult to find someone Lizfeld like outside the company. Conners had hired two managers for the South American offices, and Lizfeld had driven them over the edge within six months. Conners knew that he had to be extra careful. One more "unqualified" candidate might put his own job on the line.

Conners found three potential candidates for the Israeli position. One candidate, Joel Goldberg, was a recommendation from the headhunter Conners had commissioned. Goldberg had thirty-five years of electronics and radar experience. He had been CEO of Radar Developments Incorporated, a major electronics corporation in New York. Goldberg had taken control of Radar Developments Incorporated in 1981. By 1986, the company had tripled sales and increased profits fivefold. Goldberg had the technical knowledge to perform the job. He also had the necessary individual characteristics Conners felt would be important for this position. Goldberg had studied in Israel on a kibbutz for two years after college, spoke fluent Hebrew, and was a practicing Jew. He wanted to retire in Israel in a few years. Conners worried that Goldberg would not stay with the company long enough to establish a solid organization. Goldberg also liked running his own show, and that created a potential problem with Lizfeld.

The next candidate was Robert Kyle, Vice President of BRB's radar electronics department. Kyle had been with BRB for more than twenty years and headed two other international divisions for BRB in Japan and Canada. Kyle was familiar with the international process and the BRB corporate culture. Lizfeld had given him excellent reviews in the other two international positions. He had strong management skills and was highly respected both within the organization and in the industry. Kyle received his Ph.D. from MIT in electrical engineering and his M.B.A from Dartmouth. He had the technical expertise and was familiar with the company and its procedures. Conners was afraid of Kyle's cultural acceptance in Israel since he did not speak the language and was not familiar with Israeli attitudes. He could require Kyle to participate in extensive cultural training, but Conners still had some reservations about sending a gentile to head operations in Israel.

The last candidate was Rochelle Cohen, an Israeli who relocated to the United States in 1982. She originally relocated to assist the head of the electronics division of Yassar Aircraft, an Israeli company that opened its first international office in 1978. Cohen did very well and brought Israeli thoroughness and assertiveness to the U.S. operations. She now wanted to move back to Israel to be with her family. Additionally, her fiancé recently relocated in Israel, and she wanted to return to marry and raise a family. Cohen had experience in the international circuit, having worked in the United States, United Kingdom, and Israel, but Conners was still worried about hiring her. Although she had the political knowledge and the proper connections in the Israeli government, the problems were her young age, lack of technical expertise, and sex.

Conners contacted O'Leary to see what progress he had made. Knowing the consequences that would come from this decision, Conners realized it was going to be a difficult one to make.

U.K. Operations

Francis O'Leary reflected on his past eight years with BRB. His rise from the strife-torn east side of Belfast to BRB's corporate vice president for human resources was extraordinary. While most Irish business careers in large English firms peak at middle management, O'Leary's actually began at that point. He proved his capabilities through hard work, constant study, and an astute ability to judge the character and substance of people on first sight. His task of finding a suitable general manager for the new division in Israel offered a challenge he readily accepted.

O'Leary excelled at recruiting and hiring innovative employees who brought technical ideas with them to BRB. The management structure at BRB in England did not support internal growth of technology and innovation, so new ideas and technological advances were not rewarded with commensurate fiscal incentives. As such, turnover of experienced innovators forced O'Leary to recruit and hire innovation on a "rotating stock" basis. It was this success in hiring innovators that broke him from the shackles of middle management and thrust him to the top of the corporation. Four years ago, through a well-planned and well-executed recruiting program, O'Leary hired Rani Gilboa, a young Israeli engineer and former Israeli army officer. For Gilboa, the need for lightweight, inexpensive battlefield systems drove a desire to approach the problem from a new aspect: signal processing. After graduate study in this field, Gilboa sought and found a company that would support his concepts. That company was BRB. Gilboa's subsequent contributions to BRB's profits secured his and O'Leary's positions atop their respective disciplines within the firm.

Since that time, O'Leary had other successes hiring innovators from Israel. This stemmed largely from his tireless self-study of Israeli culture. With a feel for the Israeli people rivaling that of an "insider," O'Leary enjoyed success in pirating established innovators from Israeli firms. Now, he faced the task of recruiting and hiring a general manager for the newly established electronics division near Haifa.

Selecting the right manager would be more difficult than expected. With his knowledge of the Israeli culture, O'Leary knew intuitively that an Israeli should head the new division. Acceptance by the division's employees, ability to speak Hebrew, spousal support, and knowledge of Israeli government regulations and tax structures were vital to the success of the new division. Unfortunately, BRB's CEO preferred home country presence in the new division and directed O'Leary to recruit with that as the top priority. After O'Leary presented a strong case, however, the CEO agreed to review all candidates. Another potential problem arose when Lizfeld, the CEO, announced a hands-on management style with plans to participate actively in the management of the Israeli division. To O'Leary, this meant that Western values, along with the current innovative recruiting strategy practiced in England, would extend to Israel as well.

Until recently, O'Leary's recruiting for management positions concentrated on internal promotions. A known performer from within was a better bet than an outsider. When current employees could not meet the job requirements, O'Leary typically turned to newspapers as his primary source of candidates. The recent emergence of reputable executive placement services in England gave him an additional sourcing tool. At times, O'Leary had turned to social contacts, job centers, and the internal labor market as candidate sources, but the percentages of good leads from these were comparatively low.

After months of reading resumes, introductory letters, and job applications, three candidates emerged for the position in Israel. It was now up to O'Leary to decide the candidate he would recommend to Lizfeld.

Michael Flack worked for BRB for more than nineteen years. After graduating from Cambridge College with a degree in general engineering, Flack joined the company as a mechanical engineer. Initially, he worked in the mechanical design group of the radar division. After five years, BRB promoted Flack to engineering section manager. While in this position, he enjoyed various successes in radar miniaturization design. During his eleventh year, BRB again promoted Flack to department head in the manufacturing engineering group. Emphasis in this position shifted from design to production. During his seventeenth year, he became director of engineering design, where he was responsible for managing forty-three engineers' efforts in new-product design.

Flack had no international experience, and he was a reputed "tinkerer." He liked to spend time in the labs designing mechanical components along with his engineers. This generated tremendous esprit within his department but often resulted in inattention to his administrative responsibilities.

Rani Gilboa thought his friend Yair Shafrir was perfect for the position. Shafrir was currently vice-president of engineering at Elta Electronics in Israel. Elta is one of Israel's top radar firms, with several products proven in actual combat during the last Arab-Israeli conflict. Shafrir received his degree in electrical engineering from the University of Jerusalem. He had spent his professional career in Israel, usually changing companies to accept promotions. He had been with four companies since graduating from the university nineteen years ago. Shafrir was s strong-willed, organized individual who took pride in his record of technical management accomplishments. He had been able to complete projects on schedule and within budget over 70 percent of the time, a rare feat for an Israeli company. This record resulted mainly from the force of his personal leadership and strength of will. With his entire career spent in Israeli companies, O'Leary had little doubt that Shafrir could manage BRB's new electronics division. Culturally, he was perfect for the job. O'Leary had concerns, however, about Paul Lizfeld's injection of Western culture through his active management plan. The obstinate Shafrir, with no international business experience, might resent the interference.

A well-placed advertisement in the *London Times'* employment section drew a number of responses. One of the three final candidates responded to the ad about four weeks after it appeared in the *Times*.

Harold Michaelson was an English citizen of Jewish faith. Michaelson's family fled Poland in 1938 when Harold's father insisted that the "Nazi madman" would never attack England, especially after Prime Minister Chamberlain's successful visit to Munich. Harold was born to the newly naturalized couple in 1940. Later, he attended college in the United States, where he earned both bachelor's and master's degrees in electrical engineering at Georgia Tech. After graduating, Harold spent two years with General Electric until his father's illness forced him to return to England. He accepted an engineering position with Marconi, and he has remained with that company. Shortly after his return, his father died. Michaelson continued to take care of his mother for the next year. Mrs. Michaelson had always dreamed of living in the Jewish homeland—a dream not shared by her husband. One year after his death, she joined her sister's family in Haifa. Harold had readily accepted a position with Marconi in Israel to work on the new Israeli defense fighter LAVI. Unfortunately, cancellation of the LAVI program also canceled his chances to work in Israel for Marconi. At the time of the interview, Harold was vice president of engineering for Marconi's air radio division. He was also the youngest vice president in the corporation. His background in engineering and administrative functions, coupled with his ability to speak Hebrew, made Harold a strong candidate for the position. During the interview, he mentioned his mother's failing health and her refusal to leave Israel. He intended, if selected, to take care of her there. O'Leary wondered if that was Harold's main reason for wanting to live in Israel. Would he still want to live and work there if he lost his mother? O'Leary was anxious to discuss his candidates with John Conners.

Source: Roof, W., & Bakhtari, B. Recruiting a manager for BRB, Israel. In G. K. Stahl, M. E. Mendenhall, & G. R. Oddou (Eds.), *Readings and cases in international human resource management and organizational behavior* (5th ed., pp. 276–281). New York, NY: Routledge.

Case 7

Andrew Robinson Goes to Taiwan: The Challenges of a Short-Term Assignment

Catherine Welch

Andrew Robinson had been working as a software developer in the computer industry for 10 years and had recently joined the subsidiary of a major multinational telecommunications equipment supplier in Sydney, Telequip Australia. Andrew was born in Australia, had studied at an Australian university, did not speak a foreign language and had never worked abroad, although his family had lived abroad when he was of preschool age and while still a student he had visited parts of Asia and Europe. Andrew knew he had outstanding technical skills as a software programmer and troubleshooter, and he had accumulated extensive experience in developing software for the telecommunications industry.

When Andrew joined Telequip Australia, he was assigned to the company's network management division, which was in the process of developing a management platform for its main domestic customer. A network management platform is the nervous system of a telecommunications network. When something goes wrong in the network, the management platform sends messages to the 'brain' of the network, the control center. The platform was always designed to be generic and to be sold to other telecommunications operators in the world market. It would be Telequip Australia's first 'world product'.

Andrew worked on the network management system for the domestic customer for about 6 months. The first releases of the product had been installed when a Taiwanese telecommunications carrier, Taicom, became the first foreign company to sign a contract with Telequip Australia for the network management system. Because of the many

---

Note: This case would not have been possible without the generous and extensive input provided by Andrew Robinson.

different requirements of telecom operators, the network system would require extensive adaptation and new features to be developed, so initial estimates were that the contract would require 6 months of development before Taicom would have the new system up and running. It was anticipated that a large degree of re-use from the project for the domestic customer would be possible, particularly for the first few releases.

In addition to the software to be provided by Telequip Australia, Telequip North America was providing hardware and finance. The total value of the hardware was about 10 times the value of the Australian software.

Andrew was asked if he wanted to join the Taiwanese project and, happy at the prospect of a change, agreed. All the development work for the project would be done in Australia, with just a single manager, Jonathan Samuels, being sent to Taipei from Sydney on a full-time basis. The most senior manager on the project, Malcolm Donaghue, was based in Australia, but the understanding was that he would spend about half his time in Taipei. Because of shortages of staff and demands from other projects, most of the staff on the project were newly hired subcontractors from India with no experience of the industry.

Andrew knew that it was likely he would have to make a few short trips to Taipei to install and test software during the life of the project, but he didn't mind the idea of visiting a city he hadn't been to before. He liked Chinese food and had a lot of friends of Chinese descent, so he didn't feel that Taiwan would be too alien.

Andrew joined the project in November and in January was on the plane to Taipei for a 4-week visit. His initial few weeks on the project had been very positive and he felt that the technical aspects of the project were on track. The small development team in Australia had been making progress and hitting deadlines. The view from Taipei was very different. Taicom was not happy with progress: the system was frequently down, and even when it was running it was incapable of handling the promised load.

Andrew also had the feeling that Jonathan, although a hard worker, was not comfortable in Taipei. Although Jonathan rarely complained, he never seemed happy either. He never went out, worked 7 days a week, had not made any friends among the locals and had not made any attempts to learn Chinese. He never had a good word for his Chinese colleagues and it had not occurred to him to get business cards in Chinese. Andrew began to have his doubts about whether Jonathan was the most suitable person to act as Telequip's liaison with Taicom.

It seemed that Malcolm was also not entirely at ease in Taipei. This surprised Andrew, because Malcolm had worked in Hong Kong for some years and was the only one on the project with Asian experience. However, Malcolm's problem seemed to be that he was having trouble managing a project that now spanned two countries. He was not able to prevent further delays to the project and his only solution to a problem seemed to be to ask his staff in Taipei to work harder. He worked himself harder still. Andrew became frustrated that Malcolm did not send more work back to the development team in Australia, and that communication between staff in the two locations was so poor.

One day, Andrew's wife rang him during office hours to report that they had exceeded their limit on their credit card and she had not been able to use it. 'That doesn't sound right,' he responded, 'I haven't paid the hotel bill yet, so I don't see how we could have run up such a large amount on the card. I have been keeping track of how much I am spending.'

It transpired that the hotel had placed a hold on his card when he had checked in, pushing the amount on the card to its limit.

'Couldn't Telequip have given you a company credit card to use while you are over there?' his wife said.

'I'm afraid that's not how they work. They will reimburse me when I get back home and hand over my receipts.'

'But in the meantime I am going to have to use cash,' his wife grumbled. 'Why couldn't they have at least warned you about this? We could have increased our limit in advance.'

'It could be worse,' said Andrew. 'One of my colleagues has shown up here without a credit card at all. A couple of others had space on their cards so his hotel bill and expenses have been shared between them.'

Andrew returned to Australia after his 4-week stay in Taipei, slept 40 hours in 3 days then went back to work as normal. He and his wife had been house-hunting and on his return from Taipei found a house they liked, so signed a contract on it. Under the terms of the contract, settlement on the house would take place in May and he and his wife would move straight in.

In April, a few weeks after he had signed the contract on the house, Andrew was approached by Malcolm and asked if he would be prepared to go to Taipei for a more extended period of time. Taicom was complaining that they didn't have any visibility over the project since the work was being done in Australia, so Malcolm was convinced that Telequip needed more people on the ground in Taipei. Andrew pointed out that he had just bought a house and needed to be in Australia for settlement, but Malcolm felt confident that that could be accommodated in the schedule and assured Andrew that he could put together an attractive though unspecified financial incentive for the short-term assignment. Andrew went home to consult his wife and both agreed that since it would not be a good career move to turn Malcolm down, and since the extra money would be welcome in view of the fact they were about to start making repayments on a mortgage, Andrew should take up the assignment. 'I'll come back to Australia to help you move, anyway,' Andrew assured his wife. 'Malcolm knows about the house and knows that's something he has to work around.'

Accordingly, Andrew let Malcolm know that he would accept the assignment, but requested 2 weeks' grace so he could get himself ready. He also asked that he receive in writing the terms and conditions of his assignment. At this stage it wasn't clear how long the assignment would last, but under the terms of his visa he would not be able to stay in Taiwan for more than 60 days at a time.

Two days later, Malcolm came to him and said, 'Look, it's bad news. Taicom have told us that if we don't meet the next deadline they'll cancel the project and we'll be kicked out. I am flying out tomorrow and need some technical staff to come with me for backup. I know you said 2 weeks, but this is urgent.' Andrew didn't like the idea of having to break this latest development to his wife, but he agreed and his flight was booked. He spent the afternoon trying to finish the most urgent tasks on which he was working, leave instructions for the team he was supervising and copy his most important files on to the laptop he would be taking with him to Taipei. At 5 o'clock his personnel office e-mailed a short memo setting out his financial entitlements for the short-term assignment. It was 8 o'clock in the evening before he arrived home, by which time his wife had packed his suitcase.

On the plane he took out the document outlining his entitlements. Now that he was classed as being on a short-term assignment, rather than a business trip, the financial arrangements for his stay in Taipei had changed. He would still be paid his usual salary and would remain on the Telequip Australia payroll, but he was entitled to an additional daily per diem. Jonathan had already told him to claim the per diem at the end of each month, and the money would be paid straight into his bank account in Australia. The per diem was generous, but Andrew knew his wife wouldn't be pleased that he would still be using his personal credit card. He had at least arranged with the bank to raise his credit limit while he was back in Australia.

When he and Malcolm arrived in Taipei, a full-blown crisis had indeed developed. Taicom was very concerned about missed deadlines and, even worse, complained that the product that had been delivered so far did not meet their requirements. There was a strong sense that if Telequip did not devise a way to meet some of Taicom's grievances then the project would be cancelled. Failure of the project would have serious ramifications for the global marketing of the product. Malcolm was working 12-hour days, 7 days a week, and expected Andrew to do the same. Andrew didn't mind hard work but he wondered how long he could keep up such a demanding schedule.

Andrew was staying in a hotel but there was an expectation that he would find alternative accommodation. Telequip did not provide him with any assistance in finding an apartment, however. The whole issue of accommodation started to trouble Andrew. He didn't want to remain at a hotel, but as a foreigner with no Chinese and no knowledge of the city, how was he going to find something else? And how was he going to find the time to hunt for an apartment when he was spending such long hours at the office?

April turned into May and Andrew began to realize that he was not going to make it back to Australia in time for the move into his new house. His wife said she understood and she would manage on her own, but he knew she was upset and was finding it hard to cope. But he didn't see how he would be able to leave Taipei for a week or two. The crisis was nearing its peak, and in desperation Malcolm was transferring more and more staff from Sydney to Taipei. At one point there were 30 Telequip staff in Taipei, including many of the subcontractors who had been hired from India. Many had left behind children as well as their spouses, something which Andrew was glad he did not have to do.

Andrew was beginning to feel tired of the long hours and the sterile environment of the hotel. One night he accompanied some colleagues to a nightclub not something he would normally do at home, but he felt that he was entitled to some entertainment. The night was not a success, however. He danced with a Taiwanese woman who propositioned him, despite his protestations that he already had a wife back in Australia. He eventually managed to shake her off, but when he went back to his room early in the morning, he realized that he had lost his mobile phone on the dance floor. When his wife heard a carefully edited account of the night she was not impressed, and because he did not obtain a police report he was not able to claim the loss of his mobile phone on insurance.

Andrew had been looking for an apartment with the assistance of a Taiwanese colleague. He had looked at two flats which were spartan but adequate. However, in Taiwan, a 12-month lease is standard. He was unwilling to sign such a long-term lease and unable to negotiate a shorter one. Andrew found that Jonathan had also tried and failed to find an apartment, opting instead to stay in a serviced apartment. Their Taiwanese colleagues were amazed at how much the Telequip Australia employees were spending on five-star accommodation.

On his way to lunch one day, Andrew noticed a board in English advertising a flat for let. He phoned the number and found out that the real estate agent spoke English and that he had a different apartment on offer which was not far from where he was working. Later in the week the real estate agent took him to view the apartment. It was very basic and lacked a kitchen, but it was reasonably cheap, its owner spoke English and was prepared to agree to a 3-month lease. Andrew decided to take it. He had to provide 3 months' rent in cash, so he took out a cash advance on his credit card, and moved in as soon as the apartment had been cleaned.

Andrew's mood improved when he checked out of the hotel. At least he had overcome one hurdle and he was secretly proud of having managed such a complex transaction in a foreign city. He began eating at local restaurants rather than at the hotel, even though he often didn't understand what he was ordering. The first time he visited an eatery he would choose a meal at random. If he decided to return, he always ordered the same meal again.

The hurdles he faced in the office remained. Malcolm had returned to Sydney but had started to behave erratically and was perceived to be suffering from burnout. Control of the project had been placed in the hands of a more senior manager who was based at Telequip headquarters rather than in Australia. The long hours and the uncertainty over the project's future continued.

Approaching the end of the first release, the project looked like it was being cancelled. Much of the promised functionality was missing. As Andrew explained to his wife, 'There's a piece of functionality we promised in the contract. It doesn't fit nicely into anyone's responsibility and no one's done anything about it. The customer really needs it right now and, the problem is, it's going to take months to develop it.' He explained their planned approach.

'That sounds awfully complicated. Isn't there an easier way to do it?'

'I don't know. No one's looked for one. Maybe there is.'

There was. Three weeks later, Andrew explained, '90 per cent of the work was going to be in writing a program to display the data. But frankly, there wasn't anything in the data that couldn't be displayed in any web browser. I wrote a small program that turned each record into a file and posted it to a web page. Taicom still aren't satisfied with the release as a whole, but they've agreed to overlook the other deficiencies for the moment and we can start work on the second delivery.'

After this, life in Taipei started to settle down a little for Andrew. He took the odd day off on the weekend and explored some of the hills near his apartment. One day on the way home from work he stopped off at a coffee shop that looked fairly lively, and was invited to sit down with some students eager to practise their English and prepared to give him some tips on Chinese in return. He had bought some books on Chinese characters and could distinguish about 200 characters by this stage, although he still had great trouble working out what he was being served in restaurants and could only speak a handful of words. He had noticed that his colleagues preferred to stick to restaurants that had menus in English, and were not interested in learning any Chinese. As May turned into June they also had the humid summer to complain about.

Andrew's 60-day term was approaching its end and his wife was busily making plans for his return. Again, she was to be disappointed. He was asked to go back for another 2 months. He contemplated saying no, but the telecom industry was suffering a severe downturn at the time and Telequip Australia had recently laid off nearly 20 per cent of its staff. Perhaps because it was under pressure, the Taicom project went unscathed. Now, he thought, was not the time to make trouble and he knew he should be feeling relieved to have a job at all. There were a lot of people worse off than he was.

He told work he needed 10 days in Sydney and no one objected loudly, so he packed his bags eagerly. He really needed a break and was looking forward to a chance to rest and unwind. When he arrived home, however, he realized his wife had other plans. She wanted him to help her move some furniture upstairs, unpack boxes, start filling out their tax returns, go shopping for a new dining table, prune the roses in the garden and catch up with relatives he hadn't seen for months. There seemed to be no end to the chores awaiting him. At one point he burst out, 'Look, you have no idea how much stress I have been under. I just want a bit of time to do nothing'. His wife snapped back at him, 'And do you think life has been a holiday for me? I still had to keep working, yet somehow manage the settlement of the house all by myself and move, and unpack, and organize all the urgent repairs to this place that needed doing. And now you're about to disappear again. You can't leave me to do everything. You just don't understand what it's been like back here. There are some things I just can't do on my own, I need your help, and now's the only time I can get it.'

The personnel officer also wanted to catch up with him. She informed him that the per diem that Malcolm had arranged for Andrew's first 2-month stay in Taipei was considerably above company guidelines and would be scaled back by an unspecified amount. She promised to send him a letter outlining his new entitlements, but the letter did not arrive in time for his departure. She also told him to ring a number at an accountancy firm to check if he had any tax liability in Taipei. The accountant sent him a three-page e-mail on the matter. In part, the e-mail read:

> Based on our discussions with our Taiwanese office we understand that where an individual is seconded to work in Taiwan and receives any income from a Taiwan entity, that individual will be subject to Taiwan individual income tax regardless of the days spent in Taiwan.
>
> However, where an individual is paid by a foreign entity with no recharge to a Taiwanese entity of the compensation costs associated with the assignment, it is the number of days

spent in Taiwan which will determine whether there is a Taiwanese tax liability. Where an individual has been in Taiwan for a period of less than 90 days cumulatively during a Taiwanese tax year (being the calendar year), the employment income will be exempt and no Taipei income tax return is required.

Prima facie, owing to the International Tax Agreement (ITA) between Australia and Taiwan, where an individual:

1. is physically in Taiwan for less than 183 days (in a calendar year);

2. is paid by an employer not resident in Taiwan; and

3. their compensation costs are not being recharged to a Taiwanese entity their salary will also be exempt from tax in Taiwan.

However, even though the salary income is exempt according to the ITA, and individual must still lodge a Taiwanese tax return if their stay exceeds 90 days. Taiwanese tax is also payable at this stage but a full refund is available at a later date if all the following can be substantiated with the Taiwanese tax authorities:

1. the individual remained a tax resident of their home country (e.g. statement of residency from the Australian Tax Office);

2. Australian notices of assessment cover the relevant period; and

3. there is proof that the individual was paid and employed by a foreign company.

We understand from our Taiwan office that the process of claiming a refund is difficult even with the above substantiation. This is especially in the case of an Australian taxpayer due to the difference in tax years. Practically, the costs of claiming the refund can often outweigh taxes paid.

'So does that mean you are liable for tax in Taiwan or not?' asked his wife when she read the letter, 'and if you do have to pay tax in Taiwan but can't get a refund, or have to wait years for one, is Telequip going to reimburse you? I'm beginning to think that we're not going to do as well out of this assignment as we initially thought. Take the way you are being paid the per diem, for instance. They never pay it to you in advance. You wait a month, then put in a claim form, and then we wait around for them to give you a cheque for the amount you have claimed. But in the meantime you have racked up all those bills on your personal credit card. So in the end they owe us thousands of dollars.'

His 10-day interlude in Sydney was soon over. Back in Taipei, the routine was disturbingly familiar. Another crisis involving Taicom was brewing. This time, however, Andrew had a real sense of impending disaster. He had a sobering talk with a Taicom manager who told him that even if the system were made to work, Taicom would not use it. It simply did not provide the functionality that Taicom required.

Despite these pressures, Andrew was determined to keep some balance in his life and make sure that he take at least one day off each week. He certainly didn't want to end up like Malcolm, who probably should have been on extended sick leave but was still working. He also decided he should take the initiative to study Chinese in a more formalized fashion. He started ringing around some language schools that other expatriates had mentioned and found one with weekend classes. He had to pay for 10 weeks of classes in advance. He was unsure he would still be in Taipei for that long, so enrolled in the cheapest course he could find.

Meanwhile, his Australian colleagues were complaining about the food, the hot and humid summer, the unreasonableness of the Taicom staff and the pollution. One day was spent in suspense waiting to see if a typhoon threatening the city would hit. All the local staff stayed at home, so it was only the expatriates who gathered in the darkened, empty Taicom building. At about noon they received a call from a manager at Telequip headquarters ordering them to leave the building. In the end, the typhoon missed Taipei, but struck a village that some of the Telequip staff had visited the previous day. By this stage most of the Australians working on the Taicom project were openly expressing the hope that the project would indeed be cancelled. If the project were to fail, Andrew and his colleagues nevertheless anticipated that they would remain in Taipei for a number of weeks to wind up the project.

In mid-August, 6 weeks into Andrew's second 2-month assignment, senior Telequip Australia management announced that the company would be pulling out of the Taicom project. Telequip informed Taicom of a revised schedule that included delays of more than 6 months beyond previous estimates, which had already slipped by almost 6 months. Telequip management did not expect that the offer would be acceptable, and indeed, Taicom responded by cancelling the project. Andrew and his colleagues in Taipei were informed of the cancellation the following day. Telequip instructed its staff in Taipei to shut the system down, pack up and return home as soon as possible. Andrew and his colleagues disabled the system, collected all their belongings and left the building by the end of the day. All of them wondered if they would have jobs to return to. All felt defeated and dispirited after now having nothing to show for their months of effort. That evening Andrew ended up at a nightclub and drank until 4 a.m. with colleagues from a different but related project.

The following day, and rather hung over, Andrew was told by a Telequip secretary that she had managed to book him on a flight back to Sydney that evening. He was advised to collect the ticket from the airline's sales office in the city, after which he raced back to his apartment to pack. He caught his flight, but did not have time to retrieve his deposit from the real estate agent. A colleague who was remaining behind for a few days handled the matter on his behalf.

Back in Sydney, the Taicom team was briefed on what had happened. The Indian subcontractors were gone within an hour of the meeting. The rest of the company quickly found out through word of mouth. Morale, already low since the first round of retrenchments, plummeted even further.

'I hope this time you're back for good,' his wife said when they met at Sydney airport. 'It's truly amazing, you know. Telequip is such a large company that operates all over the world and has so much international experience. So why is it they couldn't manage to run this project in Taiwan?'

'The worst thing is,' Andrew said, 'if we had been better prepared I think we could have made this project work. I don't think it had to be a failure. The technical problems were real, but the major problem was that we weren't "buddies". We never understood them and they never understood us.'

Malcolm was retrenched the following week. Two weeks later, so were almost all of the managers and a majority of the employees who had been involved in the project, although Andrew survived. The remaining staff were reallocated and a number of other retrenchments were made elsewhere, including the whole product sales team. The 'world product' vision was dropped and Telequip Australia's focus shifted squarely to its domestic customer.

Source: Dowling, P. J., & Welch, D. E. (2004). *International human resources management: Managing people in a multinational context* (4th ed.). London: Thomson.

Case 8

Conscience or the Competitive Edge? (A)

Kate Button

Christopher K. Bart

The plane touched down at Bombay airport on time. Olivia Jones made her way through the usual immigration bureaucracy without incident and was finally ushered into a waiting limousine, complete with uniformed chauffeur and soft black leather seats. Her already considerable excitement at being in India for the first time was mounting. As she cruised the dark city streets, she asked her chauffeur why so few cars had their headlights on at night. The driver responded that most drivers believed that headlights use too much petrol! Finally, she arrived at her hotel, a black marble monolith, grandiose and decadent in its splendour, towering above the bay.

The goal of her four-day trip was to sample and select swatches of woven cotton from the mills in and around Bombay, to be used in the following season's youthwear collection of shirts, trousers, and underwear. She was thus treated with the utmost deference by her hosts, who were invariably Indian factory owners, or British agents for Indian mills. For three days she was ferried from one air-conditioned office to another, sipping iced tea or chilled lemonade, poring over leather-bound swatch catalogs, which featured every type of stripe and design possible. On the fourth day, Jones made a request that she knew would cause some anxiety in the camp. "I want to see a factory," she declared.

After much consultation and several attempts at dissuasion, she was once again ushered into a limousine and driven through a part of the city she had not previously seen. Gradually, the hotel and the western shops dissolved into the background and Jones entered downtown Bombay. All around was a sprawling shantytown, constructed from sheets of corrugated iron and panels of cardboard boxes.

Dust flew in spirals everywhere among the dirt roads and open drains. The car crawled along the unsealed roads behind carts hauled by man and beast alike, laden to overflowing with straw or city refuse—the treasure of the ghetto. More than once the limousine had to halt and wait while a lumbering white bull crossed the road.

Finally, in the very heart of the ghetto, the car came to a stop. "Are you sure you want to do this?" asked her host. Determined not to be faint-hearted, Jones got out of the car.

White-skinned, blue-eyed, and blond, clad in a city suit and stiletto-heeled shoes, and carrying a briefcase, Jones was indeed conspicuous. It was hardly surprising that the inhabitants of the area found her an interesting and amusing subject, as she teetered along the dusty street and stepped gingerly over the open sewers.

Her host led her down an alley, between the shacks and open doors and inky black interiors. Some shelters, Jones was told, were restaurants, where at lunchtime people would gather on the rush mat floors and eat rice together. In the doorway of one shack there was a table which served as a counter, laden with ancient cans of baked beans, sardines, and rusted tins of a fluorescent green substance that might have been peas. The eyes of the young man behind the counter were smiling and proud as he beckoned her forward to view his wares.

As Jones turned another corner, she saw an old man in the middle of the street, clad in a waist cloth, sitting in a large tin bucket. He had a tin can in his hand with which he poured water from the bucket over his head and shoulders. Beside him two little girls played in brilliant white nylon dresses, bedecked with ribbons and lace. They posed for her with smiling faces, delighted at having their photograph taken in their best frocks. The men and women moved around her with great dignity and grace, Jones thought.

Finally, her host led her up a precarious wooden ladder to a floor above the street. At the top Jones was warned not to stand straight as the ceiling was just 5 feet high. There, in a room not 20 feet by 40 feet, twenty men were sitting at treadle sewing machines, bent over yards of white cloth. Between them on the floor were rush mats, some occupied by sleeping workers awaiting their next shift. Jones learned that these men were on a 24-hour rotation, 12 hours on and 12 hours off, every day for 6 months of the year. For the remaining 6 months they returned to their families in the country-side to work the land, planting and building with the money they had earned in the city. The shirts they were working on were for an order she had placed 4 weeks earlier in London, an order of which she had been particularly proud because of the low price she had succeeded in negotiating. Jones reflected that this sight was the most humbling experience of her life. When she questioned her host about these conditions, she was told that they were typical for her industry—and for most of the third world, as well.

Eventually, she left the heat, dust, and din of the little shirt factory and returned to the protected, air-conditioned world of the limousine.

"What I've experienced today and the role I've played in creating that living hell will stay with me forever," she thought. Later in the day, she asked herself whether what she had seen was an inevitable consequence of pricing policies that enabled the British customer to purchase shirts at £12.99 instead of £13.99 and at the same time allowed the company to make its mandatory 56% profit margin? Were her negotiating skills—the result of many years of training—an indirect cause of the terrible conditions she had seen?

When Jones returned to the U.K., she considered her position and the options open to her as a buyer for a large, publicly traded, retail chain operating in a highly competitive environment. Her dilemma was twofold: Can an ambitious employee afford to exercise a social conscience in his or her career? And can career-minded individuals truly make a difference without jeopardizing their future?

Conscience or the Competitive Edge? (B)

Olivia Jones described her subsequent decision as follows:

"The alternatives for me were perfectly clear, if somewhat unrealistic: I could stipulate a standard of working conditions to be enforced at any factory employed, and offer to pay an inflated price for merchandise in an effort to fund the necessary improvements. This would mean having to increase the margins in other sections of the range and explaining to my controller exactly why prices had risen.

"There was, of course, no guarantee that the extra cash would make its way safely into the hands of the worker or improve his working conditions. Even exercising my greatest faith in human nature, I could see the wealthy factory owner getting increasingly fatter and some other keen and able buyer being promoted into my highly coveted position!

"I could refuse to buy from India. This would mean I would have to find alternative sources at equally low prices to justify my action. There was always Macau, where I knew conditions were worse if anything, or Hong Kong, where conditions were certainly better, from what I had seen, but prices were much higher. I had to ask myself if I would truly be improving the plight of the workers by denying them the enormous orders that I usually put through their factories. Or would I simply be salving my own conscience by righteously congratulating myself at not dealing in slave labour? Doubtless my production schedule would be snapped up eagerly by the next buyer who was hungry for cheap labour and fast turnaround.

"I could consider speaking to the powers that be and ask their advice. After all, the group was proud of its philanthropic reputation and had promoted its charity work and sponsorship of various causes, including Wimbledon Football Club and Miss World. This in mind, I approached my line manager, who laughed at my idealistic naivety and made it quite clear that I should hold my tongue if I knew what was good for me.

"It seemed I had but two choices. Either I quit the company and look for an employer which would be more responsible in its attitude towards sourcing merchandise, or I could continue to buy as before, but aware of the consequences and exercising a conscience wherever possible. I won't bother to list my excuses for opting for the latter choice.

"I believe that there is no solution, no generalization which can be used as a precedent in this type of scenario. I don't know to this day what action I could have taken to improve the lives of those individuals whom I felt I had compromised.

"Every day, in various work situations, employees, and specifically managers, come up against questions of conscience versus the status quo. It may be that you are encouraged to show prejudice against an individual or group of employees due to their race, colour or clique; maybe your boss asked you to lie to camouflage an embarrassing error and insinuate that the fault lies with someone else; maybe your employer's policy requires you to screw a client or a supplier to close a deal and maintain the bottom line.

"Each case is different and demands its own evaluation. Each man and woman must draw their own set of rules and regulations to suit their own situation and conscience.

"It takes brave individuals to jeopardize their careers for a cause but it is thanks to those who do take a stand that great feats of humanitarian work are successfully undertaken and completed. We should all evaluate the choices that are open to us and be true to ourselves. Let your conscience be your guide within the realms of reality.

"The most important lesson that I learned from the episode was that, above all, you have to learn to live with the choices that you make."

Source: Button, K., & Bart, C. K. (1994). Conscience or the competitive edge? (A, B). *Case Research Journal, 14*(1). Reprinted by permission from the *Case Research Journal.* Copyright 1994 by Button, K., Bart, C., and the North American Case Research Association. All rights reserved.

References

Abo, T. (1994). *Hybrid factory: The Japanese production system in the United States*. Oxford, UK: Oxford University Press.

Addison, J. X., & Siebert, W. S. (1994, October). Recent developments in social policy in the new European Union. *Industrial and Labor Relations Review 48*, 5–27.

Adler, N. J. (1984). Women in international management: Where are they? *California Management Review, 26*, 78–89.

Adler, N. J. (1994). Competitive frontiers: Women managers across borders. In N. J. Adler & D. N. Izraeli (Eds.), *Competitive frontiers: Women managers in a global economy* (pp. 22–42). Cambridge, MA: Blackwell.

Adler, N. J., & Ghadar, F. (1990a). International strategy from the perspective of people and culture: The North American context. In A. M. Rugman (Ed.), *Research in global strategic management: International business research for the twenty-first century* (pp. 179–205). Greenwich, CT: JAI Press.

Adler, N. J., & Ghadar, F. (1990b). Strategic human resource management: A global perspective. In R. Pieper (Ed.), *Human resource management in international comparison* (pp. 235–260). Berlin: De Gruyter.

Aguinis, H., & Glavas, A. (2012). What we know and don't know about corporate social responsibility: A review and research agenda. *Journal of Management, 38*(4), 932–968.

Aharoni, Y. (1994). How small firms can achieve competitive advantage in an interdependent world. In T. Agmon & R. Drobnick (Eds.), *Small firms in global competition* (pp. 9–18). New York: Oxford University Press.

Anderson, B. A. (2005). Expatriate selection: Good management or good luck? *International Journal of Human Resource Management, 16*, 567 583.

Antal, A. B., & Izraeli, D. (1993). A global comparison of women in management: Women managers in their homelands and as expatriates. In E. A. Fagenson (Ed.), *Women in management: Trends, issues and challenges in managerial diversity*. Newbury Park, CA: Sage.

Ariño, A., & Reuer, J. J. (2004). Designing and renegotiating strategic alliance contracts. *Academy of Management Executive, 18*, 37–48.

Arthur, M. B., & Rousseau, D. M. (Eds.). (1996). *The boundaryless career: A new employment principle for a new organizational era*. Boston, MA: Cambridge University Press.

Au, K. (1999). Intra-cultural variation: Evidence and implications for international business. *Journal of International Business Studies, 30*, 799–812.

Au, K., & Fukuda, J. (2002). Boundary spanning behavior of expatriates. *Journal of World Business, 37*, 285–296.

Aycan, Z. (2005). The interplay between cultural and institutional/structural contingencies in human resource management practices. *International Journal of Human Resource Management, 16*(7), 1083–1119.

Azumi, K., & McMillan, C. J. (1975). Culture and organizational structure: A comparison on Japanese and British organizations. *International Studies of Management and Organization, 5*(1), 35–47.

Bacon, N., & Hoque, K. (2005). HRM in the SME sector: Valuable employees and coercive networks. *International Journal of Human Resource Management, 16* (11), 1976–1999.

Bailey, J. R., Chen, C. C., & Dou, S. G. (1997). Conceptions of self and performance-related feedback in the U. S., Japan, and China. *Journal of International Business Studies, 28,* 605–625.

Baird, P. L., Geylani, P. C., & Roberts, J. A. (2012). Corporate social and financial performance re-examined: Industry effects in a linear mixed model analysis. *Journal of Business Ethics,* 109(3), 367–388.

Baliga, B. R., & Jaeger, A. M. (1984). Multinational corporations: Control systems and delegation issues. *Journal of International Business Studies, 15*(3), 25–40.

Barkema, H. G., Bell, J. H. J., & Pennings, J. M. (1996). Foreign entry, cultural barriers, and learning. *Strategic Management Journal, 17,* 151–166.

Barkema, H. G., Shenkar, O., Vermeulen, F., & Bell, J. H. J. (1997). Working abroad, working with others: How firms learn to operate international joint ventures. *Academy of Management Journal, 40,* 426–442.

Barney, J. (1991). Firm resources and sustained competitive advantage. *Journal of Management, 17*(1), 99–120.

Bartlett, C. (1986). Building and managing the transnational: The new organizational challenge. In M. Porter (Ed.), *Competition in global industries* (pp. 367–401). Boston, MA: Harvard Business School Press.

Bartlett, C. A., & Ghoshal, S. (1989). *Managing across borders: The transnational solution.* Boston, MA: Harvard Business School Press.

Bartlett, C. A., & Ghoshal, S. (1998a). Beyond strategic planning to organization learning: Lifeblood of the individualized corporation. *Strategy & Leadership, 26,* 34–39.

Bartlett, C. A., & Ghoshal, S. (1998b). *Managing across borders: The transnational solution* (2nd ed.). Boston, MA: Harvard Business Press.

Baumgarten, K. (1995). Training and development of international staff. In A.-W. Harzing & J. Van Ruysseveldt (Eds.), *International human resource management* (pp. 205–228). London: Sage.

Bean, R. (1985). *Comparative Industrial Relations.* Beckenham, UK: Croom Helm.

Beaver, W. (1995, March–April). Levis is leaving China. *Business Horizons,* 35–40.

Beechler, S. (1992, November). International management control in multinational corporations: The case of Japanese consumer electronics firms in Asia. *OECD Economic Journal,* 20–31.

Beechler, S. L., & Iaquinto, A. L. (1994). *A longitudinal study of staffing patterns in U.S. affiliates of Japanese transnational corporations.* Paper presented to the International Management Division of the Academy of Management, Dallas.

Beer, M. (1981, Winter). Performance appraisal: Dilemmas and possibilities. *Organizational Dynamics,* 25–33.

Beer, M., Spector, P. R., Lawrence, D., Mills, D. Q., & Walton, R. E. (1984). *Managing human assets.* New York: Free Press.

Belasco, J. A., & Stayer, R. C. (1994). *Flight of the buffalo: Soaring to excellence, learning to let employees lead.* New York: Grand Central Publishing.

Benson, P. G. (1978). Measuring cross-cultural adjustment: The problem of criteria. *International Journal of Intercultural Relations, 2*(1), 21–37.

Bernardin, J. H., & Cascio, W. F. (1984). Personnel appraisal and the law. In R. A. Schuler & S. A. Youngblood (Eds.), *Readings in personnel and human resource management.* St. Paul, MN: West.

Bernthal, P. R., Rogers, R. W., & Smith, A, B, (2003). *Managing performance: Building accountability for organizational success.* Pittsburgh, PA: Developmental Dimensions International.

Bhaskar-Shrinivas, P., Harrison, D. A., Shaffer, M. A., & Luk, D. M. (2005). Input-based and time-based models of international adjustment: Meta-analytic evidence and theoretical extensions. *Academy of Management Journal, 48*, 257–281.

Birkinshaw, J., Bresman, H., & Håkanson, L. (2000). Managing the post-acquisition integration process: How the human integration and task integration processes interact to foster value creation. *Journal of Management Studies, 37*, 395–425.

Birkinshaw, J., Nobel, R., & Ridderstråle, J. (2002). Knowledge as a contingency variable: Do the characteristics of knowledge predict organizational structure? *Organization Science, 13*, 274–289.

Björkman, I. (2006). International human resource management research and institutional theory. In G. Stahl & I. Björkman (Eds.), *Handbook of international human resource management* (pp. 463–474). Cheltenham, UK: Edward Elgar.

Björkman, I. (2012). Peter Hanson: Building a world-class product development centre for hi tech systems in China. In G. K. Stahl, M. E. Mendenhall, & G. R. Oddou (Eds.), *Readings and cases in international human resource management and organizational behavior* (5th ed., pp. 62–70). New York, NY: Routledge.

Björkman, I., Budhwar, P., Smale, A., & Sumelius, J. (2008). Human resource management in foreign owned subsidiaries: China versus India. *International Journal of Human Resource Management, 19*, 964–978.

Björkman, I., & Lervik, J. E. (2007). Transferring HR practices within multinational corporations. *Human Resource Management Journal, 17*, 320–335.

Black, J. S. (1990a). Factors related to the adjustment of Japanese expatriate managers in America. *Journal of Management Studies, 28*, 417–427.

Black, J. S. (1990b). Locus of control, social support, stress and adjustment in international transfers. *Asia Pacific Journal of Management, 7*(1), 1–29.

Black, J. S., & Gregersen, H. B. (1991). Antecedents to cross-cultural adjustment for expatriates in Pacific Rim assignments. *Human Relations, 44*(5), 497–515.

Black, J. S., & Gregersen, H. B. (2000). High impact training: Forging leaders for the global frontier. *Human Resource Management, 39*, 173–184.

Black, J. S., Gregersen, H. B., & Mendenhall, M. E. (1992). Toward a theoretical framework of repatriation adjustment. *Journal of International Business Studies, 22*(3), 737–760.

Black, J. S., & Mendenhall, M. (1989). A practical but theory-based framework for selecting cross-cultural training methods. *Human Resource Management, 28*(4), 511–539.

Blake, R. R., & Mouton, J. S. (1984). Overcoming group warfare. *Harvard Business Review, 62*, 98–108.

Blake, R. W. (2000). Footwear international. In H. W. Lane, J. J. DiStefano, & M. L. Maxnevski (Eds.), *International management behavior: Text, readings and cases* (4th ed. pp. 165–172). Malden, MA: Blackwell.

Bleeke, J., & Ernst, D. (1995). Is your strategic alliance really a sale? *Harvard Business Review, 73*, 97–105.

Boisot, M., & Child, J. (1996). From fiefs to clans and network capitalism: Explaining China's emerging economic order. *Administrative Science Quarterly, 41*, (4), 600–628.

Bomers, G. B. J. (1976). *Multinational corporation and industrial relations: A comparative study of West Germany and the Netherlands*. Assen/Amsterdam: Van Gorcum.

Bonache, J. (2006). The compensation of expatriates: A review and a future research agenda. In I. Björkman and G. Stahl (Eds.), *Handbook of research in international human resource management* (pp. 158–175). Cheltenham, UK: Edward Elgar.

Bonache, J., & Stirpe, L. (2012). Compensating global employees. In G. K. Stahl, I. Björkman, & S. Morris (Eds.), *Handbook of research in international human resource management*, (2nd ed., pp.162–182). Northampton, MA: Edward Elgar.

Borchert, D., & Stewart, E. (1986). *Exploring ethics*. New York: Macmillan.

Boselie, P., Farndale, E., & Paauwe, J. (2012). Performance management. In C. Brewster & W. Mayrhofer (Eds.), *Handbook of reserach on comparative human resource management* (pp. 369–392). Northampton, MA: Edward Elgar.

Boxall, P. (1995). Building the theory of comparative HRM. *Human Resource Management Journal, 5*(5), 5–17.

Boyacigiller, N. (1990). The role of expatriates in the management of interdependence, complexity and risk in multinational corporations. *Journal of International Business Studies, 21*, 357–381.

Brannen, M. Y. (2004). When Mickey loses face: Recontextualization, semantic fit, and the semiotics of foreignness. *Academy of Management Review, 29*, 593–616.

Brenner, S. N., & Molander, E. A. (1977). Is the ethics of business changing? *Harvard Business Review, 55*(1), 57–71.

Brewster, C. (2004). European perspectives on human resource management. *Human Resource Management Review, 14*, 365–382.

Brewster, C. (2006). Comparing HRM policies and practices across geographical borders. In G. Stahl & I. Björkman (Eds.), *Handbook of international human resource management* (pp. 68–90). Cheltenham, UK: Edward Elgar.

Brewster, C. (2007). Comparative HRM: European views and perspectives. *International Journal of Human Resource Management, 18*(5), 769–787.

Brewster, C., & Mayrhofer, W. (2011). Comparative human resource management. In A.-W. Harzing & A. H. Pinnington (Eds.), *International human resource management* (3rd ed., pp. 47–78). London: Sage Publications.

Briody, E. K., & Chrisman, J. B. (1991). Cultural adaptation on overseas assignments. *Human Organization, 50*(3), 264–282.

Briscoe, J. P., & Hall, D. T. (2006). The interplay of boundaryless and protean careers: Combinations and implications. *Journal of Vocational Behavior, 69*(1), 1–18.

Briscoe, D. R., & Schuler, R. S. (2004). *International human resource management: Policies & practice for the global enterprise* (2nd ed.). New York, NY: Routledge.

Briscoe, D. R., Schuler, R., & Tarique, I. (2012). *International human resource management: Policies and practices for multinational enterprises*. New York: Routledge.

Brislin, R. W., MacNab, B. R., & Nayani, F. (2008). Cross-cultural training: Applications and research. In P. B. Smith, M. F. Peterson, & D. C. Thomas (Eds.), *The handbook of cross-cultural management research* (pp. 397–410). Thousand Oaks, CA: Sage Publications.

Broad, G. (1994). Japan in Britain: The dynamics of joint consultation. *Industrial Relations Journal, 25*, 26–38.

Buck, S. (1998). *The global commons: An introduction*. Washington DC: Island Press.

Burnett, M., & Von Glinow, M. A. (2011). Total rewards in international context. In A.-W. Harzing & A. H. Pinnington (Eds.), *International human resource management*, (3rd ed., pp. 468–504). London: Sage Publications.

Burns, T., & Stalker, C. M. (1961). *The management of innovation*. London: Tavistock.

Burt, R. S. (1992). *Structural holes: The social structure of competition*. Cambridge, MA: Harvard University Press.

Button, K., & Bart, C. K. (1994). Conscience or the competitive edge? (A, B). *Case Research Journal, 14*(1).

Caligiuri, P. M. (1997). Assessing expatriate success: Beyond just being there. *New approaches to Employee Management, 4*, 117–140.

Caligiuri, P. M. (2000). The big five personality characteristics as predictors of expatriate's desire to terminate the assignment and supervisor-rated performance. *Personnel Psychology, 53*, 67–88.

Caligiuri, P. M. (2006). Developing global leaders. *Human Resource Management Review, 16*, 216–228.

Caligiuri, P. M., & Colakoglu, S. (2007). A strategic contingency approach to expatriate assignment. *Human Resource Management Journal, 17* (4), 393–410.

Caligiuri, P. M., & Di Santo, V. (2001). Global competence: What is it and can it be developed through global assignments? *Human Resource Planning, 24*(3), 27–38.

Caligiuri, P. M., & Lazarova, M. (2002). A model for the influence of social interaction and social support on female expatriates' cross-cultural adjustment. *International Journal of Human Resource Management, 13*(5), 761–772.

Caligiuri, P. M., Mencin, A., & Jiang, K. (2012). *Win-win-win: The Influence of company-sponsored volunteerism programs on stakeholders.* (Working paper).

Caligiuri, P. M., Phillips, J., Lazarova, M., Tarique, I., & Bürgi, P. (2001). The theory of met expectations applied to expatriate adjustment: The role of cross-cultural training. *International Journal of Human Resource Management, 12*, 357–372.

Caligiuri, P. M., & Tarique, I. (2006). International assignee selection and cross-cultural training and development. In G. K. Stahl & I. Björkman (Eds.), *Handbook of research in international human resource management* (pp. 302–322). Cheltenham, UK: Edward Elgar.

Caligiuri, P. M., & Tarique, I. (2012). International assignee selection and cross-cultural training and development. In G. K. Stahl, I. Björkman, & S. Morris (Eds.), *Handbook of research in international human resource management*, (2nd ed., pp. 321–342). Cheltenham, UK: Edward Elgar.

Caligiuri, P. M., & Tung, R. L. (1999). Comparing the success of male and female expatriates from a US-based multinational company. *International Journal of Human Resource Management, 10*(5), 763–782.

Calori, R., Lubatkin, M., & Very, P. (1994). Control mechanism in cross-border acquisitions: An international comparison. *Organization Studies, 15*, 361–379.

Caprar, D. V. (2011). Foreign locals: A cautionary tale on the culture of MNC local employees. *Journal of International Business Studies, 42*(5), 608–628.

Cardon, M. S., & Stevens, C. E. (2004). Managing human resources in small organizations: What do we really know? *Human Resource Management Review, 14*, 295–323.

Cardy, R. L., & Dobbins, G. H. (1994). Performance appraisal: The influence of liking on cognition. *Advances in managerial cognition and organizational information processing, 5*, 115–140.

Carlson, D. S., Upton, N., & Seaman, S. (2006). The impact of human resource practices and compensation design on performance: An analysis of family-owned SMEs. *Journal of Small Business Management, 44* (4), 531–543.

Carr, S. C., Inkson, K., & Thorn, K. (2005). From global careers to talent flow: Reinterpreting "brain drain." *Journal of World Business, 40*, 386–398.

Carter, D. E., & Baker, B. S. (1991). *Concurrent engineering: The product development environment for the 1990's.* Reading, MA: Addison-Wesley.

Cartwright, S., & Cooper, C. L. (1996). *Managing mergers, acquisitions, and strategic alliances: Integrating people and cultures.* Oxford: Butterworth-Heinemann.

Cascio, W. F. (2006). Performance management systems. In G. Stahl and I. Björkman (Eds.), *Handbook of research in international human resource management* (pp. 176–196). Cheltenham, UK: Edward Elgar.

Cascio, W. F. (2012). Global performance management systems. In G. K. Stahl, I. Björkman, & S. Morris (Eds.), *Handbook of research in international human resource management*, (2nd ed., pp.183–204). Northampton, MA: Edward Elgar.

Cascio, W. F., & Bailey, E. (1995). International HRM: The state of research and practice. In O. Shenkar (Ed.), *Global perspectives of human resource management.* Englewood Cliffs, NJ: Prentice-Hall.

Cassell, C., Nadin, S., Gray, M., & Clegg, C. (2002). Exploring human resource management practices in small and medium sized enterprises. *Personnel Review, 32*(6), 671–692.

Caudron, S., Gale, S. F., Greengard, S., & Hall, J. E. (2002). 80 people, events and trends that shaped HR. *Workforce, 81*(1), 28.

Chacko, E. (2007). From brain drain to brain gain: Reverse migration to Bangalore and Hyderabad, India's globalizing high tech cities. *GeoJournal, 68*, 131–140.

Chan, D. K. S., Gelfand, M. J., Triandis, H. C., & Tzeng, O. (1996). Tightness and looseness revisited: Some preliminary analyses in Japan and the United States. *International Journal of Psychology, 31*(1), 1–12.

Chen, C. C. (1995). New trends in reward allocation preferences: A Sino-U.S. comparison. *Academy of Management Journal, 38*, 408–428.

Child, J., & Faulkner, D. (1998). *Strategies of cooperation.* Oxford, UK: Oxford University Press.

Child, J., & Kieser, A. (1979). Organization and managerial roles in British and West German companies. In C. J. Lammers & D. J. Hickson (Eds.), *Organizations are alike and unlike.* London: Routledge and Kegan Paul.

Child, J., & Tse, D. K. (2001). China's transition and its implication for international business. *Journal of International Business Studies, 32*, 5–21.

Chinese Culture Connection (1987). Chinese values and the search for culture-free dimensions of culture. *Journal of Cross-Cultural Psychology, 18*(2), 143–164.

Church, A. T. (1982). Sojourner adjustment. *Psychological Bulletin, 91*(3), 540–572.

Chusmir, L. H., & Frontczak, N. T. (1990). International management opportunities for women: Women and men paint different pictures. *International Journal of Management, 7*(3), 295–301.

Clark, T. (Ed.). (1996). *European Human Resource Management: An introduction to comparative theory and practice.* Blackwell Business.

Clark, P. F., Stewart, J. B., & Clark, D. A. (2006). The globalization of the labor market for healthcare professionals. *International Labor Review, 145*, 37–64.

Claus, L., & Briscoe, D. (2009). Employee management across borders: A review of relevant academic literature. *International Journal of Management Reviews, 11*(2), 175–196.

Clegg, H. A. (1976). *Trade unionism under collective bargaining: A theory based on comparisons of six countries.* Oxford: B. Blackwell.

Cohen, D. (2001). Cultural variation: Considerations and implications. *Psychological Bulletin, 127*, 451–471.

Cohn, J. M., Khurana, R., & Reeves, L. (2005). Growing talent as if your business depended on it. *Harvard Business Review, 83*(10), 62–70.

Cole, N. D. (2011). Managing global talent: Solving the spousal adjustment problem. *International Journal of Human Resource Management, 22*(7), 1504–1530.

Cole, N. D. (2012). Expatriate accompanying partners: The males speak. *Asia Pacific Journal of Human Resources, 50*, 308–326.

Collings, D., & Scullion, H. (2006). Global staffing. In G. Stahl & I. Björkman (Eds.), *Handbook of international human resource management* (pp. 141–157). Cheltenham, UK: Edward Elgar.

Collings, D., & Scullion, H. (2012). Global staffing. In G. K. Stahl, I. Björkman, & S. Morris (Eds.), *Handbook of research in international human resource management,* (2nd ed., pp.142–161). Northampton, MA: Edward Elgar.

Combs, C., Yongmei, L., Hall, A., & Ketchen, D. (2006). How much do high performance work practices matter? A meta-analysis of their effects on organizational performance. *Personnel Psychology, 59*(3), 501–528.

Conner, J. (2000). Developing global leaders of tomorrow. *Human Resource Management, 39*, 147–57.

Cooke, F. L. (2011). Social responsibility, sustainability and diversity of human resources. In A.-W. Harzing & J. Van Ruysseveldt (Eds.), *International human resource management* (pp. 583–624). London: Sage.

Cooke, W. N., & Noble, D. S. (1998). Industrial relations systems and US foreign direct investment abroad. *British Journal of Industrial Relations, 36*(4), 581–609.

Creswell, J. (2001, April 30). When a merger fails: Lessons from sprint. *Fortune*, 185–187.

Crichton, A. (1968). *Personnel management in context.* London, UK: B. T. Batsford.

Croucher, R., & Cotton, E. (2009). *Global unions, global business: Global union federations and international business.* London, UK: Middlesex University Press.

Croucher, R., & Rizov, M. (2012). Union influence in post-socialist Europe. *Industrial & Labor Relations Review, 65*(3), 630–650.

Cunningham, L. X. (2011). Managing human resources in SMEs in a transition economy: Evidence from China. *International Journal of Human Resource management, 21*(12), 2120–2141.

Daniels, J. D., Radebaugh, L. H., & Sullivan, D. P. (2011). *International Business: Environments and Operations.* Upper Saddle River, NJ: Prentice-Hall/Pearson.

De Cieri, H., Dowling, P. J., & Taylor, K. F. (1991). The psychological impact of expatriate relocation on partners. *International Journal of Human Resource Management, 2*(3), 377–414.

De Leon, C. T., & McPartlin, D. (1995). Adjustment of expatriate children. In J. Selmer (Ed.), *Expatriate management: New ideas for international business* (pp. 197–214). Westport, CT: Quorum Books.

de Nijs, W. (1995). International human resource management and industrial relations: A framework for analysis. In A.-W. Harzing, & J. Van Ruysseveldt (Eds.), *International human resource management* (pp. 271–290). London, UK: Sage.

Deal, T. E., & Kennedy, A. A. (1982) *Corporate cultures: The rites and rituals of corporate life.* Harmondsworth, UK: Penguin.

Debrah, Y. A., & Rees, C. J. (2011). The development of global leaders and expatriates. In A.-W. Harzing & A. H. Pinnington (Eds.), *International Human Resource Management.* Thousand Oaks, CA: Sage.

Delios, A., & Björkman, I. (2000) Expatriate staffing in foreign subsidiaries of Japanese multinational corporations in the PRC and the United States. *International Journal of Human Resource Management, 11*(2), 278–293.

DeNisi, A. S. (1996). *Cognitive processes in performance appraisal: A research agenda with implications for practice.* London: Routledge.

Deshpande, S., & Golkar, D. (1994). HRM practices in large and small manufacturing firms, a comparative study. *Journal of Small Business Management, 32*, 49–56.

Dessler, G. (2011). *Human resource management* (13th ed.). Upper Saddle River, NJ: Prentice-Hall.

Dewettinck, K., & Remue, J. (2011). Contextualizing HRM in comparative research: The role of the Cranet network. *Human Resource Management Review, 21*, 37–49.

Diamantidis, A. D., & Chatzoglou, P. D. (2011). Human resource involvement, job related factors, and their relation with firm performance: Experiences from Greece. *The International Journal of Human Resource Management, 22*(7), 1531–1553.

Diller, J. (2008). A social conscience in the global marketplace? Labour dimensions of codes of conduct, social labeling and investor initiatives. *International Labour Review, 138*(2), 99–129.

DiMaggio, P. J., & Powell, W. W. (1983). The iron cage revisited: Institutional isomorphism and collective rationality in organizational fields. *American Sociological Review, 48*, 147–160.

Dobbin, F., Sutton, J. R., Meyer, J. W., & Scott, R. (1993). Equal opportunity law and the construction of internal labor markets. *The American Journal of Sociology, 99*(2), 396–427.

Dobbs, R., Goedhart, M., & Suonio, H. (2006). Are companies getting better at M & A? *McKinsey Quarterly.* Retrieved from http://people.stern.nyu.edu/igiddy/articles/better_mergers.pdf.

Donaldson, T. (1989). *The ethics of international business.* New York: Oxford University Press.

Donaldson, T. (1996). Values in tension: Ethics away from home. *Harvard Business Review, 74,* 48–64.

Donnelly, T., Morris, D., & Donnelly, T. (2005). Renault-Nissan: A marriage of necessity. *European Business Review, 17*(5), 428–440.

Dougherty, C. (2008, June 26). Strong economy and labor shortages are luring Polish immigrants back home. *New York Times* Retrieved from http://www.nytimes.com/2008/06/26/world/europe/26poles.html?_r=0.

Dowling, P. J. (1988). International HRM. In L. Dyer (Ed.), *Human resource management: Evolving roles and responsibilities.* Washington, DC: BNA.

Dowling, P. J., Festing, M., Engle, A. D., & Gröschl, S. (2009). *International human resource management: A Canadian perspective.* Toronto, ON: Nelson Education.

Dowling, P. J., & Welch, D. E. (2004). *International human resources management: Managing people in a multinational context* (4th ed.). London: Thomson.

Downes, M., & Thomas, A. (1999). Managing organizational assignments to build organizational knowledge. *Human Resource Planning, 22*(4), 33–48.

Doz, Y. L., & Hamel, G. (1998). *Alliance advantage: The art of creating value through partnering.* Boston, MA: Harvard Business School Press.

Du, J., & Choi, J. N. (2009). Pay for performance in emerging markets: Insights from China. *Journal of International Business Studies, 41*(4), 671–689.

Dunlop, J. (1958). *Industrial relations systems.* Carbondale, IL: Southern Illinois University Press.

Dunphy, D. (1987). Convergence/divergence: A temporal review of the Japanese enterprise and its management. *Academy of Management Review, 12,* 445–459.

Economist Intelligence Unit (2010). *Up or out: Next moves for the modern expatriate.* London, UK: Author.

Edstrom, A., & Galbraith, J. (1977). Transfer of managers as a coordination and control strategy in multinational firms. *Administrative Science Quarterly, 22,* 248–263.

Edwards, T. (1998). Multinationals, labour management and the process of reverse diffusion: A case study. *International Journal of Human Resource Management, 9,* 696–709.

Edwards, T. (2011a). The nature of international integration and human resource policies in multinational companies. *Cambridge Journal of Economics, 35,* 483–498.

Edwards, T. (2011b). The transfer of employment practices across borders in multinational companies. In A.-W. Harzing and A. H. Pinnington (Eds.), *International human resource management* (3rd ed., pp. 267–290). London, UK: Sage Publications.

Edwards, T., & Rees, C. (2006). *International human resource management: Globalization, national systems and multinational companies.* Harlow, UK: Prentice Hall.

Edwards, T., & Tempel, A. (2010). Explaining variation in reverse diffusion of HR practices: Evidence from the German and British subsidiaries of American multinationals. *Journal of World Business, 45,* 19–28.

Edwards, T., Almond, P., Clark, I., Colling, T., & Ferner, A. (2005). Reverse diffusion in US multinationals: Barriers from the American business system. *Journal of Management Studies, 42,* 1261–1286.

Edwards, T., Edwards, P., Ferner, A., Marginson, P., & Tregaskis, O. (2010). Multinational companies and the diffusion of employment practices from outside the country of origin: Explaining variation across firms. *Management International Review, 50,* 613–634.

Eisenstadt, S. N. (1973). *Tradition, change and modernity.* New York, NY: Wiley.

Ellegard, K., Jonsson, D., Engstrom, T., Johansson, M., Medbo, L., & Johansson, B. (1992). Reflective production in the final assembly of motor vehicles: An emerging Swedish challenge. *International Journal of Operations and Production Management, 12*(7–8), 117–133.

Elron, E., & Kark, R. (2000). Women managers and international assignments: Some recommendations for bridging the gap. In M. E. Mendenhall & G. Oddou (Eds.), *Readings and cases in international human resource management* (3rd ed., pp. 144–154). Cincinnati, OH: South Western.

Empson, L. (2000). Mergers between professional service firms: Exploring an undirected process of integration. *Advances in Mergers and Acquisitions, 1,* 205–237.

Enderwick, P. (1982). Labour and the theory of the multinational corporation. *Industrial Relations Journal, 13*(2), 32–43.

Enderwick, P., & Hodgson, D. (1993). Expatriate management practices of New Zealand businesses. *International Journal of Human Resource Management, 4*(2), 407–423.

English, H. B. (1958). *A comprehensive dictionary of psychological and psychoanalytical terms.* New York, NY: David McKay.

Enloe, W., & Lewin, P. (1987). Issues of integration abroad and readjustment to Japan of Japanese returnees. *International Journal of Intercultural Relations, 11*(3), 223–248.

Erez, M., & Earley, P. C. (1993). *Culture, self-identity, and work.* New York, NY: Oxford University Press.

Erez, M., & Shokef, E. (2008). The culture of global organizations. In P. B. Smith, M. F. Peterson, & D. C. Thomas (Eds.), *Handbook of cross-cultural management research* (pp. 285–300). Thousand Oaks, CA: Sage.

Evans, P. A., Doz, Y., & Laurent, A. (1989). *Human resource management in international firms.* London, UK: Macmillan.

Evans, P. A., Lank, E., & Farquhar, A. (1989). Managing human resources in the international firm: Lessons from practice. In P. A. Evans, Y. Doz, & A. Laurent (Eds.), *Human resource management in international firms: Change globalization, innovation.* London, UK: Macmillan.

Evans, P., Pucik, V., & Barsoux, J. L. (2002). *The global challenge: Frameworks for international human resource management.* New York, NY: McGraw-Hill.

Evans, P., Pucik, V., & Björkman, I. (2011). *The global challenge: International human resource management.* New York, NY: McGraw-Hill Irwin.

Farndale, E., Brewster, C., & Poutsma, E. (2008). Coordinated vs. liberal market HRM: The impact of institutionalization on multinational firms. *The International Journal of Human Resource Management, 19,* 2004–2023.

Farndale, E. F., Paauwe, J., Morris, S. S., Stahl, G. K., Stiles, P., Trevor, J., & Wright, P. (2010). Context-bound configurations of corporate HR functions in multinational corporations. *Human Resource Management, 49* (1), 45–66.

Farndale, E., Scullion H., & Sparrow, P. (2010). The role of the corporate HR function in global talent management. *Journal of World Business, 45*(2), 161–168.

Farnham, A. (1994, June 27). Global—or just globaloney? *Fortune,* 97–100.

Faulkner, D., Pitkethly, R., & Child, J. (2002). International mergers and acquisitions in the UK 1985–94: A comparison of national HRM practices. *International Journal of Human Resource Management, 13,* 106–122.

Feldman, D. C., & Brett, J. M. (1983). Coping with new jobs: A comparative study of new hires and job changers. *Academy of Management Journal, 26,* 258–272.

Feldman, D. C., & Thomas, D. C. (1992). Career management issues facing expatriates. *Journal of International Business Studies, 23,* 271–293.

Fenwick, M. (2004). International compensation and performance management. In A.-W. Harzing, & J. V. Ruysseveldt (Eds.), *International human resource management* (2nd ed., pp 307–332). London, UK: Sage.

Ferner, A., & Varul, M. (2000a). 'Vanguard' subsidiaries and the diffusion of new practices: A case study of German multinationals. *British Journal of Industrial Relations, 38,* 115–140.

Ferner, A., & Varul, M. (2000b). Internationalisation and the personnel function in German multinationals. *Human Resource Management Journal, 10,* 79–96.

Ferrell, O. C., & Fraedrich, J. (1994). *Business ethics: Ethical decision making and cases.* Boston, MA: Houghton Mifflin Company

Ferris, G., Hochwarter, W., Buckley, M. R., Harrell-Cook, G., & Fink, D. (1999). Human resource management: Some new directions. *Journal of Management, 25*(3), 385–415.

Festing, M., & Barzantny, C. (2008). Performance management in Germany and France. In A. Varma, P. S. Budhwar, & A. S. DeNisi (Eds.), *Performance management systems: A global perspective* (pp. 147–167). London, UK: Routledge.

Festing, M., Engle, A. D., Dowling, P. J., & Sahakiants, I. (2012). HRM activities: Pay and rewards. In C. Brewster & W. Mayrhofer (Eds.), *Handbook of research on comparative human resource management* (pp. 139–163). Northampton, MA: Edward Elgar.

Fink, G., Meierewert, S., & Rohr, U. (2005). The use of repatriation knowledge in organizations. *Human Resource Planning, 28,* 30–36.

Fischer, M. M., & Stirböck, C. (2006). Pan-European regional income growth and club-convergence. *The Annals of Regional Science, 40*(4), 693–721.

Fletcher, C., & Perry, F. (2001). Performance appraisal and feedback: A consideration of national culture and a review of contemporary and future trends. In N. Anderson, D. Ones, H. Sinanagil, & C. Viswesvaran (Eds.), *International handbook of work and organizational psychology* (pp. 127–144). Beverly Hills, CA: Sage Publications.

Fombrun, C., Tichy, N. M., & Devanna, M. A. (1984). *Strategic HRM.* New York, NY: Wiley.

Forster, N. (2000). The myth of the "international manager." *International Journal of Human Resources Management, 10*(1), 12–142.

Franko, L. (1973). Who manages multinational enterprises? *Columbia Journal of World Business, 8,* 30–42.

Frederick, W. C. (1991). The moral authority of transnational corporate codes. *Journal of Business Ethics, 10,* 165–177.

Freeman, R. B., & Kane, J. (1995). An alternative approach to expatriate allowances: An international citizen. *The international executive, 37*(3), 245–259.

Freeman, R. B., & Katz, L. F. (1994). Rising wage inequality: The United states vs. other advanced countries. In R. B. Freeman (Ed.), *Working under different rules.* (pp. 29–62) New York, NY: Russell Sage Foundation.

French, H. (2003). *Vanishing borders: Protecting the environment in the age of globalization.* New York, NY: Norton Paperbacks.

Friedman, M. (2002). *Capitalism and freedom: Fortieth anniversary edition.* Chicago, IL: University of Chicago Press.

Friedman, T. L. (1999). *The Lexus and the olive tree.* New York, NY: Farrar, Strauss & Giroux.

Friedman, T. L. (2005). *The world is flat: A brief history of the twenty-first century.* New York, NY: Farrar, Strauss & Giroux.

Fuentes-García, F. J., Núñez-Tabales, J. M., & Veroz-Herradón (2008). Applicability of corporate social responsibility to human resources management: Perspective from Spain. *Journal of Business Ethics, 82,* 27–44.

Fukuyama, F. (1995). Social capital and the global economy. *Foreign Affairs, 74*(5), 89–103.

Gaur, A. S., Delios, A., & Singh, K. (2007). Institutional environments, staffing strategies, and subsidiary performance. *Journal of Management, 33,* 611–636.

Gelfand, M. J., Raver, J. L., Nishii, L., Leslie, L. M., Lun, J., Lim, B. Ch., et al. (2011). Differences between tight and loose cultures: A 33-nation study. *Science, 332,* 1100–1104.

George, C. S. (1968). *The history of management thought.* Englewood Cliffs, NJ: Prentice Hall.

Gerhart, G. (2008). Cross cultural management research: Assumptions, evidence, and suggested directions. *International Journal of Cross-Cultural Management, 8,* 259–274.

Gerhart, G., & Fang, M. (2005). National culture and human resource management: Assumptions and evidence. *International Journal of Human Resource Management, 16*(6), 971–986.

Gertsen, M. C., Söderberg, A.-M., & Torp, J. E. (1998). Different approaches to understanding of culture in mergers and acquisitions. In M. C. Gertsen, A.-M. Söderberg, & J. E. Torp (Eds.), *Cultural dimensions of international mergers and acquisitions.* (pp. 17–38). Berlin: de Gruyter.

Ghauri, P. N., & Prasad, S. B. (1995). A network approach to probing Asia's interfirm linkages. *Advances in International Comparative Management, 10,* 63–77.

Ghoshal, S., & Bartlett, C. A. (1999). A New Manifesto for Management. *Sloan Management Review, 40,* 9–20.

Gibson, C. B. (1994). The implications of national culture for organization structure: An investigation of three perspectives. *Advances in International Comparative Management, 9,* 3–38.

Gibson. C. B., & Zellmer-Bruhn, M. E. (2001). Metaphors and meaning: An intercultural analysis of the concept of teamwork. *Administrative Science Quarterly, 45,* 274–303.

Global Relocation Trends Survey Report. (2010). Woodbridge, IL: Brookfield Global Relocation Services.

Global Relocation Trends Survey Report. (2011). Woodbridge, IL: Brookfield Global Relocation Services.

Global Relocation Trends Survey Report. (2012). Woodbridge, IL: Brookfield Global Relocation Services.

GMAC, NFTC, & SHRM Global Forum. (2004). *Ten years of Global Relocation Trends: 1993–2004.* Oak Brook, IL: GMAC Global Relocation Services.

Gomez-Mejia, L. R., & Welbourne, T. (1991). Compensation strategies in a global context. *Human Resource Planning, 14,* 29–42.

Gomez-Mejia, L., & Wiseman, R. M. (1997). Reframing executive compensation: An assessment and outlook. *Journal of Management, 23,* 291–375.

Gong, Y. (2003). Toward a dynamic process model of staffing composition and subsidiary outcomes in multinational enterprise. *Journal of Management, 29,* 259–280.

Gooderham, P., & Nordhaug, O. (2011). One European model of HRM? Cranet empirical contributions. *Human Resource Management Review, 21,* 27–36.

Gooderham, P. N., Nordhaug, O., & Ringdal, K. (1999). Institutional and rational determinants of organizational practices: Human resource management in European firms. *Administrative Science Quarterly, 44,* 507–531.

Gooderham, P., Nordhaug, O., Ringdal, K (2006). National embeddedness and calculative human resource management in U.S. subsidiaries in Europe and Australia. *Human Relations, 59*(11), 1491–1513.

Goulet, P. K., & Schweiger, D. M. (2006). Managing culture and human resources in mergers and acquisitions. In G. K. Stahl & I. Björkman (Eds.), *Handbook of research in international human resource management* (pp. 405–429). Cheltenham, UK: Edward Elgar.

Gregersen, H. B., & Black, J. S. (1990). A multifaceted approach to expatriate retention in international assignments. *Group and Organization Studies, 15*(4), 461–485.

Gregersen, H. B., Hite, J. M., & Black, J. S. (1996). Expatriate performance appraisal in U.S. multinational firms. *Journal of International Business Studies, 27,* 711–738.

Gregersen, H. B., Morrison, A., & Black, J. S. (1998). Developing leaders for the global frontier. *Sloan Management Review, 40,* 21–32.

Griffin, R. W., & Pustay, M. W. (2013). *International Business* (7th ed.). Upper Saddle River NJ: Prentice Hall.

Gullahorn, J. T., & Gullahorn, J. E. (1963). An extension of the U-curve hypothesis. *Journal of Social Issues, 19,* 33–47.

Gunnigle, P., Murphy, K., Cleveland, J. N., Heraty, N., & Morley, M. (2002). Localization in human resource management: Comparing American and European multinational corporations. *Advances in International Management, 14*, 259–284.

Gupta, A. K., & Govindarajan, V. (2002). Cultivating a global mindset. *Academy of Management Executive, 16*, 116–126.

Guth, R. A. (2000, Feb 29). Net lets Japanese women join workforce at home. *The Wall Street Journal*, B1, B20.

Guthridge, M., & Komm, A. B. (2008). Why multinationals struggle to manage talent. *McKinsey Quarterly, 4*, 10–13.

Guthridge, M., Komm, A. B., & Lawson, E. (2008). Making talent a strategic priority. *McKinsey Quarterly, 1*, 48–59.

Guzzo, R. A., Noonan, K. A., & Elron, E. (1994). Expatriate managers and the psychological contract. *Journal of Applied Psychology, 79*(4), 617–626.

Hall, P. A., & Gingerich, D. W. (2009). Varieties of capitalism and institutional complementarities in the political economy: An Empirical Analysis. *British Journal of Political Science, 39*, 449–482.

Hall, P. A., & Soskice, D. W. (2001). *Varieties of capitalism: The institutional foundations of comparative advantage.* Oxford, UK: Oxford University Press.

Hamill, J. (1984). Labour relations decision making in multinational corporations. *Industrial Relations Journal*, 15(2), 30–34.

Hancke, B. (2000). European works councils and industrial restructuring in the European motor industry. *European Journal of Industrial Relations, 6*(1), 35–59.

Hannon, E. (2011). International and comparative employee voice. In T. Edwards, & C. Rees (Eds.), *International human resource management: Globalization, national systems and multinational companies* (2nd ed. pp. 229–252). Harlow, Essex: Pearson Education Limited.

Harding, D., & Rouse, T. (2007). Human Due Diligence. *Harvard Business Review, 85*, 124–131.

Harpaz, I. (1990). *The meaning of work in Israel: Its nature and consequences.* New York, NY: Praeger.

Harris, H., & Brewster C. (1999). The coffee-machine system: How international selection really works. *International Journal of Human Resource Management, 10*(3), 488–500.

Harris, H. (2004). Global careers: Work-life issues and the adjustment of women international managers. *Journal of Management Development, 23*(9), 818–832.

Harris, H. (2006). Issues facing women on international assignments: A review of the research. In G. K. Stahl, & I. Björkman (Eds.), *Handbook of research in international human resource management* (pp. 265–282). Cheltenham, UK: Edward Elgar.

Harvey, M. (1982). The other side of foreign assignments: Dealing with the repatriation dilemma. *Columbia Journal of World Business, 17*(1), 53–59.

Harvey, M. (1985). The executive family: An overlooked variable in international assignments. *Columbia Journal of World Business, 20*(1), 84–92.

Harvey, M. (1989). Repatriation of corporate executives: An empirical study. *Journal of International Business Studies, 20*, 131–144.

Harvey, M. (1997). Focusing the international personnel performance appraisal process. *Human Resource Development Quarterly, 8*(1), 41–62.

Harvey, M., & Novicevic, M. M. (2006). The evolution from repatriation of managers in MNEs to "patriation" in global organizations. In G. K Stahl & I. Björkman(Eds.), *Handbook of research in international human resource management* (pp. 323–346). Cheltenham, UK: Edward Elgar.

Harvey, M., Speier, C., & Novicevic, M. M. (1999). The role of inpatriation in global staffing. *International Journal of Human Resource Management, 10*, 459–476.

Harzing, A.-W. (1995a). The persistent myth of high expatriate failure rates. *The International Journal of Human Resource Management, 6*(2), 457–474.

Harzing, A.-W. (1995b). Strategic planning in multinational corporations. In A. W. Harzing & Van Ruysseveldt (Eds.), *International Human Resource Management* (pp. 25–50). London, UK: Sage Publications.

Harzing, A.-W. (2001a). An analysis of the functions of international transfer of managers in MNCs. *Employee Relations, 23*, 581–598.

Harzing, A.-W. (2001b). Of bears, bumble-bees, and spiders: The role of expatriates in controlling foreign subsidiaries. *Journal of World Business, 36*, 366–379.

Harzing, A.-W. (2001c). Who's in charge? An empirical study of executive staffing practices in foreign subsidiaries. *Resource Management, 40*, 139–158.

Harzing, A.-W., & Noorderhaven, N. (2006). Geographical distance and the role and management of subsidiaries: The case of subsidiaries down under. *Asia Pacific Journal of Management, 23*, 167–185.

Haspeslagh, P., & Jemison, D. E. (1991). *Managing acquisitions: Creating value for corporate renewal.* New York, NY: Free Press.

Hays, R. D. (1971). Ascribed behavioral determinants of success-failure among U.S. expatriate managers. *Journal of International Business Studies, 2*(1), 40–46.

Hayton, J. C. (2003). Strategic human capital management in SMEs: An empirical study of entrepreneurial performance. *Human Resource Management, 42*(4), 375–391.

Hechanova, R., Beehr, T. A., & Christiansen, N. D. (2003). Antecedents and consequences of employees' adjustment to overseas assignment: A meta-analytic review. *Applied Psychology: An International Review, 52*(2), 213–236.

Heenan, D. A., & Perlmutter, H. V. (1979). *Multinational organizational development.* Reading, MA: Addison-Wesley.

Henderson, H. (1999). *Beyond globalization. Shaping a sustainable global economy.* West Hartford, CT: Kumarian Press.

Hilb, M. (2012). Computex corporation. In G. K. Stahl, M. E. Mendenhall, & G. R. Oddou (Eds.), *Readings and cases in international human resource management and organizational behavior* (5th ed., pp. 185–187). New York, NY: Routledge.

Hickson, D. J., & Pugh, D. S. (1995). *Management worldwide: The impact of societal culture on organizations around the globe.* London, UK: Penguin Books.

Hickson, D. J., & McMillan, C. J. (1981). *Organizations and nation: The Aston programme IV.* Farnborough, UK: Gower.

Hill, R., & Stewart, J. (2000). Human resource development in small organizations. *Journal of European Industrial Training, 24* (2–4), 105–117.

Hoffman, A. J., & Bansal, P. (2011). Retrospective, perspective and prospective: Introduction to the Oxford handbook on business and the natural environment. In P. Bansal & A. J. Hoffman (Eds.), *The Oxford handbook on business and the natural environment* (pp.3–28). Oxford, UK: Oxford University Press.

Hofstede, G. (1980). *Culture's consequences: International differences in work related values.* Beverly Hills, CA: Sage.

Hofstede, G. (1991). *Cultures and organizations: Software of the mind.* Maidenhead, UK: McGraw-Hill.

Hofstede, G. (2001). *Culture's consequences: Comparing values, behaviors, institutions, and organizations across nations* (2nd ed.). Thousand Oaks, CA: Sage.

Hofstede, G., Hofstede, G. J., & Minkow, M. (2010) *Cultures and organizations: Software of the mind.* (3rd ed.). Maidenhead, UK: McGraw-Hill.

Hofstede, G., & Minkow, M. (2010). *Cultures and organizations. Software of the mind: Intercultural cooperation and its importance for survival.* New York: McGraw Hill.

House, R. J., Hanges, P. J., Javidan, M., Dorfman, P. W., & Gupta, V. (2004). *Culture, leadership, and organizations: The GLOBE study of 62 societies.* Thousand Oaks, CA: Sage.

Houser, N., & Kloesel, C. (Eds.). (1992). *The essential Pierce: Selected philosophical writings.* Bloomington, IN: Indiana University Press.

Howard, G. (1991). Culture tales: A narrative approach to thinking, cross-cultural psychology and psychotherapy. *American Psychologist, 46,* 187–197.

Howard, M., & Willmott, M. (2001). Ethical consumption in the twenty first century. In T. Bentley & S. D. Jones (Eds.), *The moral universe* (pp. 1–8), London, UK: Demos.

Hui, H. C., & Cheng, I. W. M. (1987). Effects of second language proficiency of speakers and listeners on person perception and behavioural intention: A study of Chinese bilinguals. *International Journal of Psychology, 22,* 421–430.

Humphrey, J. (1995). The adoption of Japanese management techniques in Brazilian industry. *Journal of Management Studies, 32*(6), 767–787.

Huo, Y. P., & Von Glinow, M. A. (1995). On transplanting human resource practices to China. *International Journal of Manpower, 16*(9), 3–13.

Huselid, M. (1995). The impact of human resource management practices on turnover, productivity, and corporate financial performance. *Academy of Management Journal, 38*(3), 635–672.

Husted, B. W., & Allen, D. B. (2006). Corporate social responsibility in the multinational enterprise: Strategic and institutional approaches. *Journal of International Business Studies, 37,* 838–849.

Hyman, R. (2004). Varieties of capitalism, national industrial relations systems and transnational challenges. In A.-W. Harzing, & J. V. Ruysseveldt (Eds.), *International Human Resource Management* (2nd ed., pp. 411–432). London, UK: Sage.

Inglehart, R., & Baker, W. E. (2000). Modernization, cultural change, and the persistence of traditional values. *American Sociological Review, 65,* 19–51.

Inkpen, A. C., & Tsang, E. (2005). Social capital, networks, and knowledge transfer. *Academy of Management Review, 30,* 146–165.

Inkpen, A. C., Sundaram, A. K., & Rockwood, K. (2000). Cross-border acquisitions of U.S. technology assets. *California Management Review, 42,* 50–71.

Inkson, J. H. K., Arthur, M. B., Pringle, J., & Barry, S. (1997). Expatriate assignment versus overseas experience: Contrasting models of international human resource development. *Journal of World Business, 32*(4), 351–368.

International Confederation of Free Trade Unions (2004). *Framework agreements with multinational companies.* www.icftu.org/displaydocument.asp?Index991216332&language=EN.

International Labour Organization (2012*). World of work report: Better jobs for a better economy.* Geneva: Author.

Insch, G. S., McIntyre, N., & Napier, N. K. (2008). The expatriate glass ceiling: the second layer of glass. *Journal of Business Ethics, 83*(1), 19–28.

Jacoby, S. M. (1985). *Employing bureaucracy: Managers, unions, and the transformation of work in American industry, 1900–1945.* New York, NY: Columbia University Press.

Jemison, D. B., & Sitkin, S. B. (1986). Acquisitions: The process can be a problem. *Harvard Business Review, 64,* 107–110.

Jemison, D. B., & Sitkin, S. B. (1986). Corporate acquisitions: A process perspective. *Academy of Management Review, 11,* 145–163.

Jones, G. R. (1986). Socialization tactics, self-efficacy, and newcomers' adjustment to the organization. *Academy of Management Journal, 2,* 262–279.

Jonsen, K., Maznevski, M., & Davison, S. (2012). Global virtual teams dynamics and effectiveness. In G. K. Stahl, I. Björkman, & S. Morris (Eds.), *Handbook of research in international human resource management* (2nd ed., pp. 363–392). Cheltenham, UK: Edward Elgar.

Katz, D., & Kahn, R. L. (1978). *The social psychology of organizations.* New York, NY: Wiley & Sons.

Kay, I. T., & Shelton, M. (2000). The people problem in mergers. *McKinsey Quarterly,* (4), 26–37.

Kets de Vries, M., Vrignaud, P., & Florent-Treacy, E. (2004). The global leadership life inventory: Development and psychometric properties of a 3600-degree feedback instrument. *International Journal of Human Resource Management, 15*(3), 475–492.

Killing, P. (2003). Improving acquisition integration: Be clear on what you intend, and avoid "best of both" deals. *Perspectives for Managers*, no. 97. Lausanne: IMD.

Klein, N. (2000). *No logo: Taking aim at the brand bullies.* New York, NY: Taylor & Francis.

Kluckhohn, C., & Strodtbeck, K. (1961). *Variations in value orientations.* Westport, CT: Greenwood Press.

Kochan, T. A., McKersie, R. B., & Cappelli, P. (1984). Strategic choice and industrial relations theory. *Industrial Relations: A Journal of Economy and Society, 23*(1), 16–39.

Kogut, B., & Zander, U. (1992). Knowledge of the firm, combinative capabilities, and the replication of technology. *Organization Science, 3*, 383–397.

Köster, K., & Stahl, G. (2012). Lenovo-IBM: Bridging cultures, languages, and time zones. In G. K. Stahl, M. E. Mendenhall, & G. R. Oddou (Eds.), *Readings and cases in international human resource management and organizational behavior* (5th ed., pp. 351–365). New York, NY: Routledge.

Kosterlitz, J. (1998). Unions of the world unite. *National Journal, 30*, 1134–1154.

Kostova, T. (1999). Transnational transfer of strategic organizational practices: A contextual perspective. *Academy of Management Review, 1999*, 308–324.

Kostova, T., & Roth, K. (2002). Adoption of an organizational practice by subsidiaries of multinational corporations: Institutional and relational effects. *Academy of Management Journal, 45*, 215–233.

Kostova, T., & Roth, K. (2003). Social capital in multinational corporations and a micro-macro model of its formation. *Academy of Management Review, 28*, 297–317.

Kostova, T., & Zaheer, S. (1999). Organizational legitimacy under conditions of complexity: The case of the multinational enterprise. *Academy of Management Review, 24,* 64–81.

Kostova, T., Roth, K., & Dacin, T. (2008). Institutional theory in the study of multinational corporations: A critique and new directions. *Academy of Management Review, 33*(4), 994–1007.

KPMG (1999). *Unlocking shareholder value: Mergers & acquisitions-a global research report.* London, UK: KPMG International.

Kraimer, M. L., Shaffer, M. A., & Bolino, M. C. (2009). The influence of expatriate and repatriate experiences on career advancement and repatriate retention. *Human Resource Management, 48*(1), 27–47.

Kraimer, M. L., Shaffer, M. A., Harrison, D. A., & Ren, H. (2012). No place like home? An identity strain perspective on repatriate turnover. *Academy of Management Journal, 55*(2), 399–420.

Krishnan, H. A., Miller, A., & Judge, W. Q. (1997). Diversification and top management team complementarity: Is performance improved by merging similar or dissimilar teams? *Strategic Management Journal, 18*, 361–374.

Kristensen, P. H., & Zeitlin, J. (2005). *Local players in global games: The strategic constitution of a multinational corporation.* Oxford, UK: Oxford University Press.

Krug, J. A., & Hegarty, W. H. (1997). Postacquisition turnover among U.S. top management teams: An analysis of the effects of foreign vs. domestic acquisitions of U.S. targets. *Strategic Management Journal, 18,* 667–675.

Kühlmann, T., & Dowling, P. J. (2005). DaimlerChrysler: A case study of a cross-border merger. In G. K. Stahl & M. E. Mendenhall (Eds.), *Mergers and acquisitions: Managing culture and human resources* (pp. 351–363). Stanford, CA: Stanford University Press.

Lam, H., & Khare, A. (2010). HR's crucial role for successful CSR. *Journal of International Business Ethics, 3*(2), 3–15.

Latta, G. W., & Danielson, T. A. (2003). Treatment of expatriate tax: A look at U.S., U.K., and Canadian practices. *Compensation and benefits review, 35*, 54–59.

Lawrence, P., & Lorsch, J. (1967). Differentiation and integration in complex organizations. *Administrative Science Quarterly, 12*, 1–47.

Lawrence, T. B., & Shadnam, M. (2008). Institutional theory. In W. Donsbach (Ed.)., *The international encyclopedia of communication (Vol. V).* 2288–2293. Malden: Blackwell Publishing Ltd.

Lazerson, M. (1995). A new phoenix? *Administrative Science Quarterly, 40*, 34–59.

Lazarova, M. (2006). International human resource management in a global perspective. In M. J. Morley, N. Heraty, & D. Collings (Eds.), *International human resource management and international assignments* (pp. 24–51). Palgrave Macmillan.

Lazarova, M. B., & Cerdin, J.-L. (2007). Revisiting repatriation concerns: Organizational support versus career and contextual influences. *Journal of International Business Studies, 38*, 404–429.

Lazarova, M., Mayrhofer, W., & Brewster, C. (2013). "Plus ça change, plus c'est la même chose." A longitudinal analysis of HRM work and the profile of senior HR Managers. In E. Parry, E. Stavrou-Costea, & M. Lazarova (Eds.), *Global trends in human resource management.* New York: Palgrave Macmillian.

Lazarova, M., & Tarique, I. (2005). Knowledge transfer upon repatriation. *Journal of World Business, 40*(4), 361–373.

Lazarova, M. B., Westman, M., & Shaffer, M. A. (2010). Elucidating the positive side of the work-family interface on international assignments: A model of expatriate work and family performance. *Academy of Management Review, 35*, 93–117.

Leana, C., & Van Buren, H. (1999). Organizational social capital and employment practices. *Academy of Management Review, 24*, 538–555.

Leavitt, H. J. (2005). *Top down: Why hierarchies are here to stay and how to manage them more effectively.* Boston, MA: Harvard Business School Press.

Lee, P. N. (1987). *Industrial management and economic reform in China, 1949–1984.* New York, NY: Oxford University Press.

Leksell, L. (1981). *Headquarter-subsidiary relationships in multinational corporations.* Stockholm: Stockholm School of Economics.

Lemanski, M., Björkman, I., & Stahl, G. (2011). "How do HRM practices diffuse from MNC subsidiaries?" Unpublished manuscript, Vienna University of Economics and Business.

Leroy, F., & Ramanantsoa, B. (1997). The cognitive and behavioral dimensions of organizational learning in merger: An empirical study. *Journal of Management Studies, 34*, 871–894.

Levy, O., Beechler, S., Taylor, S., & Boyacigiller, N. A. (2007). What we talk about when we talk about "global mindset": Managerial cognition in multinational corporations. *Journal of International Business Studies, 38*, 231–258.

Lichtenstein, B., & Mendenhall, M. (2002). Non-linearity and response-ability: Emergent order in the 21st century. *Human Relations, 55*(1), 56–32.

Lincoln, J. R., Olson, J., & Hanada, M. (1978). Cultural effects of organizational structures: The case of Japanese firms in the United States. *American Sociological Review, 43*, 829–847.

Linehan, M., & Scullion, H. (2008). The development of female global managers: The role of mentoring and networking. *Journal of Business Ethics, 83*, 29–40.

Linehan, M., & Walsh, J. (2001). Key issues in the senion female international career move: A qualitative study in European context. *British Journal of Management, 12*, 85–95.

Lo, C. W. H., Egri, C. P., & Ralston, D. A. (2008). Commitment to corporate, social, and environmental responsibilities: An insight into contrasting perspectives in China and the U.S. *Organization Management Journal, 5*, 83–98.

Lorange, P., & Roos, J. (1990). Formation of cooperative ventures: Competence mix of the management teams. *Management International Review, 30*(Special issue), 69–86.

Lowe, K. B., Downes, M., & Kroeck, K. G. (1999). The impact of gender on the willingness to accept overseas assignments. *The International Journal of Human Resource Management*, 10, 223–234.

Lubatkin, M., Calori, R., Very, P., & Veiga, J. F. (1998). Managing mergers across borders: A two-nation exploration of a nationally bound administrative heritage. *Organization Science*, 9, 670–684.

Lublin, J. S. (2000, June 27). In choosing the right management model, firms seesaw between product and place. *The Wall Street Journal*, p. A1–A4.

Luce, E. (2004, September 15). IKEA's grown up plan to tackle child labour. *Financial Times*.

Lysgaard, S. (1955). Adjustment in a foreign society: Norwegian Fulbright grantees visiting the United States. *International Social Science Bulletin*, 7, 45–51.

Ma, R., & Allen, D. G. (2009). Recruiting across cultures: A value-based model of recruitment. *Human Resource Management Review*, 19(4), 334–346.

Mabey, C., & Ramirez, M. (2012). Comparing national approaches to management development. In C. Brewster & W. Mayrhofer (Eds.), *Handbook of research on comparative human resource management* (pp. 185–210). Northampton, MA: Edward Elgar Publishing, Inc.

Maitland, A. (Sept 29, 2003). No hiding place for the irresponsible business: Companies are trying to pre-empt trouble over social, environmental and ethical issues. *Financial Times*, p. 2.

Mäkelä, K., Björkman, I., & Ehrnrooth, M. (2010). How do MNCs establish their talent pools? Influences on individuals' likelihood of being labeled as talent. *Journal of World Business*, 45, 134–142.

Marginson, P., Hall, M., Hoffmann, A., & Müller, T. (2004). The impact of European works councils on management decision making in UK and US based multinationals: A Case Study Comparison. *British Journal of Industrial Relations*, 42(2), 209–233.

Marín, G. S. (2008). The influence of institutional and cultural factors on compensation practices around the world. In L. R. Gomez-Mejia & S. Werner (Eds.), Global compensation: Foundations and perspective (pp. 3–17). New York, NY: Routledge.

Marks, M. L., & Mirvis, P. H. (1998). *Joining forces: Making one plus one equal three in mergers, acquisitions, and alliances.* San Francisco, CA: Jossey-Bass.

Marks, M. L., & Mirvis, P. H. (2010). *Joining forces: Making one plus one equal three in mergers, acquisitions, and alliances* (2nd ed.). San Francisco, CA: Jossey-Bass.

Marks, M. L., & Mirvis, P. H. (2011). A framework for the human resources role in managing culture in mergers and acquisitions. *Human Resource Management*, 50, 859–877.

Markus, H. R., & Kitayama, S. (1991). Culture and the self: Implications for cognition, emotion, and motivation. *Psychological Review*, 98(2), 224–253.

Marler, J. H. (2009). Making human resources strategic by going to the net: Reality or myth? *International Journal of Human Resource Management*, 20(3), 515–527.

Marschan, R. (1996). *New structural forms and inter-unit communication in multinationals.* Helsinki: Helsinki School of Economics.

Marschan-Piekkari, R., Welch, D., & Welch, L. (1999). Adopting a common corporate language: IHRM implications. *The International Journal of Human Resource Management*, 10(3), 377–390.

Martin, R. (2006). Segmented employment relations: Post-socialist managerial capitalism and employment relations in Central and Eastern Europe. *International Journal of Human Resource Management*, 17(8), 1353–1365.

Matten, D., & Moon, J. (2008). Implicit and explicit CSR: A conceptual framework for a comparative understanding of corporate social responsibility. *Academy of Management Review*, 32, 404–424.

Mayer, D., & Cava, A. (1993). Ethics and the gender equality dilemma for U.S. multinationals. *Journal of Business Ethics, 12*, 701–708.

Mayrhofer, W., & Brewster, C. (2005). European human resource management: Researching developments over time. *Management Revue, 16*, 36–63.

Mayrhofer, H., Hartmann, L. C., Michelitsch-Riedl, G., & Kollinger, I. (2004). Flexpatriate assignment: A neglected issue in global staffing. *International Journal of Human Resource Management, 15*, 1371–1389.

Mayrhofer, W., & Scullion, H. (2002). Female expatriates in international business: Empirical evidence from the German clothing industry. *International Journal of Human Resource Management, 13*(5), 815–836.

Mayrhofer, W., Brewster, C., Morley, M. J., & Ledolter, J. (2011). Hearing a different drummer? Convergence of human resource management in Europe—A longitudinal analysis. *Human Resource Management Review, 21*, 50–67.

Mayrhofer, W., Reichel, A., & Sparrow, P. (2012). Alternative forms of international working. In G. K. Stahl, I. Björkman, & S. Morris (Eds.), *Handbook of research in international human resource management* (2nd ed., pp. 293–320). Northampton, MA: Edward Elgar.

Maznevski, M. L., DiStefano, J. J., & Nason, S. W. (1993). *The cultural perspectives questionnaire: Summary of results using CPQ3.* Paper presented at the annual meeting of Academy of International Business, Hawaii.

McCall, M. W. (1998). *High fliers: Developing the next generation of global leaders.* Boston, MA: Harvard Business School Press.

McClelland, D. C. (1962). The achievement motive in economic growth. In G. Nielson (Ed.), *Proceedings of the XIV International Congress of Applied Psychology* (Vol. 2, pp. 60–80). Oxford, England: Munksgaard.

McDonnell, A., Lamare, R., Gunnigle, P., & Lavelle, J. (2010). Developing tomorrow's leaders: Evidence of global talent management in multinational enterprises. *Journal of World Business, 45*(2), 150–160.

McGaughey, S. L., & De Cieri, H. (1999). Reassessment of convergence and divergence dynamics: Implications for International HRM. *International Journal of Human Resource Management, 10*(2), 235–250.

McNulty, Y. M., De Cieri, H., & Hutchings, K. (2009) Do global firms measure expatriate return on investment? An empirical examination of measures, barriers, and variables influencing global staffing practices. *International Journal of Human Resource Management, 20*(6), 1309–1326.

McNulty, Y. M., & Tharenou, P. (2004). Expatriate return on investment. *International Studies of Management & Organization, 34*(3), 68–95.

Meaning of Work International Research Team (1987). *The meaning of working: An international view.* New York, NY: Academic Press.

Mendenhall, M. E., Osland, J., S., Bird, A., Oddou, G. R., & Maznevski, M., L. (2008). *Global leadership: Research, practice and development.* New York: Routledge.

Mendenhall, M., & Osland, J. (2002, June). *Mapping the terrain of the global leadership construct.* Paper presented at the Academy of International Business, San Juan, Puerto Rico.

Mendenhall, M. E., & Stahl, G. K. (2000). Expatriate training and development: Where do we go from here? *Human Resource Management, 39*, 251–265.

Mendenhall, M., & Oddou, G. (1985). The dimensions of expatriate acculturation: A review. *Academy of Management Review, 10*(1), 39–47.

Mendonca, M., & Kanungo, R. N. (1994). Managing human resources: The issue of cultural fit. *Journal of Management Inquiry, 3*(2), 189–205.

Menipaz, E., & Menipaz, A. (2011). *International business.* Thousand Oaks, CA: Sage.

Metcalfe, B. D., & Rees, C. J. (2005). Theorizing advances in international human resource development. *Human Resource Development International, 8*(4), 449–465.

Meyskens, M., Von Glinow, M. A., Werther, W., & Clarke, L. (2009). The paradox of international talent: Alternative forms of international assignments. *International Journal of Human Resource Management, 20*, 1439–1450.

Michaels, E., Handfield-Jones, H., & Axelrod, B. (2001). *The war for talent.* Boston, MA: Harvard Business School Press.

Milkovich, G. T., & Bloom, M. (1998). Rethinking international compensation. *Compensation and Benefits Reviews, 30*(1), 15–23.

Milkovich, G. T., & Newman, J. M. (2008). *Compensation.* New York, NY: McGraw-Hill.

Mill, J. (1863). *Utilitarianism.* Indianapolis, IN: Bobbs-Merrill.

Miller, E. L. (1975). The job satisfaction of expatriate American managers: A function of regional location and previous international work experience. *Journal of International Business Studies,* 65–73.

Millennium Ecosystem Assessment. (2005). http://www.maweb.org/en/index.aspx.

Minbaeva, D. (2007). Knowledge transfer in multinational corporations. *Management International Review, 47*(4), 567–594.

Mirvis, P. H., & Marks, M. L. (1994). *Managing the merger: Making it work.* Upper Saddle River, NJ: Prentice Hall.

Mol, S. T., Born, M. P., Willemsen, M. E., & van der Molen, H. T. (2005). Predicting expatriate job performance for selection purposes: A quantitative review. *Journal of Cross-Cultural Psychology, 35*(5), 590–620.

Moore, F., & Rees, C. (2008). Culture against cohesion: Global corporate strategy and employee diversity in the UK plant of a German MNC. *Employee Relations, 30*(2), 176–189.

Moore, M. J. (2002). Same ticket, different trip: Supporting dual-career couples on global assignments. *Women in Management Review, 17*(2), 61–67.

Morris, M. A., & Robie, C. (2001). A meta-analysis of the effects of cross-cultural training on expatriate performance and adjustment. *International Journal of Training and Development, 5*(2), 112–125.

Morris, S. S., Snell, S. A., Wright, P. M. (2006). A resource-based view of international human resources: Toward a framework of integrative and creative capabilities. In G. K. Stahl & I. Björkman (Eds.), *Handbook of research in international human resource management* (pp. 433–449). Cheltenham, UK: Edward Elgar.

Morrison, A. J. (2000). Developing a global leadership model. *Human Resource Management, 39,* 117–131.

Muller, A., & Kolk, A. (2010). Extrinsic and intrinsic drivers of corporate social performance: Evidence from foreign and domestic firms in Mexico. *Journal of Management Studies, 47*(1), 1–26.

Muller, M. (1998). Human resource and industrial relations practices of UK and US multinationals in Germany. *International Journal of Human Resources Management, 9*(4), 732–749.

Murphy, K. R., & Cleveland, J. N. (1995). *Understanding performance appraisal: Social, organizational, and goal based perspectives.* Thousand Oaks, CA: Sage.

Murphy, K. R., & DeNisi, A. S. (2008). A model of the appraisal process. In A. Varma, P. S. Budhwar, & A. S. DeNisi (Eds.), *Performance management systems: A global perspective* (pp. 81–96). London, UK: Routledge.

Murray, V. V., Jain, H. C., & Adams, R. J. (1976). A framework for the comparative analysis of personnel administration. *Academy of Management Review, 19,* 47–57.

Nahapiet, J., & Ghoshal, S. (1998). Social capital, intellectual capital and the organizational advantage. *Academy of Management Review, 23,* 242–266.

Naisbitt, J. (1994). *Global paradox.* New York, NY: William Morrow.

Naisbitt, J., & Aburdene, P. (1990). *Megatrends 2000: Ten new directions for the 1990's.* New York, NY: Avon.

Napier, N. K. (1989). Mergers and acquisitions, human resource issues and outcomes: A review and suggested typology. *Journal of Management Studies, 26,* 271–289.

Napier, N. K., & Peterson, R. B. (1991). Expatriate re-entry: What do repatriates have to say? *Human Resource Planning, 14,* 19–28.

Napier, N. K., & Taylor, S. (2002). Experiences of women professionals abroad: Comparisons across Japan, China, and Turkey. *International Journal of Human Resource Management, 13,* 837–851.

Napier, N. K., & Thomas, D. C. (2004). *Managing relationships in transition economies.* New York, NY: Praeger.

Naumann, E. (1993). Antecedents and consequences of satisfaction and commitment among expatriate managers. *Group and Organization Management, 18*(2), 153–187.

Neuhaus, R. (1982). *International trade secretariats: Objectives, organisation, activities.* Bonn: Friedrich-Ebert-Stiftung.

Newman, K. I, & Nollen, S. D. (1996). Culture and congruence: The fit between management practices and national culture. *Journal of International Business Studies, 27,* 753–778.

Nicholson, N., & Imaizumi, A. (1993). The adjustment of Japanese expatriates to living and working in Britain. *British Journal of Management, 4,* 119–134.

Nikandrou, I., & Panayotopoulou, L. (2012). Recruitment and selection in context. In C. Brewster & W. Mayrhofer (Eds.), *Handbook of research in comparative human resource management* (pp. 121–138). UK: Edward Elgar.

Nonaka, I., & Takeuchi, H. (1995). *The knowledge-creating company: How Japanese companies create the dynamics of innovation.* New York, NY: Oxford University Press.

O'Reilly, C. A., & Pfeffer, J. (2000*). Hidden value: How great companies achieve extraordinary results with ordinary people.* Boston, MA: Harvard Business School Press.

O'Reilly, M. (1996). Expatriate pay: The state of the art. *Compensation and benefits review, 12*(1), 54–60.

Oddou, G., & Mendenhall, M. E. (2000). Expatriate performance appraisal: Problems and solutions. In M. E. Mendenhall & G. Oddou (Eds.), *Readings and cases in international human resource management* (3rd ed., pp. 213–223). Cincinnati, OH: South Western.

OECD. (2011). *OECD Guidelines for Multinational Enterprises, 2011 Edition.* OECD Publishing. http://dx.doi.org/10.1787/9789264115415-en.

Ohmae, K. (1995). *The end of the nation state.* Cambridge, MA: Free Press.

Oliver, N., & Wilkinson, B. (1992). *The Japanization of British Industry: New developments in the 1990s.* Oxford, UK: Blackwell.

Osland, J. S., & Bird, A. (2000). Beyond sophisticated stereotypes: Cultural sensemaking in context. *Academy of Management Executive, 14,* 65–79.

Osland, J. S., Bird, A., & Mendenhall, M. (2012). Developing global mindset and global leadership capabilities. In G. K. Stahl, I. Björkman, & S. Morris (Eds.), *Handbook of research in international human resource management* (2nd ed., pp. 220–252). Northampton, MA: Edward Elgar.

Osman, I., Ho, T., Galang, M. C. (2011). Are human resource departments really important? An empirical study on Malaysian small and medium enterprises (SMEs) in the service sector. *International Journal of Business and management, 6*(2), 147–153.

Ouchi, W. (1981). *Theory Z: How American business can meet the Japanese challenge.* Reading, MA: Addison-Wesley.

Paauwe, J. (2004). *HRM and performance: Achieving long-term viability.* New York, NY: Oxford University Press.

Paauwe, J., & Boselie, P. (2003). Challenging (strategic) human resource management and the relevance of the institutional setting. *Human Resource Management Journal, 13*(3), 56–70.

Paauwe, J., & Farndale, E. (2012). International human resource management and firm performance. In G. K. Stahl, I. Björkman, & S. Morris (Eds.), *Handbook of research in international human resource management* (2nd ed., pp. 97–116). Northampton, MA: Edward Elgar.

Pangarkar, A., & Kirkwood, T. (2008, September 22). Jury still out on Quebec's training law: "One-percent training" law. *Canadian HR Reporter,* 21–16.

Pappano, L. (2012, November 2). The year of the MOOC. *New York Times*. Retrieved from http://www.nytimes.com/2012/11/04/education/edlife/massive-open-online-courses-are-multiplying-at-a-rapid-pace.html?pagewanted=all.

Park, H., Russell, C., & Lee, J. (2007). National culture and environmental sustainability: A cross-cultural analysis. *Journal of Economics and Finance, 31*(1), 104–121.

Park, H., Sun, D. H., & David, J. M. (1993). Local manager selection for U.S. firms in Korea. *Multinational Business Review, 1*(2), 57–65.

Parker, B. (2005). *Introduction to globalization and business: Relationships and responsibilities.* London, UK: Sage Publications.

Parry, E., Dickmann, M., & Morley, M. (2008). North American MNCs and their HR policies in liberal and coordinated market economies. *The International Journal of Human Resource Management, 19*, 2024–2040.

Peiperl, M. A., & Jonsen, K. (2007). Global careers. In H. P. Gunz & M. A. Peiperl (Eds.), *Handbook of career studies* (pp. 350–372). Thousand Oaks, CA: Sage.

Pelto, P. J. (1968, April). The difference between tight and loose societies. *Transaction, 37*–40.

Pendleton, A., & Poutsma, E. (2012). Financial participation. In C. Brewster & W. Mayrhofer (Eds.), *Handbook of research on comparative human resource management* (pp. 345–368). Northampton, MA: Edward Elgar.

Peng, M. W. (2000). *Business strategies in transition economies.* Thousand Oaks, CA: Sage.

Peretz, H., & Rosenblatt, Z. (2011). The role of societal cultural practices in organizational training and development: A comparative study in 21 countries. *Journal of Cross Cultural Psychology, 42*, 817–831.

Perlmutter, H. V. (1969). The tortuous evolution of the multinational corporation. *Columbia Journal of World Business, 4*(1), 9–18.

Perlow, L. A. (2012). *Sleeping with your smartphone: How to break the 24/7 habit and change the way you work.* Boston, MA: Harvard Business Review Press.

Peters, T. J., & Waterman, R. H. (1982). *In search of excellence.* New York, NY: Harper & Row.

Peterson, M. F. (2004). Culture, leadership and organizations: The GLOBE study of 62 societies [Book Review]. *Administrative Science Quarterly, 8*, 641–647.

Peterson, R. B., Napier, N., & Won, S. (1995). *Expatriate management: The differential role of national multinational corporation ownership.* Paper presented at the annual meeting of the Academy of International Business, Seoul, Korea.

Phatak, A., & Habib, M. (1998). How should managers treat ethics in international business? *Thunderbird International Business Review, 40*(2), 101–117.

Pless, N. M., Maak, T., & Stahl, G. K. (2011). Developing responsible global leaders through international service-learning programs: The Ulysses experience. *Academy of Management Learning & Education, 10*(2), 237–260.

Poe, A. C. (2000). Welcome back. *HR Magazine, 45*(3), 94–105.

Poole, M. (1986). Managerial strategies and styles in industrial relations: A comparative analysis. *Journal of General Management, 12*(1), 40–53.

Porter, M. E. (1986). Changing patterns of international competition. *California Management Review, 28*(2), 9–40.

Prahalad, C. K., & Doz, Y. L. (1999). *The multinational mission: Balancing local demands and global vision.* New York, NY: The Free Press.

Psycones (2006). *Psychological contract across employment situations.* Report to the European Commission HPSE-CTY-2002–00121.

Pucik, V. (1985). Evolution of multinational human resource management. In H. V. Wortzel & L. H. Wortzel (Eds.), *Strategic management of multinational corporations: The essentials.* New York, NY: Wiley.

Pucik, V. (1988). Strategic alliances, organizational learning, and competitive advantage: The HRM agenda. *Human Resource Management, 27*, 77–93.

Pucik, V., Björkman, I., Evans, P., & Stahl, G. (2011). Human resource management in cross-border mergers and acquisitions. In A. W. Harzing & A. H. Pinnington (Eds.), *International Human Resource Management* (3rd ed., pp. 119–152). London, UK: Sage.

Pucik, V., & Evans, P. (2004). The human factor in mergers and acquisitions. In P. Morosini & U Steger (Eds.), *Managing complex mergers*. London, UK: Financial Times Management.

Pucik, V., Evans, P., Björkman, I., & Stahl, G. K. (2010). Human resource management in cross-border mergers and acquisitions. In A.-W. Harzing & A. Pinnington (Eds.), *International human resource management* (3rd ed., pp. 119–152). London, UK: Sage.

Puck, J. F., Kittler, M. G., & Wright, C. (2008). Does it really work? Re-assessing the impact of pre-departure cross-cultural training on expatriate adjustment. *The International Journal of Human Resource Management, 19*, 2182–2197.

Puck, J. F., Mohr, A. T., & Hotbrügge, D. (2006). Cultural convergence though web-based management techniques? The case of corporate web site recruiting. *Journal of International Management, 12*(2), 181–195.

Puddington, A. (2012). *Freedom in the world: The Arab uprisings and their global repercussions.* Washington, DC: Freedom House.

Pudelko, M., & Harzing, A.-W. (2007). Country-of-origin, localization, or dominance effect? An empirical investigation of HRM practices in foreign subsidiaries. *Human Resource Management, 46*, 535–559.

Puffer, S. (1996). *Business and management in Russia.* Cheltenham, UK: Edward Elgar.

Pugh, D. S., Hickson, D. J., Hinings, C. R., MacDonald, K. M., & Turner, C. (1963). Dimensions of organization structure. *Administrative Science Quarterly, 13*, 65–105.

Punnett, B. J. (1997). Towards effective management of expatriate spouses. *Journal of World Business, 32*(3), 243–257.

Punnett, B. J., Crocker, O., & Stevens, M. J. (1992). The challenge for women expatriates and spouses: Some empirical evidence. *The International Journal of Human Resource Management, 3*(3), 585–592.

Putnam, R. (1993). *Making democracy work: Civic traditions in modern Italy.* Princeton, NJ: Princeton University Press.

Radulescu, R., & Robson, M. (2013). Does labour market flexibility matter for investment? A study of manufacturing in the OECD. *Applied Economics, 45*(5), 581–592.

Redding, S. G., Norman, A., & Schlander, A. (1994). The nature of individual attachment to the organization: A review of East Asian variations. In H. C. Triandis (Ed.), *Handbook of industrial/ organizational psychology,* (2nd ed., Vol. 4). Palo Alto, CA: Consulting Psychologists Press.

Reiche, B. S. (2006). The inpatriate experience in multinational corporations: An exploratory case study in Germany. *International Journal of Human Resource Management, 17*(9), 1572–1590.

Reiche, B. S. (2011). Knowledge transfer in multinationals: The role of inpatriates' boundary spanning. *Human Resource Management, 50*(3), 365–389.

Reiche, B. S., & Harzing, A.-W. (2011). International assignments. In A.-W. Harzing & A. Pinnington (Eds.), *International human resource management* (3rd ed., pp. 187–226). London, UK: Sage.

Reiche, B. S., Kraimer, M., & Harzing, A.-W. (2011). Why do international assignees stay? *Journal of International Business Studies, 42*, 521–544.

Renesch, J. (Ed.). (1992). *New traditions in business.* San Francisco, CA: Berrett-Koehler.

Reynolds, C. (1997). Expatriate compensation in historical perspective. *Journal of World Business, 32*(3), 118–132.

Richbell, S., Szerb, L., & Vitai, Z. (2010). HRM in the Hungarian SME sector. *Employee Relations, 32*(3), 262–280.

Rizov, M., & Croucher, R. (2009). Human resource management and performance in European firms. *Cambridge Journal of Economics, 33*(2), 253–272.

Rivoli, P. (2009). *The travels of a t-shirt in the global economy* (2nd ed.). Hoboken, NJ: John Wiley & Sons.

Robertson, R. (1995). Glocalization: Time-space and homogeneity-heterogeneity. In M. Featherstone, S. Lash, & R. Robertson (Eds.), *Global modernities* (pp. 25–44). London, UK: Sage.

Robinson, S. L., & Morrison, E. W. (2000). The development of psychological contract breach and violation: A longitudinal study. *Journal of Organizational Behavior, 21*, 525–546.

Robinson, S. L., & Rousseau, D. M. (1994). Violating the psychological contract: Not the exception but the norm. *Journal of Organizational Behavior, 15*, 245–256.

Rock, C. P., & Solodkov, V. (2001). Monetary policies, banking, and trust in changing institutions: Russia's transition in the 1990s. *Journal of Economic Issues, 35*(2), 451–458.

Rogers, J., & Streeck, W. (1995). *Works councils: Consultation, representation, and cooperation in industrial relations.* London, UK: The University of Chicago Press Ltd.

Roof, W., & Bakhtari, B. Recruiting a manager for BRB, Israel. In G. K. Stahl, M. E. Mendenhall, & G. R. Oddou (Eds.), *Readings and cases in international human resource management and organizational behavior* (5th ed., pp. 276–281). New York, NY: Routledge.

Rosenzweig, P. M., & Nohria, N. (1994). Influences on human resource management practices in multinational corporations. *Journal of International Business Studies, 25*, 229–251.

Rosenzweig, P. M., & Singh, J. V. (1991). Organizational environments and the multinational enterprise. *Academy of Management Review, 16*(2), 340–361.

Rozin, P. (1998). Evolution and development of brains and cultures. *Brain and Mind, Human Frontier Science Program, Strasbourg, France*, 111–123.

Roth, K. (1995). Managing international interdependence: CEO characteristics in a resource-based framework. *Academy of Management Journal, 38*(1), 200–231.

Roth, K., & O'Donnell, S. (1996). Foreign compensation strategy: An agency theory perspective. *Academy of Management Journal, 39*, 678–703.

Rousseau, D. M. (1995). *Psychological contracts in organizations.* Thousand Oaks, CA: Sage.

Rousseau, D. M., & Schalk, R. (Eds.). (2000). *Psychological contracts in employment: Cross-national perspectives.* Thousand Oaks, CA: Sage.

Rowley, C., Poon, I. H.-F., Zhu, Y., & Warner, M. (2011). Approaches to HRM. In A.-W. Harzing & A. Pinnington (Eds.). *International human resource management* (3rd ed., pp. 153–182). London, UK: Sage Publications.

Rutherford, M. W., Buller, P. F., & McMullen, P. R. (2003). Human resource management problems over the life cycle of small to medium-sized firms. *Human Resource Management, 42*(4), 321–335.

Ryan, A. M., MaFarland, L, Baron, H., & Page, R. (1999). An international look at selection practices: National and culture as explanations of variability in practice. *Personnel Psychology, 52*(2), 359–391.

Sagiv, L., & Schwartz, S. H. (1995). Value priorities and readiness for outgroup social contact. *Journal of Personality and Social Psychology, 69*, 437–448.

Sagiv, L., & Schwartz, S. H. (2000). A new look at national culture: Illustrative applications to role stress and managerial behavior. In N. N. Ashkanasy, C. Wilderom, & M. F. Peterson (Eds.), *The handbook of organizational culture and climate.* Newbury Park, CA: Sage.

Saini, D. S., & Budhwar, P. S. (2008). Managing the human resource in Indian SMEs: The role of indigenous realties. *Journal of World Business, 43*, 417–434.

Sachdev, S. (2006). International corporate social responsibility and employment relations. In T. Edwards & C. Rees (Eds.), *International human resource management: Globalization, national systems and multinational companies* (pp. 262–284). Harlow, Essex: Pearson Education Limited.

Sachdev, S. (2011). International corporate social responsibility and HRM. In T. Edwards & C. Rees (Eds.), *International Human Resource Management: Globalization, National*

Systems and Multinational Companies (2nd ed., pp. 253–271). Harlow, Essex: Pearson Education Limited.

Salimäki, A., & Heneman, R. L. (2008) Pay for performance for global employees. In L. R. Gomez-Mejia & S. Werner (Eds.). *Global compensation: Foundations and perspective* (pp. 1568–166). New York, NY: Routledge.

Salt, J., & Miller, J. (2006). Foreign labour in the United Kingdom: Current patterns and trends. *Labour Mark Trends, 10*, 335–355.

Saxenian, A. (2005). From brain drain to brain circulation: Transnational communities and regional upgrading in India and China. *Studies in Comparative International Development (SCID), 40*(2), 35–61.

Schein, E. H. (1985). *Organizational culture and leadership.* San Francisco, CA: Jossey-Bass.

Schein, E. (1996). Career anchors revisited: Implications for career development in the 21st century. *Academy of Management Executive, 10*(4), 80–88.

Schmitt, J., & Mitukiewicz, A. (2012). Politics matter: Changes in unionisation rates in rich countries, 1960–2010. *Industrial Relations Journal, 43*(3), 260–280.

Schuler, R. S. (2001). HR issues in international joint venture and alliances. In J. Storey (Ed.), *Human Resource Management: A Critical Text* (2nd ed., pp. 314–336). London: UK ITL.

Schuler, R. S. (2001). Human resource issues and activities in international joint ventures. *International Journal of Human Resource Management, 12*, 1–52.

Schuler, R. S., & MacMillan, I. C. (1984). Gaining competitive advantage through human resource management practices. *Human Resource Management, 23*, 241–255.

Schuler, R. S., Jackson, S. E., & Luo, Y. (2004). *Managing human resource sin cross-border alliances.* London: Routledge.

Schuler, R. S., & Tarique, I. (2006). International joint venture system complexity and human resource management. In G. K. Stahl & I. Björkman (Eds.), *Handbook of research in international human resource management* (pp. 385–406). Cheltenham, UK: Edward Elgar.

Schuler, R. S., & Tarique, I. (2007). International human resource management: A North American perspective, a thematic update and suggestions for future research. *International Journal of Human Resource Management, 18*(5), 717–744.

Schuler, R.S., & Tarique, I. (2012). International joint venture system complexity and human resource management. In G. K. Stahl, I. Björkman, & S. Morris (Eds.), *Handbook of research in international human resource management*, 2nd ed. (pp. 393–414). Northampton, MA: Edward Elgar.

Schuler, R. S., & Rogovsky, N. (1998). Understanding compensation practice variations in firms: The impact of national culture. *Journal of International Business Studies, 29*, 159–177.

Schwartz, S. H. (1992). Universals in the content and structure of values: Theoretical advances and empirical tests in 20 countries. In M. P. Zanna (Ed.), *Advances in Experimental Social Psychology* (Vol. 24, pp. 1–65). San Diego, CA: Academic Press.

Schwartz, S. H. (1994). Beyond individualism/collectivism: New dimensions of values. In U. Kim, H. C. Triandis, C. Kağitçibaşi, S. C. Choi, & G. Yoon (Eds.), *Individualism and Collectivism: Theory applications and methods* (pp. 85–119). Newbury Park, CA: Sage.

Schwartz, S. H., & Bilsky, W. (1990). Toward a universal psychological structure of human values. *Journal of Personality and Social Psychology, 53*, 550–562.

Schwartz, S. H., & Sagie, G. (2000). Value consensus and importance: A cross-national study. *Journal of Cross-Cultural Psychology, 31*(4), 465–497.

Schweiger, D. M., & DeNisi, A. S. (1991). The effects of communication with employees following a merger: A longitudinal field experiment. *Academy of Management Journal, 34*, 110–135.

Schweiger, D. M., & Goulet, P. K. (2005). Facilitating acquisition integration through deep-level cultural learning interventions: A longitudinal field experiment. *Organization Studies, 26*, 1477–1499.

Schweiger, D. M., & Lippert, R. L. (2005). Integration: The critical link in M&A value creation. In G. K. Stahl & M. E. Mendenhall (Eds.), *Mergers and acquisitions: Managing culture and human resources* (pp. 17–45). Stanford, CA: Stanford University Press.

Schweiger. D. M., Atamer, T., & Calori, R. (2003). Transnational project teams and networks: Making the multinational organization more effective. *Journal of World Business, 38*, 127–140.

Scullion, H. (1991, November). Why companies prefer to use expatriates. *Personnel Management, 23*(11) pp. 32–35.

Scullion, H., & Brewster, C. (2001). The management of expatriates: Messages from Europe? *Journal of World Business, 36*(4), 36–365.

Scullion, H., & Starkey, K. (2000). In search of the changing role of the corporate human resource function in the international firm. *International Journal of Human Resource Management, 11*, 1061–1081.

Seddon, J. (1987). Assumptions, cultures and performance appraisal. *Journal of Management Development, 6*, 47–54.

Selmer, J., & Lam, H. (2004). "Third-culture kids": Future business expatriates? *Personnel Review, 33*(4), 430–445.

Selmer, J., Ebrahimi, B. P., & Mingtao, L. (2002). Career management of business expatriates from China. *International Business Review, 11*, 17–33.

Selmer, J., Torbiorn, I., & de Leon, C. T. (1998). Sequential cross-cultural training for expatriate business managers: Predeparture and post-arrival. *International Journal of Human Resource Management, 9*(5), 831–840.

Senge, P. (1990). *The fifth discipline: The art and practice of the learning organization.* New York, NY: Doubleday.

Serapio, M. G., & Cascio, W. F. (1996). End-games in international alliances. *Academy of Management Executive, 10*, 62–73.

Sethi, S. P. (1975, Spring). Dimensions of corporate social performance: An analytic framework. *California Management Review, 17*, 58–64.

Shaffer, M. A., & Harrison, D. A. (2001). Forgotten partners of international assignments: Development and test of a model of spouse adjustment. *Journal of Applied Psychology, 86*(2), 238–254.

Shaffer, M., Kraimer, M., Chen, Y.-P., & Bolino, M. C. (2012). Choices, challenges, and career consequences of global work experiences: A review and future agenda. *Journal of Management, 38*(4), 1282–1327.

Shaw, W. (1996). *Business ethics* (2nd ed.). Belmont, CA: Wadsworth.

Shepherd, D. (2003). Common bond values at the New Zealand office of AT&T. In D. C. Thomas (Ed.), *Readings and cases in international management* (pp. 92–100). Thousand Oaks, CA: Sage.

Shih, H. A., Chiang, Y. H., & Kim, I. S. (2005). Expatriate performance management from MNEs of different national origins. *International Journal of Manpower, 26*, 157–176.

Shimizu, K., Hitt, M. A., Vaidyanath, D., & Pisano, V. (2004). Theoretical foundations of cross-border mergers and acquisitions: A review of current research and recommendations for the future. *Journal of International Management, 10*, 307–353.

SHRM (2007). *Green workplace survey brief.* Alexandria, VA: Society for Human Resource Management (available online).

SHRM, BSR, & Aurosoorya (2011). *Advancing Sustainability: HR's Role.* Alexandria, VA: Society for Human Resource Management (available online).

Sidanius, J. (1993). The psychology of group conflict and the dynamics of oppression: A social dominance perspective. In S. Iyenger & W. McGuire (Eds.), *Explorations in Political Psychology.* Durham, NC: Duke University Press.

Sinangil, H. K., & Ones, D. S. (2003). Gender differences in expatriate job performance. *Applied Psychology: An International Review, 52*(3), 461–475.

Sinetar, M. (1981). Mergers, morale, and productivity. *Personnel Journal, 60*, 863–867.

Sisson, K. (2006). International employee representation: A case of industrial relations systems following the market? In T. Edwards & C. Rees (Eds.), *International human resource management: Globalization, national systems, and multinational companies* (pp. 242). Harlow, Essex: Pearson Education Limited.

Sisson, K., Arrowsmith, J., & Marginson, P. (2003). All benchmarkers now? Benchmarking and the "Europeanisation" of industrial relations. *Industrial Relations Journal, 34*(1), 15–31.

Smith, P. B., & Bond, M. H. (1999). *Social psychology: Across cultures* (2nd ed.). Needham Heights, MA: Allyn & Bacon.

Smith, P. B., & Meiskins, P. (1995). Systems, societal, and dominance effects in cross-national organizational analysis. *Work, Employment and Society, 9*, 241–26.

Smith, P. B., Dugan, S., & Trompenaars, F. (1996). National culture and the values of organizational employees: A dimensional analysis across 43 nations. *Journal of Cross-Cultural Psychology, 27*(2), 231–264.

Stahl, G. K., Mendenhall, M. E., & Oddou, G. R. (2012). *Readings and cases in international human resource management and organizational behavior* (5th ed.). New York, NY: Routledge.

Sparrow, P., Schuler, R., & Jackson, S. (1994). Convergence or divergence: Human resource practices and policies for competitive advantage worldwide. *The International Journal of Human Resource Management, 5*(2), 267–299.

Sparrow, P., Brewster, C., & Harris, H. (2004). *Globalizing human resource management.* London, UK: Routledge.

Stahl, G. K. (2008). Cultural dynamics and impact of cultural distance within mergers and acquisitions. In P. B. Smith, M. F. Peterson, & D. C. Thomas (Eds.), *The handbook of cross-cultural management research* (pp. 431–448). Thousand Oaks, CA: Sage.

Stahl, G. K., Björkman, I., Farndale, E., Morris, S. S., Paauwe, J., Stiles, P., Trevor, J., & Wright, P. M. (2007). Global talent management: How leading multinationals build and sustain their talent pipeline. *Faculty and Research Working Paper,* 34OB, INSEAD.

Stahl, G. K., & Cerdin, J.-L. (2004). Global careers in French and German multinational corporations. *Journal of Management Development, 23*, 885–902.

Stahl, G. K., Miller, E. L., & Tung, R. L. (2002). Toward a boundaryless career: A closer look at the expatriate career concept and the perceived implications of an international assignment. *Journal of World Business, 37*, 216–227.

Stahl, G. K., Pucik, V., Evans, P., & Mendenhall, M. E. (2004). Human resource management in cross-border mergers and acquisitions. In A.-W. Harzing & J. V. Ruysseveldt (Eds.), *International human resource management* (2nd ed., pp. 89–114). London, UK: Sage.

Starr, T. L., & Currie, G. (2009). "Out of sight but still in the picture": Short-term international assignments and the influential role of family. *International Journal of Human Resource Management, 20*(6), 1421–1438.

Steers, R. M., Shin, Y. K., & Ungson, G. R. (1989). *The chaebol.* New York, NY: Harper-Business.

Steiner, D. D., Gilliland, S. W. (1996). Fairness reactions to personnel selection techniques in France and the United States. *Journal of Applied Psychology, 81*(2), 134–141.

Stiles, P. (2012). The international HR department. In G. K. Stahl, I. Björkman, & S. Morris (Eds.), *Handbook of research in international human resource management* (2nd ed., pp. 36–51). Northampton, MA: Edward Elgar.

Stopford, J. M., & Wells, L. T. (1972). *Strategy and structure in multinational enterprise.* New York, NY: Basic Books.

Stroh, L. K., Dennis, L. E., & Cramer, T. C. (1994). Predictors of expatriate adjustment. *International Journal of Organizational Analysis, 2*, 176–192.

Stroh, L. K., Varma, A., & Valy-Durbin, S. J. (2000). Why are women left at home: Are they unwilling to go on international assignments. *Journal of World Business, 35* (3), 241–255.

Sutter, J. (2011). The faces of Egypt's "Revolution 2.0." *CNN online*. Retrieved from http://www.cnn.com/2011/TECH/innovation/02/21/egypt.internet.revolution/index.html.

Suutari, V. (2002). Global leader development: An emerging research agenda. *Career Devellopment International, 7*, 218–223.

Suutari, V., Brewster, C. (2000). Making their own way: International experience through self-initiated foreign assignments. *Journal of World Business, 35*(4), 417–436.

Tadmor, C. T., & Tetlock, P. E. (2006). Biculturalism: A model of the effects of second-culture exposure on acculturation and integrative complexity. *Journal of Cross-Cultural Psychology, 37*, 1733–190.

Tadmor, C. T., Galinsky, A. D., & Maddux, W. M. (2012). Getting the most out of living abroad: Bicultruralism and integrative complexity as key drivers of creative and professional success. *Journal of Personality and Social Psychology, 103*, 520–542.

Takeuchi, R. (2010). A critical review of expatriate adjustment research through a multiple stakeholder view: Progress, emerging trends, and prospects. *Journal of Management, 36*(4), 1040–1064.

Takeuchi, R., & Hannon, J. M. (1996). *The antecedents of adjustment for Japanese expatriates in the United States.* Paper presented to the annual meeting of the Academy of International Business, Banff, Canada.

Takeuchi, R., Yun, S., & Tesluk, P. E. (2002). An examination of crossover and spillover effects of spousal and expatriate cross-cultural adjustment on expatriate outcomes. *Journal of Applied Psychology, 87*(4), 655–666.

Tayeb, M. H, (2005). *International human resource management: A multinational company perspective.* Oxford, UK: Oxford University Press.

Taylor, S., & Napier, N. (1996). Working in Japan: Lessons from women expatriates. *Sloan Management Review, 37*, 76–84.

Taylor, S., & Napier, N. (2005). International HRM in the twenty-first century: Crossing boundaries, building connections. In H. Scullion & M. Linehan (Eds.), *International human resource management: A critical text* (pp. 298–318). New York, NY: Palgrave Macmillian.

Taylor, S., Beechler, S., & Napier, N. (1996). Toward an integrative model of strategic human resource management. *Academy of Management Review, 21*, 959–985.

Thomas, D. C. (1994). The boundary-spanning role of expatriates in the multinational corporation. *Advances in International Comparative Management, 9*, 145–170.

Thomas, D. C. (1998). The expatriate experience: A critical review and synthesis. *Advances in International Comparative Management, 12*, 237–273.

Thomas, D. C. (2003). *Readings and cases in international management.* Thousand Oaks, CA: Sage.

Thomas, D. C. (2008). *Cross-cultural management: Essential concepts.* Thousand Oaks, CA: Sage.

Thomas, D. C., & Fitzsimmons, S. R. (2008). Cross-cultural skills and abilities: From communication competence to cultural intelligence. In P. B. Smith, M. F. Peterson, & D. C. Thomas (Eds.), *The handbook of cross-cultural management research.* Thousand Oaks, CA: Sage Publications.

Thomas, D. C., & Inkson, K. (2008). *Cultural intelligence: Living and working globally.* San Francisco, CA: Berrett-Koehler.

Thomas, D. C., & Lazarova, M. B. (2008). Expatriate adjustment and performance: A critical review. In G. K. Stahl, I. Björkman, & S. Morris (Eds.), *Handbook of research in international human resource management* (2nd ed., pp. 247–264). Cheltenham, UK: Edward Elgar.

Thomas, D. C., & Ravlin, E. C. (1995). Responses of employees to cultural adaptation by a foreign manager. *Journal of Applied Psychology, 80*, 133–146.

Thomas, D. C., Au, K., & Ravlin, E. C. (2003). Cultural variation and the psychological contract. *Journal of Organizational Behavior, 24*, 451–471.

Thomas, D. C., Elron, E., Stahl, G., Ekelund, B. Z., Ravlin, E. C., Cerdin, J.-L., et al. (2008). Cultural intelligence: Domain and assessment. *International Journal of Cross Cultural Management, 8*(2), 123–143.

Thomas, D. C., Lazarova, M. B., & Inkson, K. (2005). Global careers: New phenomenon or new perspectives? *Journal of World Business, 40*, 340–347.

Thomas, D. C. (2010). Cultural intelligence and all that jazz: A cognitive revolution in internal management research? *Advances in International Management, 23*, 169–187.

Thomas, D. C., Fitzsimmons, S. R., Ravlin, E. C., Au, K. Y., Ekelund B. Z., & Barzantny, C. (2010). Psychological contracts across cultures. *Organization Studies, 31*(12), 1–22.

Thomson, A., Mabey, C., Storey, J., Gray, C., & Iles., P. (2001). *Changing patterns of management development*. Oxford, UK: Blackwell Publishers Ltd.

Thory, K. (2008). The internationalisation of HRM through reverse transfer: Two case studies of French multinationals in Scotland. *Human Resource Management Journal, 18*, 54–71.

Toh, S. M., & DeNisi, A. S. (2007). Host country nationals as socializing agents: A social identity approach. *Journal of Organizational Behavior, 28*, 281–301.

Torbiörn, I. (1982). *Living abroad: Personal adjustment and personnel policy in the overseas setting*. New York, NY: John Wiley & Sons.

Torbiörn, I. (1985). The structure of managerial roles in cross-cultural settings. *International Studies of Management & Organization, 85*(1), 52–74.

Towers Perrin (1992). *Priorities for competitive advantage. A worldwide human resource study*. London, UK: Author.

Tregaskis, O. (2003). Learning networks, power & legitimacy in multinational subsidiaries. *International Journal of Human Resource Management, 14*(3), 431–447.

Tregaskis, O., & Brewster, C. (2006). Converging or diverging? A comparative analysis of contingent employment practice in Europe over a 10-year period. *Journal of International Business Studies, 37*, 111–126.

Tregaskis, O., & Heraty, N. (2012). Human resource development: National embeddedness. In C. Brewster & W. Mayrhofer (Eds.), *Handbook of research on comparative human resource management* (pp. 164–184). Northampton, MA: Edward Elgar.

Triandis, H. C. (1994). Cross-cultural industrial and organizational psychology. In H. C. Triandis, M. D. Dunnette, & L. M. Hough (Eds.), *Handbook of industrial and organizational psychology* (pp. 103–172). Alto, CA: Consulting Psychologists Press.

Triandis, H. C. (1995). *Individualism and collectivism*. Boulder, CO: Westview.

Trompenaars, F. (1993). *Riding the waves of culture*. Burr Ridge, IL: Irwin.

Trompenaars, F., & Hampden-Turner, C. (1998). *Riding the waves of cultures: Understanding diversity in global business*. Upper Saddle River, NJ: Prentice-Hall.

Tsai, C.-J. (2010). HRM in SMEs: Homogeneity or heterogeneity? A study of Taiwanese high-tech firms. *The International Journal of Human Resource Management, 21*(10), 1689–1711.

Tung, R. L. (1981). Selection and training of personnel for overseas assignments. *Columbia Journal of World Business, 16*, 68–78.

Tung, R. L. (1998). A contingency framework of selection and training of expatriates revisited. *Human Resource Management Review, 8*(1), 23–37.

Tung, R. L. (2008). Brain circulation, diaspora, and international competitiveness. *European Management Journal, 26*(5), 298–304.

Tung, R. L., & Lazarova, M. (2006). Brain drain versus brain gain: An exploratory study of ex-host country nationals in Central and East Europe. *International Journal of Human Resource Management, 17*(11), 1853–1872.

Turnley, W. H., & Feldman, D. C. (1999). The impact of psychological contract violations on exit, voice, loyalty and neglect. *Human Relations, 52*, 895–922.

Ulrich, D. (1997). *Human resource champions: The next agenda for adding value and delivering results.* Boston, MA: Harvard Business School Press.

Unite, J., Parry, E., Briscoe, J. P., & Chudzikowski, K. (2012). Careers and age: Career success for older and younger workers. In J. P. Briscoe, D. T. Hall, & W. Mayrhofer (Eds.), *Careers around the world: Individual and contextual perspectives* (pp. 119–144). New York, NY: Routledge.

Vaara, E. (2003). Post-acquisition integration as sensemaking: Glimpses of ambiguity, confusion, hypocrisy, and politicization. *Journal of Management Studies, 40,* 859–894.

Vaara, E., Tienari, J., & Säntti, R. (2003). The international match: Metaphors as vehicles of social identity-building in cross-border mergers. *Human Relations, 56,* 419–452.

van der Klink, M., & Mulder, M. (1995). Human resource development and staff policy in Europe. In A.-W. Harzing & J. Van Ruysseveldt (Eds.), *International Human Resource Management* (pp. 156–178). London, UK: Sage.

van der Velde, M. E. G., Bossink, C. J. H., & Jansen, P. G. W. (2005). Gender differences in the determinants of the willingness to accept an international assignment. *Journal of Vocational Behavior, 66*(1), 81–103.

van Oudenhoven, J. P., & de Boer, T. (1995). Complementarity and similarity of partners in international mergers. *Basic and Applied Social Psychology, 17*(3), 343–356.

Vance, C. M., & Paik, Y. (2011). *Managing a global workforce: Challenges and opportunities in international human resource management.* Armonk, NY: M.E. Sharpe.

Varma, A., & Stroh, L. K. (2001). The impact of same sex LMX dyads on performance evaluations. *Human Resource Management, 12,* 84–95.

Varma, A., Budhwar, P. S., & DeNisi, A. S. (2008). *Performance management systems: A global perspective.* New York, NY: Routledge.

Varma, A., & Budhwar, P. S. (2011). Global performance management. In A-W. Harzing & A. H. Pinnington (Eds.), *International human resource management* (3rd ed., pp. 440–467). London, UK: Sage Publications.

Vernon, G. (2011). International and comparative pay and reward. In T. Edwards & C. Rees (Eds.), *International human resource management: Globalization, national systems and multinational companies* (2nd ed., pp. 207–228). Harlow, England: Pearson.

Von Glinow, M. A., & Teagarden, M. B. (1988). The transfer of human resource technology in Sino-U.S. cooperative ventures: Problems and solutions. *Human Resource Management, 27,* 201–229.

Von Glinow, M. A., & Teagarden, M. B. (2009). The future of Chinese management research: Rigour and relevance redux. *Management and Organization Review, 5,* 75–89.

Vora, D. (2008). Managerial roles in the international context. In P.B. Smith, M. F. Peterson, & D. C. Thomas (Eds.), *Handbook of cross-cultural management research* (pp. 411–430). Thousand Oaks, CA: Sage.

Wagner, T. H. (1998, April). Practices in small firms: Some evidence from Atlantic Canada. *Journal of Small Business Management,* 13–23.

Walker, C. (2011). *Nations in transit 2011. The authoritarian dead end in the former Soviet Union.* Washington, DC: Freedom House.

Ward, C., & Kennedy, A. (1993). Where's the culture in cross-cultural transition? Comparative studies of sojourner adjustment. *Journal of Cross-Cultural Psychology, 24*(2), 221–249.

Watson, J. (1997). *Golden arches east: McDonald's in East Asia.* Stanford, CA: Stanford University Press.

Weeks, K. P., Weeks, M., & Willis-Muller, K. (2009). The adjustment of expatriate teenagers. *Personnel Review, 39*(1), 24–34.

Weiss, S. E. (1993). Analysis of complex negotiations in international business: The RBC perspective. *Organization Science, 2,* 269–300.

Welch, C. L., & Welch, D. E. (2012). What do HR managers really do? HR roles on international projects. *Management International Review 52*(4), 597–617.

Welch, D. E., & Worm, V. (2006). International business travellers: A challenge for IHRM. In G. H. Stahl & I. Björkman (Eds.), *Handbook of research in international human resource management* (pp. 283–301). Cheltenham, UK: Edward Elgar.

Welch, D. E., Welch, L. S., & Worm, V. (2007). The international business traveller: A neglected but strategic human resource. *International Journal of Human Resource Management, 18*(2), 173–183.

Westney, D. E. (1993). Institutionalization theory and the multinational corporation. In S. G. E. Westney (Ed.), *Organization theory and the multinational corporation*. New York, NY: St. Martin's Press.

Whitley, R. (1999). Firms, institutions and management control: The comparative analysis of coordination and control systems. *Accounting, Organizations and Society, 24*, 507–524.

Wiechmann, D., Ryan, A. M., & Hemingway, M. (2003). Designing and implementing global staffing systems: Part 1–Leaders in global staffing. *Human Resource Management, 42*(1), 71–83.

Willis, H. L. (1984). Selection for employment in developing countries. *Personnel Administrator, 29*(7), 55.

Wilson, Y. Y., & Jones, R. G. (2008). Reducing job-irrelevant bias in performance appraisals: Compliance and beyond. *Journal of General Management, 34* (2), 57–70.

Woodall, J. (2011). International management development. In T. Edwards & C. Rees (Eds.) *International human resource management: Globalization, national systems, and multinational companies* (2nd ed., pp. 163–183). Harlow, UK: Pearson Education Ltd.

World Bank (2012). http://data.worldbank.org/indicator/NY.GNP.PCAP.PP.CD

World Trade Organization (2012). *WTO annual report*. Geneva: Author.

Wong, E. (2010, March 21). Official in China says Western-style democracy won't take root there. *New York Times*. http://www.nytimes.com/2010/03/21/world/asia/21china.html.

Wright, P. M., & Gardner, T. M. (2003). The human resource-firm relationship: Methodological and theoretical challenges. In D. Holman, T. D. Wall, P. Clegg, P. Sparrow, & A. Howard (Eds.), *The new workplace: A guide to human impact of modern working practices* (pp. 311–328). Chichester, UK: John Wiley & Sons.

Wu, L. (1999). *Guanxi: A cross-cultural comparative study*. Unpublished doctoral dissertation, University of Auckland, New Zealand.

Yamazaki, Y. (2005). Learning styles and typologies of cultural differences: A theoretical and empirical comparison. *International Journal of Intercultural Relations, 29*, 521–548.

Yan, A., Zhu, G., & Hall, D. T. (2002). International assignments for career building: A model of agency relationships and psychological contracts. *Academy of Management Review, 27*(3), 373–391.

Zhou, J., & Martocchio, J. J. (2001). Chinese and American managers' compensation award decisions: A comparative policy-capturing study. *Personnel Psychology, 54*, 115–145.

Zhu, C. J., Dowling, P. J. (2002). Staffing practices in transition: Some empirical evidence from China. *The International Journal of Human Resource Management, 13*(4), 569–597.

Index

About the Authors

David C. Thomas (PhD, University of South Carolina) is currently Professor of International Business in the School of Management at the Australian School of Business, University of New South Wales, Sydney. He is the author of eight other books including (with Kerr Inkson) the bestselling *Cultural Intelligence: Living and Working Globally* (2009, Berrett-Koehler Publishers). His book *Cross-Cultural Management: Essential Concepts* (2008, Sage Publications) was the winner of the R. Wayne Pace Human Resource Development book of the year award for 2008. In addition, he has recently edited (with Peter B. Smith and Mark Peterson) *The Handbook of Cross-Cultural Management Research* from Sage Publications. His research on cross-cultural interactions in organizational settings has appeared in numerous journals. He is currently Area Editor for Cross-Cultural Management for the *Journal of International Business Studies* and serves on the editorial boards of the *Journal of World Business*, *Journal of Organizational Behavior*, and *European Journal of Cross-Cultural Competence and Management*. His previous academic postings have included positions at the Beedie School of Business, Simon Fraser University, the Pennsylvania State University, and the University of Auckland, New Zealand, where he was also director of the Master of International Business Program. He has held visiting positions at Koç University, Istanbul, Turkey, the Chinese University of Hong Kong, the University of Hawaii, Massey University, New Zealand, and ESCEM, Tours, France. In addition to teaching at both undergraduate and post graduate level, Dr. Thomas has consulted on diversity issues with numerous organizations in North America, Europe, and Australasia.

Mila B. Lazarova is Associate Professor and Canada Research Chair in Global Workforce Management in the Beedie School of Business, Simon Fraser University, Canada. She is the Director of the Centre for Global Workforce Strategy. She received her PhD in Human Resources and Industrial Relations from Rutgers, the State University of New Jersey. Dr. Lazarova also holds a MS degree in HR/IR from Rutgers University and a MBA degree in International Business from the University of National and World Economy in Sofia, Bulgaria. Her research interests include, expatriate management, with a focus on repatriation and the career impact of international assignments; work/life balance issues related to assignments; global careers; the role of organizational career development and work/life balance practices on employee retention; and the changing role of the HR department in organizations. She also conducts research in comparative human resource management and is the Canadian contributor to CRANET, a long-term research collaboration of over 35 universities across the world that carries out a regular international comparative survey of organizational HR policies and practices. She has received two competitive research grants from the Social Sciences and Humanities Research Council of Canada in support of her work on the CRANET project. Dr. Lazarova has published her work in journals such as the *Academy of Management Review, Organization Science, Journal of International Business Studies,* and *Journal of Organizational Behavior* and has contributed numerous book chapters in edited volumes. She recently edited (with Emma Parry and Eleni Stavrou) *Global Trends in International Human Resource Management* (Palgrave Macmillian, 2013). She is currently on the editorial board of several journals, including the *Journal of International Business Studies, Journal of World Business, Human Resource Management Journal* and *the International Journal of Human Resource Management.*

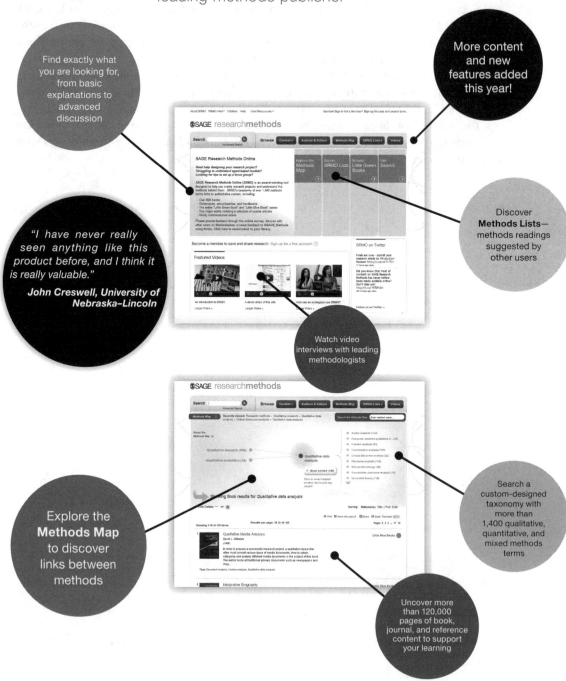

⑤SAGE research**methods**

The essential online tool for researchers from the world's leading methods publisher

Find exactly what you are looking for, from basic explanations to advanced discussion

More content and new features added this year!

"*I have never really seen anything like this product before, and I think it is really valuable.*"

John Creswell, University of Nebraska–Lincoln

Discover **Methods Lists**— methods readings suggested by other users

Watch video interviews with leading methodologists

Explore the **Methods Map** to discover links between methods

Search a custom-designed taxonomy with more than 1,400 qualitative, quantitative, and mixed methods terms

Uncover more than 120,000 pages of book, journal, and reference content to support your learning

Find out more at
www.sageresearchmethods.com